HERMAN N. WEILL was born in New York City. He completed his high school education in Switzerland with the Abitur-Diploma. He holds two undergraduate degrees from the University of Miami, Florida (A.B. and B.Ed.), and two graduate degrees from the University of Illinois (M.A. and Ph.D.). He has taught at such leading institutions of higher education as the University of Rhode Island, the University of Minnesota, and the University of Missouri. In addition to European diplomatic history, he has published works in Prussian judicial reform and other aspects of European administrative and intellectual history from the seventeenth to the twentieth centuries. He is Dean of Arts and Sciences and Professor of History at Johnson State College, Johnson, Vermont.

D1445736

European Diplomatic History

1815-1914

DOCUMENTS AND INTERPRETATIONS

EDITED, WITH ORIGINAL TRANSLATIONS,
CHAPTER INTRODUCTIONS AND SCHOLARLY NOTES

by HERMAN N. WEILL

Johnson State College

An Exposition-University Book
EXPOSITION PRESS   NEW YORK

To

DAGMAR, KAREN AND RONALD

And

In Memory of My Parents,

HENRY DAVID AND HELLA WALLACH WEILL

EXPOSITION PRESS, INC.

50 Jericho Turnpike   Jericho, New York 11753

FIRST EDITION

LIBRARY OF CONGRESS CATALOG CARD NUMBER: 74-171719

SBN 0-682-47375-8 (cloth)
SBN 0-682-47327-8 (paper)

CONTENTS

CONTENTS

3   THE UNIFICATION OF ITALY

4 THE UNIFICATION OF GERMANY

5 ORIGINS OF WORLD WAR I

PREFACE

With the United States involved in three major wars within the past thirty years alone, the need has become imperative for every citizen to develop clear concepts about diplomacy and international relations. What should the goals of our foreign policy be? What means are acceptable or unacceptable in the realization of these goals? Are wars ever justified, and if so, under what circumstances? These are just some of the vital questions which demand serious attention and thought.

This book is designed to assist the student in the formulation of these concepts. By bringing together a great variety of diplomatic documents, many of them for the first time in English translation, it makes available for analysis the European experience on the subject during the century from 1815 to 1914.

Considering how vast the documentation of that experience is, it could not be encompassed within a single volume. The editor had to be selective. Since it is people, both individually and in large groups, who devise and execute a nation's foreign policy, the primary focus of the book is, on the one hand, the rationale of individual statesmen and rulers which led to certain policy decisions, and, on the other, the context, particularly the public mood, within which these decisions were made. Hence, treaties have been kept to a minimum, and most of the space is devoted to such primary documents as ministerial conferences, personal letters, eyewitness accounts, newspaper reports, as well as to diplomatic dispatches.

A work of this kind would be impossible without the cooperation and preceding scholarly labors of many individuals. It is a pleasure to acknowledge my indebtedness to: the editors—often anonymous—of the diplomatic documents series cited in the notes; the librarians at the University of Rhode Island, Brown University, Washington University, and particularly at Harvard University where most of my research was done; Prof. Theodore S. Hamerow, who initiated me into the fascinating complexities of European diplomacy while I was a graduate student and who first suggested the need for this volume; the publications by Professors Otto Pflanze, Paul Schroeder, Gordon Craig, Brison Gooch, Harold Temperley, A. J. P. Taylor, Lynn Case, D. Mack-Smith, W. Mosse, S. William Halperin, Erich Eyck, Hajo Holborn, Fritz Fischer, William Langer, Lawrence Steefel, Joachim Remak, Sidney Fay, Bernadotte Schmitt, and Luigi Albertini; and my colleagues, students and family who constructively criticized and/or bravely endured my frequent references to the book during the years of its creation.

HERMAN N. WEILL

Johnson, Vermont
July, 1971

1

The Congress of Vienna 1

INTRODUCTION

WHEN NAPOLEON was banished to St. Helena, an era of almost continuous revolutionary upheavals and wars came to a close. During this quarter of a century, dozens of rulers had been toppled from their thrones; hundreds of thousands of men had perished in a single campaign; fortunes had been made or lost (mostly lost) in a few days. It should not occasion surprise, therefore, that the survivors, or rather those among them who could still afford to do so, celebrated the arrival of peace by plunging into a seemingly endless round of entertainments, as if they wanted to make up in a few short weeks for all the pleasures they had missed in the preceding years. The glittering array of monarchs and diplomats assembled at Vienna was no exception, and the Congress of Vienna quickly acquired the reputation of a "Dancing Congress" (*No. 1**).

Interspersed between the masked balls and sumptuous dinners, however, were numerous long and tense negotiating sessions, in which the statesmen of Europe wrestled with the complicated and often exasperating problems bequeathed to them by the era of the French Revolution and Napoleon. The outstanding statesman at Vienna, the man who was to give the subsequent era his name, was Prince Clemens von Metternich. His private letters (*No. 2*), written at the height of his influence and fame, reveal several aspects of his personality: his enormous vanity, his vindictiveness, his aristocratic contempt for the "mob," but also his physical endurance, his dedication to his work, and his gallantry toward women, especially pretty women. But these personality traits, while they help us to visualize the kind of man that Metternich was, do not explain his extraordinary position in the diplomacy of the first half of the nineteenth century. Few will deny that he possessed diplomatic skills amounting to virtuosity: a fecundity of ideas which usually included a solution to a diplomatic problem acceptable to both sides; a breadth of perspective which enabled him to grasp the manifold ramifications of a given course of policy; a superb insight into the thoughts and motives of his opponents, coupled with a willingness to meet them halfway if at all possible; patience in negotiation, and the ability to persuade others to accept his own point of view. Two other factors should not be overlooked: the unprecedented length of his career, and his articulateness. He served as Austrian Chancellor and Foreign Minister for forty years. While rulers and other statesmen came and went, Metternich seemed to be there forever. Then, too, what made him so effective was not the origin-

---

*Such references in italic type are to document numbers.—HNW.

3

ality of his political concepts, but that he was the most articulate spokesman for a philosophy which dominated the outlook of almost all the Continental monarchs, from Francis I to Alexander I, and from Charles X to Ferdinand II.

The most important immediate problem facing the statesmen at Vienna was the conclusion of peace with France. It remains to their credit that the second Peace of Paris (*No. 3*), although somewhat harsher than the first peace treaty of 1814, was still magnanimous enough to be acceptable to most Frenchmen. But while this treaty restored peace, it did not restore the victors' peace of mind. They still feared a resurgence of French power and the possibility that another attempt at French hegemony would once more plunge Europe into war. Some means had to be devised to maintain the peace which had been won at such great cost. Alexander I believed that the peace would be most readily preserved if the monarchs of Europe took a solemn pledge to base their international conduct upon the tenets of the Christian religion, and the result was the Holy Alliance (*No. 4*). But most of the diplomats thought more concrete guidelines were needed. They finally agreed that the best solution would be to renew the Quadruple Alliance, initially a wartime alliance directed against France, and that it contain a provision whereby the Great Powers would periodically assemble at a congress to concert upon the measures required to meet whatever threats to the general peace might have arisen. It was thus in the Quadruple Alliance of 1815 (*No. 5*), and particularly in its famous Article VI, that the Concert of Europe was born.

As far as Metternich was concerned, the most pernicious threat to the general peace was the revolutionary ideas which had been concocted in Paris and which, like a poisonous foam, had spread over Europe in the wake of the advancing French armies. He was convinced that if a monarch permitted any fundamental changes in the existing political structure of his state, revolutionary violence and chaos would be the inevitable consequence. A good example of this conviction is his dispatch on the dangers of reforms in Prussia (*No. 6*). This dispatch is of particular interest because the suggestions it contained were to be translated into direct action much sooner than even Metternich had anticipated. On 23 March 1819, August von Kotzebue was assassinated in Mannheim by Carl Friedrich Sand, a university student and a member of the newly founded *Burschenschaften,* or patriotic fraternities. The major points of the resulting suppressive Carlsbad Decrees, adopted unanimously by the German Diet on 20 September 1819, are almost identical with Metternich's suggestions.

When, in the following year, revolutions broke out in Spain and Naples, Metternich went one step farther and established the principle of intervention (*No. 7*). Comparing these revolutions to raging conflagrations, he insisted that the Great Powers were not only permitted, but duty-bound, to use all necessary measures, including armed force, to prevent their own houses from catching fire. In consequence, Austrian troops were sent to Naples, and French troops to Spain, to suppress these revolutions. It was at this point that the first major dissonance in the Concert of Europe became audible, for Castlereagh vigorously denied that the Powers had the right to intervene in the internal affairs of other states (*No. 8*). This dispatch marks the beginning of a new orientation in British foreign policy, which was to find England increasingly at odds with the policies pursued by Metternich and the Holy Alliance.

In the readings which conclude this chapter, two recent historians interpret the policies of Metternich and Castlereagh, respectively. Paul W. Schroeder's perceptive essay (*No. 9*) is obviously critical, although not so much of Metternich as of the exaggerated claims that his later admirers have made for him. In C. K. Webster's appreciation of Castlereagh (*No. 10*), it is interesting to note how much Castlereagh and Metternich had in common. Webster thus illuminates Metternich's policies as well as those of Castlereagh.

No. 1   La Garde: The Dancing Congress[1]

The Congress of Vienna, considered as a political gathering, has not lacked historians, but they were so intent upon recording its phases of high diplomacy as to have bestowed no thought upon its piquant and lighter social features.

.   .   .   .

Doubtless, at no time of the world's history had more grave and complex interests been discussed amidst so many fêtes. A kingdom was cut into bits or enlarged at a ball: an indemnity was granted in the course of a dinner; a constitution was planned during a hunt; now and again a cleverly-placed word or a happy and pertinent remark cemented a treaty the conclusion of which, under different circumstances, would probably have been achieved only with difficulty, and by dint of many conferences and much correspondence. Acrimonious discussions and 'dry-as-dust' statements were replaced for the time being, as if by magic, by the most polite forms in any and every transaction; and also by the promptitude which is a still more important form of politeness, unfortunately too neglected.

The Congress had assumed the character of a grand fête in honour of the general pacification. Ostensibly it was a feast of rest after the storm, but, curiously enough, it offered a programme providing for life in its most varied movements. Doubtless, the foregathering of those sovereigns, ministers, and generals who for nearly a quarter of a century had been the actors in a grand drama supposed to have run its course, besides the pomp and circumstance of the unique scene itself, showed plainly enough that they were there to decide the destinies of nations. The mind, dominated by the gravity of the questions at issue, could not altogether escape from the serious thoughts now and again obtruding themselves: but immediately afterwards the sounds of universal rejoicing brought a welcome diversion. Everyone was engrossed with pleasure. The love-passion also hovered over this assembly of kings, and had the effect of prolonging a state of abandonment and a neglect of affairs, both really inconceivable when taken in conjunction with upheavals the shock of which was still felt, and immediately before a thunderbolt which was soon to produce a singular awakening. The people themselves, apparently forgetting that when their rulers are at play, the subjects are doomed to pay in a short time the bills of such royal follies, seemed to be grateful for foibles that drew their masters down to their level.

.   .   .   .

I arrived in Vienna towards the end of September 1814, when the Congress, though it had been announced for several months, was not yet officially opened. The fêtes had, however, already commenced. . . .

The number of strangers attracted to Vienna by the Congress was estimated at close upon a hundred thousand. It ought to be said that for this memorable gathering no other city would have answered so well. Vienna is in reality the centre of Europe; at that time it was its capital. A Viennese who had happened to leave the city a few months before would have had some difficulty in identifying himself and his familiar surroundings amidst that new, gilded, and titled population which crowded the place at the time of the Congress. All the sovereigns of the North had come thither; the West and the East had sent their most notable representatives. The Emperor Alexander, still young and brilliant; the Empress Elizabeth, with her winning though somewhat melancholy grace, and the Grand Duke Constantine represented Russia. Behind these were grouped a mass of ministers, princes, and generals, especially conspicuous among them the Comtes de Nesselrode, Capo d'Istria, Pozzo di Borgo, and Stackelberg, all of whom were marked out from that hour to play important parts in the political debates of Europe. . . .

The King of Prussia was accompanied by the Princes Guillaume and Auguste. Baron de Humboldt and the Prince d'Hardemberg presided at his councils. The beautiful queen who in the negotiations of 1807 employed in vain all her seductive grace and resources of mind against the will of Napoleon, was no more.

The King of Denmark, Frédéric VI., the son of the ill-fated Caroline Mathilde, also repaired to the Congress, which, luckily for him, he was enabled to leave without his modest possessions having aroused the cupidity of this or that ambitious neighbour.

The Kings of Bavaria and Würtemberg, the Dukes of Saxe-Coburg, Hesse-Darmstadt, and Hesse-Cassel—in short, all the heads and princes of the reigning houses of Germany—were there. They also wished to take part in the political festival, and were anxious to know how the supreme tribunal would trim and shape the borders of their small States.

The King of Saxony, so ardently worshipped by his subjects, had at that time retired into Prussia, while the Allied Armies occupied his kingdom. That excellent prince, whom Napoleon called 'le plus honnête homme quit ait occupé le trône,'[2]

was only represented at the Congress by his plenipotentiaries.

The representatives of France were the Duc de Dalberg, the Comte Alexis de Noailles, M. de la Tour-du-Pin, and the Prince de Talleyrand. The last-named maintained his high reputation with great dignity under difficult circumstances, and perhaps conspicuous justice has never been done to him. The English plenipotentiaries were Lords Clancarty and Stewart, and Viscount Castlereagh.

.　.　.　.　.　.　.　.　.

The whole of this royal company met in the capital of Austria with a hospitality worthy of it, and worthy also of that memorable gathering. The Kings of Würtemberg and Denmark arrived before any of the others. The Emperor Francis proceeded as far as Schönbrunn to welcome each of them. The interview between those princes was exceedingly cordial, and free from diplomatic reserve; but the ceremony which by its pomp and splendour was evidently intended to crown the series of wonders of the Congress was the solemn entry of Emperor Alexander and the King of Prussia.

Numerous detachments of guards of honour had been posted on the routes these two monarchs were to traverse. The whole of the garrison was under arms at the approaches to and within the capital. The emperor, attended by his grand officers of state, both military and civil, the archdukes, and other princes of the blood, proceeded for some distance to meet his hosts. The meeting took place on the left bank of the Danube, at the further extremity of the Tabor bridge. There was an exchange of most affectionate and apparently most sincere greetings, and the three rulers held each other's hands for a long while.

An immense crowd lined the banks of the stream, and rent the air with cheers. Undoubtedly it was a sight as remarkable as it was unheard-of, that gathering of sovereigns tried by severe misfortune for twenty years, and who, having vanquished him who had been for such a long time victorious, seemed astonished at a triumph so dearly bought, so unexpectedly obtained.

The three monarchs, in full-dress uniforms, meanwhile mounted their horses and rode slowly on amidst the booming of the artillery. The infinite number of generals, belonging to all the nations of Europe, riding behind them, their brilliant costumes glittering in the sun, the joyous cries of the crowds, the clanging of the bells of all the steeples, the air resounding with the firing of the cannon, the sight of the population frantically hailing the return of peace—in fact, the whole scene, even the cordial demeanor of those sovereigns, constituted the most imposing and eloquent spectacle.

.   .   .   .

From that moment Vienna assumed an aspect which was as bright as it was animated. Numberless magnificent carriages traversed the city in all directions, and, in consequence of the restricted size of the capital, constantly reappeared. Most of them were preceded by those agile forerunners, in their brilliant liveries, who are no longer to be seen anywhere except in Vienna, and who, swinging their large silver-knobbed canes, seemed to fly in front of the horses. The promenades and squares teemed with soldiers of all grades, dressed in the varied uniforms of all the European armies. Added to these were the swarms of the servants of the aristocracy in their gorgeous liveries, and the people crowding at all points of vantage to catch a momentary glimpse of the military, sovereign, and diplomatic celebrities constantly shifting within the permanent frame of the varying picture. Then, when night came, the theatres, the cafés, the public resorts were filled with animated crowds, apparently bent on pleasure only, while sumptuous carriages rolled hither and

thither, lighted up by torches borne by footmen perched behind, or still preceded by runners, who had, however, exchanged their canes for flambeaux. In almost every big thoroughfare there was the sound of musical instruments discoursing joyous tunes. Noise and bustle everywhere.

.   .   .   .

The immense number of strangers had soon invaded every available hotel and private lodging. Many notabilities were obliged to take up their quarters in the outskirts. Prices ruled exorbitantly high; in order to judge of this I need only state that the rent of Lord Castlereagh's apartments was £500 per month—an unheard-of price in Vienna. It was calculated that if the Congress lasted only four months, the value of many houses would be paid to their proprietors in rent. . . .

.   .   .   .

. . . As a matter of course, my first call was due to him,[3] and on the morrow of my arrival I made my way to his home.

'You are just in time to see great doings,' he said. 'The whole of Europe is in Vienna. The tissue of politics is embroidered with fêtes, and inasmuch as at your age one is fond of joyous gatherings, balls, and pleasure, I can assure you beforehand of a series of them, because the Congress does not march to its goal; it dances. It is a royal mob. From all sides there are cries of peace, justice, equilibrium, indemnity; the last word being the new contribution of the Prince de Bénévent to the diplomatic vocabulary. Heaven alone knows who shall reduce this chaos to some semblance of order, and provide dams for the torrent of various pretensions. As for me, I am only a well-meaning and friendly spectator of the show. I shall claim nothing, unless it be a hat to replace the one I am wearing out in saluting the sovereigns I meet at every street-corner. Nevertheless, in spite of Robinson Crusoe,[4] a general and lasting peace will no doubt be concluded, for a feeling of concord has at length united the nations which were so long inimical towards each other. Their most illustrious representatives are already setting the example of it. We shall witness a thing hitherto unheard of: pleasure will bring in its wake peace, instead of strife.'

After this, he started asking me, with all the impetuosity of youth, a series of questions with reference to Paris, my travels, and my own plans, until he was interrupted by his servant informing him that his carriage was at the door.

'You'll come and dine with me to-morrow', he said; 'and then we'll go to the grand rout and ball. You'll see the most practical common-sense of Europe wearing the motley of folly. When there I'll explain to you in a few moments the curiosities of that grand piece of living tapestry composed of the most notable personages.'

. . . It was nine o'clock when we reached the imperial palace, better known as the Hofburg. That ancient residence had been specially chosen for those ingenious *momons,* character-masques in which the incognito of the domino often lent itself to political combinations in themselves masterpieces of intrigue and conception. The principal hall was magnificently lighted up, and running around it, there was a circular gallery giving access to huge rooms arranged for supper. On seats, disposed like an amphitheatre, there were crowds of ladies, some of whom merely wore dominos, while the majority represented this or that character. It would be difficult to imagine a scene more dazzling than this gathering of women, all young and beautiful, and each attired in a style most becoming to her beauty. All the centuries of the past, all the regions of the inhabited globe seemed to have appointed to meet in that graceful circle.

Several orchestras executed at regular intervals valses and polonaises: in adjoining

gallaries or rooms minuets were danced with particularly Teutonic gravity, which feature did not constitute the least comic part of the picture.

The prince had spoken the truth. Vienna at that time presented an abridged panorama of Europe, and the rout was an abridged panorama of Vienna. There could be no more curious spectacle than those masked or non-masked people, among whom, absolutely lost in the crowd, and practically defying identification, circulated all the sovereigns at that moment participating in the Congress.

The prince had a story or anecdote about each. 'There goes Emperor Alexander. The man on whose arm he is leaning is Prince Eugène Beauharnais, for whom he has a sincere affection. When Eugène arrived here with his father-in-law, the King of Bavaria, the Court hesitated about the rank to be accorded to him. The emperor spoke so positively on the subject as to secure for Eugène all the honours due to his generous character. Alexander, as you are aware, is worthy of inspiring and of extending the deepest friendship.

'Do you know the tall and noble-looking personage whom that beautiful Neapolitan girl is holding round the waist? It is the King of Prussia, whose gravity appears in no wise disturbed by the fact. For all that the clever mask may be an empress, on the other hand it is quite on the cards that she is merely a grisette who has been smuggled in.

'That colossus in the black domino, which neither disguises nor decreases his stature, is the King of Würtemberg. The man close to him is his son, the Crown Prince. His love for the Duchess d'Oldenbourg, Emperor Alexander's sister, is the cause of his stay at the Congress, rather than a concern for the grave interests which one day will be his. It is a romantic story, the *dénouement* of which we may witness before long.

'The two young fellows who just brushed

past us are the Crown Prince of Bavaria and his brother, Prince Charles. The latter's face would dispute the palm with that of Antinous. The crowd of people of different kind and garb who are disporting themselves, in every sense of the word, are, some, reigning princes, others archdukes, others again grand dignitaries of this or that empire. For, except a few Englishmen, easily picked out by their careful dress, I do not think there is a single personage here without a "handle" to his name.'

. . . .

The moment the prince left me to myself I began to wander about, and if I had made a series of appointments, I could not have met with more acquaintances hailing from Naples to St. Petersburg, and from Stockholm to Constantinople. The variety of costume and languages was truly astonishing. It was like a bazaar of all the nations of the world. Honestly, I felt that for the first time in my life I was experiencing the intoxication of a masked ball. My brain seemed to reel under the spell of the incessant music, the secrecy of disguise, the atmosphere of mystery by which it was surrounded, the general state of incognito, the uncurbed and boundless gaiety, the force of circumstances, and the irresistible seductiveness of the picture before me. I feel certain that older and stronger heads than mine would have proved equally weak.

. . . .

. . . The Austrian Court, in fact, dispensed the hospitality of its capital to its guests with truly fabulous pomp. Memory almost fails to recall, for the purpose of recording, all the brilliant details. The imagination is virtually powerless to reconstruct the dazzling splendour of the picture as a whole.

To beguile the leisure of those kings who, it would be thought, ought to have been surfeited with the counterfeits of battles,

twenty thousand picked grenadiers had been quartered at Vienna. There was, moreover, the announcement of a camp to be formed of sixty thousand troops with a view of having grand manoeuvres. The superb 'nobiliary guards' had been considerably increased by the joining of young men belonging to the most distinguished families of the monarchy. The whole of the troops had been provided with new uniforms: there was an evident desire to remove all traces of warfare, so as not to sadden those participating in the feasts and entertainments exclusively designed to celebrate peace and to promote pleasure.

All the stud farms of Germany had been requested to send their most magnificent horses. The grand dignitaries of the crown held 'open house' each day for the eminent personages of the suites of the various sovereigns. The Court had invited the Paris Opera dancers of both sexes to come to Vienna; and the Austrian Imperial Company had also been reinforced. The most celebrated actors of Germany had likewise been 'commanded,' and they appeared in new pieces, appropriate to the universal rejoicing, and calculated to prevent that joy from getting fagged.

Emperor Francis had thrown open his palace to his illustrious guests. At a rough calculation, the imperial residence held, at that particular moment, two emperors, a similar number of empresses, four kings, one queen, two heirs to thrones (one royal, the other imperial), two grand-duchesses, and three princes. The young family of the emperor had to be relegated to Schönbrunn. Attracted by the novelty of all this, an immense crowd surrounded the palace at all hours, eager to catch a glimpse of the members of a gathering unique in the annals of history.

. . . .

In order to convey an idea of the expenses of the Austrian Court, it will suffice to say that the imperial table cost fifty thousand florins per day. This was keeping 'open table' with a vengeance. Hence, it is not surprising that the extraordinary expenses of the fêtes of the Congress, during the five months of its duration, amounted to forty millions of francs. . . .

If we add to the expenses of the Court those of more than seven hundred envoys, we may get something like an accurate idea of the extraordinary consumption of all things in Vienna, and of the immense quantity of money put into circulation. In fact, the influx of strangers was such as to increase the prices of all commodities, and especially of wood for fuel, to an incredible degree. As a consequence, the Austrian Government was obliged to grant supplementary salaries to all its employés.

·   ·   ·   ·   ·   ·   ·   ·   ·

No. 2   Metternich: Private Letters—— 4 January to 21 May 1821[1]

489. *Laybach, January 4, 1821.*—On December 25, in the morning, I left Troppau, and on the morning of the 27th arrived at Vienna, where I remained till New Year's Day. I started from Vienna on January 1, in fifteen degrees of cold. Till the mountain was crossed which separates Carniola from Styria the cold continually increased; but on the opposite side of the mountain I first felt the southern air, and the ice on my carriage windows, which was half an inch thick, melted in less than a quarter of an hour. I breathed new life, as servants often get a pleasant odor when they open the doors of a banquet hall. Laybach is like the anteroom to some comfortable apartments. If Görz were not too small to accommodate a Congress, we would have settled ourselves in that town, because there the Alps are entirely passed. A man can only really live in a country where there is no winter, or not a long winter. I am still the only person here; the morning will bring an avalanche of statesmen—an avalanche that will cause no joy.

I am very well pleased with my accommodation. I have a good room to write in, a good bedroom, and a suite of reception rooms. The mistress of the house is as ugly as the seven deadly sins, and has seven children who each resemble one of the said sins.

·   ·   ·   ·   ·   ·   ·   ·   ·

Do you know an English novel called "Anastasius"? In it there is a description of the Greek character (I think in the fourth, fifth, or sixth chapter) which is very good and accurate, as indeed is everything in this book relating to Oriental and especially Greek, customs. You will find there Capo d'Istria[2] word for word, exactly as he is. It is really extraordinary that destiny should have brought us, who are of so opposite a nature, and have come into the world seven or eight hundred miles from one another, to meet upon the same ground. *Nemo propheta in patria*, says the proverb. Whether Capo d'Istria will ever be a prophet beyond his fatherland I doubt.

I should have liked Robespierre better than Abbé de Pradt, and Atilla better than Quiroga. A tyrant does not alarm me; I should know how to avoid his attacks, or bear them with honor. But the Radical maniac, the sentimental Boudoir-Philanthropist, makes me uncomfortable. I like iron and gold, but I hate tin and copper. This childish feeling is so decided in me that I never can endure plated things.

492. *January 10.*—To-day, if the earth does not break up or the heavens fall down, or the commonest and vilest ruffians destroy all good people with right and strong wills, we have won the cause. Capo d'Istria twists about like a devil in holy water; but he is in holy water and can do nothing. The chief cause of our activity today arises from my thorough agreement with the Emperor Alexander. Here, again, the tea makes its astonishing power felt.

Is there anything in the world which can to-day take the place of ink, pens, a conference table with its green cover, and a few greater or smaller bunglers?

494. *January 16.*—We shall hardly get away from here till the end of March. An army takes thirty days to march from the Po to Naples, and we must await their entry here. At any rate, the present residence here is pleasanter than the former; it is much more agreeable. We have some public amusements, as, for instance, two masked balls in the week, the first of which they say was not very lively; among five-and-forty men there was one lady, who fell asleep in a corner of the room, which did not speak much for the gallantry of the gentlemen. Moreover, there are here some very pretty women, the prettiest being Countess Thurn, who is two-and-twenty. They talk also of two other ladies, one of whom is five-and-twenty, the other five-and-thirty; the first limps, which you do not notice if she is sitting; the other has stern manners, but is of a very enthusiastic nature. This lady I will endeavor to install as the poet of our Congress.

496. *January 25.*—We are ready; the diplomatic fight is won; sound manly sense has conquered. The principle is clear and plainly set forth, and if heaven favors us the execution will be quick and successful. The evening before a battle no general can say if he will win; but he must count his troops, reconnoitre the ground, think of the retreat, and then let fly at the enemy. Providence only knows how the battle will go, but since providence has bestowed[3] on us the gift of foresight, she at least expects from us that her priceless gifts, reason and conscience, should be taken into council. From the moment when I had the inward conviction of having satisfied this expectation I was calm and content. I am not accessible to fear; I know no other than the fear lest I should mistake what is good and right. One day a thief, or perhaps a murderer, got in at my window and stood by my bed; he thought I slept, but I observed him. I allowed him to come nearer without moving, but loosened my sheets so that nothing might be in my way. One jump and I stood up, seized him, threw him out of the window, and lay down again. "He or I" was my thought. That is logic in business as with robbers. This circumstance took place in the year 1811.

I was yesterday on the Redoubt, which is dreadfully knocked about. It seems that this beautiful country has not always beautiful inhabitants. I saw only one pretty woman's face, and that belonged to a Russian cook who caused much mischief among the soldiers. As I am not a soldier, I did not prolong my stay more than a quarter of an hour.

498. *February 7.*—Every hour now brings us news from Italy which, taken altogether, shows that it will not come to a battle. I confess I shall be sorry. If it is necessary to give the insurgents a lesson it ought to be strongly expressed.[4] Nothing is useful which is merely done privately; it ought to be done openly.

At any rate the outcome of it will be a new example. For the first time for thirty years an evil will be publicly combated which has been represented to weak humanity as the highest good. Our children's children will think us very foolish, and this conviction often weighs upon my mind, for I belong to a class of men who live more in the future than in the present. My mind has an historical tinge which helps me over many present difficulties. With me the future is always before my eyes, and I believe I am far less exposed to the danger of error with regard to the future than with regard to the present.

However, I do not carry this feeling so far as to be dangerous to a man in my position. I do not overlook the present; I take it at its real value, but the present is not worth much. This is evident to me, and history has perhaps never displayed such a pitiable crowd of small personages who only busy themselves with follies. Heavens! how we shall all be abused when the day of reckoning comes—and that day will come. Then some worthy man who among the hundred thousand pamphlets and in the grocers' shops, discovers my name, will find perhaps in the year 2440 that in this far-distant time one being existed who was less wrong-headed than his contemporaries, who carried self-estimation so far as to believe themselves arrived at the culminating point of civilization.

.   .   .   .

500. *February 12.*—The Laybach Congress is to-day like a father who knows a child is about to be born to him. Will it be a boy or a girl, an angel or a monster? The poor father cannot know this till the moment of the arrival.

The star of the Russian Premier begins to decline. The breach between Capo d'Istria and the Emperor constantly increases; in a team, if one horse pulls to the right and the other to the left, the carriage will not reach its destination till the stronger has dragged off the weaker of the two. The Emperor is the stronger, and for transparent reasons.

501. *February 17.*—. . . .

.   .   .   .

I lately had a sharp contest with Capo d'Istria, and was obliged to speak to the Emperor Alexander about it. I am certain that at the end of the Neapolitan question his retirement will not be very distant.

. . . I think it natural that Nesselrode should like me; he is an honorable, right-thinking man.

.   .   .   .

502. *February 23.*—I have two days of very hard work in store for me. You cannot imagine what stormy days are to be seen in my room. Twenty or thirty persons come in and out; one wants an order, another some advice, a third an explanation; then the newsmongers, the dissatisfied, &c., &c. No one believes that the Emperor Alexander and I understand one another thoroughly, and yet it is so. The influence of the last four months has been effectual; the stronger has carried off the weaker, according to all the laws of mechanics, physics, and morals. The Russian Premier lies on the ground. Will he ever get up again?

506. *March 7.*—. . . .
. . . If I am wise, seven-eighths of the present world are mad. If I am a fool, how many wise people there are just now!

508. *March 15.*—On the 12th I was awoke very early by the news of the military insurrection in Alessandria and Turin. I said to my informant, "Well, I have expected it," got up and went to my Emperor, and then to the Emperor of Russia. We returned together to the first, and by twelve o'clock the following laconic orders were prepared and despatched:

1. The Neapolitan army is to accelerate all its operations, and not to trouble itself about what goes on in Piedmont.

2. Eighty thousand men are to march from Vienna and the neighborhood to Italy.

3. Ninety thousand men from Russia must cross our frontiers. Whereupon we separated and ate our dinner as usual.

509. *March 22.—*. . . .

This is all very pleasant: still I do not know where I shall find the time for so much hard work. Heaven has endowed me with the qualities of draught oxen. The more I work, the better I am. The last eight nights I have hardly slept more than two hours.

513. *April 3.*—I am in the strangest position I have ever been in. I have on hand an extinguished revolution and two revolutions in full blaze: one monarch who will not stir, and another who will go forward with double strides.[5] The first will not leave Florence unless I go there, and will only follow me; I may write to him ever so much, write to him through the two Emperors, let him be personally entreated by our Ambassadors—he remains deaf and dumb and gives no answer but "Send Metternich to me." The other rushes like a madman at death and the devil, listens neither to Emperors nor ambassadors, but writes letter after letter, in which there is nothing but "Send me Metternich." But meantime I cannot get away from here. I can neither get the one to go nor the other to stay. The emperors are wroth and I cross myself. This is certain. Enemies are much the most easy to manage: you run straight at them and make away with them; but friends!

.   .   .   .

515. *April 13.—* . . . .

The greatest result of the last nine months is the good understanding between the two Emperors. One thing is now certain, nothing will again divide them; I will answer for that. This result belongs entirely to me, like a child which one man and one woman have on a desert island. To have children there must be two, a woman and a man. I know certainly that in the above case I was the man on the island.

521. *May 13.*—We have brought forth a work which may be acknowledged by the most honorable man without blushing. We have made a great epoch—great because the conduct of it was very difficult. More than great is the result of the concord here established between those who possess the will and the power for action. In three months no one will speak any more of the events of March and April. All will keep silence: the good, because they always are silent; the bad, because they are not flattered by their discomfiture; the stupid, because they really do not know what has happened, and others do not tell them.

523. *May 16.*—In London, as I foresaw, no one thinks any more of the late events: a proof of how wrong one is to flatter popular feeling. If any of their apostles regard this feeling as a religion, they are at this moment, when they get such a slap in the face, bound to show their strength. But such popular feeling is only a piece of buffoonery played by bad performers. It brings inexhaustible treasures to the quacks, but to the wise not a penny. But wise men who use them tenderly are either children or jugglers, and, therefore, not wise. This feeling has with me the value of a real religion, which gives to me what fools call strength, but which, closely analyzed, is only reason, and, indeed, only that reason which is mere want of stupidity. That is my secret, but I do not betray it, because it makes people take me for an extraordinary man. I know this is the truth, but I do not wish others to know it.

525. *May 21.*—I now part from this pleasant and beautiful town that has made so much noise in the world which, like every noise, passes away. But the result is imperishable. We have accomplished good and great things. They will not, indeed, be examined into, because a man is more concerned about an eight-day's fever than busied with eight years' health. My work has much in common with that of a

physician: if the patient dies, people say the physician has killed him; if he gets well, nature has saved him. To-morrow I shall start, and after making a little digression towards the Veldeser lake with the owner of Radmannsdorf, I shall take the road by Wurzen to Vienna.

No. 3   The Second Peace of Paris——20 November 1815[1]

In the Name of the Most Holy and Undivided Treaty.[2]

THE Allied Powers having by their united efforts, and by the success of their arms, preserved France and Europe from the convulsions with which they were menaced by the late enterprise of Napoleon Bonaparte,[3] and by the revolutionary system reproduced in France, to promote its success; participating at present with His Most Christian Majesty in the desire to consolidate, by maintaining inviolate the Royal authority, and by restoring the operation of the Constitutional Charter, the order of things which had been happily re-established in France, as also in the object of restoring between France and her neighbours those relations of reciprocal confidence and goodwill which the fatal effects of the Revolution and of the system of Conquest had for so long a time disturbed: persuaded, at the same time, that this last object can only be obtained by an arrangement framed to secure to the Allies proper indemnities for the past and solid guarantees for the future, they have, in concert with His Majesty the King of France, taken into consideration the means of giving effect to this arrangement; and being satisfied that the Indemnity due to the Allied Powers cannot be either entirely Territorial or entirely Pecuniary, without prejudice to France in the one or other of her essential interests, and that it would be more fit to combine both the modes in order to avoid the inconvenience which would result, were either resorted to separately, their Imperial and Royal Majesties

have adopted this basis for their present transactions; and agreeing alike as to the necessity of retaining for a fixed time in the Frontier Provinces of France, a certain number of allied troops, they have determined to combine their different arrangements, founded upon these bases, in a Definitive Treaty. For this purpose, and to this effect, His Majesty the King of the United Kingdom of Great Britain and Ireland, for himself and his Allies[4] on the one part, and His Majesty the King of France and Navarre on the other part, have named their Plenipotentiaries to discuss, settle and sign the said Definitive Treaty; namely, His Majesty the King of the United Kingdom of Great Britain and Ireland, the Right Honourable Robert Stewart Viscount Castlereagh, Knight of the Most Noble Order of the Garter, His said Majesty's Principal Secretary of State for Foreign Affairs, etc.; and the Most Illustrious and Most Noble Lord Arthur, Duke, Marquess, and Earl of Wellington, etc.;

And His Majesty the King of France and of Navarre, the Sieur Armand Emanuel du Plessis Richelieu, Duke of Richelieu, his Minister and Secretary of State for Foreign Affairs, and President of the Council of his Ministers, &c.,

Who having exchanged their Full Powers, found to be in good and due form, have signed the following Articles:—

Frontiers of France: as in 1790.

ART. I. The Frontiers of France shall be the same as they were in the year 1790, save and except the modifications on one side and on the other, which are detailed in the present Article.

. . . .

6thly, the High Contracting Parties shall name within 3 months after the signature of the present Treaty, Commissioners to regulate everything relating to the designation of the Boundaries of the respective Countries, and as soon as the labours of the Commissioners shall have terminated, Maps shall be drawn and landmarks shall be erected, which shall point out the respective limits.

Fortresses, etc., to be placed
at disposal of Allied Powers.

ART. II. The Fortresses, Places, and Districts, which, according to the preceding Article are no longer to form part of the French territory, shall be placed at the disposal of the Allied Powers, at the periods fixed by Article IX of the Military Convention annexed to the present Treaty; and His Majesty the King of France renounces for himself, His heirs, and successors for ever, the rights of Sovereignty and property which he has hitherto exercised over the said Fortresses, Places, and Districts.

Indemnity to be Paid by France.

ART. IV. The pecuniary part of the Indemnity to be furnished by France to the Allied Powers is fixed at the sum of 700,000,000 of Francs. The modes, the periods, and the guarantees for the payment of this sum shall be regulated by a Special Convention, which shall have the same force and effect as if it were inserted, word for word, in the present Treaty.

Military Occupation by Allies
along the Frontiers of France.

ART. V. The state of uneasiness and of fermentation, which after so many violent convulsions, and particularly after the last catastrophe, France must still experience, notwithstanding the paternal intentions of her King, and the advantages secured to every class of his subjects by the Constitutional Charter, requiring, for the security of the neighbouring States, certain measures of precaution and of temporary guarantee, it has been judged indispensable to occupy, during a fixed time, by a corps of Allied Troops certain military positions along the frontiers of France, under the express reserve, that such occupation shall in no way prejudice the Sovereignty of His Most Christian Majesty, nor the state of possession, such as it is recognized and confirmed by the present Treaty. The number of these troops shall not exceed 150,000 men. The Commander-in-Chief of this army shall be nominated by the Allied Powers. This army shall occupy the Fortresses of Condé, Valenciennes, Bouchain, Cambray, Le Quesnoy, Maubeuge, Landrecies, Avesnes, Rocroy, Givet with Charlemont, Mezières, Sedan, Montmedy, Thionville, Longwy, Bitsch, and the Tête-de-Pont of Fort Louis. As the maintenance of the army destined for this service is to be provided by France, a Special Convention shall also regulate the relations of the Army of Occupation with the civil and military authorities of the country. The utmost extent of the duration of this military occupation is fixed at 5 years. It may terminate before that period if, at the end of 3 years, the Allied Sovereigns, after having, in concert with His Majesty the King of France, maturely examined their reciprocal situation and interests, and the progress which shall have been made in France in the re-establishment of order and tranquility, shall agree to acknowledge that the motives which led them to that measure have ceased to exist.[5] But whatever may be the result of this deliberation, all the Fortresses and Positions occupied by the Allied troops shall, at the expiration of 5 years, be evacuated without further delay, and given up to His Most Christian Majesty, or to his heirs and successors.

Evacuation of French Territory.

ART. VI. The Foreign Troops, not forming part of the Army of Occupation, shall evacuate the French Territory within the term fixed by Article IX of the Military Convention annexed to the present Treaty.

Period fixed for Emigration and Disposal of Property in ceded Territories.

ART. VII. In all Countries which shall change Sovereigns, as well in virtue of the present Treaty as of the arrangements which are to be made in consequence thereof, a period of 6 years from the date of the exchange of the Ratifications shall be allowed to the inhabitants, natives or foreigners, of whatever condition and nation they may be, to dispose of their Property, if they should think fit so to do, and to retire to whatever country they may choose.

Restoration of Prisoners.

ART. X. All Prisoners taken during the hostilities, as well as all hostages which may have been carried off or given, shall be restored in the shortest time possible. The same shall be the case with respect to the prisoners taken previously to the Treaty of the 30th of May, 1814, and who shall not already have been restored.

Maintenance of Treaty of 30th May, 1814, and of Final Act of Vienna Congress of 9th June, 1815.

ART. XI. The Treaty of Paris of the 30th of May, 1814, and the Final Act of the Congress of Vienna of the 9th of June 1815, are confirmed, and shall be maintained in all such of their enactments which shall not have been modified by the Articles of the present Treaty.

Ratifications.

ART. XII. The present Treaty, with the Conventions annexed thereto, shall be ratified in one Act, and the Ratifications thereof shall be exchanged in the space of two months, or sooner, if possible.

In witness whereof the respective Plenipotentiaries have signed the same, and have affixed thereunto the Seals of their Arms.

Done at Paris, this 20th day of November, in the year of Our Lord, 1815.

(L.S.) CASTLEREAGH.   (L.S.) RICHELIEU.
(L.S.) WELLINGTON.

ADDITIONAL ARTICLE.
Abolition of the Slave Trade.

Paris, 20th November, 1815

The High Contracting Powers, sincerely desiring to give effect to the measures on which they deliberated at the Congress of Vienna relative to the complete and universal abolition of the Slave Trade, and having, each in their respective dominions, prohibited, without restriction, their Colonies and Subjects from taking any part whatever in this traffic, engage to renew conjointly their efforts, with the view of securing final success to their principles which they proclaimed in the Declaration of the 4th (8th) of February, 1815, and of concerting, without loss of time, through their Ministers at the Courts of London and of Paris, the most effectual measures for the entire and definitive abolition of a Commerce so odious, and so strongly condemned by the laws of Religion and of Nature.

The present Additional Article shall have the same force and effect as if it were inserted, word for word, in the Treaty signed this day. It shall be included in the Ratification of the said Treaty.

In witness whereof the respective Plenipotentiaries have signed the same, and have affixed thereunto the Seals of their Arms.

Done at Paris, this 20th day of November, 1815.

(L.S.) CASTLEREAGH.   (L.S.) RICHELIEU.
(L.S.) WELLINGTON.

No. 4   The Holy Alliance——26 September 1815[1]

In the name of the Most Holy and Indivisible Trinity.

Holy Alliance of Sovereigns of Austria, Prussia, and Russia.

THEIR Majesties the Emperor of Austria, the King of Prussia, and the Emperor of Russia, having, in consequence of the great events which have marked the course of the three last years in Europe, and especially of the blessings which it has pleased Divine Providence to shower down upon those States which place their confidence and their hope on it alone, acquired the intimate conviction of the necessity of settling the steps to be observed by the Powers, in their reciprocal relations, upon the sublime truths which the Holy Religion of our Saviour teaches;

Government and Political Relations.

They solemnly declare that the present Act has no other object than to publish, in the face of the whole world, their fixed resolution, both in the administration of their respective States, and in their political relations with every other Government, to take for their sole guide the precepts of that Holy Religion, namely, the precepts of Justice, Christian Charity, and Peace, which, far from being applicable only to private concerns, must have an immediate influence on the councils of Princes, and guide all their steps, as being the only means of consolidating human institutions and remedying their imperfections. In consequence, their Majesties have agreed on the following Articles:—

Principles of the Christian Religion.

ART. I. Conformably to the words of the Holy Scriptures, which command all men to consider each other as brethren, the Three contracting Monarchs will remain united by the bonds of a true and indissoluble fraternity, and considering each other as fellow countrymen, they will, on all occasions and in all places, lend each other aid and assistance; and, regarding themselves towards their subjects and armies as fathers of families, they will lead them, in the same spirit of fraternity with which they are animated, to protect Religion, Peace, and Justice.

Fraternity and Affection.

ART. II. In consequence, the sole principle of force, whether between the said Governments or between their Subjects, shall be that of doing each other reciprocal service, and of testifying by unalterable good will the mutual affection with which they ought to be animated, to consider themselves all as members of one and the same Christian nation; the three allied Princes looking on themselves as merely delegated by Providence to govern three branches of the One family, namely, Austria, Prussia, and Russia, thus confessing that the Christian world, of which they and their people form a part, has in reality no other Sovereign than Him to whom alone power really belongs, because in Him alone are found all the treasures of love, science, and infinite wisdom, that is to say, God, our Divine Savior, the Word of the Most High, the Word of Life. Their Majesties consequently recommend to their people, with the most tender solicitude, as the sole means of enjoying that Peace which arises from a good conscience, and which alone is durable, to strengthen themselves every day more and more in the principles and exercise of the duties which the Divine Saviour has taught to mankind.

Accession of Foreign Powers.

ART. III. All the Powers who shall choose solemnly to avow the sacred principles which have dictated the present Act, and shall acknowledge how important it is for the happiness of nations, too long agitated, that these truths should henceforth exercise over the destinies of mankind all the influence which belongs to them, will be received with equal ardour and affection into this Holy Alliance.

Done in triplicate, and signed at Paris, the year of Grace 1815, 14th/26th September.

(L.S.) FRANCIS.
(L.S.) FREDERICK WILLIAM.
(L.S.) ALEXANDER.

[It is stated in "Martens' Treaties" that the greater part of the Christian Powers acceded to this Treaty. France acceded to it in 1815; the Netherlands and Wurtemburg did so in 1816; and Saxony, Switzerland, and the Hanse Towns in 1817. But neither the Pope nor the Sultan was invited to accede.—Ed.][2]

No. 5   The Quadruple Alliance——20 November 1815[1]

In the Name of the Most Holy and Undivided Trinity.

THE purpose of the Alliance concluded at Vienna the 25th day of March, 1815 having been happily attained by the reestablishment in France of the order of things which the last criminal attempt of Napoleon Bonaparte had momentarily subverted; Their Majesties the King of the United Kingdom of Great Britain and Ireland, the Emperor of Austria, King of Hungary and Bohemia, the Emperor of all the Russias, and the King of Prussia, considering that the repose of Europe is essentially interwoven with the confirmation of the order of things founded on the maintenance of the Royal Authority and of the Constitutional Charter, and wishing to employ all their means to prevent the general Tranquility (the object of the wishes of mankind and the constant end of their efforts), from being again disturbed; desirous moreover to draw closer the ties which unite them for the common interests of their people, have resolved to give to the principles solemnly laid down in the Treaties of Chaumont of the 1st March, 1814, and of Vienna of the 25th of March, 1815,[2] the application the most analogous to the present state of affairs, and to fix beforehand by a solemn Treaty the principles which they propose to follow, in order to guarantee Europe from dangers by which she may still be menaced; for which purpose the High Contracting Parties have named to discuss, settle and sign the conditions of this Treaty, namely;

His Majesty the King of the United Kingdom of Great Britain and Ireland, the Right Honourable Robert Stewart Viscount Castlereagh, etc., and the Most Illustrious and Most Noble Lord Arthur, Duke, Marquis and Earl of Wellington, etc.

And His Majesty the Emperor of Austria, King of Hungary and Bohemia, the Sieur Clement Wenceslas Lothaire, Prince of Metternich-Winnebourg etc., and the Sieur John Philip Baron of Wessenberg, etc., who, after having exchanged their full powers, found to be in good and due form, have agreed upon the following Articles:—

Execution of Treaties of Peace, etc., with France, of 20th November, 1815.

ART. I. The High Contracting Parties reciprocally promise to maintain, in its force and vigour, the Treaty signed this day with His Most Christian Majesty, and to see that the stipulations of the said Treaty, as well as those of the Particular Conventions which have reference thereto, shall be strictly and faithfully executed in their fullest extent.

Confirmation of Arrangements of 1814 and 1815.
Exclusion of Bonaparte Family from Supreme Power in France.
Measures of General Security.

ART. II. The High Contracting Parties, having engaged in the War which has just terminated, for the purpose of maintaining inviolably the Arrangements settled at Paris last year, for the safety and interest of Europe, have judged it advisable to renew the said Engagements by the present Act, and to confirm them as mutually obligatory, subject to the modifications contained in the Treaty signed this day with the Plenipotentiaries of His Most Christian Majesty, and particularly those by which Napoleon Bonaparte and his family, in pursuance of the Treaty of the 11th of April, 1814, have been for ever excluded from Supreme Power in France, which exclusion the Contracting Powers bind themselves, by the present Act, to maintain in full vigour, and should it be necessary, with the whole of their forces.[3] And as the same Revolutionary Principles which upheld the last criminal usurpation, might again, under other forms, convulse France, and thereby endanger the repose of other States; under these circumstances, the High Contracting Parties solemnly admitting it to be their duty to redouble their watchfulness for the tranquillity and interests of their people, engage, in case so unfortunate an event should again occur, to concert amongst themselves, and with His Most Christian Majesty, the measures which they may judge necessary to be pursued for the safety of their respective States, and for the general Tranquillity of Europe.

Military Line in France.
Renewal of Alliance of Chaumont.

ART. III. The High Contracting Parties, in agreeing with His Most Christian Majesty that a Line of Military Positions in France should be occupied by a corps of Allied Troops during a certain number of years, had in view to secure, as far as lay in their power, the effect of the stipulations contained in Articles I and II of the present Treaty, and, uniformly disposed to adopt every salutary measure calculated to secure the Tranquility of Europe by maintaining the order of things re-established in France, they engage, in case the said body of troops should be attacked or menaced with an attack on the part of France, that the said Powers should be again obliged to place themselves on a war establishment against that Power, in order to maintain either of the said stipulations, or to secure and support the great interests to which they relate, each of the High Contracting Parties shall furnish, without delay, according to the stipulations of the Treaty of Chaumont, and especially in pursuance of Articles VII and VIII of this Treaty, its full contingent of 60,000 men, in addition to the forces left in France, or such part of the said contingent as the exigency of the case may require, should be put in motion.

Additional Forces in the Event of War.
Conditions of Peace.

ART. IV. If, unfortunately, the forces stipulated in the preceding Article should be found insufficient, the High Contracting Parties will concert together, without loss of time, as to the additional number of troops to be furnished by cach for the support of the common cause; and they engage to employ, in case of need, the whole of their forces, in order to bring the War to a speedy and successful termination, reserving to themselves the right to prescribe, by common consent, such conditions of Peace as shall hold out to Europe a sufficient guarantee against the recurrence of a similar calamity.

Duration of Engagements.

ART. V. The High Contracting Parties having agreed to the dispositions laid down in the preceding Articles, for the purpose of securing the effect of their engagements during the period of the temporary occupation, declare, moreover, that even after the expiration of this measure, the said engagements shall still remain in full force and vigour, for the purpose of carrying into effect such measures as may be deemed necessary for the maintenance of the stipulations contained in Articles I and II of the present Act.

Renewal of Meetings of the Allies for Maintenance of Peace of Europe.

ART. VI. To facilitate and to secure the execution of the present Treaty, and to consolidate the connections which at the present moment so closely unite the Four Sovereigns for the happiness of the world, the High Contracting Parties have agreed to renew their Meetings at fixed periods, either under the immediate auspices of the Sovereigns themselves, or by their respective Ministers, for the purpose of consulting upon their common interests, and for the consideration of the measures which at each of those periods shall be considered the most salutary for the repose and prosperity of Nations, and for the maintenance of the Peace of Europe.

Ratifications.

ART. VII. The present Treaty shall be ratified, and the Ratifications shall be exchanged within two months, or sooner, if possible.

In faith of which the respective Plenipotentiaries have signed it, and affixed thereto the Seal of their Arms.

Done at Paris, the 20th of November, in the year of Our Lord, 1815.

(L.S.) CASTLEREAGH.   (L.S.) METTERNICH.
(L.S.) WELLINGTON.   (L.S.) WESSENBERG.

[NOTE.—Separate Treaties were signed on the same day by the Plenipotentiaries of Great Britain, Russia, and Prussia, respectively.—Ed.]

No. 6   Metternich: On Reforms in Prussia—— 14 November 1818[1]

Metternich to Prince Wittgenstein, Prussian Minister of State.

Aix, November 14, 1818.

304. I have the honor to send you, my dear Prince, the two sketches enclosed, confident as I have long been of your patriotism.

I do not come unbidden to plead for a cause strange to me. I have in these sketches laid down plainly my creed as the head of the Austrian Cabinet. Our intention is pure, like our views; we do not separate our fate from the State which in every respect is nearest to us. The moment is urgent. What to-day may yet be possible will not be so to-morrow, and assistance is only possible as long as free power is in the hands of the King.

I beg you, my dear Prince, carefully to consider both these documents. I have divided them because they belong to different branches of the administration.

The first (No. 305) is my view of the next form of administration suitable for Prussia, and rests on one single proposition:

The central representation by representatives of the people is the disintegration of the Prussian States.

It is so because such a reform takes place in no great State without leading to a revolution or following upon a revolution;

because in the Prussian State, from its geographical position and its composition, a central representation is not possible; because this State requires before everything a free and sound military strength, and this does not and cannot consist with a purely representative system.

According to my firm conviction, the King ought to go no further than the formation of provincial Diets in a very carefully considered, circumscribed form. If the idea of a central representative body, chosen from the different Diets, is referred to by me, this is because a similar idea already exists in the Royal declaration, which is known to the public and is the only one possible. Beyond this all is pure revolution. Will these very limited ideas not also lead to revolution? This question the King should ponder deeply before he decides.

The second paper (No. 306) is no less important in its object, and is as urgent as the first in its application. It needs no comment, for fact speaks daily for my proposition.

I have, under the seal of secrecy, imparted these two projects to the Chancellor of State, Prince Hardenberg. I put the present copies into your hands, my dear Prince, and I leave it to your judgment whether you will submit them to his Majesty. In the first audience granted me by his Majesty some propositions were received with such free and outspoken conviction that his Majesty made me wish to write them down. I believe, too, that I fulfill a duty to my own Fatherland in offering our true and impartial opinion on the position and the dangers of our closest allies. Receive, my dear Prince, this proof of confidence, &c. &c.

On the Position of the Prussian States.

305. It would be superfluous to enter upon a consideration of the importance of the existence of Prussia for the whole of the European State-system. This springs from the nature of things; it is founded on the present condition of Europe, and this universal admission is manifested by the late negotiations.[2]

But for Austria the existence of Prussia has a special and peculiar value.

In a similar position with respect to neighboring States; the chief members of a Bund[3] which has the right to reckon on their support, and the duty of rendering the same support to them in return, the two States can never separate their interests without danger and difficulty to both. They must together prosper or together suffer; the peace, the strength, or the weakness of the one will always react for good or evil on the other.

The strength of States rests on two fundamental conditions—their political and their administrative conformation.

The first is at the present time more than ever beyond the calculation, as beyond the will, of Governments. The limits of States are of late years firmly and inviolably fixed by diplomatic negotiations. What might be improved in them lies consequently beyond the sphere of discussion. Political repose rests on fraternization between monarchs, and on the principle of maintaining that which is. To oppose these fundamental principles would be to shake the edifice to its very foundations; the consequences of such an undertaking must certainly be to any State more productive of danger than utility.

But the form of administration remains in the hands of the Government wherever the power has not been given away. The efforts of parties are constantly directed to lead Governments astray from this truth. The revolutionists always calculate on the paternal feeling of the reigning princes; wisdom, however, bids the monarch, above all, to maintain the right, to protect his people from theoretical projects, and to prove and consider everything, and make choice of the best.

Wherever the limit has not yet been

overstepped—that is to say, wherever the monarch can still act independently—the carrying out of this last principle is quite possible, and this holds good for Prussia. The course now chosen by the King will decide much more than the fate of his own kingdom. What an incalculable influence the next internal organization of the Prussian States must have on Germany and Austria is self-evident. This is felt by the unelected representatives of the so-called voice of the people. The party has so far remained true and consistent in its course. It has sought in Prussia the support for its lever, and perhaps has found it only too readily. The moment has arrived for the King to give his verdict. His decision may be the certain triumph of the revolution over the whole of Europe, or may save and maintain the peace of Prussia and the world.

What will the King do? This question may, perhaps, be answered in a few sentences.

The main condition of every form, its utility or its worthlessness, will be determined by a true knowledge of the body to which it is to be applied.

The Prussian States, although united under one sceptre, consist of many different portions, separated by geographical position, climate, race, or language. It has in this respect much similarity with the Austrian, although the position of the latter is in every way more advantageous. The separate parts of the Austrian monarchy are more solid; their geographical position is better; they all form a well-rounded whole. Of the two kingdoms Austria would herself be more suited for a pure representative system than Prussia, if the differences of her populations in language and habits were not too important. How can that which is impossible to be carried out in Austria succeed in Prussia?

Under the existing circumstances in the two monarchies the certain result of the attempt would be that in the desire for a really representative central system, the kingdom would fall into separate parts—parts which have not then to be made, but which are already there as parts, and show more substantial differences than even Holland or the Netherlands.

The success of the central representation in this kingdom does not need consideration; the introduction of it has given to all Europe a great and decisive proof of the uselessness of such a scheme in a whole formed of such essentially different parts, and in this way it may have done some good.

In another respect the kingdom of the Netherlands offers a second experience which is not to be despised. This kingdom requires above all for its maintenance a strong military power, and this very important condition of its existence as well as that of Prussia is enfeebled by its constitution, as would be the case in Prussia if a central representation were introduced. This has been felt by the civil party in Prussia, which has long ago raised its voice against the army, and proposed a senseless system of a mere arming of the people in the place of the standing army. The Prussian State would approach its internal dissolution if ever the King of Prussia should appear, not at the head of an army, but as the leader of seven or eight separate masses of men.

Promises, however, have been made on the part of the Government; they must be redeemed. The pressure of the people is to obtain some guarantee against despotism, especially on the part of the Germans, from a remembrance of former times, and from the dreadful abuse of power of which the German princes, in their arrogance, have been guilty since the year 1806. This pressure was originally for the restoration of government by Diet, until overpowered by the voices of the revolutionists, it made its appearance in the form of a desire for a central representative system. It is easy to imagine from the obscure ideas of the majority as to the real nature of popular representation to what delusion this gives rise; and if the national mind has really changed, it becomes all the more incumbent on the monarchs to examine everything, and to resolve only what is truly good.

The king has promised a purely representative system. He will accordingly give to his people the guarantees which alone are suitable to his kingdom.

The Prussian monarchy may be divided naturally into several divisions:

1. The Marks of Brandenburg;
2. The Kingdom of Prussia;
3. The Grand Duchy of Posen;
4. The Duchy of Silesia;
5. The Duchy of Saxony;
6. The Duchy of Westphalia;
7. The Grand Duchy of the Lower Rhine.

It is still to be considered to what divisions Pomerania, Lower Saxony, and Berg will be joined. They are at any rate not fitted to form single States, and it is probable that Pomerania will be united to the Marks, Lower Saxony to the Duchy of Saxony, and Berg to Westphalia.

Each of these provinces is entitled to take part in a representative system by Diet, but these Diets are by no means to be cast in exactly the same forms without regard to their local concerns, which are, for instance, in the Grand Duchy of the Lower Rhine very different from others, as Silesia, the Marks, &c. &c. By an enlightened regard for local concerns, the surest foundation will be laid for the happiness of each State in itself and the welfare of all the States as a whole.

Such Diets should be formed before anything else is done.

If ever the Budget question or legislation in the highest sense should make a central representation advantageous to the State, or if the solution of this question should be hereafter unavoidable, an expedient might be found by choosing not less than three members to be sent from each Diet, expressly called together for that purpose.

This central body would at least be more easy to guide aright than a combination of deputies strange or even hostile to each other, who would never be brought to agree in one political aim.

The following main points will suffice to show briefly our views:

1. The Prussian State shall continue to exist in the form of separate provinces.

The executive power to reside in the King. He will have ministers at the head of the different departments, and a Council of State.

Each province to have an Upper and a Lower administrative board.

2. Each province to be represented in a way suitable to its local relations.

The presidents of the Diets to be named by the King.

The principal features of the action of the Diets will be as follows:

In their assemblies, legally summoned, they shall have the right to transmit to the Government all requests and remonstrances on matters concerning the welfare of the province, the Diet, or single individuals.

It will rest with them to distribute the taxes according to legal principles, to watch over the just division of the public burdens in the provinces and prevent all abuse and injustice in this respect.

3. The King will introduce this system of representation and reserve to himself the subsequent decision as to the co-operation of the provincial Diets by means of a central representation composed from them for the passing of the Budget and higher legislation.

The Government must be careful, before the introduction of Diets, to arrange the provinces in their different parts and regulate their administration, and a central representation can only be the result of such arrangements.

4. It is no doubt a question worthy of consideration, what connection there might

be between a Council of State in the extensive form of the Prussian Council and the central representation as chosen from the different Diets, and whether some members of the Council of State, as such, might become members of the central representation.

On Education, Gymnastic Establishments, and Liberty of the Press.
(Supplement to No. 304.)

306. As important perhaps for the decision of the Prussian Government are the questions arising from the intrigues of the various peace-disturbing parties in Prussia as well as Germany.

The means of checking the growing evil are twofold. The first and principal the King will find in his own will; the second, in the closest agreement with Austria. The first refers to the Prussian State itself; the second to a common course to be followed at the Diet.[4] These last might gain in safety by an agreement between the two chief German States, and confidential conferences with the chief Courts before they can with advantage be brought before the Diet.

The subjects which we think necessary to point out here are:

I. The question of Education.
II. The establishments for Gymnastics.
III. The Liberty of the Press.

I. EDUCATION.

No impartial observer can now doubt that the innovators in Germany—and most of them are found among the learned caste —have relinquished the hope of actively influencing the present generation with their revolutionary spirit, and still more of moving them to action. The characteristic features of the Germans will always hinder the success of such an attempt. The German is cold, prudent, and faithful. He speculates more than he acts, especially when the action involves a rending of the civil and domestic ties. The patriotism of the Germans has various aims; there are in the common fatherland separate voices of the people; provincial patriotism is the nearest to the German citizen: he grasps it from the cradle, and thirty generations have shown no reason why it should not be honored as the deepest and most natural feeling, for the Brandenburger and the Austrian, the Bavarian and the Hessian, are all alike Germans. The political formation of States often operates on the mind of the people for centuries longer than the institutions themselves exist; the remembrance of the German Empire, too, is still fresh and vivid, particularly in the lower classes. Even if there is no more an Empire, there is still a Germany, and the nucleus of ancient provinces under ancient Princes.

Conscious of the futility of the undertaking, the plan of the innovators—for they act on a settled plan—has taken quite a different character, a character which suits itself to the feeling and personal relations of the leaders: that which the present generation cannot perform is reserved for the next, and in order that the next generation may not follow the footsteps of its predecessors, the youth must be seized as he leaves boyhood, and he must undergo a revolutionary training.

Where the revolution in its coarsest form cannot pervert and incite to insurrection the already educated, a people shall be educated for revolution.

This plan is followed at some of the German universities, and if we have not the necessary information to enable us to judge exactly how far many professors at the Prussian universities join in it, we believe we are not wrong in considering it more than probable that they do so.

The Royal Prussian Government is well aware of the signification of the German *Burschenschaft,* and that the mischief cannot be too soon checked is beyond a doubt. But that this can only be accomplished by the united action of the German Governments is just as certain.

II. GYMNASTIC ESTABLISHMENTS.

The mischief here is closely connected with life at the universities: the inventors, the invention, and the execution belong to Prussia.

The gymnastic establishment is a real preparatory school of university disorders. There the boy is formed into the youth, as in the higher school—the university—the youth is formed into the man.

We here declare our firm conviction that it has become a duty of State for the King thoroughly and entirely to destroy this evil. Palliative measures are no longer sufficient. The whole institution in every shape must be closed and done away with, offenders being made liable to legal censure.

As the institution was founded and still exists in Berlin itself, and as the branch institutions seem all to depend on and spring from the mother institution, the evil must there be uprooted. If offshots continue to exist, this will be a fit subject for con-sultation with those German Governments which may not be clear-sighted enough, and may further encourage the evil.

III. LIBERTY OF THE PRESS.

This point, the most difficult of all, can only be regulated by a close agreement between Austria and Prussia, and by this means with the other German Govern-ments—if, indeed, it possibly can be regu-lated.

Every measure must be grounded on the following principles:

1. The broadest views as to real substan-tial works;

2. The most decided difference between such works and pamphlets and journals;

3. Respect for the independence of the single States forming the Bund, and the certainty that no State may remain in the Bund which does not possess some efficient law on this subject, whether it be preventive or repressive.

No. 7   Metternich: On the Right of Intervention—— 8 and 31 December 1820[1]

Circular Despatch of the Courts of Austria, Russia, and Prussia, to their Ambassadors and Agents at the German and Northern Courts, Troppau, December 8, 1820.

484. The events of March 8 in Spain, and July 2 in Naples, and the catastrophe in Portugal, must cause in all those who have to care for the peace of States a deep feeling of grief and anxiety, and, at the same time, a necessity for meeting, in order to consider in common how best to meet the evils which threaten to break out all over Europe.

It was natural that these feelings should be very active in those particular Powers which had lately conquered revolution, and now saw it raising its head again; and also natural that these Powers, in resisting the revolution for the third time, should resort to the same means which they had used so happily in the memorable combat which delivered Europe from a twenty years' yoke.

Everything justified the hope that this union, formed under the most dangerous circumstances, crowned with the most brilli-ant success, fostered by the negotiations of 1814, 1815, and 1818, as it had released the European continent from the military despotism of the representative of revolu-tion, and brought peace to the world, would be able to curb a new force not less tyran-nical and not less to be despised—the power of rebellion and outrage.

These were the motives, and the purpose, of the meeting in Troppau. The former are so evident that they do not require an explanation: the latter is so honorable and beneficial that doubtless the wishes of all honorable men will follow the allied Courts in their noble career.

The business which is imposed on them by the most sacred obligations is great and difficult; but a happy presentiment bids them hope for the attainment of their aim by a firm maintenance of the spirit of those treaties to which Europe owes peace and unity among her States.

The Powers exercise an indisputable right in contemplating common measures of safety against States in which the Government has been overthrown by rebellion, and which, if only as an example, must consequently be treated as hostile to all lawful constitutions and Governments. The exercise of this right becomes still more urgent when revolutionists endeavor to spread to neighboring countries the misfortunes which they had brought upon themselves, scattering rebellion and confusion around.

Such a position, such proceedings are an evident violation of contract, which guarantees to all the European Governments, besides the inviolability of their territories, the enjoyment of those peaceful relations which exclude the possibility of encroachment on either side.

The allied Courts took incontestable fact as their starting-point, and those ministers who could be at Troppau itself supplied with definite instructions from their monarchs, therefore made an agreement as to the principles to be followed as to States whose form of government has been violently disturbed, and as to the peaceful or forcible measures to be adopted to lead such States back into the Bund.[2]

The results of their deliberations they communicated to the Courts of Paris and London, that those Courts might take them into consideration.

Since the Neapolitan revolution takes daily fresh root; since no other endangers so directly the peace of the neighboring States; since no other can be acted upon so immediately, the necessity of proceeding on the above-mentioned principles with regard to the kingdom of Both the Sicilies soon became evident.

To bring about conciliatory measures to that end, the monarchs assembled at Troppau resolved to invite the King of Both Sicilies to meet them at Laybach, a step which would free the will of his Majesty from every outward constraint, and put the King in the position of a mediator between his deluded and erring subjects and the States whose peace was threatened by them. Since the monarchs were determined not to acknowledge Governments created by open rebellion, they could enter into a negotiation with the person of the King only. Their ministers and agents in Naples have received the necessary instructions for that purpose.

France and England have been asked to take part in this step, and it is to be expected that they will not refuse their consent, since the principle on which the invitation rests is in perfect harmony with the agreements formerly concluded by them, and is also a pledge of the most upright and peaceable feelings.[3]

The system established between Austria, Prussia, and Russia is no new one; it rests on the same maxims which formed the foundation of the agreements by which the union of the European States in the Bund has been effected. The hearty concord existing between the Courts which form the centre of this confederation can only be strengthened by it. The Bund will be maintained on the same footing as that on which it was placed by the Powers to whom it owes its existence, and as it has been gradually accepted by all, from the conviction entertained of its evident and undoubted advantages.

No further proof, however, is required

that the Powers have not been guided in their resolutions by the thought of conquest or the desire of interfering with the internal affairs of other Governments. They want nothing but to maintain peace, to free Europe from the scourge of revolution, and to avert, or shorten as much as possible, the mischief arising from the violation of all the principles of order and morality. Under such conditions they think themselves justified in claiming the unanimous approbation of the world as a reward for their cares and their efforts.

*Metternich to Count Rechberg,
Vienna, December 31, 1820.*

485. I take advantage, my dear Count, of the first moment at my disposal, which is the last of my stay here, to give you some account of what has been done and what is going to be done. . . .

Here are the facts in all their simplicity.

Any catastrophe such as that of Naples presents different periods, whether regarded from a domestic or foreign point of view. The revolt breaks out; it is indubitable and evident; it is the beginning of a conflagration; if they are in good order, take your fire-engines there; ask no questions; do not hesitate; extinguish the fire; success will be certain. Do not take empty fire-engines, but let them be well filled.

Then comes the second period. The revolt takes the appearance of Reform. A feeble sovereign swears to put a knife to his throat. A chorus of Liberals and Radicals join in his hymns; the sovereign is praised to the skies; and the people seem to adore him. Milk and honey are to flow in all the veins of the State abandoned to anarchy; tyrants alone could hinder the development of so fine a work!

This is the history of the months of July to November.

Our fire-engines were not full in July, otherwise we should have set to work immediately.

In the second period, it did not seem to us that our neutral attitude was sufficient; the Naples affair threatened Italy, Austria, Europe equally. It is therefore for the latter to declare itself in principle with us. We take upon ourselves the material part. To go to Naples is nothing at any time, but to remain at Naples and re-establish order in the kingdom of the Two Sicilies is certainly more difficult.

Europe has frankly and well seconded us. We, who were free to hold whatever language we liked, have spoken: those of our allies who could do the same have done so. Those who are more bound by forms have acted according to our principles. The Neapolitan revolt and all its charms have been put in quarantine. You have done more than even the great English and French. You have sent back the agent of the Carbonari who came to boast to you of the happiness of his country; you have done this, my dear Count, and it was worthy of you.

Agreed in their principles at Troppau, the three Cabinets have carried them into effect. The idea of inviting the King to meet us at Laybach was acceptable. This invitation was made on very simple but the only correct grounds. You know the autograph letters of the Sovereigns: they are all friendly, for no one is an enemy of the King. The *ostensible* instructions for our plenipotentiaries were more precise. They were ordered to declare:

1st. That the Powers would never recognize anything which is the work of the rebellion.

2nd. That before resorting to extreme measures, they desire to exhaust every means of conciliation, *not between the rebellion and lawful power, but between the real interests of the kingdom and those of Italy and Europe.* That, knowing but one proper instrument for a work so great and salutary, his Majesty the King was invited to meet the three monarchs.

3rd. That at Naples it is asserted that

the King is free. That the King, being free, should feel it his duty to take upon himself this great work; that if the King did not come he would be surrendered.

4th. That as the King's person is not on this occasion to be replaced by any other, the invitation is personal. That our ambassadors would in consequence refuse passports to any other individual, were it even a Prince of the Royal House; that on the other hand, it would depend upon the King to be accompanied by whomsoever his Majesty should think fit.

. . . .

No. 8   Castlereagh: England Denies the Right of Intervention——19 January 1821[1]

CIRCULAR Despatch to British Missions at Foreign Courts.

Foreign Office, 19th January, 1821.

SIR,

I should not have felt it necessary to have made any communication to you, in the present state of the discussions begun at Troppau and transferred to Laybach, had it not been for a Circular Communication, which has been addressed by the Courts of Austria, Prussia, and Russia to their several Missions,[2] and which His Majesty's Government conceive, if not adverted to, might (however unintentionally) convey, upon the subject therein alluded to, very erroneous impressions of the past, as well as of the present, sentiments of the British Government.

It has become therefore necessary to inform you, that the King has felt Himself obliged to decline becoming a Party to the measures in question.

These measures embrace two distinct objects:—1st, The establishment of certain General Principles for the regulation of the future political conduct of the Allies in the cases therein described:—2ndly, The proposed mode of dealing, under these principles, with the existing affairs of Naples.

The system of measures proposed under the former head, if to be reciprocally acted upon, would be in direct repugnance to the fundamental Laws of this Country.—

But even if this decisive objection did not exist, the British Government would nevertheless regard the principles on which these measures rest, to be such as could not be safely admitted as a system of International Law. They are of opinion that their adoption would inevitably sanction, and, in the hands of less beneficent Monarchs, might hereafter lead to, a much more frequent and extensive interference in the internal transactions of States, than they are persuaded is intended by the August Parties from whom they proceed, or can be reconcileable either with the general interest, or with the efficient authority and dignity, of independent Sovereigns. They do not regard the Alliance as entitled, under existing Treaties, to assume, in their character as Allies, any such general powers, nor do they conceive that such extraordinary powers could be assumed, in virtue of any fresh Diplomatic Transaction amongst the Allied Courts, without their either attributing to themselves a supremacy incompatible with the rights of other States, or, if to be acquired through the special accession of such States, without introducing a federative system in Europe, not only unwieldy and ineffectual to its object, but leading to many most serious inconveniences.

With respect to the particular case of Naples, the British Government, at the very earliest moment, did not hesitate to express their strong disapprobation of the mode and circumstances, under which that Revolution was understood to have been effected; but they, at the same time, expressly declared to the several Allied Courts, that they should not consider themselves as either called upon, or justified, to advise an interference on the part of this Country: They fully admitted, however, that other European States, and especially Austria and the Italian Powers, might feel themselves differently circumstanced; and they professed that it was not their purpose to prejudge the question as it might affect them, or to interfere with the course which such States might think fit to adopt, with a view to their own security, provided only that they were ready to give every reasonable assurance that their views were not directed to purposes of aggrandisement subversive of the Territorial System of Europe, as established by the late Treaties.

Upon these principles the conduct of His Majesty's Government with regard to the Neapolitan Question has been, from the first moment, uniformly regulated, and copies of the successive instructions sent to the British Authorities at Naples for their guidance have been from time to time transmitted for the information of the Allied Governments.

With regard to the expectation which is expressed in the Circular above alluded to, of the assent of the Courts of London and Paris to the more general measures proposed for their adoption founded, as it is alleged, upon existing Treaties; in justification of its own consistency and good faith, the British Government, in withholding such assent, must protest against any such interpretation being put upon the Treaties in question, as is therein assumed.

They have never understood these Treaties to impose any such obligations; and they have, on various occasions, both in Parliament and in their intercourse with the Allied Governments, distinctly maintained the negative of such a proposition: That they have acted with all possible

explicitness upon this subject, would at once appear from reference to the deliberations at Paris in 1815,[3] previous to the conclusion of the Treaty of Alliance[4] at Aix-la-Chapelle in 1818;—and subsequently in certain discussions which took place in the course of the last year.

After having removed the misconception to which the passage of the Circular in question, if passed over in silence, might give countenance; and having stated in general terms, without however entering into the argument, the dissent of His Majesty's Government from the general principle upon which the Circular in question is founded, it should be clearly understood that no Government can be more prepared than the British Government is, to uphold the right of any State or States to interfere, where their own immediate security or essential interests are seriously endangered by the internal transactions of another State.—But as they regard the assumption of such right, as only to be justified by the strongest necessity, and to be limited and regulated thereby, they cannot admit that this right can receive a general and indiscriminate application to all Revolutionary Movements, without reference to their immediate bearing upon some particular State or States, or be made prospectively the basis of an Alliance.—They regard its exercise as an exception to general principles of the greatest value and importance, and as one that only properly grows out of the circumstances of the special case; but they at the same time consider that exceptions of this description never can, without the utmost danger, be so far reduced to rule, as to be incorporated into the ordinary diplomacy of States, or into the institutes of the Law of Nations.

As it appears that certain of the Ministers of the three Courts have already communicated this Circular Despatch to the Courts to which they are accredited, I leave it to your discretion to make a corresponding communication, on the part of your

Government, regulating your language in conformity to the principles laid down in the present despatch. You will take care, however, in making such communication, to do justice, in the name of your Government, to the purity of intention, which has no doubt actuated these August Courts in the adoption of the course of measures which they are pursuing. The difference of sentiment which prevails between them and the Court of London on this matter, you may declare, can make no alteration whatever in the cordiality and harmony of the Alliance on any other subject, or abate their common zeal in giving the most complete effect to all their existing engagements.

I am, etc.

CASTLEREAGH.

No. 9　　Paul W. Schroeder: Metternich—— European Statesman or Austrian Diplomat?[1]

.　.　.　.　.　.　.　.　.　.

It cannot be denied, then, that Metternich displayed diplomatic talents of a high order, amounting almost to genius. In this respect, no one in the nineteenth century matched him except Bismarck. More open to dispute are the questions of what ends Metternich sought to achieve with his diplomacy, and how worthwhile these ends were. Few even of Metternich's detractors would deny his diplomatic skill, while his defenders, notably his eminent biographer, Heinrich Ritter von Srbik, insist that something better and deeper is required to account for Metternich's achievements than mere diplomatic skill and maneuvering.[2]

Before attempting to add my bit to the acrid and not wholly edifying controversy over Metternich, I wish to stress two points by way of precaution. First, my own interpretation covers only Metternich's foreign policy during 1820-1823, and is thus at most a limited contribution to a general interpretation of Metternich's policy. This condition applies to all the rest of this chapter, even where it is not explicitly stated. Second, the evaluation of Metternich's policy given here is intended to be simply descriptive and historical, not moral. Even where I use words unavoidably charged with moral connotation (e.g., "repressive," "standstill") in characterizing Metternich's policy, the intent is to give an accurate description, not a moral judgment.

Plainly, it would be presumptuous as well as futile for me to attempt in a brief space a point-by-point analysis and critique of Srbik's interpretation of Metternich. Srbik's main thesis, however, has become familiar and widely accepted, and has influenced to a greater or lesser extent such historians as Hugo Hantsch, Werner Näf, Constantin de Grunwald, Hans Rieben, and, most recently, Henry A. Kissinger.[3] According to this interpretation, Metternich was a man of many faults and shortcomings, indeed, but withal a political figure far removed from the blind reactionary pictured by nineteenth-century historians. Despite grave mistakes, he was, all in all, a constructive European statesman. His program for Austria and Europe was based on a system of coherent principles, not a patchwork of day-to-day diplomatic maneuvers; his policy was highly conservative, but definitely not reactionary.[4]

The objection to this construction of Metternich, in my opinion, is that, though persuasive and convincing at first appearance, it does not, when applied to the period under consideration, seem to fit the evidence at hand. My own impression, in dealing with Metternich from 1820 to 1823, is that, instead of finding the long-range principles and plans of a constructive European statesman, one is continually confronted in the documents with the shortrange maneuvers and expedients of a repressive Austrian diplomat. Three basic questions regarding Metternich's policy and attitudes in this period may explain and defend this conclusion. First, was his policy constructive? Second, was it "European"? Third, was it genuinely conservative? The answer to each question, properly understood and qualified, must, I believe, be in the negative.

As to the first, Metternich's policy in this period was not constructive for the simple reason that he was not trying to construct anything. His aim was not to make things happen, but to prevent things from happening; not to meet problems in some positive way, but simply to restrain and prevent political action, change, innovation, and movement of all kinds. . . .

.   .   .   .

To argue, as I have, that Metternich's policy was one of repression and standstillism is not to imply that everything he did was wrong. His actions in the Russo-Turk crisis or the French-Spanish imbroglio, for example, might well be justified as the defense of a *status quo* which was better than any practicable change. It is quite arguable that Austria's internal weaknesses, together with the personality of her Emperor, made a policy of standstillism the only one possible. The only point here is that it is hard to see how such a purely negative policy can be labeled "constructive."

.   .   .   .

One need not judge Metternich by modern standards of the welfare state to arrive at an unfavorable verdict on his approach to fundamental problems of state. He lagged behind the better standards of his own time. His own emissaries—De Menz, Daiser, and Brunetti—showed insights and programs better than his. If enlightened despotism, as has been said, was the deathbed repentance of absolute monarchy, Metternich, in this period at least, never repented. He showed no great zeal for the aims of enlightened despotism—the promotion of industry and agriculture, the advancement of education and learning, the elevation of the physical lot of the worker and the peasant, and the development of the resources of the state—while he repudiated its fundamental premise—that the state and its monarch exist to promote the welfare of its subjects—as part of the false philosophy and philanthropy of the eighteenth century.[5]

It may be objected that this appraisal leaves out Metternich's most important contribution to statecraft, his contribution to the maintenance of European peace and order. His most vital insight was the recognition that liberalism and nationalism, left unchecked, would lead to the wars and anarchy of the twentieth century. A clear evidence of his statesmanship was his effort to meet this danger by attempting to preserve the unity of the great powers, by espousing a principle of intervention against revolution, and by promoting the beginnings of a confederation of Europe.[6] Whatever the shortcomings of Metternich's outlook on domestic issues, in other words, his program was genuinely and constructively European.

Certainly there is something to this thesis. That is, Metternich was undoubtedly "European" in a sense that Palmerston or Clemenceau was not. He valued five-power unity and international accord and could never bring himself, as Canning did, to rejoice that the era of congresses was over and that the old politics of national ambition and balance of power were back in vogue. It is, I feel, important to keep in mind the fact that Metternich was an early-nineteenth-century aristocratic internationalist in outlook, not a twentieth-century democratic one. . . . The European society and civilization which he claimed to defend are hardly distinguishable from the narrow, highly aristocratic society within which he ruled and prospered. The dangers he foresaw were not those of totalitarian democracy and total war, but simply those of successful middle-class revolution, which represented for him the great abyss, beyond which all was dark and incalculable. The impending chaos, anarchy, and dissolution of society against which he so incessantly warned meant simply the overthrow of absolute monarchy and aristocratic rule in favor of constitutions, representative government, and middle-class predominance. Yet all the limitations in Metternich's international outlook do not deny him the status of a genuine nineteenth-century European. No one could expect him, in his time, to be a Robert Schuman or a Paul-Henri Spaak. Certainly he saw clearly that the conservative ideals and social order he represented were European and international in character and scope, and had to be defended on an international basis. Too much importance has been attached, in my opinion, to Metternich's statement, "Europe has for a long time held for me the significance of a fatherland,"[7] but it does contain a kernel of truth.

It is one thing to recognize that Metternich's outlook was European. It is quite another, however, to argue that his *policy* in this period was also European, i.e., that his chief aims were the maintenance of five-power unity and the promotion of European principles and institutions in the direction of a confederation of Europe. There is, in my opinion, no real evidence to sustain this latter contention, and a good deal of evidence pointing in the opposite direction. One can demonstrate quite clearly that Metternich consistently followed a policy of defending and advancing his country's interests (as, of course, any statesman must). That he was willing at any time to sacrifice, subordinate, or even deemphasize Austrian interests to maintain European unity or advance European goals appears doubtful.

He was not, for instance, ready to make sacrifices to maintain the unity of the Concert of Powers. To picture Metternich as struggling in vain to hold the alliance together against the separatist tendencies of England and France is, in my view, a serious misconception. However much Metternich talked about allied harmony and exhorted England and France to adhere to the common cause, the fact is that he deliberately chose a policy which he knew would drive at least one of them, and possibly both, out of the alliance, because this policy would enable him to form a separate, intimate coalition with Russia and Prussia more suitable for Austrian interests.

.   .   .   .

It is equally difficult to see European principles or federative polity in the institutions which Metternich attempted to establish. Whatever the German Confederation and the abortive Italian League might conceivably have led to in the way of European confederation, they were assuredly not intended by Metternich as means to this end. Indeed, their purpose was just the opposite—to reinforce an exclusively Austrian hegemony in Central Europe, and to prevent German or Italian unification or federation.[8] . . .

Nor do some of Metternich's diplomatic practices conform to the picture of the European statesman concerned to promote harmony among the powers. However much he proclaimed to France that Austria had no intention of trying, in the old discredited manner, to create a sphere of influence in Italy, his persistent efforts to reinforce and extend Austrian hegemony in Italy were bound to produce the conviction in France that this was exactly what Austria was doing. Metternich's practice of sowing suspicion and distrust between different powers in the Concert in order to align one or the other power more closely with Austria was likewise hardly conducive to Allied unity. . . . At the Congress of Verona, finally, he carried off the virtuosic feat of arousing and maintaining Russian suspicion of France, French suspicion of Russia, and English suspicion of both France and Russia, all at the same time.[9] In the same style, and of the same doubtful value to European solidarity, was Metternich's policy of attempting to unseat people he disliked from their posts within other governments. Some of the targets of his intrigues were, in England, Charles Stuart, Lord Burghersh, and Canning; in France, the Duke of Dalberg, La Tour du Pin, and Pasquier; in Prussia, Humboldt and Hardenberg; and in Russia, Tatistchev, Stroganov, Pozzo di Borgo and Capodistrias.

One need not moralize about these practices. Only when Metternich is presented as the European statesman *par excellence* and the assertion is made and repeated that Europe and the unity of the alliance were uppermost in his thought and action do these aspects of his diplomacy become hard to understand. For they are precisely the sort of practices which Castlereagh, for one, sought to avoid because he believed they were detrimental to Allied unity.[10] When, however, Metternich is seen primarily as an Austrian diplomat with Austrian interests to defend, these practices become wholly understandable, if not admirable, tools of his trade. Indeed, there is not a single major aspect of his policy in this period which is not best and most simply understood as an effort to secure power, peace, and internal security for the fragile Austrian monarchy. . . .

The third basic question, "Was Metternich a conservative?" is probably the most difficult to answer, precisely because of the wealth of definitions and connotations which the word "conservative" bears. If one defines as conservative any philosophy or policy which identifies itself with the existing order and seeks to maintain it, then Metternich was certainly a conservative, and indeed the outstanding representative of conservatism in his time. If, however, one tries to distinguish between policies of conservatism, standstillism, and reaction, the question becomes much more complicated. For according to the commonplace definitions of a liberal as one who welcomes change in society and tries to promote it, a conservative as one who accepts change and tries to restrain and guide it, a "stand-patter" as one who resists change and tries to retain what exists unchanged, and a reactionary as one who rejects change and tries to restore an order already past, Metternich's policy appears in this period to be occasionally one of reaction,[11] usually one of standstillism, and seldom if ever one of conservatism. To use the German terms for which there seem to be no precise English equivalents, his was a policy of *Beharren*, not *Erhaltung*.

That Metternich's policy during this era was essentially a negative, repressive one of resistance to change has already been argued at some length. The only point which might be added to that thesis here is that this policy does not seem to have been only a temporary expedient forced upon Metternich by the revolutionary events of the time, but rather to have been coherent with his general outlook. It is impossible to avoid the impression that Metternich equated change and reform with subversion and revolution. He viewed the world in Zoroastrian terms as an arena of perpetual struggle between two world-governing principles, that of order and good versus that of evil and anarchy. Every existing right was not merely legitimate but holy (a favorite Metternichean phrase is "the sanctity of all existing rights"); every call for change or attempt at change made by anyone except a legitimate sovereign was not merely illegitimate but wickedly presumptuous. All the good men of right principles, sound reasoning, loyalty, and courage were on Metternich's side; only knaves, malcontents, and fools were on the other. All liberals, however moderate, were really revolutionaries; all demands for a constitution or for reforms, however limited, were really steps toward anarchy and revolution. . . .

. . . .

The fact that Metternich sometimes conceded in principle the admissibility of political change (as in the proposed Act of Guarantee at Troppau) does not bear great weight, first of all because, as has already been argued, the whole role of principles in his policy is a dubious one. . . . Not rancor or prejudice, then, but a prudent skepticism warns one against leaning heavily on a Metternichean statement of principle unless it has been translated into practice.

And precisely this did not happen. Theoretically, Metternich conceded the admissibility of change, provided that it was initiated from above by the legitimate sovereign (a right, incidentally, which a legitimist could hardly deny to a monarch). In practice, however, this theoretical admission played no role at all in Metternich's policy. His private counsel to every sovereign was to make no changes at all in fundamental institutions, and all other changes only in the interest of repressing agitation and revolution. . . .

. . . .

No evidence, therefore, tells seriously against the view that Metternich's political theory in this period was that of absolutism, complete with divine right and passive obedience. However much he spoke of "tempered monarchy" and ancient forms, it altered in no way his insistence that all power in the state belonged indivisibly and inalienably to the king, the sole divinely-ordained source of all authority, against whose will there could be no possible justified resistance or revolt. No advisory bodies could exist, no ministers function

in the state other than at the royal pleasure. Liberty meant simply the freedom of the king's will; autocratic governments were therefore free governments and constitutional regimes were *ipso facto* unfree. The national will was the will of the sovereign. Kings were made to govern, and people to be governed. Two things, to be ruled firmly and to enjoy material prosperity, represented the sum total of popular capabilities, needs, and aspirations. "The mass of the people," remarked Metternich, citing Napoleon as his authority, "is always inert; they suffer their burdens in silence; and material benefits are regarded and enjoyed by them as well-being."[12]

It bears repeating that no one need become exercised over this rather cynical but commonly-held doctrine of the early nineteenth century. It is so little surprising that Metternich shared it that the point would scarcely be worth making had not the rehabilitation of Metternich proceeded to the point where some would make of him a political philosopher with conservative principles of timeless validity.[13] Against this tendency, it may be useful to point out once more that Metternich was basically a rigid absolutist whose political outlook was tied to a system of government and society which may once have had its grandeur and fitness, but which even by Metternich's time, was becoming outworn, and by our own is completely anachronistic. It does Metternich no good service to take very seriously his boastful claims to modernity. His famous lament that he was born in the wrong century and would have been better off seeing the light of day either a century earlier or later is only partly justified. In the seventeenth or eighteenth century, he would certainly have been at home. In his own age, he achieved undeniable stature, perhaps even greatness, as the outstanding representative and defender of a dying order. But in the twentieth century, he could only have been a Von Papen.

To say all this is certainly not to return

to Metternich as the blind monster sometimes portrayed in nineteenth-century historiography,[14] or even Viktor Bibl's more recent "demon of Austria," a Metternich without a single redeeming quality, responsible for everything that has gone wrong with Austria since 1809.[15] No one can deny to Metternich the virtues of moderation, caution, and love of peace, nor the qualities of courage (in his own way) and outstanding diplomatic skill. Often his diplomacy was very successful; sometimes his influence and policy worked for good, though on the whole their results for Austria and Europe were hardly good in the long run. Metternich also must bear only part of the responsibility for the standstill policy followed by Austria. Certainly the character of Francis I, the peculiar makeup of the Habsburg Empire, and possibly even the folk characteristics of the Austrian people were factors of equal or greater importance.[16] Finally, if it has any bearing, one may readily admit that the repressive policies of Metternich look very mild alongside the tyranny of a Hitler or Stalin.[17]

Tyranny, like most things, is much more highly developed and organized in the twentieth century—and Metternich was never a tyrant in the real sense of the word.

The only view to which one must return if the interpretation set out here is correct is something like that of Charles Dupuis, who contended early in the twentieth century that Metternich led the Concert of Europe more as a good Austrian than as a good European, and that this was an important factor in the system's decline.[18] My own interpretation involves simply seeing Metternich, for this period at least, as less statesman than diplomat; as less European than Austrian; as less a constructive conservative than a repressive "stand-patter"; as less profound and earnest than clever but essentially cynical and superficial; and also, perhaps, as less the philosopher-king and forerunner of European unity than the *grand seigneur,* outstanding in certain abilities but typical of his class in his general outlook, and dedicating his efforts to preserving and enjoying the old regime.

No. 10   C. K. Webster: The Foreign Policy of Castlereagh, 1815-1822[1]

.   .   .   .

One conclusion is at any rate quite clear. That Castlereagh was not only courageous and laborious, but also amongst the foremost of his age in diplomatic skill and resource is now generally accepted, and is proved by an overwhelming mass of testimony. The great qualities of which Castlereagh gave evidence in the period 1812-1815[2] are, indeed, scarcely so apparent in these later years. When, however, all these circumstances are taken into account, his technical ability is seen to be of the highest

kind, and the manner in which he obtained his ends shows again and again the touch of a master-hand. He was at his best perhaps during the Conference of Aix-la-Chapelle, where the decisions finally taken were almost exactly those laid down in his instructions, in spite of the difficulties raised, not only by the continental statesmen but also by his own Cabinet. In the end, Castlereagh had not only obtained what he wanted, but had obtained it in such a manner as to silence by sheer force of argument and conviction those who had disagreed with him. Nor had he left in any one that resentment and suspicion which a too obviously displayed triumph often incurs and thus defeats its own ends.

Such successes Castlereagh could only achieve, however, when he was able to come into personal contact with European statesmen. It was only then that his energy, resource and powers of persuasion were able to find full opportunity. He had thus, it must be admitted, to incur a severe diplomatic defeat during the Conferences of Troppau and Laibach. Yet the manner in which he retrieved the domestic and foreign situation in 1821-22, and obtained once more a commanding position in Britain and Europe is evidence enough that his abilities remained unimpaired until the final catastrophe.[3]

Whatever he thought of the objects of his policy, it must be allowed, therefore, that he was a diplomatist of the very highest class. His knowledge of men and affairs, his physical and moral courage, his persuasive and convincing character in conversation, his ability to appreciate the point of view of an opponent and find means to reconcile it with his own, above all, his capacity to make those with whom he came into contact trust his judgment in those transactions between States, where the future is obscure and risks must always be run, make him rank as one of the ablest of British Foreign Ministers.

A great diplomatist can, however, be a very bad statesman. It is the ends which men seek by which they must be judged. No amount of technical ability will compensate for a failure to appreciate what is right and what is possible. Few have surpassed Metternich in diplomatic skill, yet his career has been almost universally condemned because he used it to maintain a harmful and repulsive hegemony over central Europe. Was Castlereagh any wiser? It is not sufficient answer to point out that he failed to make his wider schemes permanent. How far had he the right to attempt to put them into practice? Above all, was

his conception of the European Alliance one worthy of a sincere and farsighted statesman? If so, why did it fail, and were the causes such as Castlereagh could have foreseen and prevented? On the answer to these questions will depend the place which will ultimately be his in history, and must be shortly discussed here.

It is as well to remind ourselves once more at the outset that the Alliance grew out of the necessities of the greatest war in which Britain had ever engaged and was meant to protect her from her ancient and inveterate enemy. It was only this aspect of it that enabled Castlereagh to obtain for it the consent of his countrymen. He thus grafted his new conception of diplomacy on a vigorous sentiment of the British people and obtained for it some measure of support. As his relations with the Cabinet clearly reveal throughout these years, he could not have secured their consent on any other terms. The skill with which he carried out the delicate negotiations necessary cannot be too highly praised. He was leading to a new conception of international diplomacy men who were quite incapable of appreciating all the issues involved in the new scheme which he had devised.

That the idea of Diplomacy by Conference was itself a great conception and one well adapted to the needs of Europe and Britain, few will deny. The only objection that can be urged against it is that it was in advance of the age. But the statesman who determined to try and make the new idea, which, as has since been clearly proved, is essential to the preservation of European peace, is surely entitled to lasting honour. A situation had arisen which promised to make it a success. The desire for peace amongst the European peoples and the habit of confidential intercourse, which their rulers had contracted during the final stages of the war, appeared to make more possible what would have been previously regarded as only an idle dream. Castlereagh, who had succeeded in overcoming the apparently hopeless obstacles in the way of a European coalition in 1813-14, had perhaps some right to expect that he could obtain an even greater triumph in the years of peace.

Much success he certainly did obtain. By the system of the Alliance the difficult problems connected with the European settlement were overcome with surprising ease. France could certainly not have been brought back into the community of nations with such unanimity and safety unless the European Alliance had been in existence. After 1818 the Quadruple Alliance[4] against France was to be maintained, indeed, but allowed to sleep in the Chancery safes unless awakened by some flagrant act of aggression. Meanwhile, all the Great Powers were bound together in an association, which was apparently based upon practical interests, which had been tested by experience and which might become gradually of overwhelming importance. Even as late as July, 1820, Adams could describe the political system of Europe as "a compact between the five Principal European Powers . . . for the preservation of universal peace," conclude that "it has proved effectual to its purposes by an experience of five years," and anticipate that "as a compact between governments it is not improbable that the European Alliance will last as long as some of the states who are parties to it."[5]

Castlereagh might be pardoned for taking a similar view. Yet in a little over two years it was realised that the great experiment was over and that Europe had come back to that state of nature, in which Canning so rejoiced, of every country for itself and God for them all.

The reasons of the failure will have already occurred to those who have read this book. They were many, some inevitable, others possibly avoidable. To determine the exact influence of each is a task beyond the powers of history, whose generalisations are nearly always untrue, so complicated are the facts of human nature which it is

called upon to explain. It may not be out of place, however, to attempt to summarise here some of the conclusions which appear to result from the evidence which we possess.

In the first place then it may be pointed out that the European Alliance depended, to a large degree, on the personal connections established between the European rulers at a particular moment. Its aims and objects were never formulated; it never obtained the stability of a definite constitution. It was enshrined only in the vague words of Article VI. of the Treaty of November 20, 1815.[6] Such had been and continued to be Castlereagh's conception of Diplomacy by Conference—a mere agreement on the part of the Great Powers to meet together from time to time to discuss international affairs. He had devised it in fact to suit a Britain and a Europe in which he himself would possess a commanding position, and he was justified by the fact that so long as he lived the system continued in spite of the inconvenient and unexpected events of 1820-21. But no system which depends on the personal connections of a particular individual can hope to survive for long. In relying too much on his own diplomatic skill and experience Castlereagh made it almost impossible for a successor to continue his policy. As has been seen, he realised this fact only too poignantly when he felt his own strength failing.

It may be doubted, however, whether any attempt to formulate the system in such a manner as to ensure its permanance would have stood any chance of success in that age. The objects of the Alliance were merely conservative. None of the statesmen accepted the fact that the world must change, though some of them, especially Metternich, had perceived that some such process was going on. Their conception of politics, economics and social life was a static one, and if the Alliance had been formulated it was only this idea to which expression could have been given. In a Europe in which a new national life was beginning to arise, as the result of the French Revolution, new methods of education and other mysterious and still unascertained forces, an Alliance, whose only object was to preserve the *status quo* from destruction by force, was bound to fail, even if the statesmen had been prepared to accept an elaborate constitution drawn to meet every emergency that could be foreseen.

Nor had the rulers the right to impose such restrictions on their peoples. Even Castlereagh and Richelieu[7] only represented a minority of their countrymen. The three autocratic monarchies were even less able to express the wishes of their subjects. So great an advance in the European polity could only have been successful if it had been brought about by the pressure of an enlightened and enthusiastic public opinion in the various countries concerned. Had Castlereagh, for example, been sustained in his attempt by the same organised and powerful body of opinion as supported the Abolition of the Slave Trade, how different his position would have been!

But such an expedient was the last on which Castlereagh would have relied. He lacked both the capacity and the desire to win the support of the mass of his countrymen to his policy. To Parliament he had indeed to submit, and he recognised also that there was a public opinion outside Parliament which was the ultimate arbiter of the policy of the nation. But it never occurred to him, as it did in some sense to his successor, to appeal to it boldly and with sincerity and make it realise the truths of which he was himself convinced. This was a fatal weakness, and made the task which Castlereagh had set before himself a hopeless one from the first. For, as has been seen, the Alliance not only never commanded popular support, but was never understood by contemporary opinion. The confusion with the Holy Alliance,[8] the attacks of the Opposition, and the revolutionary outbreaks in Southern Europe completely obscured that aspect of the Alliance which Castlereagh wished to emphasise. Castlereagh's cumbrous speeches were quite incapable of bringing home to his countrymen these new ideas. In the rest of Europe the appeal was even less possible. In France the European Alliance was naturally associated with the Quadruple Alliance, directed against her, out of which it had grown, and in the other countries of Europe the mass of men were only very faintly conscious of their interest in it.

Castlereagh, like most statesmen of his age, had indeed but little trust in democracy. It was associated in his mind with 'revolution,' and revolution meant violence, murder, and aggression—that aspect of the French Revolution which had necessarily impressed itself most strongly on the minds of its opponents. How strongly that emotion was felt by that generation, it is difficult now to realise. For revolution was associated not only with the overthrow of the *ancien régime* in France, but with the Napoleonic domination of Europe, which had succeeded it. When the revolutions in Southern Europe came, therefore, it sometimes seemed to those who had overcome the French Revolution as if Britain and Europe were again in even greater danger than before. Even in 1818 Canning could write of Britain, "The dangers in my conception are greater than in 1793; the means of resistance and the sense of necessity comparatively nothing." After the Neapolitan revolution he applied the same comparison to Europe.[9] Castlereagh had the same fears, and, as he had more responsibility at the critical time, they affected him perhaps even more. How much his Cabinet and Parliament agreed with him is seen in the manner in which the repressive Acts of 1819 were accepted by them. It was scarcely possible for one so situated to lay the foundations of the Alliance on popular understanding and consent.[10]

Nevertheless Castlereagh was far from submitting to the theories of Alexander and Metternich. His protests in 1820-21 against the use of the Alliance to put down revolution were obviously genuine and not made merely to satisfy public opinion. He saw at once that, if the new instrument were thus used, it would soon cease to function in the sense in which he desired it. No one could have asserted more strongly than he did that the Alliance had no concern with the domestic policy of any state. The State Paper of 1820 is only one of a series of documents, which emphasise this point and culminate in the public protest of the circular of January 19, 1821.[11] There can be no question but that Castlereagh felt just as strongly about it as Canning. The difference between them was that Castlereagh wished to preserve the new system of Conferences, and was, therefore, prepared to forget what had happened at Troppau and Laibach in order to perpetuate his scheme. His presence at Vienna in 1822 might have made the Alliance once more accept this doctrine, as it had done at Aix-la-Chapelle. Canning had no desire to bring back to its proper functions an institution with which not his own reputation but that of his predecessor was connected.

But even if Castlereagh had succeeded at Verona, it is difficult to see how his success could have been more than temporary. To the three Eastern monarchies there was no possibility of any compromise with democratic institutions such as the aristocracy of Britain and France had already been forced to make. While Castlereagh thought the Carlsbad Decrees useful and necessary, and condemned the foolish and irresponsible democrats of Naples and Spain, he was by no means unwilling to try and use his influence to obtain in those countries some form of Parliamentary institutions better adapted, according to British ideas, to their necessities. In Naples, Spain, and Portugal, he hoped that the Crown and the democrats would come to some agreement and erect a more workable form of government. But it was impossible for such ideas to be accepted by Metternich and the new Alexander that existed after Troppau. There was no possibility of permanence in an association of such autocracies with constitutional governments. The rift between Eastern and Western Europe was bound to destroy the Alliance.

When, indeed, the Alliance had apparently been used at Troppau and Laibach to overthrow the revolutionary governments in Naples and Piedmont its end was already near. The protests, which Britain made, were considered as directed against the Alliance itself, and not merely against the use to which Alexander and Metternich had contrived to put it. Castlereagh, indeed, took the greatest pains to distinguish between the illegitimate objects for which the Eastern Powers tried to use the Alliance and the legitimate aims, which had been defined in the Treaties which he had signed and, indeed, largely devised. But such a distinction, though clear enough to impartial analysis could be easily obscured by emotional rhetoric or malevolent design. Henceforward it was extraordinarily difficult to make his main object apparent. Only a striking success at Verona would have shown the world that the Alliance was meant to restrain the Great Powers rather than to oppress the Small.

Castlereagh never solved the difficult problem of relations between the Small and the Great Powers of Europe. The distinction was one which had only just been realised, and had never been clearly formulated. It was, indeed, to thwart all the efforts of the publicists and lawyers throughout the nineteenth century, and has only been solved, perhaps, in our own day by the gradual appreciation of the logic of facts. To have brought all the Small Powers into the Alliance as Capo d'Istria and the Tsar at one time thought of doing, would clearly have been to make the machine unworkable.

Yet it was obvious that, apart from the question of revolutions, the interests of the Small Powers were deeply affected by the Alliance. So long, indeed, as the Great Powers were united, the rest might protest against their exclusion, but they had no alternative but to obey. Castlereagh saw clearly the dangers of this situation, but he could find no real solution. He proposed to avoid them by a diplomatic and tactful treatment of those States which were necessarily excluded from the Alliance. But this course could not be expected to satisfy the Small Powers, and the result was that they adopted an attitude of hostility towards an institution which reduced their influence and importance in Europe. This undoubtedly contributed to the failure of the Alliance to appeal to elements of public opinion from which it might have been expected to obtain support.

At the best, moreover, the Alliance could only work very spasmodically in an age in which communications were so difficult. The Tsar might be glad for an excuse to leave Russia for several months, but the Foreign Minister of a constitutional State, with whose Government he could only communicate at long intervals when abroad, found it very difficult to spare the necessary time. Castlereagh had to be brought back from the Congress of Vienna to defend his colleagues from the attacks of the Opposition. Had the Queen died a little earlier and necessitated the summoning of Parliament, he might have been forced to return in similar fashion from Aix-la-Chapelle. It was obviously impossible for him to attend at Troppau and Laibach even if he had desired. The Hanover interview was only obtained because George had necessarily to visit his continental dominions at least once in his reign. It has been seen how difficult it was for Castlereagh to arrange for his journey to Vienna in 1822. It was scarcely possible under such conditions to make the Conferences a normal organ of European diplomacy. The European States had at-tained a unity such as they had never before possessed, but it needed new developments in communications and transport before they could express it in political institutions.

If these circumstances were sufficient to make impossible the continuance of the European Alliance as Castlereagh had planned it, they made the grandiose and sentimental schemes of the Tsar appear entirely ridiculous. The extravagance of Alexander's ideas was indeed one of the chief reasons why the Alliance so soon ceased to appeal to reasonable men. It can hardly be doubted that the Tsar was sincere. Most of the evidence, at any rate, points in that direction. But the manner in which he attempted to turn the simple idea of Diplomacy by Conference into a guarantee of thrones and governments did almost as much harm to Castlereagh's plans as a more hostile attitude. Castlereagh was able to defeat these schemes during his lifetime, but their mere existence made much harder his task of persuading the British Cabinet to agree to his own plans. Not for the last time the practical statesman found the unbalanced and emotional enthusiast one of the principal obstacles in the path of peace.

For all these reasons, therefore, it must be admitted that Castlereagh was attempting an impossible task. Yet the end which he set before himself was so noble, and the effort which he made to overcome his manifold and overwhelming difficulties was so gallant and persistent, that it is difficult to avoid paying a tribute to his courageous statesmanship. Politics, and especially international politics, so rarely produce men who rise above a weak opportunism, that the spectacle of a man trying almost single-handed to put into practical shape a new conception of international diplomacy is one that compels admiration. Few men could have obtained even the measure of success which was his, and that was only won by almost unparalleled devotion to duty. Castlereagh undoubtedly gave up his life to the cause of international peace.

Did he sacrifice to this endeavour the special interests of his own country? It was Canning's contention that Castlereagh had laid too much stress on European interests, that he was, in fact, not sufficiently a patriot. This is a strange charge to make against one who had conducted the final stages of the most glorious period in the history of his country, and negotiated a peace which laid, broad and deep, the foundations of a new Empire overseas. Yet the charge appealed to Castlereagh's contemporaries and has often been repeated by historians. There is obviously some measure of truth in it. Throughout his career Castlereagh was always more ready than his colleagues to sacrifice some minor point of British interests to what he considered the more important interest of general goodwill among nations. This characteristic was clearly seen in the treatment of France in 1814-15. It is apparent also in these later years, especially in his dealings with the United States. That for over one hundred years Britain remained at peace with these two countries, in spite of many occasions of acute controversy, must be considered as in part the result of his wisdom and restraint. No one cared less than Castlereagh for that kind of prestige which is obtained by flaunting a diplomatic victory. When he had obtained his own way he was anxious that it should be accepted by other countries as their way also. His policy of cooperation and conciliation prevented him from indulging in those appeals to patriotic sentiment which never fail to win popular applause.

Castlereagh was, however, a careful steward of his country's interests. If he subordinated minor points to the cause of international peace, he never gave way on what he regarded as essential. So far as material interests are concerned, it is difficult to see what he could have done to make more permanent and extensive the power of the British Empire. Nor did he ever cease to maintain British influence in those portions of the world where it was considered that British interests necessitated its special exercise. The connections with Portugal, Spain, Constantinople, and Persia were kept specially close during these years, though care was taken to prevent, if possible, a diplomatic contest with Britain's rivals. Over reviving France, Castlereagh was naturally especially watchful. Yet how wise was the policy which he advocated with success in 1819! He became, it is true, more suspicious and hostile in 1821-22. But he still hoped to reconcile the interests of the two countries, even in problems where they appeared to be most apart. He undoubtedly intended, if possible, to act with her rather than against her, even in the questions of Spain and the Spanish Colonies.

It is true, however, that Castlereagh did not obtain for this country the prestige and influence which she obtained under Canning and other Foreign Ministers, by the encouragement of liberal movements on the Continent. He was, indeed, on the other side. The ridiculous shapes which these movements assumed were especially repugnant to his practical commonsense, and he sacrificed them ruthlessly to what he conceived to be the greater interest of Europe —peace and rest after the storms of recent years. Such attempts as he made to persuade the rulers of that age to treat their subjects with more wisdom and humanity and even allow them some form of constitutional government were never avowed. Lord Salisbury defended this attitude in 1861. "If he had only constructed," he wrote, "a few brilliant periods about nationality or freedom or given a little wordy sympathy to Greece or Spain or the South American republics, the world would have heard much less of the horrors of his policy."[12] Castlereagh was, indeed, incapable of such hypocrisy. He never held out his hand to any nation or party unless he saw some way to produce a practical result. Nevertheless it is his greatest condemnation that he failed to appreciate the fact that nationality and self-government were the master forces of the nineteenth century, and that, until they were given room for development, all schemes for international peace would be of no avail. Only when those under the inspiration of these great ideas could be disciplined and taught by experience some of the practical wisdom to which Castlereagh rightly attached so much importance, could his schemes for international cooperation be accomplished and his country obtain the only kind of influence in the European policy, which can be durable and of advantage to the Power which possesses it.

It is this fact which has deprived Castlereagh of the credit and honour which is rightly his. If he avoided the extravagances and crudities of his opponents and worked for great ends, which many of them could not perceive, with wonderful patience and diplomatic skill, he failed to associate his ideas with the deepest emotions of his age. No statesman can succeed who does not steer his vessel into the main stream, however skilfully he may navigate the shallows. His cargo of ideas is soon left behind in the race. So it was with Castlereagh, and thus much of his labour was in vain.

But not all. For though the ideas of international conferences between the Great Powers was never revived in the shape in which he had devised it, and did not remain part of the Treaty obligations of the Great Powers, yet its influence never wholly disappeared. The 'Concert of Europe' is a direct descendant of the European Alliance; and, though the 'Concert of Europe' was too vague and spasmodic a machine to focus the forces that make towards peace and prevent the final catastrophe, yet it was to render great service to Europe in the course of the century. For this and for the work which he did to overcome the particular difficulties of his age, Castlereagh is entitled to the gratitude not only of his own countrymen but of humanity.

The man to whom that gratitude is due we shall never know intimately. The curtain of reserve was never raised until the personality behind it was no longer the Castlereagh who had played so great a part in European affairs. Yet behind the smiling, inscrutable and splendid presence a glimpse can sometimes be caught of a character that would have been singularly winning and attractive if it had not been oppressed by a too conscious sense of duty and responsibility. No statesman ever gave himself more completely to the public service. He sacrificed to it not only his comfort and his health, but all those personal and intimate emotions which are the greatest part of the lives of most men, however exalted their state. If we can learn from his failures, the sacrifice will not have been made in vain.

Notes

No. 1, pp. 5-10

[1] Comte A. de La Garde-Chambonas, *Anecdotal Recollections of the Congress of Vienna,* introduction and notes by the Comte Fleury, translated by the author of 'An Englishman in Paris' (London, 1902), pp. 1-8, 13-18, 27-30.

[2] "The most honest man to have occupied the throne."–HNW.

[3] The author refers here to the Prince de Ligne, to whom he was distantly related. The Prince introduced him at the Congress as his cousin. –HNW.

[4] This is an allusion to Napoleon, who had been banished to the island of Elba.–HNW.

No. 2, pp. 10-14

[1] Fürst Clemens Lothar Wenzel von Metternich-Winneburg, *Memoirs of Prince Metternich,* published by Prince Richard Metternich, edited

by M. A. de Klinkowström, translated by Mrs. Alexander Napier and Gerard W. Smith, 5 vols. (New York, 1881), II, 338-352. Hereafter cited as Metternich, *Memoirs*.

[2] At the time Russian Prime Minister, who disagreed with Metternich's policies.—HNW.

[3] This is a misprint; it should read "has *not* bestowed on us." See the original German edition, III, 426.—HNW.

[4] Metternich here refers to the Neapolitan Revolution.—HNW.

[5] The Grand-Duke of Tuscany and Duke of Modena.—Ed.

No. 3, pp. 14-17

[1] Sir Edward Hertslet (ed.), *The Map of Europe by Treaty; Showing the Various Political and Territorial Changes which Have Taken Place since the General Peace of 1814*, 4 vols. (London, 1875-1891), I, 342-350. Hereafter cited as Hertslet (ed.), *Map of Europe*.

[2] A misprint; should read "Trinity."—HNW.

[3] Bonaparte escaped from Elba on the night of the 25th of February, 1815, and landed in France on the 1st of March.—Ed.

[4] Austria, Russia, and Prussia acceded to this treaty on the same day.—HNW.

[5] The military occupation was brought to an end by a Convention signed at the Congress of Aix-la-Chappelle on 9 October 1818; at this time, the indemnity was also reduced to 265,000,000 francs. See Hertslet (ed.), *Map of Europe*, I, 557-568 and 576-578.—HNW.

No. 4, pp. 17-18

[1] Hertslet (ed.), *Map of Europe*, I, 317-319.

[2] Great Britain was invited to accede. However, the Prince Regent, upon the urging of Castlereagh, politely declined, assuring the three Sovereigns that he entirely concurred in the principles expressed in the Treaty, but that the British Constitution precluded his formal accession to it.—HNW.

No. 5, pp. 18-20

[1] Hertslet (ed.), *Map of Europe*, I, 372-375.

[2] The Treaties of Chaumont, arranged by Castlereagh, provided primarily that none of the Allied Powers would enter into a separate peace with France, and that they would defend, with armed force, if necessary, the terms of the peace treaties against any future French infringements. The Treaty of Vienna, signed only three weeks after Napoleon's return from Elba, renewed the Treaties of Chaumont. Both Treaties are reprinted in Hertslet (ed.), *Map of Europe*, III, 2043-2048 and 2058-2059, respectively.—HNW.

[3] Prince Louis Napoleon Bonaparte was proclaimed President of the French Republic, 20th December, 1848, and Emperor of the French, by the title of Napoleon III, on the 2nd December, 1852. These titles were recognized by all the Powers of Europe.—Ed.

No. 6, pp. 20-25

[1] Metternich, *Memoirs*, II, 140-147.

[2] This refers to the Congress of Aix-la-Chapelle, which was about to be concluded.—HNW.

[3] The German Confederation.—HNW.

[4] The permanent meeting in Frankfurt of the representatives of the member-states of the German Confederation.—HNW.

No. 7, pp. 25-28

[1] Metternich, *Memoirs*, II, 316-319.

[2] This term usually refers to the German Confederation, but in this context means the European community of nations.—HNW.

[3] England, according to a despatch dated January 17, 1821, declined to join in the measure in question. Not so France, whose king wrote to the King of Naples urging him to accept the invitation of the allied monarchs.—Ed.

No. 8, pp. 28-30

[1] Hertslet (ed.), *Map of Europe*, I, 664-666.

[2] See *No. 7*, above.—HNW.

[3] See *No. 3*, above.—HNW.

[4] See *No. 5*, above.—HNW.

No. 9, pp. 30-35

[1] Paul W. Schroeder, *Metternich's Diplomacy at Its Zenith, 1820-1823* (Austin, Texas, c. 1962), pp. 240-244, 249-251, 254-258, 260-266. Copyright by Paul W. Schroeder. Reprinted by permission of the author.

[2] Srbik, *Metternich*, I, 317-320; Srbik, "Ideengehalt des Systems," *Historische Zeitschrift*, CXXXI (1925), 240-241; Arnold O. Meyer, "Der Streit um Metternich," *ibid.*, CLVII (1938), 76.

[3] Hugo Hantsch, *Die Geschichte Österreichs*, II, 303-307; Näf, *Staat und Staatsgedanke*, 15-21; Constantin de Grunwald, *La Vie de Metternich*, 197-212; Rieben, *Metternich's Europapolitik*, 9-22; and Henry A. Kissinger, *A World Restored: Metternich, Castlereagh and the Problems of Peace, 1812-1822*.

4 Srbik, *Metternich,* I, 88-93, 122-128, 324-327, 350-420, *et passim.*

5 See Metternich's memoir titled "Napoléon Bonaparte. Écrit en l'année 1820," Varia, Frankreich, Fasc. 93. The works of Count Corti give ample evidence that not only Francis I, as Srbik would have it (*Metternich,* I, 438), but also Metternich regarded the state as patrimony. See, for example, Corti's *Rise of the House of Rothschild,* 349-363, and his *Metternich und die Frauen,* II, 283-284.

6 Hantsch, *Geschichte Österreichs,* II, 307.

7 This statement is quoted by Bertier de Sauvigny in his *Metternich et son temps* (p. 91) with the comment that these are words "for which he doubtless can be forgiven a great deal."

8 The two outstanding authorities on the Italian League, Bettanini and Grossmann (see Chapter I, note 8), concur in their estimate of the purpose of the scheme, although they disagree rather sharply on its merits. Bettanini upholds the Piedmontese position in the Sardinian-Austrian dispute over the League, while Grossmann defends Austrian policy; yet both agree that the clash was not between Austrian federative policy and Sardinian nationalism, but between two egocentric policies, both motivated by interests of state.

9 See Chapter VII. Also see Lebzeltern (St. Petersburg, April 29, 1822) to Metternich, Berichte, Russland, Fasc. 29, No. 37C; Metternich (Vienna, April 4, 1823) to Vincent, Weisungen, Frankreich, Fasc. 354, Nos. 2 and 4.

10 Webster, *Foreign Policy of Castlereagh,* 64-68.

11 While I believe Metternich's policy may on occasion be legitimately termed "reactionary," the word bears such an ineradicable bad moral connotation that I intend to avoid its use where possible.

12 Memoir by Metternich, "Napoléon Bonaparte. Écrit en l'année 1820," Varia, Frankreich, Fasc. 93.

13 Among his biographers, this tendency is most noticeable in Hélène du Coudray's *Metternich* and Algernon Cecil's *Metternich, 1773-1859: A Study of His Period and His Personality.* Such works as Peter Viereck's *Conservatism Revisited: The Revolt against Revolt;* the same writer's "New Views on Metternich," *Review of Politics,* XIII (April 1951), 211-

228; Albert Garreau's *Saint Empire;* and Bela Menczer's "Metternich and Donoso Cortes," *Dublin Review,* No. 444 (1948), 19-51, go even further in this direction.

14 A particularly bad example of this is found in William Roscoe Thayer, *The Dawn of Italian Independence: Italy from the Congress of Vienna, 1814, to the Fall of Venice, 1849.*

15 Viktor Bibl, *Metternich, der Dämon Österreichs,* 23-24, 354-367.

16 On the causes of the breakdown of the pre-1848 order in Austria, see Josef Redlich, *Das österreichische Staats- und Reichproblem. Geschichtliche Darstellung der inneren Politik der Habsburgischen Monarchie von 1848 bis zum Untergang des Reiches,* 67-79.

17 Golo Mann, for example, writes of the Carlsbad decrees: "When their wording is carefully examined today one can only recall sadly and enviously the time when such decrees passed for the most monstrous example of despotism and reaction."—*Secretary of Europe,* 267.

18 Dupuis, *Principe d'équilibre,* 154-157.

No. 10, pp. 35-42

1 C.[harles] K. Webster, *The Foreign Policy of Castlereagh, 1815-1822: Britain and the European Alliance* (London, 1925), pp. 493-505. Reprinted by permission of the publishers, G. Bell and Sons, Ltd.

2 See the same author's *The Foreign Policy of Castlereagh, 1812-1815: Britain and the Reconstruction of Europe* (London, 1931).—HNW.

3 His death by suicide in 1822.—HNW.

4 See *No. 5,* above.—HNW.

5 W. C. Ford, *Writings of J. Q. Adams,* vii. 47.

6 See *No. 5,* above.—HNW.

7 French Prime Minister from 1815 to 1818 and from 1820 to 1821.—HNW.

8 See *No. 4,* above.—HNW.

9 Canning to Bagot, Aug. 24, 1818, Oct. 25, 1820: Captain Bagot, *George Canning and his Friends,* ii. 82, 103.

10 Castlereagh left a codicil to his will allowing his wife to sell her diamonds if necessary. As Clanwilliam pointed out to Stewart, in the intimate letter previously quoted, this direction could only be meant as a safeguard against successful revolution in Britain.

11 See *No. 8,* above.—HNW.

12 Salisbury, *Essays, Biographical,* 53

The Crimean War

2

INTRODUCTION

I F EVER there was a needless war, the Crimean War seems to have been it. Not a single one of the responsible statesmen in any of the participating countries really wanted a war, and some of them—for instance, Lord Aberdeen—reproached themselves until the day they died that they had not done more to prevent it. It was a war caused by ill-considered threats which personal and national prestige insisted had to be made good, by a "show of force" which unexpectedly and tragically turned into the use of force, by indecision, shortsightedness, and public hysteria.

The ostensible cause of the Crimean War was the eruption of open fighting between Greek Orthodox and Roman Catholic, or Latin, Christians over the Holy Places in and near Jerusalem. Bad blood had existed between these two groups for centuries, at least as far back as the Great Schism of 1054, and, under ordinary circumstances, almost no one in Europe would have paid much attention to this latest in a long series of clashes. What forced them to take notice, however, was the intervention of France in behalf of the Latin Christian, and of Russia in behalf of the Greek Orthodox, subjects of the Sultan.

Napoleon III was anxious to increase his prestige, and to lead France back to the glory and influence she had enjoyed under his illustrious uncle. The timid foreign policy of Louis Philippe, which had bored France to tears, was to be replaced by an aggressive assertion of French interests. By taking up the cause of the Latin Christians, Napoleon also hoped to obtain the political support of the strong Clerical Party in France. Pressure was exerted upon the Sultan. A French naval squadron appeared off the Syrian coast. The Sultan took the hint, and, in 1852, issued a firman, or royal decree, which substantially increased the privileges of the Latin Christians at the Holy Places.

This success incensed not only the 12,000,000 Greek Orthodox subjects of the Sultan, but Tsar Nicholas I, as well. Nicholas believed that Russian prestige would suffer an irreparable blow if he did not protect the interests of his coreligionists. He was also determined to block an expansion of French influence in this region. He would counter threat with threat, and force with force (*No. 11*). First, Russian military units were mobilized and ordered to advance upon the Turkish Principalities in the Balkans (*No. 12*). Next, Prince Menchikoff, a brusque and overbearing man, was appointed Russian ambassador to the Porte. Upon his arrival in Constantinople, he deliberately insulted the Turkish Foreign Minister (*No. 13*), leading to the latter's resignation. He then presented the Russian

45

demands: the Greek Orthodox were to be given complete equality with the Latin Christians at the Holy Places, and the Tsar was to be granted a permanent protectorate over all the Greek Orthodox in the Ottoman Empire (*No. 14*). When the Porte agreed to the first of these demands, but balked at the second, which would have given Russia the opportunity to interfere in Turkish affairs anytime it pleased, Menchikoff broke off diplomatic relations with Turkey and left Constantinople (*No. 15*). Russia thereupon presented Turkey with an ultimatum that unless all of her demands were met, Russian troops would occupy the Danubian Principalities (*No. 16*).

As this ultimatum and the Tsar's military instructions (*No. 17*) make clear, Nicholas had no intention of precipitating a war with Turkey. Having dealt with the Turks for almost three decades, he was genuinely convinced that they would yield only to a display of force. He was also encouraged to act so forcefully by his belief that France, if she decided to back Turkey against Russia, would be diplomatically isolated. Austria and Prussia, the other two members of the Holy Alliance, had been following Russia's lead for many years, and Nicholas was confident that they would continue to do so. As for England, the Tsar, on the occasion of a visit in June, 1844, had discussed the Eastern Question with Queen Victoria and several of her ministers, including Lord Aberdeen, who was then Foreign Secretary. Upon his return to St. Petersburg, he informed Count Nesselrode, the Russian Chancellor and Foreign Minister, of the agreement he had reached with the British government. Nesselrode wrote up a memorandum of the agreement (*No. 18*), which Aberdeen later confirmed as an accurate summary. With Aberdeen now Prime Minister, Nicholas took it for granted that the agreement of 1844 was still valid, and, in conversations with Sir Seymour, the British ambassador at St. Petersburg, made several proposals to implement it (*No. 19*).

The Tsar's assessment of both the English and the Austrian attitudes turned out to be grievously mistaken. Nicholas appears to have been woefully ignorant of the workings of the British parliamentary system of government. As the autocratic ruler of all the Russias, he was the sole person to determine Russian policy, and his word was binding upon his successors. No British minister had such power. The agreement of 1844—if such it can be called, for its wording was so vague and imprecise that it hardly deserved the appellation—had not even been communicated to, much less approved by, Parliament, and therefore had no binding force upon successive British governments. Furthermore, Aberdeen, although he was Prime Minister and friendly disposed toward Russia, lacked the determination and political skill to translate these assets into a policy of cooperation with the Tsar. But even an abler man than Aberdeen might have found the task beyond his strength. The anti-Russian currents in England, as Baron Brunnow, the Russian ambassador at London, quite accurately pointed out (*No. 20*), were too numerous and deep: a coalition ministry; a divided Cabinet; a weak Parliament; a hostile press; an increasingly irrational public. He might have added, among others, England's growing commercial interests in the Middle East and its imperial ties with India, both of which appeared to be threatened by Russia's Turkish policy, and the pressures exerted by Napoleon to get England to make a common front against Russia.

Aberdeen attempted to navigate these currents by eagerly fostering the diplomatic negotiations initiated at Vienna to find a compromise satisfactory to all the Powers. At the same time, however, he let himself be persuaded to a British "show of force" at Constantinople. Lord Stratford de Redcliffe, formerly Stratford Canning, an irascible man and a known Russophobe, with many years of service as British ambassador at the Porte, was reappointed to that post (*No. 21*). A short time later, following Napoleon's lead (*No. 22*), the British and French fleets in the Mediterranean were ordered to Besika Bay, just off the entrance to the Dardanelles, and placed at Stratford's disposal (*Nos. 23 and 24*). These two crucial decisions, with the latter, by an ironic coincidence, being reached on the same day as the Russian ultimatum to Turkey, brought the unwanted war appreciably closer. The Sultan had been seriously considering ways of mollifying the Tsar. Although a stormy debate still rages over Stratford's activities at Constantinople, there can be little doubt that his arrival, combined with that of the British and French fleets at Besika Bay, stiffened the resistance of the Turks. They rejected the Russian ultimatum (*No. 25*), as well as the Vienna Note of 28 July 1853, the diplomatic compromise which had been reached at Vienna. They then demanded the Russian evacuation of the Danubian Principalities. When Russia refused to comply, they declared war against her (*No. 26*), which was followed by the Russian declaration of war against Turkey (*No. 27*).

The outbreak of war caused consternation in many circles. Aberdeen still clung to the forlorn hope that some solution could be found which would enable England to stay out of the war, but the aforementioned currents pulled England inexorably into the maelstrom. This process, painful to some, can be clearly traced in the editorials of *The* [London] *Times* (*No. 28*). The British public evinced no such scruples (*No. 29*). Its passionate Russophobia, nurtured for many years, was inflamed to a fever pitch by the "massacre" of Sinope (*No. 30*). When its clamor for war went unheeded, the ugly rumor spread that the Prince Consort was in the Tsar's pay and was holding back the Cabinet (*No. 31*). The government finally yielded. The message on a state of war with Russia (*No. 32*) was welcomed with great rejoicing by the majority of Englishmen, including the Poet Laureate (*No. 33*). The few courageous voices raised in protest against the war, such as John Bright's (*No. 34*), fell on deaf ears.

Once the war was joined, it became obvious that neither side could win a quick, decisive victory. England's naval supremacy was of little avail against Russia's landbased power, and with Prussia and Austria interposed between the combatants, the Allied armies had no direct avenue of attack. The choice of the Crimea seems to have occurred almost in desperation, to obtain a battlefield somewhere, anywhere, rather than for its strategic importance. The situation would have changed drastically if Austria could have been persuaded to join the Allies, and the latter launched a vigorous diplomatic campaign to enlist her in their ranks. After some procrastination, Austria became more amenable, and even went so far as to sign an alliance with the Western Powers, but then she refused to join in the war against Russia. The explanation by the Austrian historian Heinrich Friedjung of the reasons for this tortuous and disastrous policy (*No. 35*) is not completely satisfactory, but is the best available. Without active Austrian participation, the war dragged on, taking a fearful toll in lives and treasure. Perhaps the most important factors which finally caused the belligerents to sign the Peace of Paris (*No. 36*) were the death of Nicholas and the willingness of his successor, Alexander II, to negotiate on more reasonable terms; and the disinclination of Napoleon, after the fall of Sebastopol, to trust any further in the uncertain fortunes of war.

No. 11   Russia Is Determined to Meet French Force
With Force————15 January and 21 February 1853[1]

Sir G. H. Seymour to Lord John Russell.
(*Received January 23.*)

St. Petersburgh, January 13, 1853.
My Lord,

I CALLED yesterday, by his desire, upon the Chancellor, who had the kindness to read to me the long and very important instruction upon the present position of affairs, which is about to be addressed to Baron de Brunnow.[2] The draft bore marks of having been already sanctioned by the Emperor, and the despatch will be sent off by messenger to London to-morrow or the next day. This interesting paper, of which I should be able to give but an imperfect sketch, will be communicated to you by the Russian Mission, and will, I am willing to believe, be left in your Lordship's hands.

The chief points touched upon appeared to me the following:—

That since the question of the Holy Places had been noticed by the Russian Minister to the Earl of Malmesbury it had assumed a new character; that the acts of injustice towards the Greek Church, which it had been desired to prevent, had been perpetrated, and, consequently, that now the object must be to find a remedy for those wrongs; that the success of the French negotiations at Constantinople was to be ascribed solely to intrigue and violence,— violence, which had been supposed to be the *ultima ratio* of kings, being, it had been seen, the means which the present ruler of France was in the habit of employing in the first instance; that the Emperor was as solicitous as he ever had been to prevent the overthrow of Turkey, the state of that country being, indeed, very precarious, but the maintenance of Turkey as it now exists being, perhaps, more suited to the interests of Russia, and, at all events, more favourable to the maintenance of peace, than exposure to those chances of disagreement among the Powers, which might ensue upon the downfall of the Turkish Empire. Nevertheless, that his Imperial Majesty's rights, secured to him and to the Greek Church, could not be withheld with impunity; but that he was prepared to seek satisfaction through diplomatic means.

At the same time, as force had been employed in extorting concessions from the Porte, and as a moral influence, which may still prevail, had thus been created in her favour by France, it is necessary that the same means should be prepared by the Imperial Government, and the rather as there was danger of the Turks continuing to act, as they had been seen lately to do, under fear and compulsion.

.   .   .   .

Memorandum by the Tsar.[3]

St. Petersburgh, 21 February 1853.

.   .   .   .

But, in order that the Emperor may continue to concur in that system of forbearance, to abstain from any demonstrations—from any peremptory language—it would be necessary that this system should be equally observed by all the Powers at once. France has adopted another. By menace she obtained, in opposition to the letter of the Treaties, the admission of a ship of the line into the Dardanelles. At the cannon's mouth she twice presented her claims and her demands for indemnity at Tripoli, and afterwards at Constantinople.

Again, in the contest respecting the holy places, by menace she effected the abrogation of the firman and that of the solemn promises which the Sultan had given the Emperor. With regard to all these acts of violence England observed a complete silence. She neither offered support to the Porte nor addressed remonstrances to the French Government. The consequence is very evident. The Porte necessarily concluded from this that from France alone it has everything to hope, as well as everything to fear, and that it can evade with impunity the demands of Austria and of Russia. It is thus that Austria and Russia, in order to obtain justice, have seen themselves compelled in their turn, against their will, to act by intimidation, since they have to do with a Government which only yields to a peremptory attitude; and it is thus that by its own fault, or rather by that of those who have weakened it in the first instance, the Porte is urged on in a course which enfeebles it still more.

.   .   .   .

No. 12   Russian Military Units Advance on the Turkish Frontier——January 1853[1]

Sir G. H. Seymour to Lord John Russell.
(Received January 19.)

St. Petersburgh, January 6, 1853.
(Extract.)

I BELIEVE that I may state to your Lordship, that measures have been taken by the Russian Government to ensure the 5th Corps d'Armée being placed in a state of preparation for active service.

I propose taking an early opportunity of speaking to the Chancellor upon the subject of the information which I now feel authorised in submitting to your Lordship, with the observation that I cannot help connecting these military preparations with the threat partly made by the French Government of sending an expedition to Syria in the event of satisfaction not being obtained for the claims of the Latin Church.

Sir G. H. Seymour to Lord John Russell.
(Received January 19.)

St. Petersburgh, January 7, 1853.
(Extract.)

ORDERS have been despatched to the 5th Corps d'Armée to advance to the frontiers of the Danubian Provinces, without waiting for their reserves; and the 4th Corps, under the command of General Count Dannenberg, and now stationed in Volhynia, will be ordered to hold itself in readiness to march if necessary.

Each of these Corps consists of twenty-four regiments, and, as your Lordship is aware, each Russian regiment is composed of three battalions (each of about 1000 men), of which one battalion forms the reserve.

General Lüder's Corps d'Armée, accordingly, being now 48,000 strong, will receive a reinforcement of 24,000 men soon after its arrival at its destination, and supposing the 4th Corps to follow, the whole force will amount, at least according to official returns, to 144,000 men.

Lord Cowley[2] to Lord John Russell.
(Received January 21.)

Paris, January 20, 1853.

(Extract.)

M. DROUYN DE LHUYS[3] informed me yesterday that he had received advices from St. Petersburgh, announcing that the Emperor of Russia had ordered a large concentration of troops on the frontiers bordering on Turkey.

This display of force will not prevent the French Government, according to M.

Drouyn de Lhuys' assurances, from terminating the question of the Sacred Places.

·   ·   ·   ·   ·   ·   ·   ·   ·

No. 13   Prince Menchikoff's Arrival in Constantinople—— 4 March 1853[1]

Colonel Rose[2] to Lord John Russell.
(Received March 19.)

Constantinople, March 7, 1853.
(Extract.)

CIRCUMSTANCES connected with the mission of Prince Menchikoff have gradually come to light, and cause grave apprehensions for the independence, if not the destiny, of Turkey.

No expense or efforts have been spared for the purpose of imparting to the Russian Embassy all the advantages which accrue from personal influence, display, and entertainment.

Prince Menchikoff is an Admiral and Minister of the Marine, and he is accompanied by the Chancellor's son, Prince Galitzin, the Emperor's Aide-de-Camp, and a large suite.

·   ·   ·   ·   ·   ·   ·   ·   ·

Unfortunately Prince Menchikoff's first public act evinced entire disregard on his part of the Sultan's dignity and rights, which, combined with the hostile attitude of Russia, created the impression that coercion, rather than conciliatory negotiation, would distinguish his Exellency's mission.

His Exellency transmitted his credentials to Fuad Effendi, and the next day, with his whole Embassy, waited on the Grand Vizier at the Porte; it is an invariable rule that a new Ambassador makes the second visit of ceremony to the Minister for Foreign Affairs. But Prince Menchikoff, after leav-ing the Grand Vizier, although invited by Kiamil Bey, the "Introducteur des Ambassadeurs," to visit Fuad Effendi, whose apartment adjoins those of the Grand Vizier declined to do so: and Prince Menchikoff, passing by the line of troops and Kavasses, and the very door of Fuad Effendi, which had been opened to receive him, left the Porte.

The affront was the more galling, because great preparations had been made for the purpose of receiving the Russian Ambassador with marked honours, and a great concourse of people, particularly Greeks, had assembled for the purpose of witnessing the ceremony.

The incident made a great and most painful sensation. The Grand Vizier expressed to me his indignation at the premeditated affront which had been offered to his Sovereign; and the Sultan's irritation was excessive.

M. Benedetti and myself at once saw all the bearing and intention of the affront. Prince Menchikoff wished, at his first start, to create an intimidating and commanding influence, to show that any man, even a Cabinet Minister, who had offended Russia, would be humiliated and punished even in the midst of the Sultan's Court, and without previous communication to His Majesty. Prince Menchikoff wished to take the cleverest man out of the Ministry, humiliate it, upset it, and establish in its place a Ministry favourable to his views.

·   ·   ·   ·   ·   ·   ·   ·   ·

No. 14   Prince Menchikoff's Demands——
22 March to 5 May 1853[1]

The Earl of Clarendon to
Sir G. H. Seymour.

Foreign Office, May 31, 1853.

Sir,

Prince Menchikoff, in his note of the 5th of May, recapitulated the proposals he had previously made to the Porte on the 22nd March and 19th April; but in addition to those of the 22nd March relating to the holy places,[2] Prince Menchikoff simultaneously made other proposals far more important and comprehensive in their character, accompanied with warnings of the danger which Rifaat Pasha[3] would incur if any of those proposals were permitted to transpire.

These last proposals amounted in substance to the conclusion of a Treaty stipulating that Russia should enjoy the exclusive right of intervening for the effectual protection of all the members of the Greek Church, and of the interests of the churches themselves; that the privileges of the Patriarchs should be effectually confirmed, and that the Patriarchs should hold their preferment for life independently of the Porte's approval; the protection of Greek pilgrims in Palestine; the construction of a Russian church at Jerusalem; and the confirmation and enforcement of all Imperial rescripts granted from time to time to Russia. These demands were put forward as an explanation of the Treaty of Kainardji, and necessary for its complete execution.

·   ·   ·   ·   ·   ·   ·   ·   ·   ·

No. 15   Prince Menchikoff Breaks Off Diplomatic
Relations with Turkey——18 May 1853[1]

Prince Menshikov to the Chancellor
[Nesselrode].

Buyukder, 9/21 May 1853.

On 6/18 May, I sent to the Porte the Note, of which a copy is enclosed, announcing that I was leaving Constantinople, followed by the whole mission.

Here are the events which have preceded this rupture:

The Sultan had ordered a grand council to meet on the 5th/17th in order to resolve upon the final determination to be made concerning my Ultimatum. This council was composed of all the ministers and great dignitaries of the Porte, those still active as well as retired, and included, among others, the old Hosrew and Fuad-Effendi, five governors of provinces, Sheik-ul-Islam and the principal leaders, forming a total of 48 persons.

On the day before and during the hours of the morning which preceded the meeting, Lord Redcliffe was seen visiting, with an alacrity hardly consistent with his position, most of these dignitaries in order to persuade them to vote against us and to adopt the draft of a reply which had been concocted at the British embassy and already previously transmitted to the former Grand Vizier Mehmet-Aly. The majority spoke out in agreement with Lord Redcliffe's view, and the well-intentioned members of the council were overwhelmed and accused of being Moscow fellow-travellers.

On the following day, 6/18, Reshid Pasha came to see me, and was embarrassed to discuss the subject.

Responding to my sharp question, he told me that it had been decreed:

to proclaim a supreme decision assuring the status quo of the Holy Places of Jerusalem, which would not be changed in any way without a previous understanding between the Russian and French Cabinets;

to give to the patriarch of Constantinople a royal decree of assurances on the maintenance of the cult;

to address to me an explanatory Note in conclusion of the negotiation, and

to propose to me a royal edict, having the force and validity of a treaty, which would grant a site for the construction of a Russian church and hospice at Jerusalem.

After a sharp and clear refusal to accept, expressed in strong words, I demanded to see the documents; but Reshid replied with embarrassment that he had not brought them with him because their wording had to be submitted that very morning to the same council for its approval. Thereupon I declared to this minister that I was finally breaking off diplomatic relations with the Porte, and that I would leave Constantinople with the whole mission.

The Note mentioned above followed closely upon Reshid's departure, and was delivered to him during the meeting of the council, which persisted in its conclusions of the day before, after having decided to take defensive measures while at the same time to protect Russian commerce, to reassure the clergy, and to use favourable proceedings toward the Christians.

During the sharp, abrupt, and not very verbose interview I had with the Minister of Foreign Affairs, he seemed to be ashamed of the proposals which he had to make to me, and he confessed his powerlessness in bringing under control a position which he had found to be all set and which his recent assumption of office had not given him time to modify.

While this conference was taking place, Lord Redcliffe, who had already seen Reshid in the morning, waited for him in a caique out in the middle of the Bosporus, and he saw him again for the third time after the meeting of the council, whose debates were closely watched by an English assistant who remained nearby. There, my dear Count, is what the British representatives have the effrontery to call the independence of the Turkish Government.

I am, etc.

No. 16   The Russian Ultimatum to Turkey——31 May 1853[1]

The Chancellor [Nesselrode] to
Reshid Pasha,
Minister of Foreign Affairs.

St. Petersburg, 19/31 May 1853.

The Emperor, my August Master, has just been informed that his ambassador had to leave Constantinople as a result of the peremptory refusal by the Porte to give to the Imperial Russian Court the minimum pledges necessary to reassure it about the protective intentions of the Ottoman government with regard to the Orthodox cult and churches in Turkey.

After a fruitless sojourn of three months; after having exhausted, orally and in writing, every possibility which the truth, goodwill, and a spirit of conciliation could have demanded of him; finally, after having attempted to allay all the ill-founded scruples and all the susceptibilities of the Porte by successive modifications, to which he had consented within the terms and the form of the guarantees which he had been charged to demand, Prince Menchikoff had to reach the decision which the Emperor learns of with sorrow, but which His Majesty could not but fully approve.

Your Excellency is too well-informed not to foresee the consequences of the interruption of our relations with the government of His Highness. You are too devoted to the true and permanent interests of your Sovereign and of his Empire not to feel profound regrets in the presence of events which can erupt, and for which the responsibility will rest entirely on those who provoke them.

Furthermore, in addressing this letter to Your Excellency today, I have no other purpose than to enable you, to the degree that you are still in a position to do so, to render a very important service to your Sovereign. Submit once more, Sir, the true state of affairs to His Highness; the moderation and the justice of the Russian demands; the very grave offense which is given to the Emperor by opposing his so constantly friendly and generous intentions with groundless suspicion and an inexcusable refusal.

The dignity of His Majesty, the interests of his Empire, the call of his conscience, do not permit him to accept such proceedings, in return for all those which he yet wishes to have for Turkey. He must seek to obtain amends for them, and to provide against their repetition in the future.

In a few weeks, his troops will receive the order to cross the frontiers of the Empire, not to fight a war with the Sultan—a war which it is repugnant to His Majesty to undertake against a Sovereign whom he has always been pleased to consider as a sincere ally and a well-intentioned neighbor —but to have material guarantees up to that moment when the Ottoman government, brought back to more equitable views, will give to Russia the moral warranties which, for two years, she has demanded in vain through her representatives at Constantinople, and, most recently, through her ambassador.

The draft of a Note, which Prince Menchikoff drew up prior to his departure and which he delivered to you, is still in your possession. Let Your Excellency make haste, after having obtained the agreement of His Highness the Sultan, to sign this Note, without changes, and to transmit it in not more than eight days to our ambassador at Odessa, where he should still be.

I most earnestly wish that, at this decisive moment, the advice which I tender to your Excellency with the confidence inspired in me by your wisdom and your patriotism, be appreciated by you as well as by your colleagues in the Divan, and that, in the interests of the peace which we should all be equally desirous to preserve, it be followed without hesitation nor delay.

No. 17   The Tsar's Military Instructions——9 June 1853[1]

. . . In a letter in his own handwriting, Emperor Nicholas informed Prince M.D. Gorchakow over a month before, namely, on May 28, 1853, that he would try to avoid a war with Turkey, not only because of the destructive Turkish climate, but also because, if we wish to avoid the final destruction of the Turkish Empire, any military action would have an uncertain objective. However, in the event that our last attempt to persuade the Ottoman Porte to accept the terms offered by us fails, then we will be forced to have recourse to compulsory steps which, depending upon the course of events, will be executed in the following order:

First Stage: Upon receiving the final refusal of the Porte to accept our terms, we will have to transfer our troops to the Moldavian border, and, by crossing the Pruth, occupy the Danubian Principalities. We will not declare war, but explain that our troops will retain these regions, as a guarantee, until Turkey satisfies the rightful demands of Russia. The following units are to be deployed in the occupation of the Principalities: the 4th Infantry Corps, part of the 15th Infantry Division, the 5th Light Cavalry Division, and several Cossack regiments. In accomplishing this mission, care is to be exercised not to cross the Danube and to avoid any military contact with the enemy. Only if the Turks themselves cross the left bank of the Danube, and, refusing to retreat before our troops, start a battle, then we should act accordingly. The best way to prevent such a collision would be to occupy the Principalities quickly with a light cavalry vanguard, to be followed by the infantry at close range. It will not be advisable to let the troops advance beyond Galatz because, if the Turks should muster a squadron at Babadag, it could, without our resistance at the lower Danube, break through into our territory. In addition, the position of the 15th Division on the lower Danube, the presence of our fleet there, and the construction of a bridge at Ismail will keep the Turks in dismay guessing if we intend to cross the Danube at that point, as we did in 1828.

The Black Sea Fleet will remain near our coast. Only the cruisers will form a separate squadron, to keep an eye on the Turks and on other foreign fleets; it will try to avoid any fights.

With these dispositions, extending a chain of Cossack posts along the Danube, supported by reserves, and selecting sound camp positions for the other troops, we will wait and see what impression our occupation of the Principalities will make upon the Turks.

Second Stage: If the obstinacy of the Ottoman Porte should compel us to increase our punitive steps, then it is intended, without crossing the Danube, to declare a blockade of the Bosporus, and, depending upon the circumstances, to allow our cruisers to seize any Turkish vessels on the Black Sea. At the same time, it will be required to warn the Turkish government that its continued stubbornness will result in declaring the independence of the Danubian Principalities and of Serbia.

It is desirable that the Austrians, who share our views, should occupy Herzegovina and Serbia.

Third Stage: If, however, our threats will have no effect on the enemy, then it will be time for further action. In this case, the recognition of the independence of the Principalities will, no doubt, be the beginning of the dismemberment of the Ottoman Empire.

These are the thoughts of Emperor Nicholas in this period when disagreements emerged between Russia and Turkey which, at the time, did not menace a general European war.

No. 18   The Nesselrode Memorandum——1844[1]

RUSSIA and England are mutually penetrated with the conviction that it is for their common interest that the Ottoman Porte should maintain itself in the state of independence and of territorial possession which at present constitutes that Empire, as that political combination is the one which is most compatible with the general interest of the maintenance of peace.

Being agreed on this principle, Russia and England have an equal interest in uniting their efforts in order to keep up the existence of the Ottoman Empire, and to avert all the dangers which can place in jeopardy its safety.

.   .   .   .

However, they must not conceal from themselves how many elements of dissolution that Empire contains within itself. Unforeseen circumstances may hasten its fall, without its being in the power of the friendly Cabinets to prevent it.

As it is not given to human foresight to settle beforehand a plan of action for such or such unlooked-for case, it would be premature to discuss eventualities which may never be realized.

In the uncertainty which hovers over the future, a single fundamental idea seems to admit of a really practical application; it is that the danger which may result from a catastrophe in Turkey will be much diminished, if, in the event of its occurring, Russia and England have come to an understanding as to the course to be taken by them in common.

That understanding will be the more beneficial, inasmuch as it will have the full assent of Austria. Between her and Russia there exists already an entire conformity of principles in regard to the affairs of Turkey, in a common interest of conservatism and of peace.

In order to render their union more efficacious, there would remain nothing to be desired but that England should be seen to associate herself thereto with the same view.

The reason which recommends the establishment of this agreement is very simple.

On land Russia exercises in regard to Turkey a preponderant action.

On sea England occupies the same position.

Isolated, the action of these two Powers might do much mischief. United, it can produce a real benefit: thence, the advantage of coming to a previous understanding before having recourse to action.

This notion was in principle agreed upon during the Emperor's last residence in London. The result was the eventual engagement, that if anything unforeseen occurred in Turkey, Russia and England should previously concert together as to the course which they should pursue in common.

The object for which Russia and England will have to come to an understanding may be expressed in the following manner:

1. To seek to maintain the existence of the Ottoman Empire in its present state, so long as that political combination shall be possible.

2. If we foresee that it must crumble to pieces, to enter into previous concert as to everything relating to the establishment of a new order of things, intended to replace that which now exists, and in conjunction with each other to see that the change which may have occurred in the internal situation of that Empire shall not injuriously affect either the security of their own States and the rights which the Treaties assure to them respectively, or the maintenance of the balance of power in Europe.

For the purpose thus stated, the policy of Russia and of Austria, as we have already said, is closely united by the principle of perfect identity. If England, as the principle Maritime Power, acts in concert with them, it is to be supposed that France will find herself obliged to act in conformity with the course agreed upon between St. Petersburgh, London, and Vienna.

Conflict between the Great Powers being thus obviated, it is to be hoped that the peace of Europe will be maintained even in the midst of such serious circumstances. It is to secure this object of common interest, if the case occurs, that, as the Emperor agreed with Her Britannic Majesty's Ministers during his residence in England, the previous understanding which Russia and England shall establish between themselves must be directed.

No. 19   The Seymour Conversations——January to April 1853[1]

Sir G. H. Seymour to Lord John Russell.
(Received January 23.)

(SECRET AND CONFIDENTIAL.)

St. Petersburgh, January 11, 1853.
My Lord,

ON the evening of the 9th instant I had the honour of seeing the Emperor at the palace of the Grand Duchess Helen, who, it appeared, had kindly requested permission to invite Lady Seymour and myself to meet the Imperial family.

The Emperor came up to me, in the most gracious manner, to say that he had heard with great pleasure of Her Majesty's Government having been definitively formed, adding that he trusted the Ministry would be of long duration.

His Imperial Majesty desired me particularly to convey this assurance to the Earl of Aberdeen, with whom, he said, he had been acquainted for nearly forty years, and for whom he entertained equal regard and esteem. His Majesty desired to be brought to the kind recollection of his Lordship.

You know my feelings, the Emperor said, with regard to England. What I have told you before I say again: it was intended that the two countries should be upon terms of close amity; and I feel sure that this will continue to be the case. You have now been a certain time here, and, as you have seen, there have been very few points upon which we have disagreed; our interests, in fact, are upon almost all questions the same.

. . . .

. . . He said, however, at first with a little hesitation, but, as he proceeded, in an open and unhesitating manner, The affairs of Turkey are in a very disorganized condition; the country itself seems to be falling to pieces (menace ruine): the fall will be a great misfortune, and it is very important that England and Russia should come to a perfectly good understanding upon these affairs, and that neither should take any decisive step of which the other is not apprised.

. . . .

"Stay," the Emperor said, as if proceeding with his remark, "stay; we have on our hands a sick man—a very sick man: it will be, I tell you frankly, a great misfortune if, one of these days, he should slip away from us, especially before all necessary arrangements were made. But, however, this is not the time to speak to you on that matter."

. . . .

Sir G. H. Seymour to Lord John Russell.
(Received February 6.)

(SECRET AND CONFIDENTIAL.)

St. Petersburgh, January 22, 1853.
My Lord,

ON the 14th instant, in consequence of a summons which I received from the Chancellor, I waited upon the Emperor, and had the honour of holding with His Imperial Majesty the very interesting conversation of which it will be my duty to offer your Lordship an account, which, if imperfect, will, at all events, not be incorrect.

. . . .

Now Turkey, in the condition which I have described, has by degrees fallen into such a state of decrepitude that, as I told you the other night, eager as we all are for the prolonged existence of the man (and that I am as desirous as you can be for the continuance of his life, I beg you to believe), he may suddenly die upon our hands (nous rester sur les bras); we cannot resuscitate what is dead; if the Turkish Empire falls, it falls to rise no more; and I put it to you, therefore, whether it is not better to be provided beforehand for a contingency, than to incur the chaos, confusion, and the certainty of an European war, all of which must attend the catastrophe if it should occur unexpectedly, and before some ulterior system has been sketched; this is the point to which I am desirous that you should call the attention of your Government.

. . . .

. . .; still it is of the greatest importance that we should understand one another, and not allow events to take us by surprise; "now I desire to speak to you as a friend and as a *gentleman;* if England and I arrive at an understanding of this matter, as regards the rest, it matters little to me; it is indifferent to me what others do or think. Frankly, then, I tell you plainly, that if England thinks of establishing herself one of these days at Constantinople, I will not allow it. I do not attribute this intention to you, but it is better on these occasions to speak plainly; for my part, I am equally disposed to take the engagement not to establish myself there, as proprietor that is to say, for as occupier I do not say: it might happen that circumstances, if no previous provision were made, if everything should be left to chance, might place me in the position of occupying Constantinople."

. . . .

With regard to a French expedition to the Sultan's dominions, His Majesty intimated that such a step would bring affairs to an immediate crisis; that a sense of honour would compel him to send his forces into Turkey without delay or hesitation; that if the result of such advance should prove to be the overthrow of the Great Turk (le Grand Turc), he should regret the event, but should feel that he had acted as he was compelled to do.

. . . .

The other topics touched upon by the Emperor are mentioned in another despatch. With regard to the extremely important overture to which this report relates, I will only observe, that as it is my duty to record impressions, as well as facts and statements, I am bound to say, that if words, tone, and manner offer any criterion by which intentions are to be judged, the Emperor is prepared to act with perfect fairness and openness towards Her Majesty's Government. His Majesty has, no doubt, his own objects in view; and he is, in my opinion, too strong a believer in the imminence of dangers in Turkey. I am, however, impressed with the belief, that in carrying out those objects, as in guarding against those dangers, His Majesty is sincerely desirous of acting in harmony with Her Majesty's Government.

. . . .

Lord John Russell to
Sir G. H. Seymour.

(SECRET AND CONFIDENTIAL.)

Foreign Office, February 9, 1853.
Sir,

I HAVE received, and laid before the Queen, your secret and confidential despatch of the 22nd of January.

Her Majesty, upon this as upon former occasions, is happy to acknowledge the moderation, the frankness, and the friendly disposition of His Imperial Majesty.

Her Majesty has directed me to reply in the same spirit of temperate, candid, and amicable discussion.

The question raised by His Imperial Majesty is a very serious one. It is, supposing the contingency of the dissolution of the Turkish Empire to be probable, or even imminent, whether it is not better to be provided beforehand for a contingency, than to incur the chaos, confusion, and the certainty of an European war, all of which must attend the catastrophe if it should occur unexpectedly, and before some ulterior system has been sketched; this is the point, said His Imperial Majesty, to which I am desirous that you should call the attention of your Government.

In considering this grave question, the first reflection which occurs to Her Majesty's Government is that no actual crisis has occurred which renders necessary a solution of this vast European problem. Disputes have arisen respecting the Holy Places, but these are without the sphere of the internal government of Turkey, and concern Russia and France rather than the Sublime Porte.

.   .   .   .

On the part of Great Britain, Her Majesty's Government at once declare that they renounce all intention or wish to hold Constantinople. His Imperial Majesty may be quite secure upon this head. They are likewise ready to give an assurance that they will enter into no agreement to provide for the contingency of the fall of Turkey without previous communication with the Emperor of Russia.

Upon the whole, then, Her Majesty's Government are persuaded that no course of policy can be adopted more wise, more disinterested, more beneficial to Europe than that which His Imperial Majesty has so long followed, and which will render his name more illustrious than that of the most famous Sovereigns who have sought immortality by unprovoked conquest and ephemeral glory.

.   .   .   .

Sir G. H. Seymour to Lord John Russell.
(Received March 6.)

(SECRET AND CONFIDENTIAL.)

St. Petersburgh, February 21, 1853.
(Extract.)

THE Emperor came up to me last night, at a party of the Grand Duchess Hereditary's, and in the most gracious manner took me apart, saying that he desired to speak to me.

.   .   .   .

Well, the Emperor continued, so you have got your answer, and you are to bring it to me to-morrow?

I am to have that honour, Sir, I answered; but your Majesty is aware that the nature of the reply is very exactly what I had led you to expect.

So I was sorry to hear; but I think your Government does not well understand my object. I am not so eager about what shall be done when the sick man dies, as I am to determine with England what shall not be done upon that event taking place.

But, Sir, I replied, allow me to observe, that we have no reason to think that the sick man (to use your Majesty's expression) is dying. We are as much interested as we believe your Majesty to be in his continuing to live; while for myself, I will venture to remark that experience shows me that countries do not die in such a hurry. Turkey will remain for many a year, unless some unforeseen crisis should occur. It is precisely, Sir, for the avoidance of all circumstances likely to produce such a crisis, that Her Majesty's Government reckons upon your generous assistance.

Then, rejoined the Emperor, I will tell you, that if your Government has been led to believe that Turkey retains any elements of existence, your Government must have received incorrect information. I repeat to you that the sick man is dying; and we can never allow such an event to take us by surprise. We must come to some understanding; and this we should do, I am convinced, if I could hold but ten minutes' conversation with your Ministers—with Lord Aberdeen, for instance, who knows me so well, who has full confidence in me, as I have in him. And remember, I do not ask for a Treaty or a Protocol; a general understanding is all I require—that between gentlemen is sufficient; and in this case I am certain that the confidence would be as great on the side of the Queen's Ministers as on mine.

.   .   .   .

Sir G. H. Seymour to Lord John Russell.
(Received March 6.)

(SECRET AND CONFIDENTIAL.)

St. Petersburgh, February 22, 1853.
(Extract.)

I HAD the honour of waiting yesterday upon the Emperor, and of holding with his Majesty one of the most interesting conversations in which I ever found myself engaged. My only regret is my inability to report in full detail a dialogue which lasted an hour and twelve minutes.

.   .   .   .

. . . I said, Perhaps your Majesty would be good enough to explain your own ideas upon this negative policy. This His Majesty for some time declined doing; he ended, however, by saying: Well, there are several things which I never will tolerate: I will begin by ourselves. I will not tolerate the permanent occupation of Constantinople by the Russians; having said this, I will say that it never shall be held by the English, or French, or any other great nation. Again, I never will permit an attempt at the reconstruction of a Byzantine Empire, or such an extension of Greece as would render her

a powerful State; still less will I permit the breaking up of Turkey into little republics, asylums for the Kossuths and Mazzinis, and other revolutionists of Europe; rather than submit to any of these arrangements I would go to war, and as long as I have a man and a musket left would carry it on. These, the Emperor said, are at once some ideas. . . .

.   .   .   .

In a word, the Emperor went on to observe, As I before told you, all I want is a good understanding with England, and this not as to what shall, but as to what shall not be done; this point arrived at, the English Government and I, I and the English Government, having entire confidence in one another's views, I care nothing about the rest.

I remarked that I felt confident that Her Majesty's Government could be as little disposed as His Imperial Majesty to tolerate the presence of the French at Constantinople; and being desirous, if possible, of ascertaining whether there were any understanding between the Cabinets of St. Petersburg and Vienna, I added, But your Majesty has forgotten Austria; now all these Eastern questions affect her very nearly; she of course would expect to be consulted.

Oh! replied the Emperor, greatly to my surprise, but you must understand that when I speak of Russia, I speak of Austria as well; what suits the one suits the other; our interests as regards Turkey are perfectly identical.

.   .   .   .

You see how I am behaving towards the Sultan. This gentleman (ce monsieur) breaks his written word to me, and acts in a manner extremely displeasing to me, and I have contented myself with despatching an Ambassador to Constantinople to demand reparation: certainly I could send an army there if I chose, there is nothing to stop them; but I have contented myself with such a show of force as will prove that I have no intention of being trifled with.

.   .   .   .

. . .; and the Emperor continued, It may be fair to tell you that if any attempts at exterminating those people should be made by Omar Pasha, and should a general rising of the Christians take place in consequence, the Sultan will in all probability lose his throne; in this case he falls to rise no more. I wish to support his authority, but if he loses it, it is gone for ever. The Turkish Empire is a thing to be tolerated, not to be reconstructed; in such a cause I protest to you I will not allow a pistol to be fired.

The Emperor went on to say that in event of the dissolution of the Ottoman Empire, he thought it might be less difficult to arrive at a satisfactory territorial arrangement than was commonly believed. The Principalities are, he said, in fact an independent State under my protection: this might so continue. Servia might receive the same form of Government. So again with Bulgaria: there seems to be no reason why this province should not form an independent State.

As to Egypt, I quite understand the importance to England of that territory. I can then only say, that if, in the event of a distribution of the Ottoman succession upon the fall of the Empire, you should take possession of Egypt, I shall have no objections to offer. I would say the same thing of Candia: that island might suit you, and I do not know why it should not become an English possession.

.   .   .   .

Sir G. H. Seymour to the Earl of Clarendon.
(Received March 19.)

(SECRET AND CONFIDENTIAL.)

St. Petersburg, March 9, 1853.
(Extract.)

WHEN I waited upon Count Nesselrode on the 7th instant, his Excellency said that, in pursuance of orders which he had received from the Emperor, he had to place in my hands a very confidential memorandum, which His Imperial Majesty had caused to be drawn up, and which was intended as an answer to, or a comment upon, the communication which I had made to His Imperial Majesty on the 21st ultimo.

.   .   .   .

MEMORANDUM

February 21, 1853.

THE Emperor has, with the liveliest interest and real satisfaction, made himself acquainted with the secret and confidential despatch which Sir Hamilton Seymour communicated to him. He duly appreciates the frankness which has dictated it. He has found therein a fresh proof of the friendly sentiments which Her Majesty the Queen entertains for him.

In conversing familiarly with the British Envoy on the causes which, from one day to another, may bring on the fall of the Ottoman Empire, it had by no means entered into the Emperor's thoughts to propose for this contingency a plan by which Russia and England should dispose beforehand of the provinces ruled by the Sultan—a system altogether arranged; still less a formal agreement to be concluded between the two Cabinets. It was purely and simply the Emperor's notion that each party should confidentially state to the other, less what it wishes than what it does not wish; what would be contrary to English interests, what would be contrary to Russian interests; in order that, the case occurring, they might avoid acting in opposition to each other.

There is in this neither plans of partition, nor Convention to be binding on the other Courts. It is merely an interchange of opinions, and the Emperor sees no necessity of talking about it before the time. It is precisely for that reason that he took especial care not to make it the object of an official communication from one Cabinet to another. By confining himself to speaking of it himself, in the shape of familiar conversation, to the Queen's Representative, he selected the most friendly and confidential form of opening himself with frankness to Her Britannic Majesty, being desirous that the result, whatsoever it might be, of these communications should remain, as it ought to be, a secret between the two Sovereigns.

. . . .

In short, the Emperor cannot but congratulate himself at having given occasion for this intimate interchange of confidential communications between Her Majesty and himself. He has found therein valuable assurances, of which he takes note with a lively satisfaction. The two Sovereigns have frankly explained to each other what in the extreme case of which they have been treating their respective interests cannot endure. England understands that Russia cannot suffer the establishment at Constantinople of a Christian Power sufficiently strong to control and disquiet her. She declares that for herself she renounces any intention or desire to possess Constantinople. The Emperor equally disclaims any wish or design of establishing himself there. England promises that she will enter into no arrangement for determining the measures to be taken in the event of the fall of the Turkish Empire without a previous understanding with the Emperor. The Emperor, on his side, willingly contracts the same engagement. As he is aware that in such a case he can equally reckon upon Austria, who is bound by her promises to concert with him, he regards with less apprehension the catastrophe which he still desires to prevent and avert as much as it shall depend on him to do so.

No less precious to him are the proofs of friendship and personal confidence on the part of Her Majesty the Queen, which

Sir Hamilton Seymour has been directed on this occasion to impart to him. He sees in them the surest guarantee against the contingency which his foresight had deemed it right to point out to that of the English Government.

*The Earl of Clarendon
to Sir G. H. Seymour.*

(SECRET AND CONFIDENTIAL.)

Foreign Office, March 23, 1853.

Sir,

YOUR despatches of the 21st and 22nd ultimo have been laid before the Queen, and I am commanded to express Her Majesty's entire approval of the discretion and judgment displayed by you in the conversations which you had the honour to hold with the Emperor.

I need not assure you that the opinions of His Imperial Majesty have received from Her Majesty's Government the anxious and deliberate consideration that their importance demands. . . .

. . . .

Her Majesty's Government believe that Turkey only requires forebearance on the part of its allies, and a determination not to press their claims in a manner humiliating to the dignity and independence of the Sultan,—that friendly support, in short, that, with States as with individuals, the weak are entitled to expect from the strong, —in order not only to prolong its existence, but to remove all cause of alarm respecting its dissolution.

It is in this work of benevolence and of sound European policy that Her Majesty's Government are desirous of cooperating with the Emperor; they feel entire confidence in the rectitude of His Imperial Majesty's intentions, and as they have the satisfaction of thinking that the interests of Russia and England in the East are completely identical, they entertain an earnest hope that a similar policy there will prevail, and tend to strengthen the alliance between the two countries, which it is alike the object of Her Majesty and Her Majesty's Government to promote.

*The Earl of Clarendon
to Sir G. H. Seymour.*

(SECRET AND CONFIDENTIAL.)

Foreign Office, April 5, 1853.

Sir,

YOUR despatches of the 9th, 10th, and 12th ultimo have been laid before the Queen.

.   .   .   .

As regards the holy places, you are aware of the instructions given to Colonel Rose for his guidance at the Porte, and of the despatch addressed to Her Majesty's Ambassador at Paris, which was communicated to the French Government, and I have further to inform you that Viscount Stratford de Redcliffe was instructed to bear in mind that Her Majesty's Government, without professing to give an opinion on the subject, were not insensible to the superior claims of Russia, both as respected the treaty obligations of Turkey, and the loss of moral influence that the Emperor would sustain throughout his dominions, if, in the position occupied by His Imperial Majesty with reference to the Greek Church, he was to yield any privileges it had hitherto enjoyed to the Latin Church, of which the Emperor of the French claimed to be the protector.

.   .   .   .

Sir G. H. Seymour to the Earl of Clarendon.
(Received May 2.)

(SECRET AND CONFIDENTIAL.)

St. Petersburgh, April 20, 1853.
(Extract.)

THE Emperor on rising from table when I had the honour of dining at the Palace on the 18th instant, desired me to follow him into the next room.

His Majesty then said that he had wished to state to me the real and sincere satisfaction which he received from your Lordship's despatch marked Secret and Confidential of the 23rd ultimo.

It had been, His Majesty said, most agreeable to him to find that the overtures which he had addressed to Her Majesty's Government had been responded to in the same friendly spirit in which they were made; that, to use a former expression, there was nothing in which he placed so much reliance as "la parole d'un gentilhomme"; that he felt that the relations of the two Courts stood upon a better basis now that a clear understanding had been obtained as to points which, if left in doubt, might have been productive of misintelligence, and, as His Majesty was pleased to add, he felt obliged to me for having contributed towards bringing about this friendly *entente.*

And His Majesty said, I beg you to understand that what I have pledged myself to will be equally binding upon my successor; there now exist memorandums of my intentions, and whatever I have promised, my son, if the changes alluded to should occur in his time, will be as ready to perform as his father would have been.

.   .   .   .

His Majesty, after observing that according to the accounts just received (those of the 29th ultimo) little or no progress had been made towards an adjustment of difficulties at Constantinople, said that as yet he had not moved a ship or a battalion; that he had not done so from motives of consideration for the Sultan and from economical motives; but that he would repeat that he had no intention of being trifled with, and that if the Turks did not yield to reason, they would have to give way to an approach of danger.

No. 20   The Russian Ambassador Appraises the British
Cabinet and Public— —25 May 1853[1]

Baron Brunnow to Count Nesselrode.

London, 13/25 May 1853.

When things become complicated, my dear Count, you prefer that they be faced squarely. This is what I am doing in this letter addressed to you.

I will begin by giving you an exact idea of the disposition of the Cabinet. It is divided; but the majority is against us.

Aberdeen is, in the main, our only friend; however, he is beginning to weaken. He will resist his colleagues as long as he can; he will try to slow down the march of events in the hope that, with the benefit of time, some remedy will appear; but he will end up, I am afraid, by being *overwhelmed;* then he will look upon a retreat as his last resource. You can see that this is without benefit for us.

Clarendon would be perfect if he were not haunted by an extreme fear of the newspapers, of the two Houses, and, in general, of public opinion. He has his reputation *to make;* and he believes that he would compromise it if he surrendered to what is called *"the unreasonable Russian demands."* In addition, he is afraid to appear more faint-hearted against us than Palmerston would have been in his place. Finally, he does not want to provoke an open quarrel with Stratford Canning by disavowing him. The result of all this is that Clarendon, without entertaining the least hostility against us, becomes our antagonist because of his sole fear of discrediting himself in the eyes of the public if he were to retreat before Russia.

Lord John Russell is not evil, but he is malicious. He enjoys seeing Aberdeen entangled with Austria in Italy and with Russia in Turkey. He will do nothing to help him out of his dilemma. Perhaps he foresees, not without pleasure, the prospect of the Prime Minister's retreat!

Sir James Graham follows Lord Aberdeen's lead. But, as First Lord of the Admiralty, he regrets the passive role which, until now, has been imposed upon the squadron at Malta! He does not like to see it stay at anchor in the face of the events which are about to occur. He, too, fears the "what will people say!"

Palmerston—you know him. I do not have to say anything about him. His followers say that he is the only one who can lead England out of the present crisis with honor! He will make things as difficult as possible for Clarendon, and will block, if he can, an accommodation between England and us in order to place the Foreign Secretary in a situation which is, perhaps, over his head.

The other members of the Cabinet let things drift along. The Whigs are, generally, in favor of some form of resistance; the Peelites lean toward temporizing. Lord Landsdown[e][2] would regret to see Aberdeen succumb under the weight of the present crisis; but he will support him—*feebly.* He will do us more harm than good by advising the Prime Minister not to appear to be *too Russian,* as he is already accused of being!

This is the situation in the Cabinet. It has become more troublesome since the newspapers have all come out against us. Please have a report prepared for you on the latest manifestations of the press. Too much importance should not be attached to it. But it is always a symptom which is not to be disdained.

The attitude of the two Houses is not in our favor. The cry of *"unreasonable Russian demands"* shuts up even those who, habitually, are the most reasonable. I must draw your attention to a singular circumstance which will influence the Houses in a sense unfavorable to us. Here it is. When the Whigs were in power and the Peelites in opposition, the latter became our natural auxiliaries in keeping the adventurous policy of Palmerston at bay! This state of affairs has changed.[3] We will not have the talented men of the Peelite Party at our disposal any more, to defend our cause before Parliament. I expect little from Disraeli. He will make fun of Aberdeen, by impressing upon him that he was in the wrong: at first, by placing too blind a confidence in us, and then, by becoming angry with us solely because he had been duped by his own credulity. Such sarcasms could do more harm than good. In any case, we have nothing to gain from them.

The City, very tranquil and calm until now, begins to show signs of uneasiness.

The public, in a body, is stupid enough to be thankful to the government of Her Britannic Majesty that it did not let itself be *intimidated* by the so-called Russian menaces! Finally:

The Court is keenly absorbed in a situation whose consequences could affect the affairs of the Continent in general. The Queen is very disturbed about it. She demonstrates more foresight than most of her ministers!

After painting this picture, without making the colors any *gloomier* than they are, I will render an account of my last interview with Lord Clarendon. . . .

No. 21   Stratford's Instructions——25 February 1853[1]

The Earl of Clarendon to
Lord Stratford de Redcliffe.

Foreign Office, February 25, 1853.

(Extract.)

THE Queen has been pleased to direct that at this critical period of the fate of the Ottoman Empire your Excellency should return to your Embassy for a special purpose, and charged with special instructions.

Your Excellency is aware that the preservation of the independence and integrity of Turkey enters into the general and established system of European policy; that the principle is solemnly declared and sanctioned by the Convention of 1841, and is acknowledged by all the great Powers of Europe.

The object of your Excellency's mission at this time is to counsel prudence to the Porte, and forebearance to those Powers who are urging her compliance with their demands. You are instructed to use every effort to ward off a Turkish war, and to persuade the Powers interested to look to an amicable termination of existing disputes.

.   .   .   .

It remains only for me to say, that in the event, which Her Majesty's Government earnestly hope may not arise, of imminent danger to the existence of the Turkish Government, your Excellency will in such case despatch a messenger at once to Malta, requesting the Admiral to hold himself in readiness, but you will not direct him to approach the Dardanelles without positive instructions from Her Majesty's Government.

No. 22   The French Fleet Is Ordered to Salamis——
25 March 1853[1]

The Earl of Clarendon to Lord Cowley.

Foreign Office, March 29, 1853.

(Extract.)

ON the 25th instant Count Walewski[2] informed me, by the direction of his Government, that the French fleet had orders to proceed to Salamis, and that communications of a satisfactory nature (as reported in your Excellency's despatch of the 24th instant) had been received from Russia with respect to the instructions given to Prince Menchikoff concerning the Holy Places.

Count Walewski said that the French Admiral was directed not to proceed further than Salamis, and that the fleet was sent there not as a menace to Russia, but as a measure of precaution; . . . .

I told Count Walewski that I saw no reason for altering the opinion I had more than once expressed to him, and that I still thought the orders for the sailing of the fleet were given hastily and without sufficient reason; and that, although I hoped the two Governments would always act together when their policy and their interests were identical, yet I must frankly say that the recent proceedings of the French Government were not the best calculated to secure that desirable result; for the fleet had been ordered to sail without consultation or communication with us, . . .

No. 23   The British Fleet Is Placed at Stratford's Disposal——
31 May 1853[1]

*The Earl of Clarendon
to Lord Stratford de Redcliffe.*

Foreign Office, May 31, 1853.

My Lord,

THE latest despatch received at this office from your Excellency is dated the 15th instant, and Her Majesty's Government are therefore uninformed respecting the negotiations which took place between the 15th and the 22nd, on which day Prince Menchikoff quitted Constantinople, nor do they yet know whether the rupture between the Russian Ambassador and the Porte was of a character to preclude all hope that negotiations might be resumed.

Nevertheless the departure of Prince Menchikoff, followed by the entire Russian Mission, is a fact in itself of such grave importance, the military preparations of Russia on the Turkish frontier are upon a scale of such vast magnitude, and the danger which threatens the Porte may be so imminent, that it appears indispensable to take measures for the protection of the Sultan, and to aid his Highness in repelling any attack that may be made upon his territory.

I have accordingly to inform your Excellency that by Her Majesty's commands the fleet now stationed at Malta is placed at the disposal of your Excellency, and that orders will be sent to Admiral Dundas to conform to the requisitions he may receive from you, and to repair to such place as you may direct in the event of your considering the presence of a British force absolutely essential to the safety of the Turkish Empire. Her Majesty's Government, however, are desirous that your Excellency should distinctly understand that in coming to this determination they by no means intend to depart from the moderate and conciliatory course which they have always adopted between the Porte and its allies; but in the use of the power now confided you, involving as it may do the momentous question of peace or war, Her Majesty's Government place the fullest reliance on the discretion of your Excellency.

A declaration of war by Russia against Turkey, the embarkation of troops at Sevastopol, or any other well-established fact denoting intentions of unmistakeable hostility, would in the opinion of Her Majesty's Government entirely justify your Excellency in sending for the fleet, which however would not pass the Dardanelles except on the express demand of the Sultan; but the use of force should only be resorted to as a last and unavoidable resource for the protection of Turkey against an unprovoked

attack, and in defence of her independence, which England is bound to maintain.

I am, etc.
(Signed) CLARENDON.

The Earl of Clarendon to the
Lords Commissioners of the Admiralty.

Foreign Office, June 2, 1853.

My Lords,

I HAVE received the Queen's commands to acquaint your Lordships that, in the present critical state of Turkish affairs, it is Her Majesty's pleasure that Her Majesty's fleet, now stationed at Malta, should proceed forthwith to the neighbourhood of the Dardanelles, and that Vice-Admiral Dundas should be instructed to send a fast steamer to Constantinople to enable Viscount Stratford de Redcliffe to communicate with him without loss of time, and should further be instructed to comply with any requisition in regard to the movements and operations of the fleet under his orders which he may receive from Her Majesty's Ambassador.

I have at the same time the honour to transmit to your Lordships, for your information, a copy of a despatch which I have addressed to Viscount Stratford de Redcliffe placing the fleet at his disposal.

I am, etc.
(Signed) CLARENDON.

No. 24   The French Fleet Is Ordered to Join the British
                 Fleet at Besika Bay——4 June 1853[1]

Lord Cowley to the Earl of Clarendon.
(Received June 6.)

Paris, June 5, 1853.

(Extract.)

M. DROUYN DE LHUYS has just in-

formed me that he saw the Emperor yesterday, and that, after acquainting His Majesty with the resolution taken by Her Majesty's Government, in consequence of the intelligence lately received both from Constantinople and St. Petersburgh, to order Admiral Dundas to approach the Dardanelles, and to place himself under the orders of Lord Stratford de Redcliffe, he stated to His Majesty the strong desire which your Lordship had expressed, that the two Governments should act entirely in concert for the maintenance of the independence of the Porte, and of the integrity of the Ottoman Empire.

His Majesty inquired whether it was certain that Admiral Dundas had been actually ordered to leave Malta, and on being assured of the fact, acquiesced in telegraphic orders being sent to Marseilles, to order the "Chaptal" to get under weigh

with despatches for Admiral de la Susse and M. de la Cour.[2]

. . . .

In the despatches transmitted by the "Chaptal," M. de la Cour is referred to these instructions; he is told that Her Majesty's fleet is placed under Lord Stratford's directions, and that the two fleets will rendezvous at Besika Bay,[3] there to await orders from Constantinople.

Admiral de la Susse is desired to make for Besika Bay, where he is told he will find the English fleet.

No. 25   Turkey Rejects the Russian Ultimatum——16 June 1853[1]

Reshid Pasha to the Imperial Chancellor [Nesselrode].

Constantinople, 4/16 June 1853.

I have hastened to submit to His Majesty, my August Master, the despatch which Your Excellency has done me the honor of addressing to me on the 19th May of this year.[2]

His Majesty the Sultan has always shown, on every occasion, the highest respect for His Majesty the Emperor of Russia, whom he considers as his sincere ally and as a well-intentioned neighbor. The Sublime Porte, by no means doubting the generous intentions of the Emperor, has felt profound sorrow at the interruption of relations which, unfortunately, came about because the real impossiblity in which it found itself in regard to the question raised by Prince Menchikoff of recording the religious privileges granted to the Greek rite in a diplomatic engagement has not, perhaps, been well understood. Nevertheless, it has the consolation of seeing that, for its part, it has by no means contributed

to bring about a similar state of affairs. In effect, the Ottoman government has demonstrated, from the beginning, the friendliest disposition and all accomodation relating to all of the questions which Prince Menchikoff, following the orders of the Emperor, had been charged with regulating. And even in a question as delicate as that of the religious privileges of the Greek Church, still inspired by its peaceful feelings and not rejecting the assurances which could have made the doubts disappear which might have been raised in this regard and reduced them to nothing, the Porte, trusting above all in the known sagacity of Prince Menchikoff, hoped that the ambassador would be satisfied with the draft of a Note which had been delivered to him most recently and which contained all of the assurances demanded. However that may be, this regrettable fact has occurred.

It is true that His Highness Prince Menchikoff has, the second time, abridged the minute of the royal decree which he had presented at first, and, in presenting, at the end, a draft of a Note, he made several changes, either in the terms or in the wording and in the title of the document; but it still contained the sense of an engagement. And since such a diplomatic engagement cannot be in accordance with either the independence of the Ottoman government or with the rights of its sovereign authority, one can hardly ascribe to such motives based on a real impossibility, presented on this point by the Sublime Porte, the title of a refusal and transform this into a question of honor for His Majesty the Emperor of Russia.

Furthermore, if one complains of this impossibility, by attributing it to a sentiment of defiance, does not Russia, in refusing to take into account any of the numerous assurances offered by the Sublime Porte in the most solemn manner, and in declaring that it was indispensable to record them in an act having the force of an engagement, rather give patent proof of its lack of confidence in the Ottoman government? And does not the latter, in its turn, have the right to complain about this?

However, to respond to these two points it relies upon the well-known sense of justice of His Majesty the Emperor of Russia, as well as upon the sound judgment and the eminently peaceful sentiments of Your Excellency which, moreover, everyone has been able to recognize and to appreciate.

His Majesty the Sultan, through an imperial decree provided with his august *Hatti-chérif,* has just confirmed once more the privileges, rights, and immunities enjoyed *ab antiquo* by the religious and the Churches of the Greek rite.

The Sublime Porte will never hesitate to maintain and to give the assurances contained and promised in the draft of the Note delivered to Prince Menchikoff shortly before his departure. The despatch received from Your Excellency mentions the intention of having the frontier crossed by Russian troops. Such a declaration is incompatible with the assurances of peace and of good will by His Majesty the Emperor. It is, truly, so contrary to what one has the right to expect on the part of a friendly Power that the Sublime Porte is at a loss how to accept it.

The military preparations and the defense works ordered by the Porte, as it has officially notified the Powers, are thus only necessitated by the raising of considerable Russian forces; they only constitute a purely defensive measure. The government of the Sultan, having no hostile intentions whatsoever against Russia, expresses the desire that the ancient relations, which His Majesty regards as so valuable and whose advantages are so numerous and so manifest for both parties, be re-established in their original state.

I trust that the Court of Russia will appreciate, with a sentiment of sanguine consideration, the sincere and loyal intentions of the Sublime Porte, and will take into account the real impossibility with which it is faced to defer to the wishes which have been expressed to it. If this impossibility is appreciated, as it deserves to be, then I can assure Your Excellency that the Sublime Porte will not hesitate to instruct an extraordinary ambassador to travel to St. Petersburg in order to renew negotiations there and to seek, in concert with the government of His Majesty the Emperor of Russia, an accomodation which, while being agreeable to His Majesty, would also be of such a nature that the Porte could accept it, without impairing in any way either the foundations of his independence or the Sovereign authority of His Majesty the Sultan.

Your Excellency can take it for granted that I, for my own part, fervently wish for such a result. I like to believe that you, in your turn, do likewise.

I am, Your Excellency, etc.

No. 26 Turkey Declares War Against Russia——
4 October 1853[1]

UNDER existing circumstances it would be superfluous to recapitulate from the commencement the narrative of the difference which has arisen between the Sublime Porte and Russia, to enter into a fresh detail of the different stages of this difference, as well as to recite the opinions and views of the Government of His Majesty the Sultan, which have been made public by the official documents published from time to time.

Notwithstanding our desire not to revert to the urgent motives which led to the modifications introduced by the Sublime Porte into the draft of note prepared at Vienna,[2] motives which have, moreover, been previously set forth in an explanatory note, fresh representations having been made, subsequently to the refusal of Russia to accept those same modifications, in favour of the adoption of the said draft without alteration, the Ottoman Government finding it at the present time utterly impossible to adopt the draft of note in question, and being compelled to declare War, deems it to be its duty to set forth the imperative reasons of this important determination, as well as those which have constrained it to adapt its conduct in this instance to the recommendations of the Great Powers its Allies, although it has never ceased to appreciate the benevolent character of their observations.

The principal points which the Government of His Majesty the Sultan will in the first place notice, are these: that, at the outset, there was nothing in its conduct to give occasion for complaint, and that, animated with the desire of preserving peace, it has acted with a remarkable spirit of moderation and conciliation from the commencement of the difference up to the present time. It is easy to prove these facts to all who do not deviate from the paths of justice and equity.

Even though Russia might have had a ground of complaint in regard to the question of the Holy Places,[3] she ought to have confined her measures and representations within the limits of that single question, and not put forth pretensions which the object of her claims could not bear out. Moreover, she ought not to have had recourse to measures of intimidation, such as those of sending her troops to the frontiers and of making maritime preparations at Sevastopol, in regard to a question which might have been amicably settled between the two Powers. However, it is clear that the contrary of all this has taken place.

The question of the Holy Places had been settled to the satisfaction of all parties: the Government of His Majesty the Sultan had shown itself to be favourably disposed on the subject of the assurances required as to that question, and as to certain other demands relative to Jerusalem. In fine, there was no ground for putting forward on the part of Russia any further demand. Is it not to seek occasion for War to insist, as she does, on the question of the privileges of the Greek Church which have been bestowed by the Ottoman Government, privileges which it considers it a matter of honour, of dignity, and of its sovereign authority to uphold, and in regard to which it cannot admit of the interference or supervision of any Government? Has not Russia occupied with a considerable force the Principalities of Moldavia and Wallachia, declaring that those provinces should serve her for a guarantee until such time as she should have obtained what she requires? Was not this act justly considered by the Porte as an infraction of Treaties, and consequently as a *casus belli*? Could the other Powers themselves entertain any other opinion of it? Who, then, can doubt that Russia is the aggressor? Was it possible that the Sublime Porte, which has always observed with notorious fidelity all its Treaties, should have infringed them to such a degree as to induce Russia to adopt so violent a course as that of herself violating these Treaties? Or, have there occurred within the Ottoman Empire, in disregard of the promise explicity recorded in the Treaty of Kainardji,[4] such acts as the demolition of Christian churches, or have any obstacles been offered to the exercise of the Christian religion?

The Ottoman Cabinet, without wishing to enter into longer details on these points, entertains no doubt that the High Powers, its Allies, will find and consider what has been mentioned to be altogether correct and true.

In regard to the non-acceptance by the Sublime Porte of the Vienna draft of note in its unaltered form, it is to be observed that that draft, without being altogether the same as Prince Menchikoff's note, and while it comprised indeed some paragraphs of the Sublime Porte's own draft of note, does not on the whole, either in letter or in spirit, differ essentially from that of Prince Menchikoff.

.   .   .   .

The very language of the officers and agents of Russia who have declared that the intention of their Government was no other than to discharge the office of advocate with the Sublime Porte so often as proceedings contrary to the existing privileges should take place, is an evident proof of the correctness of the opinion of the Ottoman Government.

If the Government of His Majesty the Sultan has deemed it necessary to require assurances, even should the modifications of the Vienna note which it proposed itself have been admitted, how could it, in conscience, be at ease if the Vienna note was maintained in its integrity and without modifications? The Sublime Porte, by accepting that which it has publicly declared it would not accept without compulsion, would compromise its dignity in the estimation of the other Powers; it would sacrifice it in the estimation even of its own subjects; it would commit a moral and material suicide.

Although the refusal of Russia to acquiesce in the modifications required by the Sublime Porte was based on a question of honour, it cannot be denied that the real cause for the refusal of Russia is merely her desire not to substitute explicit terms for vague expressions, which might furnish her with a further pretext for interference. Such a conduct consequently obliges the Porte on its side to persist in its refusal.

The reasons which have decided the Ottoman Government to make its modifications having been appreciated by the Representatives of the 4 Powers, it is proved that the Sublime Porte was altogether in the right in not adopting the Vienna note without alteration.

.   .   .   .

If it is alleged that the eagerness with which a draft has been framed in Europe results from the tardiness of the Sublime Porte to propose an arrangement; the Government of His Majesty the Sultan is compelled to justify itself by stating the following facts:—

Before the entrance of the Russian troops into the two Principalities, certain of the Representatives of the Powers, influenced by the sincere desire of preventing the occupation of those Provinces, represented to the Sublime Porte the necessity of drawing up a draft in which the draft of note of the Sublime Porte and that of Prince Menchikoff should be blended together.

Subsequently, the Representatives of the Powers submitted confidentially to the Porte various plans of arrangement. None of these last meeting the views of the Imperial Government, the Ottoman Cabinet was on the point of entering into negotiations with the Representatives of the Powers in regard to a draft drawn up by itself in conformity with their suggestion. At this moment news having arrived of the passage of the Pruth by the Russians,[5] the aspect of the question became changed. The draft of note proposed by the Sublime Porte was necessarily laid aside; and the Cabinets, after the Protest of the Sublime Porte,[6] were requested to express their sentiments on this violation of Treaties.

On the one hand, the Ottoman Cabinet had to wait for the answers; and on the other, it drew up, at the suggestion of the Representatives of the Powers, a draft of arrangement which was sent to Vienna. As the only answer to all this, appeared the draft note drawn up at Vienna.

Be that as it may, the Ottoman Government, being reasonably apprehensive of anything which might imply, in favour of Russia, a Right of Intervention in Religious Matters, could do no more than give assurances calculated to dispel the doubts which had led to the discussion; and after so many preparations and sacrifices, it certainly will not accept propositions which could not be accepted during Prince Menchikoff's stay at Constantinople. Since the Cabinet of St. Petersburgh is not satisfied with the assurances which have been offered to it; since the benevolent efforts of the High Powers have been fruitless; since, finally, the Porte can no longer tolerate or endure the existing state of things, as well as the prolonged occupation of the Moldo-Wallachian Principalities, which are integral parts of its Empire; the Ottoman Cabinet, with the fixed and laudable intention of defending the sacred Rights of Sovereignty and the Independence of its Government, will resort to just Reprisals against a violation of Treaties which it looks upon as a *casus belli*. It, therefore, officially makes known that the Government of His Majesty the Sultan is obliged to declare War, and that it has given the most positive instructions to his Excellency Omer Pasha to call upon Prince Gortchakoff to evacuate the Principalities, and to commence hostilities if, within 15 days after the arrival of his letter at the Russian headquarters, a negative answer should reach him.

It is well understood that if Prince Gortchakoff's answer is in the negative, the Russian agents must quit the Ottoman dominions, and that the Commercial Relations of the respective subjects of the two Governments must be interrupted.

The Sublime Porte, however, does not consider it just that, agreeably to ancient usage, an embargo should be laid on Russian merchant-vessels. Accordingly, they will be warned to proceed, within a period to be fixed hereafter, to the Black Sea or to the Mediterranean, as they may choose. Moreover, the Imperial Government, being unwilling to interrupt the Commercial Relations of the subjects of friendly Powers, will leave the Straits open to their mercantile marine during the War.

Moharrem 1, 1270 [4th October, 1853].

No. 27   The Russian Declaration of War Against Turkey——1 November 1853[1]

By the Grace of God, We, Nicolas I, Emperor and Autocrat of All the Russias, etc.

Make known:

By our Manifesto of the 14th June of the present year, we acquainted our well-beloved and faithful subjects with the motives which have compelled us to demand of the Ottoman Porte inviolable guarantees in favour of the sacred rights of the Orthodox Church.

We likewise announced to them that all our efforts to recall the Porte, by means of friendly persuasion, to sentiments of equity, and to faithful observance of Treaties, had been ineffectual; and that we had consequently deemed it indispensable to advance our troops into the Danubian Principalities. But in adopting this measure we still entertained the hope that the Porte would admit its errors and would determine to conform to our just demands.

Our expectation has been deceived.

To no purpose even have the Principal Powers of Europe sought by their exhortations to shake the blind obstinacy of the Ottoman Government. It has replied to the pacific efforts made by Europe, as well as to our forbearance, by a Declaration of War,[2] and by a Proclamation replete with false accusations against Russia. Finally, embodying in the ranks of its army the Revolutionists of all countries, the Porte has commenced hostilities on the Danube.[3]

Russia is challenged to the fight; nothing, therefore, remains for her, but, in confident reliance upon God, to have recourse to arms in order to compel the Ottoman Government to respect Treaties, and obtain from it reparation by which it has responded to our most moderate demands, and to our legitimate solicitude for the defence of the Orthodox faith in the East which is equally professed by the Russian people.

We are firmly convinced that our faithful subjects will join in the fervent prayers which we address to the Most High, that His hand may be pleased to bless our arms in the holy and just cause which has ever found ardent defenders in our pious ancestors.

"In Thee, LORD, have I trusted: let me never be confounded."

Given at Tsarskoe-Selo, this 20th of October, in the year 1853, and the 28th of our Reign.

NICOLAS

[Conferences were held at Vienna between the Representatives of Great Britain, Austria, France, and Prussia, and Protocols were signed on the 5th December, 1853; and on the 13th January, 2nd February, and 5th March, 1854; with the object of stopping the War between Russia and Turkey by Friendly Intervention, but they led to no result. Ed.]

No. 28 Editorials in **The** [London] **Times——**
1 September to 13 December 1853

Thursday, September 1, 1853 (p. 6).

. . . .

But the Philo-Turks are not satisfied—they are ready for a declaration of war, which will abrogate all these treaties, and they are willing to risk the existence of the Ottoman Empire and the welfare of the Christian population on the success of an army of Moslems, collected from Asia, collected from Africa, but now encamped in Europe, and already more formidable to the Turkish Government and the inhabitants of the country than to their enemies. Do those who would applaud the rejection of M. DROUYN DE LHUYS'[1] note approve a policy that threatens to set in motion this brutal force, with all its horrible consequences? Among those consequences, the most just would be the ruin likely to recoil on the authors of such a scheme; for we cannot suppose that the elements of Christianity and civilization would succumb to the Bashi-bozouks, or other ferocious tribes now lying or marching between Shumla and Adrianople. When Russia assumed a menacing attitude, having deceived and attempted to overreach her allies and compromised the peace of Europe, we were entirely of opinion that the most energetic measures might be required, and ought to be taken, if necessary, by the Western Powers, to defeat her pretensions and to resist her progress, and this country was prepared to meet that danger, not from any strong sympathy for Turkish barbarism, but from a unanimous hostility to Russian aggression. That demonstration proved successful, for Europe was unanimous, and Russia was

reduced more speedily than had been anticipated to accept the offered terms.[2] In the interest of peace and in the real interests of Turkey it is as important to prevent the SULTAN from making war on Russia as it was to prevent Russia from making war on the SULTAN. We care little for one or the other party; our concern is with that cause of civilization, freedom, and peace, which has nothing to gain from the triumph of either side, though it has much to lose by a rupture; and we support the terms of compromise recommended by the Four Powers, because they afford an honourable path out of a difficult position without increasing the weakness of one side or the preponderance of the other.

Thursday, September 22, 1853 (p. 8).

In another part of our impression[3] will be found a despatch from Count NESSELRODE to Baron MAYENDORFF,[4] expressing some of the reasons alleged by the CZAR for refusing to accede to the Turkish modifications.[5] This document will not require much comment. . . .

. . . .

. . . and it is but too probable that the next mail may inform us of the actual resort to arms.

It cannot be forgotten, indeed, that such a result is no more than a natural consequence of the aggression of Russia. We may say that hostilities were already commenced when the Danubian Principalities were occupied by a Russian army, for, if an armed invasion of a foreign territory does not constitute an act of war, it will be hard to say what does so. The Turks would be clearly justified in crossing the Danube, in expelling the Russians from Wallachia and Moldavia, and even in following up by offensive demonstrations an expedition so openly provoked. If they could accomplish this by their own unaided strength, the most difficult of State problems would at once be solved; but few persons acquainted with the subject will venture to doubt that the event of such proceedings would be to bring the Russians, after one or more campaigns, to the gates of Constantinople. This consummation it is the paramount interest of combined Europe to avert, but it is clear that intervention could be much more conveniently effected before the sword has been drawn than when the CZAR has been brought within reach of his prize with the title of conquest, and after the chances of war.

Friday, September 23, 1853 (p. 6).

.   .   .   .

The present offence, however, of Russia consists, not so much in her demands upon Turkey, as in her enforcement of those demands by armed aggression. There could certainly be no great impropriety in a requisition by a Christian State, on behalf of other Christians suffering wrong, nor could it be easy to impeach such a proceeding by any imputation of clandestine motives. But, when the Emperor NICHO-LAS backed his application by the seizure of the Danubian Principalities, and proclaimed his intention of retaining this territory until his demands were satisfied, he not only outraged public law, but disclosed the true spirit of his intervention. As a matter of right the British Government would have an equal, if not a better title, to bring the Cabinet of Madrid to reason by similar measures. On this plea, and with the precedent of Russia before us, we might advance from Gibraltar and occupy the valley of the Guadalquiver until the Spanish Government had consented, in the terms

of the modified Note, "to allow our fellow-Christians the same advantages as are granted to all other Christians, being Spanish subjects." This proceeding would probably be regarded by Europe with amazement and indignation; but it would really be little more than the CZAR has already done upon a pretext by no means stronger.

Monday, September 26, 1853 (p. 8).

.   .   .   .

We trust indeed, that our prowess may never be brought to the test, for a war with Russia would be quite as injurious to our trade as to hers. In war, however it may be conducted, it is always the more mercantile, the more wealthy, and the more civilized Power that suffers the most,—precisely as a gentleman suffers most in a personal encounter with a boor. We should pay in a hundred ways. Therefore, if we assert our strength, it is only because we are dealing with a Power that requires arguments of this sort. Russia's first argument is to march an army into Turkey, and occupy two provinces, in order to indicate what she will do with the rest. With such a Power, which confesses, or rather boasts, to be illogical, and which meets the arguments of diplomacy with the fact of an invasion, little else can be done than point to that wondrous array of floating castles, one day a holyday pageant, the next day the scourge of a despot, and, possibly, the doom of an empire. If any other apology be necessary for thus anticipating the horrors of war, it is found in the unselfish justice of our cause. . . .

Thursday, November 24, 1853 (p. 6).

.   .   .   .

Without reopening the general question of the Ottoman polity, it is sufficient to understand that the cause of the Turks in the present quarrel has been abetted by

Powers strong enough to sustain it; that the aggressions of Russia will be resisted, and the rights of the PORTE preserved. Under such circumstances it is difficult to see why the war on the Danube should be prolonged, or why the belligerents should indulge in hostilities which will probably exert little influence on the ultimate result. Undoubtedly the Turks may inflict some blows on the reputation of the CZAR, but, if they cannot disturb its reality, and if the shock of war recoils upon themselves, the interests, not only of humanity and peace, but of the Ottoman empire itself, might have been better served by forbearance. The object of the contest is to eject the CZAR from the Danubian Principalities. Diplomacy certainly failed in accomplishing this purpose during a four months' trial, but whether war will be more speedily efficacious remains yet to be seen.

Monday, December 5, 1853 (p. 6).

. . . .

. . . No doubt, it has become difficult for the Emperor NICHOLAS to recede, and, for the sake of peace, it is wiser to facilitate his retreat than to insist upon a surrender. But every day's delay has strengthened the united determination of the other Powers to oppose his pretensions, and, if it were true that he had taken the desperate resolution of breaking off all further negotiations, he would throw down the glove to a great portion of Europe. Of the success of these negotiations we have ceased, from the experience of the last few months, to entertain any confident hope, but they will at least have exhausted every means of preserving peace, they have consolidated the efforts of the Great Powers interested in restoring peace and they will completely throw on Russia, if they fail, the disgrace and the penalty of the unjust and unnecessary war.[6]

Tuesday, December 13, 1853 (p. 6).

The intelligence from the seat of war, which we received yesterday with hesitation,[7] has now been corroborated by several channels, and by a positive announcement in the official journal of France. War has begun in earnest. . . . We have thought it our duty to uphold and defend the cause of peace, as long as peace was compatible with the honour and dignity of the country, and we feel no regret that to the very last we have adhered to a course of policy which a just concern for the best interests of England and of the civilized world prescribed. But we have never concealed our opinion that the events occurring in the East might ere long compel us to meet by more resolute measures a sterner alternative; and we have repeatedly urged upon the Governments of England and France the necessity of being prepared with a plan of operations adapted to such an emergency. If the intelligence last received be confirmed in the manner in which it is related to us, the time for these resolutions to take effect is already come.

. . . .

Whatever doubt may still prevail as to the circumstances which preceded this action and the mode in which it was fought, there can be very little as to its naval and political consequences. It tends to give the Russian navy an ascendancy on the Black Sea which the Turks have hitherto disputed; and it calls upon the maritime allies of the PORTE in very positive language to supply that naval protection of which she more than ever stands in need. . . . A more violent and offensive measure could not have been resorted to; . . .

The effect this event will have in Europe is not less serious. It dispels the hopes we have been led to entertain of pacification, for we cannot share the opinion that this success will lower in any degree the temper or pretensions of Russia; and it imposes upon the allied fleets more peremptory duties. . . . Having exhausted every means that forbearance and ingenuity could suggest for the restoration of peace, but having at the same time pledged the honour and the naval forces of England to bring this dispute to a successful termination by other means, if all negotiations for peace should fail, it would be unworthy of the position we occupy in the world, and the peculiar obligations we have contracted in this question, to hesitate when the course is clear before us. The English people are resolved that Russia shall not dictate conditions to Europe, or convert the Black Sea, with all the various interests encompassing its shores, into a Russian lake. They desire that a course of consummate hypocrisy should be punished by a signal defeat, and that a stop should be put to these aggressions. The Emperor of Russia, who began this war without a pretext, is carrying it on without disguise, and it therefore becomes the imperative duty of the Four Powers, who have so recently recorded their determination to put an end to it, to take all the measures which that object may demand.

No. 29   A Public Meeting at the London Tavern—— 7 October 1853[1]

Last night a public meeting was held at the London Tavern "to support the cause of Turkish independence against Russian aggression." It was announced in the advertisement calling the meeting, that "several noblemen, members of Parliament, and other influential gentlemen" would attend; and this, together with the interest attaching to the question, brought together a crowded, and, as the event showed, an enthusiastic audience. Long before the hour of meeting the hall was crowded to inconvenience, and great numbers of people were unable to gain admittance from want of room. Among the gentlemen on the platform were Lord Dudley Stuart, M.P., Sir C. Napier, Mr. Blackett, M.P., Mr. D. Urquhart, Mr. Prout, Mr. Nicholay, Professor Newman, Captain Mayne Reed, etc.

On the motion of Mr. Prout, Lord Dudley C. Stuart was unanimously called on to preside.

Lord D. STUART, on taking the chair, was received with loud cheering.—He said, he could assure them that the spirit which he saw animate the meeting set his heart on fire, and gave him courage on the great occasion which had called them together (cheers); because he saw that he was addressing a body of men who, with the spirit of Englishmen, were resolved to maintain the honour and the good faith of their country (great cheering), and not to allow themselves to be insulted or their rights trampled on by the machinations of tyrants. (Renewed cheering.) He understood that thousands had gone away from the door unable to gain admission. He was exceedingly sorry that such should be the case, and he could only say that when the meeting was summoned for 7 o'clock the committee and himself could not foresee that such would be the eagerness of the inhabitants of the metropolis to be present that they would assemble in numbers so great an hour before the time. (Cheers.) They were met on a great, an important and most solemn occasion, to consider the present crisis of affairs in Europe, as they affected the honour and the interests of this country (loud cheers), and to come to some conclusion as to what it behoved the free and independent people of England to do at such a juncture. (Cheers.) He apprehended that the object of their assembling that evening was to make some demonstration which would have the effect of guiding the Government to a course honourable to the country, if they required to be so guided; or, if they were determined to take a bold and manly course—a course different from that which had marked their proceedings hitherto (cheers)—to give them the free and enlightened support of the intelligence of this great metropolis. (Cheers.) They wished to give expression to the feeling which he saw manifested on the present occasion, and which had been exhibited in different parts of the country, for they were not the first to move on this question, and he could not suppose that the opinions of a meeting so numerous and so influential could be without a corresponding effect on the Government of the country. (Cheers.) However, if such should not be the case, they would at least have the satisfaction of having done their duty, and it would not be said throughout the world that in this metropolis, in this focus of ardent love for liberty, there were no men ready to protest against Russian encroachment, and to call upon the Government to come forward boldly in behalf of the injured but generous Sultan. (Great cheering.) They would show that if Governments and Cabinets, and persons in high station, were so overcome by the cares, or the pleasures, or the tinsel of this life, and the enjoyments of their position, as not to care for what was passing in other countries, the inhabitants of this metropolis would be no party to such base and pusillanimous misconduct. (Great cheering.) Now, what was the crisis which had called them together that night? They had seen the Emperor of Russia at the head of his millions of armed serfs pursuing the course which his predecessors had long recognized as their settled policy, committing aggressions upon Turkey, and thereby proceeding by degrees towards universal dominion and the slavery of the world. (Great cheering.) Russia, as was her wont, had put forward all kinds of flimsy pretences, and she had, among others, urged the hypocritical ground that she was actuated by a regard for religion. (Cheers.)

She had endeavoured to represent the dispute about the Holy Places of Jerusalem as the foundation of the present quarrel; but Russia had professed herself satisfied with the concessions made to her on that subject, though he for one could not see that she had any grievance whatever, to complain of. But this point having been settled, and the Russian Government having given assurances which our Ministers were green enough to believe (laughter), Prince Menschikoff, with characteristic want of faith on the part of Russia, put forth a claim which would have given to the Czar a right of sovereignty over all the population of Turkey that professed the Greek religion. (Cheers.) The Turks, nothing intimidated, gave the resolute answer that they would agree to nothing of the kind, and Prince Menschikoff, after leaving the question open to the last day, and giving more last days, finding himself unable to prevail with the Sultan, was obliged to leave the Turkish capital; and the autocrat, who could brook no opposition to his will, informed the Turkish Government that, if his demands were not conceded, he would march his troops into the Danubian Principalities. And he did so, while the Governments of France and England assured the Sultan that there could be no doubt the Emperor of Russia had by that step committed an act of war (laughter), as if there could be the slightest doubt that the possession of the territory of another country by any power was an act of war. (Hear, hear.) The Russian forces still remained in those provinces, tyrannizing over the independent and enlightened inhabitants, who were able to say they had never been conquered, and who had placed themselves voluntarily under the rule of the Sultan by the most sacred treaties. (Hear, hear.) Count Nesselrode had the audacity to declare that the reason why Russia occupied those provinces was that the fleets of England and France had gone to the mouth of the Dardanelles,—a statement so contrary to the truth that only one word could describe it, the use of which was not agreeable to ears polite. The language of Russia has been sufficiently described by a learned member of the House of Peers, one who was no enemy to the liberty of nations, though he had been brought up with the enemies of despotism, when he said the despatch of Count Nesselrode was the most odious, insulting, and fallacious document it had ever been his misfortune to read. (Hear, hear.) Did those great Western Powers order their fleets to go into the Black Sea to commit reprisals for the unjust attack of Russia? Why, they entered on a conference at Vienna. (A laugh.) Of all places Vienna was the last place to hold a conference at. (Loud cheers.) Everybody knew that the Court of Vienna was nothing now but the tool of Russia; that whatever was done by Austria was sure to be done so as to give satisfaction and contentment at St. Petersburgh. At the conferences the Russian ambassador was not formally admitted, but the Prime Minister of Austria, Count Buol, had married Count Meyendorff's sister, and it was not a violent supposition that those two persons, representing the Emperors of Russia and of Austria, should have a good understanding. With the ambassador of the Sultan no communication took place. He had no Ministerial brother-in-law. But the note was sent to Constantinople, and the Sultan was expected immediately to sign it. The Sultan objected for the same reason that the Czar consented. ("Exactly.") The Czar said, "oh yes; this gives me all I want." The Sultan said, "I might as well have agreed to the note of Prince Menschikoff." Austria turned round and said she could not agree to anything of the kind proposed by Turkey, and she sided with Russia; and Russia would make no concession, but insisted on the original convention being agreed to pure and simple. Further conference had been held at Olmütz; the Austrian and Russian Emperors had been reviewing their troops, and performing all that kind of military parade, or perhaps he might better call it tomfoolery. But at these conferences the Earl of Westmorland[2] was present. ("Shame!") The French Government, with a better appreciation of its dignity and independence, would not allow its ambassador to go there (hear, hear); and he could not but say that throughout this transaction the Government of France had played a loftier and more honourable part than that of England, because it had always been understood that France was for more vigorous counsels. France was for repelling wrong and insisting on right; and, if she did not act on those noble intentions, it was because she was overpersuaded by the Cabinet headed by Lord Aberdeen. ("Aberdeen!") The crisis in which Europe was placed was one of great gravity. It was now reported, that after the conference, Russia still continuing to insist on her unjustifiable demands, Lord John[3] had taken the step which he would have taken long ago if he had not been overpersuaded,—that he had taken the bold course of declaring war, and it remained to be seen what England and France were going to do. It was said that the two fleets had been ordered up the Dardanelles to Constantinople. He sincerely trusted that statement was correct. In reviewing the conduct of the Government he could not help condemning it. He was not one of those who wanted war for the sake of war. When entered on without necessity it was a great crime; but he did not want that this country should accept dishonour rather than war. (Loud cheers.) He recollected the language of Burke with respect to Poland when it was first partitioned—how that great and far-seeing statesman reproached the Government of the day for not interfering, and said it ought never to be forgotten that the purchase of present quiet at the price of future security was most degrading. That was what those were doing who wanted peace at all price. You could not have peace always; you would not have it long if you submitted to wrong. It was that which was true humanity, true Christianity, true piety, because it diminished bloodshed. When a great injustice was done, and persevered in, and you could not prevent it by any other means, you must resort to force. He feared that they had come to that point—that they must decide between war and dishonour. Who had brought them to that point? Was it not the Government of this country? Yes. If they had had an energetic Government, and a farseeing man at the helm (cries of "Palmerston")— if they had had such a man as Lord Palmerston[4] (great cheering, which was renewed) he did not think the Emperor of Russia would ever have ventured to address his untenable demands to Turkey; he did not think he would have been marching out of the Danubian provinces now, because he was sure he never would have ventured to enter them; he would have remained on the other side of the Pruth, in his own dominions. He thought the noble lord whom he had mentioned the greatest statesman of the present day; but he did not think it would be necessary to have had that distinguished man at the head of affairs to prevent what had happened. Any Minister except him they had now would be enough. He did not believe Lord Malmesbury, an old friend of his, would have submitted. Since last year this country had lost a great man—the immortal Wellington. He would not have permitted encroachment. Had he been alive the Czar would not have ventured. Were they not bound to come forward for that gallant country Turkey, oppressed as she had been? It was for their interest to do so. But, if it were not for their interest, they would be bound to do so by honour first of all. This was the cause of commercial liberality, of chivalrous generosity. He wished there was as much religious equality in London as in Turkey. As regarded commerce, the liberality of the Turks was well-known, while

Russia and Austria had prohibitive tariffs. He had seen a man here who was himself a living witness of the generosity of Turkey—namely, Kossuth (great cheering), who was defended by the Sultan against the bloodhounds of St. Petersburg.

Professor NEWMAN moved the first resolution, which was as follows:—

"That the series of Russian aggressions convinces this meeting that there is in the Russian Cabinet a fixed purpose not only to subdue Turkey, but to domineer over all Europe, and extirpate all freedom. We look upon this as the true reason why no diplomatic settlement of the Turco-Russian quarrel was or is possible, and we lament that the British Government has wasted much valuable time, damaged the just cause of the Turks, inflicted upon commerce months of needless depression, and (worst of all) inspired universal suspicion of the good faith of England, in a vain effort to negotiate with an unscrupulous and violent power which acted while we talked, and which, if now momentarily appeased, would only become more dangerous on some early occasion."

. . . .

Mr. BLACKETT, M.P., seconded the resolution, and observed that the only claim he had upon their attention was the fact that he represented a town (Newcastle) which took a very deep interest in this question, and which had already met and expressed its views regarding it—a circumstance of which he thought he had some reason to be proud. (Cheers.) . . . . He thought the warmest panegyrist of the Government would hardly deny that up to this time the consequence had been failure, the most absolute and entire. (Cheers.) It was said, he knew, that the Government as well as the people were about to turn a new leaf on the question, but if it was true that the fleets had been sent through the Dardanelles, to act as the allies of the Sultan, then they could have no greater justification of the present meeting, than that the Government were at last pursuing the course which the people had from the first held to be the true one. (Cheers.) . . . God forbid he should depreciate the evils of war, but when he thought of the immense misfortune to the human race which an extension of Russian despotism would create—when he thought of the overthrow of the balance of power, and the extension of Russian territory, attended as it ever had been with high tariffs and prohibitory duties—when he reflected on the injury to British commerce that would follow—when he reflected on these and other evils, he thought it more than probable that the cost of a war would be but a moderate insurance against the intolerable calamities of the so-called peace. (Cheers.) But when he thought of those higher considerations that ought to influence them—of the solemn compact by which this country had been pledged to Turkey—of the assurance which our Ministers had held out of their determination to maintain the integrity of Turkey—of the right on the side of the Sultan—and many other considerations, there was no one but would agree with him in the hope that England might be true to her ancient honour, and that the Government might not belie the spirit of their countrymen. (Cheers.)

.   .   .   .

The resolution was carried unanimously.

Mr. NICHOLAY moved the second resolution, which was as follows:—

"That this meeting applauds the glorious patriotic spirit of the Turkish people at the present crisis, and would deplore any attempt on the part of the British Government to suppress that spirit as an act of unparalleled infamy; especially considering the many solemn ways in which England had bound herself to maintain the Turkish independence."

.   .   .   .

Mr. D. URQUHART said . . . that the facts which had come before the public satisfied the meeting that the men who had advised Her Majesty were not competent to deal with the emergency (cheers); . . . . This was not a question between Russia and Turkey, but between Russia and England. (Cheers.) . . .

. . . the resolution was carried.

Captain MAYNE REID moved;—

"That not only does the interest, but the duty and honour of England, call upon our Government to discard all secret and dynastic diplomacy, and render, unconditionally, to Turkey prompt, decisive, and effective aid."

He expressed his objections to secret diplomacy. There was not a phrase more repugnant to the hearts of Englishmen. There was dishonesty in the sound. There was positive and palpable meanness in the thought. And what had this secret diplomacy done for England? The tricksters of foreign countries had out-tricked our diplomacy. How England should call to its aid those juggling tricks he could not understand. It was the duty of the country to demand what was right. There was a rumour abroad that a high personage in this realm[5] had been meddling with the diplomacy of this country. For the sake of the character that individual held, for the character of a gentleman, he trusted that the report was not true. He would not say, "For God's sake don't nail the man's ears to the pump"; but he would first denounce that individual as the meanest citizen in our country. . . .

.   .   .   .

The resolution was then agreed to.

Mr. PROUT moved—

"That this meeting is of opinion that Austria, by reason of her previous course of policy, and of her recent perfidious behaviour towards Turkey, ought to be regarded by us as an enemy, and not cherished as an ally."

Mr. NICHOLLS seconded the resolution, which, after a few words from Mr. TRELAWNY, was unanimously adopted.

Mr. ELT moved—

"That an address, embodying the foregoing resolutions, be intrusted to a deputation to be presented to Her Majesty."

Mr. MOORE seconded the resolution, which was agreed to.

Mr. HODGES moved, "That a copy of the foregoing resolutions be transmitted to the Turkish Ambassador," which motion having been seconded, was also carried unanimously.

The proceedings then terminated.

No. 30　　News of the Battle of Sinope Reaches London———
　　　　　12 December 1853[1]

LATEST INTELLIGENCE.

RUSSIA AND TURKEY.

A RUSSIAN VICTORY.

We have received the following telegraphic despatch from our correspondent at Vienna, and have no doubt that it was there considered authentic.

Until it is confirmed, however, we are not inclined to place implicit reliance upon it.

The latest intelligence from Constantinople, *via* Marseilles, is to the 26th ult., and at that date the Turkish squadron, which had entered the Black Sea contrary to the advice of the British Ambassador, had returned in safety to the Bosphorus without having encountered any portion of the Russian fleet.

It is, of course, possible that it may have again put to sea, or that another squadron may be referred to; but, if an engagement of such importance had indeed taken place, and with such lamentable results, it is difficult to believe that our correspondent's

statement would not have received some confirmation from other sources:—

(BY SUBMARINE AND EUROPEAN TELEGRAPH.)

VIENNA, Saturday Evening, 6 o'clock.

"On the 30th of November six Russian ships of the line, under Admiral Machinoff, attacked a Turkish squadron at Sinope, and, notwithstanding the violent fire of the land batteries in the roads, in an hour and a-half completely destroyed seven Turkish frigates, one steam-frigate, two schooners, and three transport ships.

"An attempt was made to take the Turkish flagship, with Osman Pasha on board, to Sebastopol, but as she began to sink while at sea Osman Pasha and the crew were taken on board the Russian ships.

"The Russian flagship had suffered so much that it could hardly reach Sebastopol.

A despatch from Odessa of the 5th inst., which reached Paris by way of Vienna, confirms the above intelligence, without giving further details. The number of Turkish vessels captured or sunk is quoted at 12.

"Prince Menschikoff immediately left Odessa for St. Petersburg, to communicate the news of the victory to the Emperor."

No. 31   An Attack on Prince Albert[1]

The Turkish war both near and far,
  Has played the very deuce then,
And Little AL, the royal pal,
  They say has turned a Russian;
Old Aberdeen, as may be seen
  Looks woeful pale and yellow,
And Old John Bull had his belly full,
  Of dirty Russian tallow.

CHORUS

We'll send him home & make him groan
  Oh, AL you've played the deuce then,
The German lad has acted sad,
  And turned tail with the Russians.

When AL came home you're all aware,
  He brought with him no riches,
He had scarce a rag upon his back,
  And great holes in his breeches;
Oh, England on him pity took,
  And changed his sad condition,
And soon he planned, you understand,
  The National Exhibition.

The Coburgs came from far and near,
  With their Dispatch's, all dirt,
A begging for the Russian Bear,
  To blooming lovely Albert;
To keep old nick, the devil's limb,
  and on to Turkey lead him,
To massacre the innocent Turks,
  And rob them of their freedom.

Last Monday night, all in a fright,
  AL out of bed did tumble,
The German lad was raving mad.
  HOW he did groan and grumble;
He cried to Vic, I've cut my stick,
  To St. Petersburg go right slap,

When Vic, tis said, jumped out of bed,
  And wopp'd him with her night-cap.

There with the bolster round the room
  Vic gave him dreadful lashes,
She scratched his face & broke his nose,
  And pull'd out his moustachous;
You German dog, you shall be flogged,
  She hallo'd like a Prussian,
How could you dare to interfere.
  And turn a cursed Russian?

Bad luck they say both night and day,
  To the Cobugs and the humbugs,
The witermbugs, the Scarembugs,
  And all the German horse-rugs;
And the old bug of Aberdeen,
  The Peterbugs and Prussians,
May Providence protect the Turks,
  And massacre the Russians.

You jolly Turks now go to work,
  And show the Bear your power.
It is rumoured over Briton's isle,
  That A—is in the Tower;
The Postmen some suspicion had,
  And opened the two letters,
'Twas a pity sad the German lad,
  Should not have known much better.

Well now my friends to make an end,
  From tyrants guard our own coast,
I'll tell you what between you and I,
  The Tower ditch and the gate-post;
I think that AL has been used well,
  Since first he came to England
And had no cause to obstruct the laws,
  Or in politics be mingling.

Let France and England go to work,
  Shun Austrians and Prussians,

Assist the poor and injured Turks,
  And smother all the Russians;
Chain up the bear and make him stare,
  And so keep my Davy,
We'll sing Old England three times three
  The Army and the Navy.

CHORUS

I will tell thee AL, we never shall,
  Although you played the deuce then,
Allow the Turks to be run down
  By the dirty, greasey Russians.

No. 32 Message on a State of War between France, Great Britain, and Russia——27 March 1854[1]

THE Government of the Emperor and that of Her Britannic Majesty, had declared to the Cabinet of St. Petersburgh that, should the Differences with the Sublime Porte not be restricted within purely Diplomatic Limits, and that, should the Evacuation of the Principalities of Moldavia and Wallachia not be immediately commenced and completed by a fixed date, they would be compelled to consider an answer in the negative or silence as a Declaration of War.

The Cabinet of St. Petersburgh having decided not to answer the above communication, the Emperor desires to inform you of that resolution, which constitutes Russia in a state of War with us, the responsibility of which rests entirely on that Power.

By order of the Emperor,
ACHILLE FOULD,
The Minister of State.

No. 33 The Poet Laureate Welcomes the War[1]

I

My life has crept so long on a broken wing
Thro' cells of madness, haunts of horror and fear,
That I come to be grateful at last for a little thing.
My mood is changed, for it fell at a time of year
When the face of night is fair on the dewy downs,
And the shining daffodil dies, and the Charioteer
And starry Gemini hang like glorious crowns
Over Orion's grave low down in the west,
That like a silent lightning under the stars
She seem'd to divide in a dream from a band of the blest,
And spoke of a hope for the world in the coming wars—
'And in that hope, dear soul, let trouble have rest,
Knowing I tarry for thee,' and pointed to Mars
As he glow'd like a ruddy shield on the Lion's breast.

II

And it was but a dream, yet it yielded a dear delight
To have look'd, tho' but in a dream, upon eyes so fair,

That had been in a weary world my one
thing bright;

And it was but a dream, yet it lighten'd
my despair

When I thought that a war would arise
in defence of the right,

That an iron tyranny now should bend or
cease,

The glory of manhood stand on his ancient
height,

Nor Britain's one sole God be the million-
aire.

No more shall commerce be all in all, and
Peace

Pipe on her pastoral hillock a languid note,

And watch her harvest ripen, her herd increase,

Nor the cannon-bullet rust on a slothful
shore,

And the cobweb woven across the cannon's
throat

Shall shake its threaded tears in the wind
no more.

III

And as months ran on and rumor of battle
grew,

'It is time, it is time, O passionate heart,'
said I,—

For I cleaved to a cause that I felt to be
pure and true,—

'It is time, O passionate heart and morbid
eye,

That old hysterical mock-disease should
die.'

And I stood on a giant deck and mixt my
breath

With a loyal people shouting a battle-cry,

Till I saw the dreary phantom arise and fly

Far into the North, and battle, and seas
of death.

IV

Let it go or stay, so I wake to the higher
aims

Of a land that has lost for a little her lust
of gold,

And love of a peace that was full of wrongs
and shames,

Horrible, hateful, monstrous, not to be told;

And hail once more to the banner of battle
unroll'd!

Tho' many a light shall darken, and many
shall weep

For those that are crush'd in the clash of
jarring claims,

Yet God's just wrath shall be wreak'd on
a giant liar,

And many a darkness into the light shall
leap,

And shine in the sudden making of splendid
names,

And noble thought be freer under the sun,

And the heart of a people beat with one
desire;

For the peace, that I deem'd no peace, is
over and done,

And now by the side of the Black and the
Baltic deep,

And deathful-grinning mouths of the
fortress, flames

The blood-red blossom of war with a heart
of fire.

V

Let it flame or fade, and the war roll down
like a wind,

We have proved we have hearts in a cause,
we are noble still,

And myself have awaked, as it seems, to
the better mind.

It is better to fight for the good than to rail
at the ill;

I have felt with my native land, I am one
with my kind,

I embrace the purpose of God, and the
doom assign'd.

No. 34   John Bright: A Lonely, but Eloquent, Protest Against the War——29 October 1854[1]

Rhyl, North Wales, Oct. 29.

My dear Sir,—

. . . .

I have said nothing here of the fact that all these troubles have sprung out of demands made by France upon the Turkish Government,[2] and urged in language more insulting than any which has been shown to have been used by Prince Menschikoff. I have said nothing of the diplomatic war which has been raging for many years past in Constantinople, and in which England has been behind no other Power in attempting to subject the Porte to foreign influences. I have said nothing of the abundant evidence there is that we are not only at war with Russia, but with all the Christian population of the Turkish empire, and that we are building up our Eastern policy on a false foundation—namely, on the perpetual maintenance of the most immoral and filthy of all despotisms over one of the fairest portions of the earth which it has desolated, and over a population it has degraded but has not been able to destroy. I have said nothing of the wretched delusion that we are fighting for civilization in supporting the Turk against the Russian and against the subject Christian population of Turkey. I have said nothing about our pretended sacrifices for freedom in this war, in which one great and now dominant ally is a monarch who, last in Europe, struck down a free constitution, and dispersed by military violence a national Representative Assembly.[3]

My doctrine would have been non-intervention in this case. The danger of the Russian power was a phantom; the necessity of permanently upholding the Mahometan rule in Europe is an absurdity. Our love for civilization, when we subject the Greeks and Christians to the Turks, is a sham; and our sacrifices for freedom, when working out the behests of the Emperor of the French and coaxing Austria to help us, is a pitiful imposture. The evils of non-intervention were remote and vague, and could neither be weighed nor described in any accurate terms. The good we can judge something of already, by estimating the cost of a contrary policy. And what is that cost? War in the north and south of Europe, threatening to involve every country of Europe. Many, perhaps fifty millions sterling, in the course of expenditure by this country alone, to be raised from the taxes of a people whose extrication from ignorance and poverty can only be hoped for from the continuance of peace. The disturbance of trade throughout the world, the derangement of monetary affairs, and difficulties and ruin to thousands of families. Another year of high prices of food, notwithstanding a full harvest in England, chiefly because war interferes with imports, and we have declared our principal foreign food-growers to be our enemies. The loss of human life to an enormous extent.[4] Many thousands of our own countrymen have already perished of pestilence and in the field; and hundreds, perhaps thousands, of English families will be plunged into sorrow, as a part of the penalty to be paid for the folly of the nation and its rulers.

When the time comes for the 'inquisition for blood,' who shall answer for these things? You have read the tidings from the Crimea; you have perhaps shuddered at the slaughter; you remember the terrific picture,—I speak not of the battle, and the charge, and the tumultuous excitement of the conflict, but of the field after the battle, —Russians in their frenzy, or their terror, shooting Englishmen who would have offered them water to quench their agony of thirst; Englishmen, in crowds, rifling the pockets of the men they had slain or wounded, taking their few shillings or roubles, and discovering among the plunder of the stiffening corpses images of the "Virgin and the Child." You have read this, and your imagination has followed the fearful details. This is war,—every crime which human nature can commit or imagine, every horror it can perpetrate or suffer; and this it is which our Christian Government recklessly plunges into, and which so many of our countryment at this moment think it patriotic to applaud! You must excuse me if I cannot go with you. I will have no part in this terrible crime. My

hands shall be unstained with the blood which is being shed. The necessity of maintaining themselves in office may influence an Administration; delusions may mislead a people; *Vatel* may afford you a law and a defence;[5] but no respect for men who form a Government, no regard I have for 'going with the stream,' and no fear of being deemed wanting in patriotism, shall influence me in favour of a policy which, in my conscience, I believe to be as criminal before God as it is destructive of the true interest of my country.

I have only to ask you to forgive me for writing so long a letter. You have forced it from me, and I would not have written it did I not so much appreciate your sincerity and your good intentions towards me.

Believe me to be, very sincerely yours,

JOHN BRIGHT.

Absalom Watkin, Esq., Manchester.

No. 35   Heinrich Friedjung: The Crimean War and Austrian Policy[1]

. . . It was on this occasion[2] that Emperor Nicholas wanted to sound out Metternich as to whether Austria was willing to join him in advancing against the Turks. "Prince Metternich," he remarked to him across the dinner table, "what is your opinion of the Turk? He is a sick man, isn't he?" The Chancellor, using the fact that he was hard-of-hearing as a convenient diplomatic device, acted as if he had not heard, even when the remark was repeated. When the Tsar addressed the question to him for the third time, Metternich brought the conversation to an end with the elegant reply: "Does Your Majesty make this inquiry of the physician or of the heir?"

.   .   .   .

The Tsar wanted to bring all these misunderstandings with Austria to an end by

sending his confidant, Count Orlow, to Vienna;[3] thus he wanted to assure himself of Austria's neutrality before his army crossed the Danube. . . . This time he demanded the assurance of unconditional neutrality on the part of Austria, meaning that he would be free to extend his dominion over the Balkan peninsula; in return, he would guarantee to the Emperor of Austria all his lands, and would also persuade the German Confederation and Prussia to give the same guarantee. What would happen after the war with the European parts of Turkey?

This time the Russian Court expressed itself more clearly than it had before, did not say anything of the maintenance of the Ottoman Empire, but proposed the founding of quasi-sovereign states; in order to win over Austria, the protectorate over them was to be exercised jointly by the two imperial Powers. Thus this suggestion presupposed the support by Austria of the insurrections in the peninsula. In Vienna, however, the joint exercise of a protectorate was not considered worth much, and Emperor Francis Joseph replied to Count Orlow very correctly that such an arrangement would practically give complete sovereignty to the Russian Court because of its ethnic and religious ties with the Southslavs. Orlow, himself, was aware how insufficient the offer was, and he openly admitted it to Hübner[4] at the time of the Congress of Paris. Therefore, he went one step further and promised in the name of his monarch that the latter would not determine anything at the conclusion of peace without having received the aproval of the Emperor of Austria. That, too, was found to be insufficient, apparently because it did not seem wise to calmly wait until the Russians were at the gates of Constantinople. Emperor Francis Joseph replied with a counter-proposal, which adverted to the previous assurances of the Tsar. The Russians were not to cross the Danube, but instead were to conduct the war exclusively in Asia; at the conclusion of peace, the territorial limits of Turkey were not to be touched. If the Tsar rejected these conditions, then Austria retained its freedom of action. But these were, from the Russian viewpoint, harsh demands, and to have met them would have been equivalent to abandoning designs to which they had by now become closely attached. Orlow could not make such a promise, and therefore had to consider his mission as having failed. Buol[5] had told him even more emphatically than the monarch that Austria could not tolerate the expansion of Russian power over the Balkan peninsula. . . .

.   .   .   .

. . . a thorough investigation shows that the Austrian policy of 1853 did not fail through deceit but through weakness, that

one did not want to deceive the Tsar but feared his wrath and did not point out to him with manly candour the necessary consequences of his actions. Count Buol, in 1854, when he saw how obstinately the Tsar pursued the struggle against the western Powers, went to the other extreme, that is, he spoke rudely to Russia and treated it roughly. A statesman often feels it necessary to be inconsistent; but it is a bad mistake to have obviously earned such a reproach, a greater mistake in any case than even calculated and well-prepared faithlessness.

.   .   .   .

It is worth the effort to take a closer look at the man who, as Austrian minister, threw Prussia's friendship to the winds and transformed Russia from a proven ally into a bitter opponent.

It would be questionable if one were to believe the description of Count Buol-Schauenstein given by the two Russian ambassadors at Vienna, Meyendorf and Gortschakow. According to them, he was a man without honor and faith, and the real reason why he turned away from Russia and toward the West was his naked fear of the threats of France and England. His brother-in-law, Meyendorf, who bitterly complained about him,[6] had no grounds for claiming that he was deceived by him, for Buol had frightened him from February 1854 on by the vehemence of his language; but he had not wanted to believe that the Emperor could be influenced by his minister to take hostile measures. "Buol's fear of France" also plays a conspicuously large rôle in the book[7] about the Crimean War which Gortschakow commissioned. The hostile characterization of Buol, with which we are here confronted, represents revenge for all the disappointments and hostilities which the Russian statesman had to suffer in Vienna.

In contrast to this, the Prussian ambassadors at Vienna, who did not like Buol

either, did not judge his character unfavorably. Arnim defended him against the exaggerated suspicion of him which prevailed in Berlin; Alvensleben, who had been sent to Vienna to watch over Arnim, declared that Buol, though not skillful, was relatively truthful; and Edwin v. Manteuffel, the cousin of the Minister, reports with satisfaction from one of his missions to Vienna the open and candid language of Buol.[8] It is obvious that the French and English were well satisfied with the minister, and the Duke of Coburg, the partisan of English policy, even calls him "a steadfast, reliable man with very conservative, reasonable views." The truth of the matter is that, as far as honor and faith in diplomacy is concerned, the ministers of those days, such as Manteuffel, Palmerston, and Cavour, were not exactly models of virtue either, and that Buol possessed the average honesty of the political men of his time, although admittedly not more. He regrettably lacked the reliability in negotiations and the conclusion of treaties through which Metternich or Bismarck distinguished themselves.
. . . He was haughty and ill-tempered, in moments of rage capable of controlling himself only with great difficulty; he did not hesitate to make sarcastic and bitter judgments, all attributes which do not fit in with the description of him given by the Russians.[9] But he lacked persistence, so that Beust, following up a remark made by Metternich, compared him to a knife without a cutting edge. . . .

. . . .

The objective which Vienna sought to reach was enticing enough: Russia was to be forced to accept the Four Points,[10] and at the conclusion of peace, Austria was to obtain sovereignty over the whole lower Danube to the Black Sea. The intention was not to incorporate the Danubian Principalities, but to obtain from Europe a protectorate with full occupation rights; . . .

. . . .

. . . [But Buol] was fully aware that such grand designs could only be achieved with considerable effort and with the help of the western Powers. Since Russia had to pass through the contested areas to reach Constantinople, the Tsar would never have ceded them voluntarily to Austria. On the other hand, it was known in Vienna that Napoleon III entertained the notion of convincing the Vienna Cabinet to surrender Lombardy in exchange for Moldavia and Wallachia. Thus Buol was in complete agreement with the naval Powers, just as he was generally of the opinion that no alliance would be as advantageous to Austria as one with France.[11]

. . . .

There is an obvious miscalculation in the plans of the men who wanted to plunge Austria into the struggle with Russia and designate it as the heir of the latter in the Balkan peninsula. All of them, Buol and Bach,[12] Hübner and Prokesch,[13] expected something incredible from their country: they not only wanted it to maintain its rule in Italy, not only to remain dominant in Germany while continuing to humiliate Prussia, but on top of that to make great conquests in the Balkan peninsula, first in Wallachia and Moldavia, and then, as Hübner's diaries prove, in Bosnia and Serbia, and thus subjugate everything up to the Balkans. This was supposed to be accomplished in opposition to Russia, if necessary after a war with this Power. Since Hungary also had to be kept under control, the objective was chosen with almost fantastic audacity. For the supporters of such a policy had to remember that one day all the neighbors of the Habsburg monarchy, Russians and Prussians, Italians and Southslavs, would join together to rid themselves of their rule. But then Austria, in all probability, had to collapse, militarily and economically. Even now the finances were completely inadequate. In order to mobilize against Russia, not only did a forced loan from the citizens of the state have to be proclaimed, but, since the money did not come in fast enough, the state railways had to be squandered at a low price to a French company. The overestimation of Austria's strength was also the major cause of the defeats and losses which occurred in 1859 and 1866.

. . . .

. . . Palmerston arrived in Paris at this time, and complained about Austria's unreliability.[14] When Hübner, at their first encounter, asked him: "It is said, my lord, that you do not love us," he dryly told him: "It's Austria's policy which I don't love," . . . It was probably due to Palmerston's influence that, on 23 November, Napoleon answered Emperor Francis Joseph's letter in a sharp tone,[15] and gave him the choice of either signing the treaty of alliance or of breaking completely with the western Powers. Both Paris and London wondered whether Austria, which twice now had initiated negotiations for a triple alliance, intended to make fun of France and England. The excuses of Buol and Hübner were in vain—the Vienna Cabinet was held by the two Powers in an iron grip. Finally, they presented a formal ultimatum which would have sealed Austria's isolation: the ambassadors of France and England, Baron Bourqueney and Lord Westmoreland, threatened to demand their passports and to depart if the treaty were not at last signed.[16]

. . . .

Days of terrible pressure upon the Vienna Cabinet followed the ultimatum of the western Powers. Count Buol was entangled in his own promises, and if the Emperor refused to sign the treaty, he saw only one escape: his resignation. The best service he could have rendered to his monarch would have been to have left the government immediately and without any subterfuges, instead of forcing the latter to make such a decision. In that way, the western

Powers would have been given a certain satisfaction, and his successor would have had greater freedom of action. It was senseless to promise armed support against Russia, even only under certain conditions, when the Emperor could never be persuaded to send his troops into battle. Buol should have sensed this at last, and made way for someone who would have tried to reach a compromise with Russia.

If a similar situation had occurred in a country with a parliamentary form of government, Buol would have been forced to leave the Cabinet. It has often been maintained that such states could not conduct their foreign policy with as much unity and determination as could absolute empires, even though the examples of England and the United States of America prove the contrary. What is certain, however, is that a minister who pursued policies which were as contradictory as those of Count Buol-Schauenstein could not have maintained himself before a parliament.

Emperor Francis Joseph yielded, even though reluctantly, to the condition made by Buol under which he would remain, and the treaty was signed on 2 December. Apparently the minister allayed the Emperor's misgivings by pointing out that, considering the flexible ifs and buts of the draft, he was still free to opt for war or for peace. What probably decided the matter was the thought that, after having alienated Russia, it would be serious, indeed, if now a break with the western Powers should also occur.

Emperor Napoleon had been awaiting the results of the negotiations with great anxiety; . . . . As Hübner reports, on 3 December, when it appeared that the matter had not yet been decided, he was thoughtful and sullen at the dinner-table; but when, upon leaving the table, the impatiently awaited despatch arrived, he lost his composure completely, ran over to the Empress, hugged her and pressed her to his breast. The reaction of the English Cabinet, and particularly of Palmerston, was rather different. At this time he stood on the sideline, and was not Foreign Secretary but Home Secretary; but he was fully informed on the affair, and, with his usual perspicacity, saw through the disagreeable proceedings at the Vienna Court. On 27 November, he said to Hübner: "We will now sign a treaty of alliance. It will be a stillborn infant. If we do so, it is against our will, and we are only giving in to the urging of the Emperor Napoleon. Under an alliance I understand your participation in the war. But you will never go to war against Russia, and the sole result of this treaty will be tension between Austria and the western Powers." This prediction of the politically shrewd Englishman was to be fulfilled word for word.

Meanwhile, the impression that the treaty made in Europe was profound and lasting. . . . it was, indeed, a turning-point in the diplomatic history of Europe when Austria concluded an offensive and defensive alliance with the Tsar's opponents, even though it was only a conditional one; as a matter of fact, the treaty of 2 December 1854, although it was not carried out, represented the death-knell of the Holy Alliance system founded by Metternich.

The event was so interpreted in Berlin and in Petersburg. In both places the treaty was felt to be a slap in the face, and the accusation was made that one had been rudely deceived by Austria. . . . The King [of Prussia] . . . , in his first bitter anger, wanted to mobilize a few divisions against Austria. . . . A short time later, on 27 January 1855, the King wrote to the Duke of Coburg the bitter words: "After the shameless deceit by Austria (28 November and 2 December) I refuse to negotiate with *that* Power *any more,* the lesson was too *strong.*" The indignation at the other German Courts was just as great. . . .

More profound and longer-lasting was the indignation of Russia. The Tsar expressed his bitter anger by ordering that the statue and portrait of the Emperor Francis Joseph be removed from his study; according to the story which his nephew, the Grand-Duke of Saxony-Weimar, later often repeated to his intimate circle, he gave away the former to his valet. It is well known that at this time the Tsar told the Austrian ambassador that he and Sobieski had been the most stupid kings of Poland because they had saved Austria. Gortschakow was thunderstruck when Buol personally told him that the treaty had been concluded. According to the report which the Austrian minister made of this interview, he passionately cried out:[17] "I'm finished, my role is at an end; I can't do anything else but resign. . . . Just yesterday I sent a courier to Petersburg with a despatch which reported an entirely different situation. You are inflicting a mortal wound upon my Cabinet, I must ask for my passports." Gortschakow, for his part, also saw to it that the emotional conversation was described.[18] According to his version, Buol was greatly embarrassed and tried excuses; he was led to make the serious admission that he could not act otherwise because he had been confronted with the choice between an immediate break with the western Powers and the treaty of alliance. He thereupon had to hear the sharp retort of the Russian ambassador: he could not follow a train of thought by the Vienna cabinet which took as its point of departure the feeling of fear. The deportment of Count Buol was pitiable, maintains the hardly impartial report about these events which he later caused to be published.

Gortschakow never forgot the bitterness of these hours, and he enjoyed his revenge in full measure when, in 1859 and 1866, he abandoned Austria to its fate. In the winter of 1854/1855, he was so dominated by his violent rage against Austria that he failed to see that the vacillation of the Vienna Cabinet was the result of weakness and indecision. . . .

.   .   .   .

From this point on,[19] the Austrian government insisted that it had done everything which the treaty of 2 December had obligated it to do. It was therein specified that the three allied Powers would agree on the conditions of peace, and would then, if necessary, force Russia to accept them. Well then—the agreement had taken place between Buol, Drouyn de l'Huys,[20] and Russell,[21] and Russia was willing to accept it; it was not the fault of the Vienna Cabinet that the governments at London and Paris rejected the work of their negotiators. Emperor Francis Joseph, in particular, thought that he had kept his promise; he was not obligated to draw his sword for exaggerated demands made by the western Powers. . . .

Formally, no objections can be made against this interpretation of the December treaty, particularly if one considers the well-known circumstances under which it had come about. Nevertheless, minute gradations of the law and of treaty obligations are not very important in determining international relations. The western Powers maintained that the concluded offensive and defensive alliance had a deeper meaning, and was intended to remain in force until the war had been brought to an end. They declared themselves deceived, and accused the Vienna Cabinet of withdrawing only because it wished to share in the spoils of Russia's defeats without having seriously committed its own forces. Thus the result was that, while Austria had quarrelled with Russia to the point of irreconcilability, its relations with France and England became more reserved, at times even hostile. . . .

. . . .

The appearance of a friendly alliance, which Austria tried to preserve, gave Palmerston the opportunity for sarcastic comments. In a speech in Parliament, he once said, almost innocently: "Austria marches with us up to a certain point,"—then, after a pause: "it marches with us—but only morally," whereupon his audience broke out in loud laughter. . . .

. . . .

For Napoleon III wished to bring the war to an end, and he resisted England's pressure for a new campaign which was to have completely crushed Russia's forces; London recommended the landing of an army corps in the Caucasus in order to induce the only recently subjugated inhabitants of the mountains to revolt, next, a vigorous attack in the Baltic, and, finally, the total conquest of the Crimea, where the Russian army, owing to the stubbornness of its commander, Prince Gortschakow,[22] still retained a good position.

The French Emperor was right in thinking that this would take him farther and farther away from French interest; furthermore, it was unwise to jeopardize his hard-won military laurels. Therefore, he dropped hints, which he made sure became known in Petersburg, to the effect that he would be a magnanimous victor and that he was ready for a reconciliation with the Russians; they only had to agree to a peace which would be in accordance with the wishes of Europe and the expectations of his people.

Thus, while his prestige became ever greater with friend and foe, his enmity was dangerous for Austria, and particularly then when he by-passed Vienna and approached Russia directly. Then the Habsburg monarchy would come under fire from two sides, and would have to look to its own defenses against the national forces in Germany, Italy, and Hungary. It had achieved the singular accomplishment of standing all alone in Europe. But that danger was apparent because the Vienna Cabinet received information about a web of secret negotiations whose threads stretched from Petersburg to Paris. . . .

. . . Buol parried the blow, . . . The Austrian minister reached an understanding with the French ambassador in Vienna and they agreed on the conditions of a future peace; but this time, Vienna was really serious, and not only Buol, but Emperor Francis Joseph, too, pledged his word that Austria would then send an ultimatum to Petersburg, and, if this were rejected by Russia, it would break off diplomatic relations with that Power.

The Emperor of Austria remained consistent in declaring even now that he would go no farther, and that his participation in the war was out of the question. But the step which he intended to take already forced the Tsar to again move a number of troops to the western border, and so fortune continued to favor the new enterprises of the allies, who, at this time, also concluded an alliance with Sweden. . . .

. . . .

The struggle in the Black Sea was the last war fought for the European balance of power; the prize of victory was not an immediate advantage, but the prevention of Russian hegemony. This purpose was achieved, and the prophesy of the first Napoleon: in fifty years, Europe will be either republican or Cossack, remained unfulfilled. Once again English policy succeeded in gaining a large state on the Continent for a war which brought the latter little advantage, but which strengthened Albion's naval supremacy. In this respect, Austria ceded its place to France, and its profit would have been obvious if it had not plunged into unnecessary expenses and received a setback in the Danubian principalities.

Nowadays, one is inclined to underestimate the result of the Crimean War because Russia, since 1870, has again taken military possession of the Black Sea, and, after the victorious war of 1878, has reached the Danube border once more. But as a matter-of-fact the war prevented the Tsar from acquiring sovereignty over Turkey, and, since then, Russia has not again

openly dared to lay claim to Constantinople. In 1877, it took up arms in order to achieve the freedom of the Slavs in the Balkans, and Europe took the Tsar-Liberator at his word so that his troops had to evacuate the peninsula completely by 1880. . . .

It was Austria which benefitted the most from all of this. The Crimean War humbled the too powerful neighbor, and freed Austria from the tutelage to which it had been subjected since the Russians marched into Hungary in 1849. But even if this were disregarded, then the liberation of the lower Danube itself was a fortunate circumstance; this, according to Hübner's expression, was the trophy which the Austrian plenipotentiaries brought home from the Congress of Paris.

But the debit side of the ledger was bad enough. Fortune had smiled upon Austria, yet its statesmen had poured out her gifts unwisely. After the war, the Habsburg monarchy stood all alone in Europe, and in the East as well as in the West, in the North as well as in the South, rose bitter enemies or rivals ready to pounce. The old alliances had been torn apart, even the rudiments of new ones did not exist.

This was a far greater disadvantage than the failure of the Austrian designs on Moldavia and Wallachia. For these countries could hardly have been retained during the crises of the next decade, their possession would rather have accelerated the catastrophes of the Empire. Austria had a surfeit of dissatisfied nationalities, an addition would not have improved its health.

In this lay the mistake of the policy which urged an alliance with France in order to wrest control of the lower Danube from Russia. The moment the Russian army had been withdrawn from Moldavia and Wallachia, one had to think of a compromise with the northern Empire; to have neglected to do so and to have prevented it was the fault of Count Buol. His method led inevitably, whether he was fully aware of it or not, to a war with Russia—to a dangerous, useless clash, and one which would have created new complications even if its outcome had been fortunate.

In this respect, Emperor Francis Joseph

possessed the correct instinct, and although it is difficult to understand why, nevertheless, he gave Count Buol a free hand for so long, it remains to his credit to have spared his Empire from such a fateful clash of arms.

.   .   .   .

No. 36   The Peace of Paris——30 March 1856[1, 2]

Integrity and Independence of Ottoman Empire.

In the Name of Almighty God.

THEIR Majesties the Queen of the United Kingdom of Great Britain and Ireland, the Emperor of the French, the Emperor of All the Russias, the King of Sardinia, and the Emperor of the Ottomans, animated by the desire of putting an end to the calamities of War, and wishing to prevent the return of the complications which occasioned it, resolved to come to an understanding with His Majesty the Emperor of Austria as to the bases on which Peace might be re-established and consolidated, by securing, through effectual and reciprocal guarantees, the Independence and Integrity of the Ottoman Empire.

.   .   .   .

Restoration of Sebastopol, Balaklava, Kamiesch, Eupatoria, Kertch, Jenikale, Kinburn, etc., to Russia.

ART. IV. Their Majesties the Queen of the United Kingdom of Great Britain and Ireland, the Emperor of the French, the King of Sardinia, and the Sultan, engage to restore to His Majesty the Emperor of All the Russias, the Towns and Ports of Sebastopol, Balaklava, Kamiesch, Eupatoria, Kertch, Jenikale, Kinburn, as well

as all other Territories occupied by the Allied Troops.

Admission of the Sublime Porte into the European System. Guarantee of Independence of Ottoman Empire.

ART. VII. Her Majesty the Queen of the United Kingdom of Great Britain and Ireland, His Majesty the Emperor of Austria, His Majesty the Emperor of the French, His Majesty the King of Prussia, His Majesty the Emperor of All the Russias, and His Majesty the King of Sardinia, declare the Sublime Porte admitted to participate in the advantages of the Public Law and System (*Concert*) of Europe. Their Majesties engage, each on his part, to respect the Independence and the Territorial Integrity of the Ottoman Empire; Guarantee in common the strict observance of that engagement; and will, in consequence, consider any act tending to its violation as a question of general interest.

Meditation in event of Misunderstanding between the Sublime Porte and one or more of the Contracting Powers.

ART. VIII. If there should arise between the Sublime Porte and one or more of the other Signing Powers, any misunderstanding which might endanger the maintenance of their relations, the Sublime Porte, and each of such Powers, before having recourse to the use of force, shall afford the other Contracting Parties the opportunity of preventing such an extremity by means of their Mediation.

Neutralisation of the Black Sea.[3]

ART. XI. The Black Sea is Neutralised; its Waters and its Ports, thrown open to the Mercantile Marine of every Nation, are formally and in perpetuity interdicted to the Flag of War, either of the Powers possessing its Coasts, or of any other Power, with the exceptions mentioned in Articles XIV and XIX of the present Treaty.[4]

Military-Maritime Arsenals not to be Established or Maintained on Coasts of Black Sea.[5]

ART. XIII. The Black Sea being Neutralised according to the terms of Article XI, the maintenance or establishment upon its Coast of Military-Maritime Arsenals becomes alike unnecessary and purposeless; in consequence, His Majesty the Emperor of All the Russias, and His Imperial Majesty the Sultan, engage not to establish or to maintain upon that Coast any Military-Maritime Arsenals.

Free Navigation of the Danube.

ART. XV. The Act of the Congress of Vienna, having established the principles intended to regulate the Navigation of Rivers which separate or traverse different States, the Contracting Powers stipulate among themselves that those principles shall in future be equally applied to the Danube and its Mouths. They declare that its arrangement henceforth forms a part of the Public Law of Europe, and take it under their Guarantee.

Duties and Regulations of Police and Quarantine in the Danube.

The Navigation of the Danube cannot be subjected to any impediment or charge not expressly provided for by the Stipulations contained in the following Articles: in consequence, there shall not be levied any Toll founded solely upon the fact of the Navigation of the River, nor any Duty upon the Goods which may be on board of Vessels. The Regulations of Police and of Quarantine to be established for the safety of the States separated or traversed by that River, shall be so framed as to facilitate, as much as possible, the passage of Vessels. With the exception of such Regulations, no obstacle whatever shall be opposed to Free Navigation.

Rectification of Frontier of Bessarabia.

ART. XX. In exchange for the Towns, Ports, and Territories enumerated in Article IV of the present Treaty, and in order more fully to secure the Freedom of the Navigation of the Danube, His Majesty the Emperor of All the Russias consents to the rectification of his Frontier in Bessarabia.

The new Frontier shall begin from the Black Sea, one kilometre to the east of the Lake Bourna Sola, shall run perpendicularly to the Akerman Road, shall follow that road to the Val de Trajan, pass to the south of Bolgrad, ascend the course of the River Yalpuck to the Height of Saratsika, and terminate at Katamori on the Pruth. Above that point the old Frontier between the Two Empires shall not undergo any modification.

Delegates to trace New Frontier.

Delegates of the Contracting Powers shall fix, in its details, the Line of the new Frontier.

.   .   .   .

Notes

No. 11, pp. 48-49

[1] Great Britain, Parliament. House of Commons. Session of 1854. *Parliamentary Papers,* Vol. 71: *Eastern Papers,* Pt. I, p. 59, and Pt. V, p. 16. Hereafter cited as *Brit. Parliam. Papers* (1854).

[2] Russian Ambassador at London.—HNW.

[3] This Memorandum was enclosed with a dispatch sent by Seymour to Clarendon on 9 March 1853.—HNW.

No. 12, pp. 49-50

[1] *Brit. Parliam. Papers* (1854), Vol. 71, Pt. I, pp. 56, 57.

[2] British Ambassador at Paris.—HNW.

[3] French Foreign Minister.—HNW.

No. 13, pp. 50-51

[1] *Brit. Parliam. Papers* (1854), Vol. 71, Pt. I, pp. 86-87.

[2] British *chargé d'affaires* at Constantinople. —HNW.

No. 14, p. 51

[1] *Brit. Parliam. Papers* (1854), Vol. 71, Pt. I, p. 202.

[2] Nesselrode had admitted to Seymour, "That as regards the holy places, an arrangement had been made [with Turkey] which was satisfactory both to Prince Menchikoff and to M. de la Cour; . . . ." Seymour to Clarendon, May 14, 1853, *ibid.,* pp. 201-202.—HNW.

[3] Turkish Foreign Minister.—HNW.

No. 15, pp. 51-52

[1] A.[ndrei] M. Zaionchkovskii (ed.), *Vostochnaia Voina, 1853-1856,* 2 vols. in 5 (St. Petersburg, 1908-1913), Vol. 1-2, pp. 428-429. Hereafter cited as Zaionchkovskii (ed.), *Vostochnaia Voina.* Translated by Herman N. Weill.

No. 16, pp. 52-53

[1] Zaionchkovskii (ed.), *Vostochnaia Voina,* Vol. 1-2, pp. 441-442. Translated by Herman N. Weill.

No. 17, pp. 53-54

[1] M.[odest] I. Bogdanovich, *Vostochnaia Voina, 1853-1856,* 4 vols. (2nd. rev. ed., St. Peters-

burg, 1877), I, 88-90. Translated by Mrs. Gilbert Arons and Herman N. Weill.

No. 18, pp. 54-56

[1] *Brit. Parliam. Papers* (1854), Vol. 71, Pt. VI, pp. 2-4.

No. 19, pp. 56-63

[1] *Brit. Parliam. Papers* (1854), Vol. 71, Pt. V, pp. 1-17, 19-20, 22-24.

No. 20, pp. 63-64

[1] Zaionchkovskii (ed.), *Vostochnaia Voina,* Vol. II-1, pp. 22-23. Translated by Herman N. Weill.

[2] A prominent politician, Lord Landsdowne had refused the Queen's invitation to form a government in 1852, and served, instead, as a minister without portfolio under Aberdeen.— HNW.

[3] Aberdeen headed a coalition ministry of Whigs and Peelites. Disraeli was the most prominent member of the Opposition.—HNW.

No. 21, pp. 64-65

[1] *Brit. Parliam. Papers* (1854), Vol. 71, Pt. I, pp. 80-82.

No. 22, p. 65

[1] *Brit. Parliam. Papers* (1854), Vol. 71, Pt. I, p. 98.

[2] French Ambassador at London.—HNW.

No. 23, pp. 65-66

[1] *Brit. Parliam. Papers* (1854), Vol. 71, Pt. I, pp. 199, 210.

No. 24, pp. 66-67

[1] *Brit. Parliam. Papers* (1854), Vol. 71, Pt. I, pp. 225-226.

[2] French Ambassador at Constantinople.— HNW.

[3] Just off the Dardanelles.—HNW.

No. 25, pp. 67-69

[1] Zaionchkovskii (ed.), *Vostochnaia Voina,* Vol. I-2, pp. 443-444. Translated by Herman N. Weill.

[2] See *No. 16,* above—HNW.

No. 26, pp. 69-72

[1] Hertslet (ed.), *Map of Europe*, II, 1171-1176.

[2] The Vienna Note of 28 July 1853.—HNW.

[3] The first published despatch respecting the question of the Holy Places at Jerusalem, or the Rights and Privileges of the Latin and Greek Churches in Turkey, was dated 20th May, 1850. See Papers laid before Parliament in 1854, Part I.—Ed.

[4] The Russian demands were, in part, justified by this treaty, concluded on 21 July 1774.—HNW.

[5] The Russians crossed the Pruth at Souleni on the 3rd July, 1853.—Ed.

[6] On the 14th July, 1853, the Porte protested against the occupation of the Principalities by Russia.—Ed.

No. 27, pp. 72-73

[1] Hertslet (ed.), *Map of Europe*, II, 1177-1178.

[2] See *No. 26*, above.—HNW.

[3] The Turkish army crossed the Danube at Widdin, and occupied Kalafat on the 3rd November, 1853.—Ed.

No. 28, pp. 73-76

[1] French Foreign Minister.—HNW.

[2] The Vienna Note of July 28, 1853.—HNW.

[3] *Ibid.*, p. 9; this dispatch, dated September 7, 1853, had found its way into the German press, and was published by the *Zeit* in Berlin on September 18, 1853,—HNW.

[4] Russian Ambassador at Vienna.—HNW.

[5] The gist of the despatch was that since Russia had accepted the Vienna Note without any alterations, Turkey must do the same.—HNW.

[6] This refers to the Russo-Turkish War, not to the Crimean War.—HNW.

[7] See *No. 30*, below.—HNW.

No. 29, pp. 76-81

[1] *The* [London] *Times*, October 8, 1853, p. 5.

[2] British Ambassador at Vienna.—HNW.

[3] Lord John Russell, who had been Foreign Secretary from December, 1852, to February, 1853 but was then Lord President of the Council.—HNW.

[4] Longtime Foreign Secretary, but then Home Secretary.—HNW.

[5] The speaker refers to Prince Albert.—HNW.

No. 30, pp. 81-82

[1] *The* [London] *Times*, Monday, December 12, 1853, p. 6.

No. 31, pp. 82-83

[1] From *Lovely Albert!*, a broadside preserved in the British Museum; by courtesy of the British Museum.

No. 32, p. 83

[1] Hertslet (ed.), *Map of Europe*, II, 1186.

No. 33, pp. 83-85

[1] Alfred Lord Tennyson, *Maud*, Part Three. (1854).

No. 34, pp. 85-86

[1] "Mr. Bright Upon the War," *The* [London] *Times*, November 4, 1854, p. 10.

[2] France had successfully interceded with the Sultan in behalf of the "Latin" Christians in 1851-1852.—HNW.

[3] Napoleon III's *coup d'état* in 1851.—HNW.

[4] It is estimated that over 500,000 men lost their lives in the Crimean War.—HNW.

[5] Bright's letter had been written in reply to one from Mr. Watkin, in which the latter had maintained that one could not object to the Crimean War on legal grounds since it came within Vatel's definition of international law. Vatel (more commonly spelled Vattel) was a Swiss jurist who had published a lengthy treatise on international law—*Le Droit des Gens* (1759)—which, in its turn, was based on Christian Wolff's famous *Jus Gentium* (1749). —HNW.

No. 35, pp. 86-93

[1] *Der Krimkrieg und die österreichische Politik* (Stuttgart and Berlin, 1907), pp. 5, 17-18, 46, 101-109, 122-128, 160-162, 173-174, 187-189. Translated by Herman N. Weill.

[2] The meeting at Münchengrätz in 1833.—HNW.

[3] Orlow was in Vienna from January 29 to February 8, 1854.—HNW.

[4] Austrian Ambassador at Paris.—HNW.

[5] Austrian Chancellor and Foreign Minister.—HNW.

[6] Gerlach reports that Meyendorf is to have said: "My brother-in-law Buol is the biggest political son-of-a-bitch that I have ever en-

countered and that it is at all possible to be; he admits his fear of France, if he has to go to war he prefers to fight against Russia rather than against France." (Letters between Bismarck and Gerlach, 17 October and 15 November 1854.) Why an Austrian minister, who prefers an alliance with France rather than with Russia, should be a son-of-a-bitch cannot be understood from any other than a Russian viewpoint.

7 Baron Jomini's *Étude diplomatique sur la guerre de la Crimée* (2 vols., St. Petersburg, 1878), which Friedjung had mentioned earlier. —HNW.

8 Arnim to Manteuffel, 24 December 1853.— Manteuffel to Bismarck, 2 April 1855.—Gerlach: *Denkwürdigkeiten*, II, p. 249.—Edwin v. Manteuffel to the Minister Manteuffel, October 1854.

9 For this reason Hübner complains (19 December 1856) at the time of a clash with France: "Count Coudenhoven brings me despatches from Vienna which don't make any sense at all. The useless fits of anger, this exaggerated suspicion, only serve to arouse angry feelings. 'Clever, but neither broad nor deep,' as Prince Metternich very accurately said of Buol."

10 These were peace conditions drawn up by Austria and agreed to by England and France at Vienna in August 1854. They were rejected by Russia, although they subsequently became the basis for the Peace of Paris.—HNW.

11 Bismarck wrote on 13 October to Berlin: "To steal a few stinking Wallachians they have no compunction (in Vienna) to risk all the hard-won confidence in Germany and to threaten the German allies with French bayonets."

12 Austrian Minister of the Interior.—HNW.

13 Austrian general and diplomat (Ambassador at Frankfurt, 1853-1855).—HNW.

14 In the following passages, Friedjung discusses the Triple Alliance between Austria, France, and England, which was signed in Vienna on 2 December 1854.—HNW.

15 The Russians had been making strenuous efforts to ensure Austria's continued neutrality. They seemed to have succeeded, for in the letter here referred to, Francis Joseph had made several objections to the alliance and given the impression that Austria was about to back out.—HNW.

16 What actually transpired, which had only been generally known before (e.g., Bismarck to Manteuffel, 5 December 1854), has now been revealed by Hübner, and also by the reports of Arnim and Gortschakow in H. v. Lucius, *Rôle politique de la Prusse pendant la guerre de Crimée*, p. 61.

17 Harcourt: *Les quatres ministères de M. Drouyn de l'Huys*, Paris 1882.

18 *Étude diplomatique*, II, p. 191.

19 After signing the Triple Alliance, Austria, as Palmerston had predicted, did not declare war against Russia but, instead, convened another peace conference (March-May, 1855). This time, the conditions were accepted by Russia, but rejected by the French and English governments.—HNW.

20 Foreign Minister and French plenipotentiary at the conference.—HNW.

21 Lord John Russell, British plenipotentiary at the conference, and at this time Colonial Secretary.—HNW.

22 Prince Michael Gortschakow, a first cousin of the diplomat, Prince Alexander Gortschakow, mentioned above.—HNW.

No. 36, pp. 93-94

1 Hertslet (ed.), *Map of Europe*, II, 1251, 1254-1257, 1259.

2 An Armistice was concluded between the Belligerent Powers on the 14th March, 1856. —Ed.

3 Abrogated by the General Treaty of 13th March, 1871.—Ed.

4 The exceptions were small coastal service ships.—HNW.

5 Same as n. 3.

The Unification of Italy

3

INTRODUCTION

AMONG THE many crucial international repercussions of the Crimean War, the one which was to have the most important bearing upon central Europe was the serious weakening of the Austrian position. Russia, which had rushed to Austria's assistance to crush the Revolutions of 1848 and to re-establish her influence in Germany at Olmütz, had now become decidedly hostile. France and England were still smarting over her refusal to enter the war on their side. The war had also revealed Austria's internal division, her economic weakness, and the mediocrity of her political leaders.

This radical change in Austria's position did not escape the attention of Cavour, Sardinia's brilliant statesman. He knew from the bitter experiences of 1848 that no political changes would occur in Italy until Austria had been forced to withdraw from the peninsula. Yet 1848 had also shown that the Italians could not accomplish Austria's withdrawal by themselves. France and England were the two countries most likely to furnish the needed assistance, and Cavour set out to obtain it. Sardinia entered the Crimean War on the side of the Allies. In return, Napoleon III allowed Cavour to use the Congress of Paris as a rostrum from which to denounce the Austrian presence in Italy (*No. 37*).

After this auspicious beginning, Cavour set to work in earnest to win Napoleon over. His arguments fell upon receptive ears, for not only had Napoleon been a Carbonari himself in his youth, but, as the essays written long before he came to power show (*No. 38*), he was keenly aware that the drive by nationalities for autonomy was one of the most powerful political forces of his time. Furthermore, intent as he was to annul the treaties of 1815, he knew that he could not do so until he had defeated Austria, their most ardent champion. Yet there were other factors which had to be weighed carefully. Would French public opinion support a war in Italy? What were the ramifications of a threat to, or the eventual loss of, the Pope's territorial possessions in Italy? Should France receive compensation for her support, and, if so, in what form? What would be the likely reaction of the other Powers?

To Cavour's increasing exasperation, Napoleon pondered the complex problem for almost two years. He was finally jolted into action by an attempt against his life by Orsini, an Italian patriot (*No. 39*). Orsini's defense at his trial, and his moving letter appealing to the Emperor to free Italy, gave Napoleon the opportunity to arouse French public opinion against Austria. He ordered that the details of the trial and the contents of the letter be published.

Then, at the famous meeting with Cavour at Plombières (*No. 40*), the two men plotted a war against Austria. Having reached agreement (*No. 41*), a Franco-Sardinian Alliance was signed (*No. 42*), and Cavour began to prepare for the war (*No. 43*).

These preparations were to remain strictly secret, but such secrecy could not be maintained. Before long, the other Powers, including Austria, had a rather accurate notion of what was afoot. To avoid a war, England offered her mediation, and Russia suggested that a European Congress be convened to discuss the Italian problem. Austria rejected England's offer, and dragged her feet on Russia's suggestion so that the proposed Congress never met. Instead, although fully aware that a challenge to Sardinia was very likely to be a challenge to France as well, she threw down the gauntlet to Sardinia. The rationale behind this fateful decision has continued to puzzle historians. The minutes of the conferences of the Austrian Council of Ministers (*No. 44*), while they do not provide a definitive answer, at least throw considerable light upon the state of mind of Emperor Francis Joseph and of his chief advisers. When the Austrian ultimatum (*No. 45*) received a noncommittal Sardinian reply (*No. 46*), Austria declared war (*No. 47*), which was followed by the Sardinian and French proclamations of war (*Nos. 48 and 49*). England opted for neutrality (*No. 50*), although it soon became clear, especially after Palmerston became Prime Minister, that its sympathies were on the side of the Italians.

The War of 1859 lasted less than three months. Shortly after the Battle of Solferino, Napoleon suddenly decided to sign a preliminary peace with Austria at Villafranca (*No. 51*). Cavour, outraged at this violation of the Franco-Sardinian Alliance, resigned in protest. It was at this point that events took a turn which neither Cavour nor Napoleon had foreseen, for what they had essentially planned as a territorial rearrangement of northern Italy now quickly developed into a movement for the unification of all of Italy. The ground had been well prepared by the numerous patriotic societies, and particularly by Mazzini's lifelong efforts for a free and independent Italy. In central Italy, the outbreak of the war was interpreted as the starting signal for such a general unification. Revolutions deposed the local rulers. Plebiscites were then held, which resulted in overwhelming majorities in favor of annexation to Sardinia. This presented Cavour, who had returned to power in January, 1860, with a problem, for the agreements reached at Plombières had not provided for such an eventuality. Napoleon finally agreed to the annexations (*No. 52*) in return for cession of Savoy and Nice (*No. 53*).

But the wave of national sentiment had now reached floodtide proportions, and could not be stopped there. Garibaldi and his Redshirts, in an amazing *tour de force,* liberated the Kingdom of Naples (*No. 54*). He was determined to complete his self-appointed task by freeing Rome and Venetia, but with French troops protecting the Pope and Austria still in possession of Venetia, such a move was bound to result in foreign intervention. Cavour solved the problem by persuading the King of Sardinia to lead his troops through the Papal States to Naples. Here, in a magnificent gesture of patriotism and self-denial, Garibaldi turned over his command to the King and retired to his island home of Caprera. In the plebiscites held in these regions, the vast majority voted to unite with the new Italy (*No. 55*), and, on 17 March 1861, Victor Emmanuel was proclaimed King of Italy (*No. 56*).

No. 37   The Italian Problem at the Congress of Paris——
8 April 1856[1]

Protocol No. 22.—Sitting of April 8, 1856.

Present:

The Plenipotentiaries of Austria,
      "   France,
      "   Great Britain,
      "   Prussia,
      "   Russia,
      "   Sardinia,
      "   Turkey.

THE Protocol of the preceding sitting is read and approved.

. . . .

Count Walewski [France] says that it is desirable that the Plenipotentiaries, before they separate, should interchange their ideas on different subjects which require to be settled, and which it might be advantageous to take up in order to prevent fresh complications. Although specially assembled for settling the Eastern question, the Congress, according to the first Plenipotentiary of France, might reproach itself for not having taken advantage of the circumstance which brings together the Representatives of the principal Powers of Europe, to clear up certain questions, to lay down certain principles, to express intentions, in fine to make certain declarations, always and solely with the view of ensuring the future tranquillity of the world, by dispelling the clouds which are still seen looming on the political horizon before they become menacing.

. . . .

The first Plenipotentiary of France then observes[2] that the Pontifical States are equally in an abnormal state; that the necessity for not leaving the country to anarchy had decided France as well as Austria to comply with the demand of the Holy See by causing Rome to be occupied by her troops, while the Austrian troops occupied the Legations.

He states that France had a twofold motive for complying without hesitation with the demand of the Holy See, as a Catholic Power and as an European Power. The title of eldest son of the church which is the boast of the Sovereign of France makes it a duty for the Emperor to afford aid and support to the Sovereign Pontiff; the tranquillity of the Roman States and that of the whole of Italy affects too closely the maintenance of social order in Europe for France not to have an overbearing interest in securing it by all the means in her power. But, on the other hand, it is impossible to overlook the abnormal condition of a Power which, in order to maintain itself, requires to be supported by foreign troops.

Count Walewski does not hesitate to declare, and he trusts that Count Buol [Austria] will join in the declaration, that not only is France ready to withdraw her troops, but that she earnestly desires to recall them so soon as that can be done without inconvenience as regards the internal tranquility of the country and the authority of the Pontifical Government, in the prosperity of which the Emperor, his august Sovereign, takes the most lively interest.

The first Plenipotentiary of France represents how desirable it is for the balance of power in Europe that the Roman Government should be consolidated in sufficient strength for the French and Austrian troops to be able, without inconvenience, to evacuate the Pontifical States, and he considers that a wish expressed in this sense might not be without advantage. In any case he does not doubt that the assurances which might be given by France and Austria as to their real intentions in this respect would have a salutary influence.

Following up the same order of ideas, Count Walewski asks himself if it is not to be desired that certain Governments of the Italian Peninsula, by well-devised acts of clemency, and by rallying to themselves minds gone astray and not perverted, should put an end to a system which is directly opposed to its object, and which instead of reaching the enemies of public order, has the effect of weakening the Governments, and of furnishing partisans to popular faction. In his opinion it would render a signal service to the Government of the Two Sicilies, as well as to the cause of order in the Italian Peninsula, to enlighten that Government as to the false course in which it is engaged. He is of opinion that warnings conceived in this sense, and proceeding from the Powers represented in the Congress, would be the better received by the Neapolitan Government, as that Government could not doubt the motives which dictated them.

.   .   .   .

The Earl of Clarendon [Great Britain] sharing the opinions expressed by Count Walewski, declares that, like France, England proposes to recall the troops which she was obliged to send to Greece so soon as she shall be able to do so without inconvenience to the public tranquillity; . . .

The first Plenipotentiary of Great Britain remarks that the Treaty of March 30 opens a new era; that as the Emperor had said to the Congress on receiving it after the signature of the Treaty, this era is that of peace; but in order to be consistent nothing should be omitted to render that peace solid and lasting; that, representing the principal Powers of Europe, the Congress would fail

in its duty if, on separating, it sanctioned by its silence a state of things which is injurious to the political equilibrium, and which is far from securing peace from all danger in one of the most interesting countries of Europe.

We have just provided, continues the Earl of Clarendon, for the evacuation of the different territories occupied by foreign armies during the war; we have just taken the solemn engagement to effect the evacuation within the shortest period; how would it be possible for us not seriously to advert to occupations which took place before the war, and to abstain from devising means for putting an end to them?

The first Plenipotentiary of Great Britain does not consider it of any use to inquire as to the causes which have brought in foreign armies upon various points of Italy, but he considers that even admitting that those causes were legitimate, it is not the less true, he says, that the result is an abnormal and irregular state of things, which can be justified only by extreme necessity, and which should come to an end as soon as that necessity is no longer imperiously felt; that nevertheless, if endeavours are not made to put an end to that necessity, it will continue to exist; that if we are content to depend upon the armed force instead of seeking to apply a remedy to the just causes of discontent, it is certain that a system little honourable for the Governments, and lamentable for the people, will be perpetuated. He conceives that the administration of the Roman States presents inconveniences from whence dangers may arise which the Congress has the right to attempt to avert; that to neglect them would be to run the risk of labouring for the benefit of the revolution which all the Governments condemn and wish to prevent. The problem which it is a matter of urgency to solve, consists, he conceives, in combining the retreat of the foreign troops with the maintenance of tranquillity, and the solution depends on the organisation of an administration which by reviving confidence would render the Government independent of foreign support; that support never succeeding in maintaining a Government to which the public sentiment is hostile, and there would result from it, in his opinion, a part which France and Austria would not wish their armies to perform. For the well-being of the Pontifical States, as also for the interest of the sovereign authority of the Pope, it would therefore, in his opinion, be advantageous to recommend the secularisation of the Government, and the organisation of an administrative system in harmony with the spirit of the age, and having for its object the happiness of the people. He admits that this reform might perhaps offer in Rome itself, at the present moment, certain difficulties; but he thinks that it might easily be accomplished in the Legations.

The first plenipotentiary of Great Britain observes that for the last eight years Bologna has been in a state of siege, and that the rural districts are harassed by brigands: it may be hoped, he thinks, that by establishing in this part of the Roman States an administrative and judicial system, at once secular and distinct, and that by organizing there a national armed force, security and confidence would rapidly be restored, and the Austrian troops might shortly withdraw without having to apprehend the return of fresh troubles; it is at least an experiment which, in his opinion, ought to be attempted, and this remedy proposed for indisputable evils ought to be submitted by the Congress to the serious consideration of the Pope.

As regards the Neapolitan Government, the first Plenipotentiary of Great Britain is desirous of imitating the example given him by Count Walewski by passing over in silence acts which have obtained such grievous notoriety. He is of opinion that it must doubtless be admitted in principle that no Government has the right to interfere in the internal affairs of other States, but he considers there are cases in which the exception to this rule becomes equally a right and a duty. The Neapolitan Government seems to him to have conferred this right, and to have imposed this duty upon Europe; and as the Governments represented in the Congress are all equally desirous to support the monarchical principle and to repel revolution, it is a duty to lift up the voice against a system which keeps up revolutionary ferment among the masses instead of seeking to moderate it. "We do not wish," he says, "that peace should be disturbed, and there is no peace without justice; we ought then to make known to the King of Naples the wish of the Congress for the amelioration of his system of Government—a wish which cannot remain without effect—and require of him an amnesty in favour of the persons who have been condemned or who are imprisoned without trial for political offences."

.   .   .   .

Count Orloff [Russia] observes that the powers with which he is furnished having for their sole object the restoration of peace, he does not consider himself authorized to take part in a discussion which his instructions had not provided for.

Count Buol [Austria] congratulates himself on seeing the Governments of France and England disposed to put an end, as speedily as possible, to the occupation of Greece. Austria, he gives the assurance, wishes most sincerely for the prosperity of that kingdom, and is equally desirous with France that all the States of Europe should enjoy, under the protection of public law, their political independence and complete prosperity. . . .

.   .   .   .

. . . It would be impossible for him, indeed, to discuss the internal situation of independent States, which are not represented at the Congress. The Plenipotentiaries have received no other commission than to apply themselves to the affairs of the Levant, and they have not been convened for the purpose of making known to independent Sovereigns wishes in regard to the internal organization of their States; the full powers deposited among the acts of the Congress prove this. The instructions of the Austrian Plenipotentiaries, at all events, having defined the object of the mission which has been intrusted to them, they would not be at liberty to take part in a discussion which those instructions have not anticipated.

For the same reasons, Count Buol conceives that he must abstain from entering into the order of ideas adverted to by the first Plenipotentiary of Great Britain, and from giving explanations upon the duration of the occupation of the Roman States by the Austrian troops, although adhering entirely and completely to the words uttered by the first Plenipotentiary of France on this subject.

Count Walewski [France] observes that there is no question either of adopting definitive resolutions or of entering into engagements, still less of interfering directly with the internal affairs of Governments represented or not represented at the Congress, but merely of consolidating, of completing the work of peace, by taking into serious consideration beforehand the fresh complications which might arise, either from the indefinite and unjustifiable prolongation of certain foreign occupations, or from an unseasonable[3] and impolitic system of severity, or from a turbulent licentiousness at variance with international duties.

Baron Hübner [Austria] replies that the Plenipotentiaries of Austria are not authorized either to give an assurance or to express wishes: the reduction of the Austrian army in the Legations sufficiently shows, in his opinion, that the Imperial Cabinet intends to withdraw its troops as soon as such a measure shall be considered opportune.

Baron Manteuffel [Prussia] declares that he knows enough of the intentions of the King, his august Master, not to hesitate to express his opinion on the question on which the Congress is engaged, although he has no instructions on the subject.

.   .   .   .

As for the steps which it might be considered advantageous to take, in what relates to the state of affairs in the Kingdom of the Two Sicilies, Baron Manteuffel observes that such steps might present various inconveniences. He says that it might be well to ask one's self whether admonitions such as those which have been proposed, would not excite in the country a spirit of opposition and revolutionary movements, instead of answering to the ideas which it had been contemplated to carry out, certainly with a benevolent intention. He does not deem it proper to enter upon an examination of the actual situation of the Pontifical States. He confines himself to expressing the desire that it may be possible to place the Government in a condition which would henceforth render superfluous the occupation of foreign troops. . . .

Count Cavour [Sardinia] does not mean to question the right of each Plenipotentiary not to take part in the discussion of a question which is not contemplated by his instructions; it is nevertheless, he thinks, of the utmost importance that the opinion manifested by certain Powers, in regard to the occupation of the Roman States, should be recorded in the Protocol.

The first Plenipotentiary of Sardinia states that the occupation of the Roman States by the Austrian troops assumes every day more of a permanent character; that it has lasted seven years, and that, nevertheless, no indication appears which would lead to the supposition that it will cease at a more or less early period; that the causes which gave rise to it are still in existence; that the state of the country which they occupy is, assuredly, not improved, and that in order to be satisfied of this, it is enough to remark that Austria considers herself obliged to maintain, in its utmost severity, the state of siege at Bologna, although it dates from the occupation itself. He observes that the presence of the Austrian troops in the Legations and in the Duchy of Parma, destroys the balance of power in Italy, and constitutes a real danger for Sardinia. The Plenipotentiaries of Sardinia, he says, deem it, therefore, a duty to point out to the attention of Europe a state of things so abnormal as that which results from the indefinite occupation of a great part of Italy by Austrian troops.

As regards the question of Naples, Count Cavour shares entirely the opinions expressed by Count Walewski [France] and the Earl of Clarendon [Great Britain] and he conceives that it is in the highest degree important to suggest modifications which, by appeasing passions, would render less difficult the regular progress of affairs in the other States of the Peninsula.

Baron Hübner [Austria] on his part, says that the first Plenipotentiary of Sardinia has spoken only of the Austrian occupation, and kept silence in regard to that of France; that nevertheless the two occupations took place at the same time and with the same object; that it was impossible to admit the argument drawn by Count Cavour, from the permanency of the state of siege at Bologna; that if an exceptional state of things is still necessary in that city while it has long since ceased at Rome and Ancona, this appears at the utmost to prove that the dispositions of the people of Rome and of Ancona are more satisfactory than those of the city of Bologna. He remarks that in Italy it is not only the Roman States which are occupied by foreign troops; that the Communes of Menton and of Roquebrune, forming part of the Principality of

Monaco, have been for the last eight years occupied by Sardinia, and that the only difference which exists between the two occupations is, that the Austrians and the French were invited by the Sovereign of the country, while the Sardinian troops entered the territory of the Prince of Monaco contrary to his wishes, and maintain themselves therein, notwithstanding the remonstrances of the Sovereign of the country.

In reply to Baron Hübner, Count Cavour [Sardinia] says that he is desirous that the French occupation should cease as well as the Austrian, but that he cannot help considering the one as being far more dangerous than the other for the independent States of Italy. He adds that a small corps d'armée, at a great distance from France, is menacing for no one; whereas it is very alarming to see Austria resting on Ferrara and on Placentia, the fortifications of which she is enlarging, contrary to the spirit if not to the letter of the Treaties of Vienna, and extending herself along the Adriatic as far as Ancona.

As for Monaco, Count Cavour declares that Sardinia is ready to withdraw the fifty men who occupy Menton, if the Prince is in a condition to return to the country without exposing himself to the most serious dangers. Besides, he does not consider that Sardinia can be accused of having contributed to the overthrow of the ancient Government, in order to occupy those States, since the Prince has not been able to maintain his authority in the single town of Monaco, which Sardinia occupied in 1848, in virtue of the Treaties.

. . . .

Count Walewski [France] congratulates himself on having induced the Plenipotentiaries to interchange their ideas on the questions which have been discussed. He had supposed that it might have been possible, perhaps with advantage, to express themselves in a more complete manner on some of the subjects which have fixed the attention of the Congress. "But such as it is," he says, "the interchange of ideas which has taken place, is not without advantage."

The first Plenipotentiary of France states that the result of it is, in effect:—

1. That no one has contested the necessity of seriously deliberating as to the means for improving the situation of Greece, and that the three protecting Courts have recognised the importance of coming to an understanding among themselves in this respect.

2. That the Plenipotentiaries of Austria have acceded to the wish expressed by the Plenipotentiaries of France for the evacuation of the Pontifical States by the French and Austrian troops, as soon as it can be effected without prejudice to the tranquillity of the country and to the consolidation of the authority of the Holy See.

3. That the greater part of the Plenipotentiaries have not questioned the good effect which would result from measures of clemency, opportunely adopted by the Governments of the Italian Peninsula, and especially by that of the Two Sicilies.

.   .   .   .

(The signatures follow.)[4]

No. 38   The Ideas of Napoleon III: Essays——1832 to 1844[1]

.   .   .   .

What a country needs above all is independence, liberty, stability, the supremacy of merit, and a broadly-based economic well-being. The best government shall be the one where any abuse of power can always be corrected, where, without a social upheaval, without an effusion of blood, both the laws and the head of state can be changed, for one generation can not compel future generations to obey its laws.

In order that *independence* be assured, the government must be strong, and for it to be strong, it must enjoy the confidence of the people so that it can have a large and well-disciplined army without being accused of tyranny, so that it could arm the whole nation without being afraid of seeing itself overthrown.

In order to be *free*, which is only one consequence of independence, everyone, without distinction, must be allowed to participate in the election of national representatives; the masses, who can never be corrupted and who neither flatter nor dissimulate, must be the constant spring from which all power flows.

.   .   .   .

One speaks of eternal battles, of interminable struggles, and yet it would be easy for rulers to consolidate peace forever: let them observe the relations and customs of the diverse nations among themselves, let them grant them their nationality and the institutions which they demand, and they shall have found the true political balance. Then all men shall be brothers, and they shall embrace each other, rejoicing over tyranny dethroned, over the earth consoled, and over humanity gratified.[2]

When the fate of arms had made Napoleon [I] master of the greater part of the Continent, he wanted to use his conquests for the establishment of a European confederation.

Prompt in recognizing the trend of civilization, the Emperor accelerated its development by executing at once what was only concealed in the distant decrees of Providence. His genius made him foresee that the rivalry which divides the different nations of Europe would disappear in the face of a well-understood general interest.

The more perfect the world becomes, the higher the barriers which divide mankind, the larger the number of countries which the same interests tend to reunite.

.   .   .   .

"Whenever battles take place in Europe," Napoleon has said, "they are civil wars."

"The Holy Alliance is an idea which has been stolen from me," that is to say, the Holy Alliance of peoples through their kings, and not that of the kings against the peoples: this is the immense difference between his idea and the manner in which it has been realized. Napoleon had displaced the rulers in the momentary interest of the peoples; in 1815, the peoples were displaced in the particular interest of the rulers. The statesmen of this era, consulting only rancor or passions, based an European equilibrium upon the rivalries of the Great Powers, instead of founding it upon general interests; therefore, their system collapsed everywhere.

The policy of the Emperor, on the contrary, consisted in founding a solid European association by making his system rest upon complete nationalities and upon satisfied general interests. If fortune had not forsaken him, he would have had all of the means in his hands to constitute Europe; he had kept in reserve entire countries which he could have used to attain his goal. Dutchmen, Romans, Piedmontese, inhabitants of Bremen and of Hamburg, all of you who were so astonished to find yourselves French, you returned to the atmosphere of nationality which becomes your antecedents and your position; and France, in ceding the rights which victory had given her over you, also acted in her own interest; for her interest can not be separated from that of civilized peoples. To cement

the European association, the Emperor, according to his own words, would have had an European code of laws adopted, an European Superior Court of Appeals, redressing errors for everyone just as the Superior Court of Appeals in France redresses the errors of the lower tribunals. He would have founded an European Institute to animate, direct, and coordinate all of the learned societies in Europe. The uniformity of legislation would have been obtained through his powerful intervention.

The last great transformation would thus have been accomplished for our Continent. And just as, in principle, communal interests were placed above individual interests; then, the interests of the city above the interests of the countryside, the interests of the province above the interests of the city; finally, the interests of the nation above the interests of the province; so, in the same way, European interests would have dominated national interests; and humanity would have been gratified; for Providence can not have intended that a nation could only be happy at the expense of the others, and that there should exist in Europe only victors and vanquished and not reconciled members of the same and great family.

.   .   .   .

It is with the feeling left by a delightful dream that one contemplates the scene of happiness and of stability that Europe would have presented if the vast projects of the Emperor had been accomplished. Each country, circumscribed by its natural borders, united with its neighbor by ties of interest and of friendship, would have enjoyed, within its area, the benefits of independence, of peace, and of liberty. The rulers, freed from fear and from suspicion, would have exerted themselves only to improve the condition of their peoples and to introduce among them all the advantages of civilization!

Instead of this, what have we now in

Europe? Everyone, in going to sleep at night, fears what the morrow will bring; for the germ of evil is everywhere, and every honest soul almost dreads the good because of the sacrifices which would be required to attain it.

Men of liberty, who have rejoiced at the downfall of Napoleon, your error has been disastrous! How many years shall yet pass, how many struggles and sacrifices, until you shall have reached the point to which Napoleon had brought you!

And you, statesmen of the Congress of Vienna, who were rulers of the world on the ruins of the Empire, your role could have been glorious, you did not understand it! You have aroused, in the name of liberty and even of license, the peoples against Napoleon; you have placed him under the ban of Europe as a despot and a tyrant; you claim to have set the nations free and to have assured their tranquillity. They believed you for a moment; but nothing solid is ever constructed upon a lie and upon an error! Napoleon had bridged the revolutionary abyss; by overthrowing him, you destroyed that bridge. Take care that you are not swallowed up by this abyss!

. . . .

The period of the Empire was a war to the death against the old European system. The old system triumphed; but, in spite of Napoleon's downfall, the Napoleonic ideas have sprung up everywhere. Even the victors appropriated the ideas of the vanquished, and the peoples strain every effort to rebuild what Napoleon had established among them.

In France, the realization of the Emperor's ideas, under different names or in different forms, is ceaselessly demanded. If a great measure or a great work is carried out, it is generally a project of Napoleon's which is being carried out or accomplished. Every act by those in power, every proposal by the Chambers, is always placed under the aegis of Napoleon in order to become popular; and an entire system is constructed upon a word which he uttered casually.

Italy, Poland, have tried to recover that national organization which Napoleon had given them.

Spain pours forth streams of its children's blood in order to re-establish the institutions which the agreement of Bayonne had guaranteed in 1808. The disorders under which it suffers are only the reaction which follows of itself against their resistance to the Emperor.

. . . .

In conclusion, let us repeat, the Napoleonic idea is not at all an idea of war, but a social, industrial, commercial, humanitarian idea. If, to some men, it always appears to be accompanied by the thunder of combat, this is because it was indeed beclouded for too long by the smoke of cannon and the dust of battle. But today the clouds have disappeared, and one can glimpse, beyond the glory of arms, a civil glory which is greater and longer-lasting.

May the spirit of the Emperor thus rest in peace! The memory of him grows larger every day. Every wave which breaks upon the rock of Saint Helena carries with it, blown by the breath of Europe, an homage to his memory, a regret to his ashes, and the echo of Longwood repeats over his tomb: "THE FREE PEOPLES ARE WORKING EVERYWHERE TO RE-CREATE YOUR WORK!"[3]

A controversy has been raging for twelve years emphasizing, by turns, the advantages of an English alliance or of a Russian alliance, as if it were absolutely necessary that France should be closely bound to one of these two Great Powers. . . . Here is what Emperor Napoleon said:

"France is, through her geographical position, the fertility of her soil, and the intelligent energy of her inhabitants, the arbiter of European society; she departs from the role which nature assigns her when she becomes a conqueror; she steps down from it when she complies with the obligations of any alliance whatsoever. She is to the nations of Europe what the lion is to the beings who surround him. She can not make a move without being either protective or destructive; she bestows the support of her power, but she never exchanges it, in her own interest, for the assistance which she may need for her defense. Her own power is always sufficient, even then when she finds herself momentarily weakened by the affliction of nations: internal divisions. For she needs only one convulsive effort to punish her enemies for having dared to challenge her to combat.

. . . .

"When one has, at one and the same time, the honor and the good fortune to be France, all of the implications of this favorable position must be understood: and, from the *sun-nation* that one is, never change into a *satellite-nation*."

. . . .

What has been happening during the last twelve years proves the truth and the profundity of Napoleon's opinion.[4]

We would say, then, that today a government must derive its moral force from a *principle* and its physical force from an *organization*. It is then that the new regime shall have as solid a base as the old, for the adoption of a principle recognized by everyone will gain public opinion for it; by establishing a vast organization, everyone will willingly work for it. Let us suppose, for example, that a government openly accepts the principle of the sovereignty of the people, that is to say, of elections, every soul shall be for it; for does an individual, a caste, a party exist which would dare to attack this right, the legal product of the will of an entire people? Let us further suppose that it organizes the nation

by giving everyone precise rights and duties, that is to say, a place in the community, a rung on the social ladder, it would have formed all of the people into solid regiments and assured that true order which has for its foundation equality before the law and for its rule a hierarchy of merit.

"Enlist a coward," said Voltaire, "in the regiment of the Grey Musketeers, and you change him instantly into a brave man." The same applies in politics. Give the most anarchistic proletarian some rights, a legal place in society, and you change him instantly into a man of order, devoted to the public cause, for you are giving him interests to defend.

"Men are what institutions make them: and, on the other hand, institutions must be in keeping with what civilization demands that men should be."[5]

. . . .

We hear it repeated endlessly that peace is a benefit and war a calamity; no one doubts this truth. But what is not said often enough is that, if war is often a necessity when one has a great cause to defend, it is, on the contrary, a crime to conduct it by caprice, without having a great result as an objective, an immense advantage as a reason.

Well then, does the government assure peace and make it profitable for the country; does it not, on the contrary, compromise it every day? This is what it is important to examine.

Those in power boast of the tranquillity which exists; but to kill a people by plunging it into a lethargic sleep, to wrap it in its past glory as in a shroud, to disorganize it by corruption, and to yet make that sleep so artificial, that disorganization so hideous, that everyone anticipates with fear, but with certainty, the moment of his awakening, this is not to institute peace but to establish momentarily in the country the tranquillity of the cemetery!

. . . .

To establish peace upon solid foundations does not mean maintaining an artificial tranquillity for a few years; it means working to make the hatreds between nations disappear by favoring the interests, the tendencies of each people; it means creating an equitable equilibrium among the Great Powers; it means, in short, following the policy of Henry IV and not the disastrous march of the Stuarts and of Louis XV.

Open the memoirs of Sully and see what great ideas the man possessed who had pacified France and founded religious liberty! To establish solidly the European equilibrium, Henry IV foresaw that all nations had to be equal in power, and that none should dominate the others by its preponderance; he foresaw that for peoples as for individuals, only equality is the source of all justice. . . .

. . . .

Let us say, then, in concluding, to those who govern us: You are not men of peace; for you are incapable of either conceiving or of executing one of those great projects which assure the tranquillity of the world. You have compromised the future of France by leaving her isolated in Europe and by exhausting the country with military works which do not even have war as their object; within the country, you have divided us; externally, you have re-united all of our enemies in the same sentiment of defiance and of hatred. You have left all of the important questions in a state of litigation, and yet, as you know, there are questions of independence and of honor which must be resolved sooner or later and which cannot be suppressed. . . .

No! you are not men of peace; and if, one day, war breaks out, it is you who shall be responsible for it; for it is you who shall have made it inevitable. The real author of a war, a celebrated writer has said, is not the one who declares it, but the one who has made it necessary by a policy without grandeur, without dignity, without good faith.[6]

No. 39   Orsini's Attempt to Assassinate Napoleon III—— January to March 1858

LATEST INTELLIGENCE.[1]

ATTEMPT

TO

ASSASSINATE

THE

EMPEROR NAPOLEON.

(BY SUBMARINE AND BRITISH TELEGRAPH.)

We have received the following telegram from our Paris correspondent dated Paris, Thursday, Jan. 14, 10[2] p.m.:—

"The Emperor was fired at this evening at half-past 9 o'clock while he was entering the Italian Opera in the Rue Lepelletier.

"Some persons in the street were wounded.

"The Emperor showed himself to the people at the doors of the opera-house.

"He was received with enthusiastic cheering.

"He remained till the end of the opera.

"On his return at midnight he was hailed by the enthusiastic cheers of an immense multitude, which was waiting for him in the streets."

THE ATTEMPTED ASSASSINATION OF THE EMPEROR NAPOLEON.[3]

(FROM OUR OWN CORRESPONDENT.)

Paris, Friday, Jan., 15, 6 P.M.

You will have received before this intelligence of the atrocious attempt made by some miscreants on the Emperor's life last night, at the door of the opera-house, in the Rue Lepelletier. . . .

It was known some days previous that His Majesty purposed visiting the Opera last night. As is customary on such occasions, the entrance of the Rue Lepelletier was illuminated with gas stands, the house of the Court tradesman that stands at the right hand as you enter from the Boulevards, and also the front of the theatre. As is usual, a crowd of people thronged the Boulevards and the street to see the *cortège*. About 9 o'clock the Imperial carriage arrived, preceded by another with the attendants, and followed by an ordinary escort of Lancers. The Emperor, Empress, and General Roguet, the Aide-de-Camp on duty, occupied the same carriage. On arriving at the theatre, near which some groups of spectators were standing, a loud explosion was heard, followed at the interval of a few seconds by another, and again a third—the last the loudest of all. A rush of the people on the Boulevards took place down the Rue Lepelletier, anxious to know what was the matter. For some minutes all was confusion, but the mounted guards on duty did their utmost to prevent the crowd from filling the streets. It was known that the Emperor had been fired at, and rumours flew about of something still more disastrous. So far as the Emperor was personally concerned, however, all apprehension was soon removed, and an immense and enthusiastic shout told those who were at a distance that His Majesty was unhurt. In order to tranquillize the people the Emperor, on quitting his carriage, presented himself at the door, and again on the balcony.

On entering his box he and the Empress were, as you may suppose, most enthusiastically cheered.

The assassins had provided themselves with hollow projectiles of the most deadly description, and contrived to fling them on the ground under the carriage, where they instantly exploded, and spread destruction among the bystanders. One of the carriage horses was killed on the spot, the other wounded; the carriage itself was broken to pieces; General Roguet, who sat in front, was wounded slightly, it is said, and the two footmen who stood behind, dangerously hurt. A bullet, or fragment of the shell, passed through the Emperor's hat but did not touch him. The Empress was also untouched. At the moment of the explosion, which was tremendous, the row of gaslights running down the front of the theatre, and those at the wings, were extinguished; for some time the place was in utter darkness, while the windows of three or four houses opposite were dashed into fragments. I need not dwell on the consternation which prevailed. As quick as lightning the news flew to every corner of the city. All Paris appeared to be in movement. The night was dark and cold, though not wet, and, thronged as the Boulevards were before, crowds now poured ceaselessly down the great thoroughfare from every street and all in the direction of the Rue Lepelletier. . . .

. . . .

. . . The number of persons taken into custody, I am told, amounted to 27 up to 2 o'clock this day, three or four of whom are believed to be the chiefs. They are most of them, if not all, Italians. One of them was a Colonel in the Roman (Republican) service. In consequence of a telegraphic despatch received yesterday from the French Minister at Brussels, one person was arrested before the Emperor went to the opera. The Roman Colonel is named Pierri, or, at least, such is the name on his passport, which was regularly oiséd by the Belgian Consul. The name of another of them is Orsini or Corsini—all probably feigned names. One of them speaks English. . . .

. . . .

THE ATTEMPT TO ASSASSINATE THE EMPEROR OF THE FRENCH.[4]

(FROM OUR OWN CORRESPONDENT.)

Paris, Thursday, Feb. 25, 6 P.M.
Although it was generally known that the Assize Court would be accessible to no one who was not provided with a ticket, or at least that the space reserved for ordinary spectators would be extremely restricted and that the chances of admission were very slight indeed, yet neither that nor the intense cold prevented crowds from moving in a continuous stream towards the Palace of Justice from the early hour of 7 this morning. . . .

. . . .

At a-quarter past 10 the burly form of Marshal Magnan was recognized among the crowd, and almost at the same moment the prisoners were introduced. Each was led by two gendarmes, and were placed in order after each other:—Orsini, Rudio, Pierri, and Gomez. Their appearance, as might be expected, drew off attention from every other object to fix it on them. Every eye-glass and opera-glass was directed to the bench of the accused, and particularly to Orsini. The prisoners were dressed in black, but this was the only resemblance between them. Of the four, Orsini is certainly the most worthy of remark. He is of middle stature, rather stout, full in face, as in body. Without being what may be called *distingué* his bearing at all events contrasts with that of his companions, and gives him the air of a man of the superior classes. He wore neither beard nor moustache, but

only whiskers. If he wore a white neckcloth instead of a black one he would be taken for an advocate or an *avoué*, or an *employé* of the upper ranks.

. . . .

The examination of the prisoners then began. . . .

. . . .

. . . Orsini was then interrogated:—
"The President.—You first made admissions, and then you retracted them. Finally, on the 9th of February you addressed a letter to the Attorney-General in which you protest your innocence."
"Orsini.—I have in fact an explanation to give. I have long endeavoured to effect the independence of my country, and this idea has occupied my mind without any feeling of hatred against France being mixed up with it. All my hatred was against the Austrians, who since 1815 have never ceased to persecute us and plunder us. I have never ceased to struggle against Austrian domination, and this is the only crime of which I have been guilty. In 1848 I hoped with all Italy that the end of Austrian domination had arrived. A Constituent Assembly having been convoked at Rome I was elected to form part of it. There, seeing a French Army landed, we thought it came as a friend, but when we saw it came as an enemy we were painfully astonished. An engagement having placed a certain number of French soldiers in our hands, we took advantage of an armistice which the French General accorded us to restore him his prisoners. This surrender took place at the advanced posts to the cry of '*Vive la France! Vive l'Italie!*' At a later period every one knows how the engagements, the promises, and the armistice were kept. But in spite of that the political men who then directed affairs at Rome did not cease to show attachment towards France, so persuaded were we all that that war was

the act of the Government and not of the nation.

"The President.—The freedom allowed to the defence ought to make us tolerate such words; but we will revert to them.

"Orsini.—Be it so; but if I be allowed to explain I shall do so with the same moderation as I have hitherto shown. To return to our sentiments towards France, I will say we consider her as so foreign to what passed at Rome, that in all the conspiracies which have taken place at Rome since the duration of the occupation measures were always taken and orders given that in case of executions or in case of success the French army should be spared. The fall of the Roman Republic becoming an accomplished fact, I have not ceased to labour for the liberation of my country. Instead of placing myself, as Mazzini, in the way of conspiracies which sent out a score or so of armed men in the street, where they are stupidly shot down, I wished at first to pursue my object by legal means. When in England I wrote and spoke to the public in favour of political intervention. I applied to the authorities, and I addressed petitions to the Queen for the same purpose. Seeing that all those steps ended in nothing, the faith I had in my cause urged me to find out the reasons of my failure. I will not now detail the reasons which convinced me that the Emperor Napoleon has an interest diametrically opposed to the independence of Italy. Once convinced that this was the great stumbling-block to our independence, I confess that I resolved to kill him. I make this avowal frankly. I should have preferred executing this design alone, but close access to the Emperor was not easy, and I was therefore obliged to seek associates. After having approved my plans and given their consent and assistance these men abandon me to-day, and it is their testimony which has led to my capture by you. I will not show reprisals. I will not recriminate on them. I pardon them, and I offer my head as a sacrifice to my country. Before my judges I will only occupy myself with one thing—my character. Let me not be judged by the declarations of these men. I do not accuse them. But fear, which is a dangerous counsellor, has forced on them a system of allegations which are not in conformity with the truth. The regard which I have for the guilty sufficiently explains what my conscience prescribes towards an innocent person. Mr. Allsop is pursued as an accomplice. Well then, I am bound to say that Mr. Allsop has never had any knowledge of this project of assassination. He assisted me in the making of the bombs, in the belief that they were to be employed in an insurrectionary attempt in Italy. As to M. Bernard, the respect I owe to truth does not permit me to affirm that I have not told him that the bombs were to be employed in France, but I cannot still assert that I told him so. I oftener conversed with him about Italy, than about France."

This exposition of his plans was made by the prisoner with the utmost calmness; there was nothing inflated in his tone, and there appeared little or no affectation in his manner. . . .

(BY SUBMARINE AND BRITISH TELEGRAPH.)

We have received the following telegram from our Paris correspondent:—

Paris, Friday, Feb. 26, 10 P.M.
"The jury has given a verdict of *Guilty* as regards the four accused.

"The Court has pronounced sentence of death on Orsini, Rudio,[5] and Pierri.

"Gomez is sentenced to penal servitude for life."

FRANCE.[6]

(FROM OUR OWN CORRESPONDENT.)

Paris, Monday, March 1, 6 P.M.
. . . The subjoined letter to the Emperor, as published in the *Moniteur* with the rest

of the proceedings, has produced an unpleasant impression on the representatives of some of the German States, and it certainly will not promote goodwill between the Court of Vienna and that of the Tuileries. It is still the topic of severe remark in diplomatic circles:—

"To NAPOLEON III., EMPEROR OF THE FRENCH.

"The depositions which I have made against myself in the course of the political proceedings which have been instituted on the occasion of the attempt of the 14th of January are sufficient to send me to the scaffold, and I shall submit to my fate without asking for pardon, both because I will not humiliate myself before him who has destroyed in the bud the liberty of my unhappy country and because, in the situation in which I am now placed, death for me will be a relief.

"Being near the close of my career, I wish, however, to make a last effort to assist Italy, whose independence has hitherto made me pass through so many perils and submit to every sacrifice. She is the constant object of all my affections, and it is that idea which I wish to set forth in the words which I address to your Majesty.

"In order to maintain the balance of power in Europe it is necessary to render Italy independent, or to tighten the chains by which Austria holds her in bondage. Shall I ask that for her deliverance the blood of Frenchmen shall be shed for the Italians? No, I do not go so far as that. Italy asks that France shall not intervene against her, and that France shall not allow Germany to support Austria in the struggles in which she may perhaps be soon engaged. This is precisely what your Majesty can do, if you are so inclined; on your will, therefore, depends the welfare or the misfortune of my country,—the life or death of a nation to which Europe is in a great measure indebted for her civilization.

"Such is the prayer which from my cell I dare to address to your Majesty, not despairing but that my feeble voice may be heard; I beseech your Majesty to restore to Italy the independence which her children lost in 1849 through the very fault of the French. Let your Majesty call to mind that the Italians, among whom was my father, joyfully shed their blood for Napoleon the Great, wherever he pleased to lead them; that they were faithful to him until his fall; and that, so long as Italy is not independent, the tranquillity of Europe and that of your Majesty will always be vain illusions.

"May your Majesty not reject the last prayer of a patriot on the steps of the scaffold! May you deliver my country, and the blessings of 25,000,000 citizens will follow you to posterity!

"FELICE ORSINI.

"Prison of Mazas, Feb. 11."

.   .   .   .

. . . The publicity which the trial, including the speech of M. Jules Favre,[7] has obtained, has been, it is but just to add, at the special desire and order of the Emperor. The Advocate-General submitted to the Minister of the Interior two sets of proof sheets containing the report of the *Gazette des Tribunaux* and the *Droit*. One set was that which was corrected for publication, and the other as it issued full and complete from the pens of the shorthand-writers. The Minister submitted them in turn to the Emperor, who gave orders that nothing should be suppressed in the reports, and that M. Jules Favre's speech, which was the most difficult to deal with, should be given in full. Perhaps one or two sentences were omitted, but otherwise it was published in the *Moniteur* nearly as he spoke it.

.   .   .   .

FRANCE.[8]

EXECUTION OF ORSINI AND PIERRI.

(FROM OUR OWN CORRESPONDENT.)

Paris, Saturday, March 13, 6 P.M.

. . . .

The prison clock struck 7 [a.m.]; before the last sound died away the door leading to the scaffold opened as of itself. The Abbé Hugon entreated Pierri to profit by the few moments still left to collect his thoughts and assume a calmer attitude. He promised to be calm, but said he should chant a patriotic hymn; and it is said that he actually began to sing the well-known "Mourir pour la Patrie."[9] Leaning on the Abbé Hugon he mounted [the] 15 steps of the scaffold, still repeating the verses of the song.

Orsini was supported by the Chaplain of the Conciergerie, and his calmness never abandoned him for a moment. When he appeared on the platform it could be seen, from the movement of his body and of his head, though covered with the veil, that he was looking out for the crowd, and probably intended addressing them. But they were too far off. The greffier then directed the usher to read the sentence of the Court condemning the prisoners to the death of parricides. The usher, who was an old man, over 60, was evidently much moved at having to perform this duty, and he trembled as much from emotion as from cold as he read the document, which no one listened to.

After this formality was terminated Orsini and Pierri embraced their spiritual attendants, and pressed their lips on the crucifix offered to them. They then gave themselves up to the headsman. Pierri was attached to the plank in an instant. He was executed first. The moment his veil was raised, and before his head was laid on the block, it is affirmed that he cried *"Vive l'Italie—Vive la République!"*

Orsini was then taken in hand. His veil was raised, and his countenance still betrayed no emotion. Before he was fastened to the plank he turned in the direction of the distant crowd, and, it is said, cried *"Vive la France!"* It was but five minutes past 7 when the second head fell into the basket. A cold shudder ran among those whose attention was fixed upon what was passing on the scaffold, and for an instant there was deep silence. It passed off, however, very soon. When all was over men went to their work, and parties who had gone together to the spot from distant quarters of the town hastened home to breakfast. The morning was becoming clearer every moment. The troops began to move as if about to leave the ground. The guillotine was lowered and taken off; the crowds gradually thinned; some few groups still lingered about the spot; but the cold was bitter, and the snow began to fall, and in a few hours the place was deserted.

The number of deaths from the attempt for which these wretched men suffered now amounts, I am assured, to 14.

. . . .

No. 40   Cavour Meets Napoleon III at Plombieres——— 20 July 1858[1]

Cavour to King Victor Emmanuel.

Baden, [Germany], 24 July 1858.

Sire,

The ciphered letter which I sent to Your Majesty from Plombiéres can have given Your Majesty only a very incomplete idea of the long conversations which I held with the Emperor. I think that, consequently, Your Majesty will be impatient to receive an exact and detailed account of them. Having just left France, this is what I hasten to do through this letter, which I will send to Your Majesty through M. Tosi, attached to the Legation in Bern.

The Emperor, as soon as I entered his study, touched upon the question which had been the reason for my journey. He began by saying that he was determined to support Sardinia with all of his forces in a war against Austria, provided that the war was undertaken in a non-revolutionary cause which could be justified in the eyes of diplomacy and, more importantly, of public opinion in France and in Europe.

Since the quest for such a cause presented the major difficulty to be resolved before we could come to an agreement, I thought I had to deal with the question before any of the others. I proposed at first to emphasize the grievances caused by the unreliable execution on Austria's part of her commercial treaty with us. To this the Emperor replied: that a commercial question of mediocre importance could not be the cause of a great war destined to change the map of Europe. I then proposed to advance once more the causes which had determined us to protest at the Congress of Paris[2] against the illegitimate extension of Austria's power in Italy; that is to say, the treaty of 47 between Austria and the Dukes of Parma and of Modena; the prolonged occupation of the Romagna and of the Legations, the new fortifications constructed around Piacenza.

The Emperor did not agree to this proposal. He remarked that, since the grievances which we had brought forward in 1856 had not been judged sufficient to bring about the intervention of France and of England in our favor, one would not understand how they could now justify an appeal to arms. "Besides," he added, "as long as my troops are in Rome, I can hardly demand that Austria withdraw hers from Ancona and from Bologna." The objection was justified. I thus had to give up my second proposal; I did so regretfully, for there was something frank and audacious about it which went perfectly with the noble and generous character of Your Majesty and of the people which you govern.

My position became embarrassing, for I had nothing else to propose that was well-defined. The Emperor came to my aid, and together we set about going over all the states of Italy in order to seek that cause of war which was so difficult to find. After having journeyed up and down the whole peninsula without success, we arrived, almost without realizing it, at Massa and Carrara, and there we discovered what we had been so intensely searching for. Having given the Emperor an exact description of this unfortunate country, of which he already possessed rather precise knowledge, we agreed that a petition by the inhabitants to Your Majesty would be provoked in order to demand your protection and to even require the annexation of these Duchies to Sardinia. Your Majesty would not accept the proposed forfeiture, but, taking the side of these oppressed people, would address a haughty and menacing Note to the Duke of Modena. The Duke, relying upon the support of Austria, would reply to it in an impertinent manner. Thereupon Your Majesty would occupy Massa and the war would begin.

Since it would be the Duke of Modena who would have caused it, the Emperor thinks that the war would be popular not only in France, but also in England and in the rest of Europe, in view of the fact that this prince is considered, rightly or wrongly, as the scapegoat of despotism. Moreover, since the Duke of Modena has not recognized any of the sovereigns who have reigned in France since 1830, the Emperor has less reason to be circumspect with him than with any other prince.

This first problem solved, the Emperor said to me: Before going any farther, we have to think about two grave difficulties which we will encounter in Italy: the Pope and the King of Naples. I have to be careful about them: the first in order not to raise the Catholics in France against me, the second in order to retain the sympathy of Russia which makes it a sort of a point of honor to protect King Ferdinand.

I replied to the Emperor that, as to the Pope, it would be easy for him to maintain the latter's tranquil possession of Rome by means of the French garrison which was already stationed there, permitting him to let the Romagnas rise in revolt; that since the Pope had not wished to follow in their regard the advice which he had given him, he could not take it amiss that these districts should profit from the first favorable opportunity to rid themselves of a detestable system of government which the Court of Rome had obstinately refused to reform; —That, as to the King of Naples, one did not have to bother about him, unless he should side with Austria: providing, however that his subjects should not be interfered with if, profitting from the moment, they should throw off his paternal domination.

This answer satisfied the Emperor, and we passed to the great question: What would be the objective of the war?

The Emperor admitted without difficulty that the Austrians had to be completely chased out of Italy, and that not a square inch of ground could be left to them on this side of the Alps and of the Isonzo. But thereafter, how was Italy to be organized? After lengthy discussions, whose details I will spare Your Majesty, we just about agreed on the following points, although recognizing that they were susceptible to modifications by the events of the war. The Valley of the Po, the Romagna, and the Legations are to constitute the Kingdom of Upper Italy, over which the House of Savoy shall rule. The Pope shall retain Rome and its surrounding territory. The rest of the Papal States, together with Tuscany, shall form the Kingdom of Central Italy. The territorial limits of the Kingdom of Naples shall not be changed. The four Italian states, following the model of the Germanic Confederation, shall form a confederation whose presidency shall be given to the Pope to console him for the loss of the largest part of the Papal States.

This arrangement appeared to me completely acceptable. For Your Majesty, in being Sovereign legally over the richest and strongest half of Italy, would be sovereign in fact over the whole peninsula.

As to the choice of sovereigns to be placed in Florence and in Naples in the very probable case that Your Majesty's uncle and his cousin should make the wise decision to retire to Austria, the question has been left unanswered; nevertheless, the Emperor did not conceal the fact that he would be pleased to see Murat reascend his father's throne [at Naples]; and I, for my part, indicated that the Duchess of Parma could occupy, at least for the time being, the Pitti Palace [at Florence]. This latter idea pleased the Emperor no end, for he seems to be particularly concerned that he should not be accused of persecuting the Duchess of Parma, who is a princess of the Bourbon family.

After having settled the future fate of Italy, the Emperor asked me what France would receive, and whether Your Majesty would cede Savoy and the County of Nice. I replied that Your Majesty, adhering to the principle of nationalities, understood that it followed that Savoy must be re-united with France; that, consequently, you were prepared to make this sacrifice even though it would cost you dearly to give up a country which contained the cradle of your family and a people which had given your ancestors so many proofs of its af-fection and of its devotion.—That, as to Nice, the question was different, for the people of Nice belonged, by their origin, their language, and their habits, more to Piedmont than to France, and that, con-sequently, their accession to the Empire would be contrary to the very principle for whose triumph we were about to resort to arms.—Thereupon the Emperor stroked his mustache several times and only added that these were for him strictly secondary questions which there would be time to deal with later on.

Passing then to an examination of the means to insure that the war should have a favorable outcome, the Emperor observed that an effort must be made to isolate Aus-tria and to face only her alone; that it was for this reason that he insisted so strongly that it be motivated by a cause which would not alarm the other Continental Powers and which would be popular in England. The Emperor seemed to be con-vinced that the one which we had adopted would fulfill this double objective. The Emperor counts positively with the neutral-ity of England; he recommended to me that we make every effort to influence pub-lic opinion in that country to force its

government, which is its slave, not to un-dertake anything in Austria's favor. He counts equally with the Prince of Prussia's antipathy against the Austrians for Prussia not to come out against us. As to Russia, he has the promise of Emperor Alexander, given formally and repeated several times, that he would not interfere with his projects in Italy. If the Emperor does not delude himself, as I am led to believe he does not from everything he has told me, the ques-tion would be reduced to a war between France and us on one side, and Austria on the other.

However, the Emperor considers that the question, even reduced to these propor-tions, is nevertheless of extreme importance and still presents immense difficulties. It cannot be gainsaid that Austria has enor-mous military resources. The wars fought by the [First] Empire were the best proof. Napoleon could well defeat her in Italy and Germany for fifteen years, he could well destroy a great number of her armies, take provinces away from her and impose crush-ing war taxes upon her; he always found her again on the field of battle, ready to recommence the struggle. And one is forced to recognize that at the end of the wars of the Empire, at the terrible battle of Leipzig, it was once more the Austrian battalions who contributed the most to the defeat of the French army. Therefore, to win two or three battles in the valleys of the Po and of the Tagliamento will not be sufficient to force Austria to give up Italy, one would, of necessity, have to penetrate into the center of the Empire, and, with the sword pointed at its heart, that is to say, at Vienna itself, force her to sign a peace under the conditions previously agreed upon.

Very considerable forces are indispens-able to attain this objective. The Emperor estimates them at a minimum of 300,000 men, and I believe he is right. 100,000 men will be needed to blockade the fortresses along the Mincio and the Adige and to guard the passes in the Tyrol; 200,000 men would march upon Vienna through Carinthia and Styria. France would furnish 200,000 men, Sardinia and the other Italian provinces the remaining 100,000. Perhaps the Italian contingent will appear too small to Your Majesty; but if you consider that the numbers mentioned are combat forces, troops of the line, you will recognize that, in order to have 100,000 men available, 150,000 will have to be mobilized.

The Emperor appeared to me to have very equitable ideas on the manner in which the war should be fought and on the role which the two countries should play in it. He recognized that France should concentrate its forces especially on Spezia and on the right bank of the Po, until one had become the master of the length of this river by forcing the Austrians to shut themselves up in the fortresses. Thus there would be two great armies, one to be commanded by Your Majesty and the other by the Emperor in person.

Having reached agreement on the military question, we did so as well on the financial question which, I must acquaint Your Majesty, is the one with which the Emperor is especially preoccupied. However, he consents to furnish us the war material which we should need, and to facilitate for us the negotiation of a loan at Paris. As to the assistance of the Italian provinces in money and in goods, the Emperor believes that one should avail oneself of them while also being sparing of them up to a certain point.—The questions which I have had the honor of summarizing as succinctly as possible for Your Majesty were the object of a conversation with the Emperor which lasted from 11 o'clock in the morning to 3 o'clock in the afternoon. At three o'clock, the Emperor took leave of me, asking me to return at 4 o'clock to go with him on a carriage ride.

At the indicated hour, we entered an elegant phaeton drawn by American horses which the Emperor guided himself, and, followed by a single servant, he led me for three hours amidst the valleys and the forests which make the Vosges one of the most picturesque parts of France.

Hardly had we left the streets of Plombières behind us than the Emperor broached the subject of Prince Napoleon's marriage by asking me what Your Majesty's intentions were in this respect. . . .

The Emperor replied that he eagerly desired the marriage of his cousin with Princess Clotilda; that an alliance with the family of Savoy would be, of all those possible, the one that he would prefer; . . . .

The Emperor returned several times to the question of the marriage. . . .

In my replies to the Emperor, I was always careful not to offend him, while also avoiding any kind of commitment. At the end of the day, at the moment when we parted, the Emperor said to me: "I understand that the King should be reluctant to give his daughter in marriage while she is so young, and I will not insist at all that the marriage take place at once; I will be quite disposed to wait a year or more if necessary. The only thing I want is to know where I stand; therefore, will you kindly ask the King to consult his daughter and to give me some positive indication of his intentions. If he consents to the marriage, let him fix the date; I do not ask for any other commitment than our word mutually given and received." Thereupon we took leave of each other. The Emperor, while shaking my hand, said to me by way of farewell: "Have confidence in me, as I have confidence in you."

Your Majesty can see that I have faithfully followed your instructions. Since the Emperor did not at all make Princess Clotilda's marriage a condition *sine qua non* of the alliance, I have not made the least commitment on this subject nor contracted any kind of obligation. Now I beg Your Majesty to allow me to express, frankly and precisely, my opinion on a question upon which may depend the success of the most glorious enterprise, of the greatest work which has been attempted in many a year.

The Emperor has not made the marriage of Princess Clotilda with his cousin a condition *sine qua non* of the alliance; but it was quite clear that it was very important to him. If the marriage does not take place, if Your Majesty refuses the Emperor's proposals without a plausible reason, what will happen? Will the alliance be broken? It is possible, but I do not think that this will occur. The alliance will take place. But the Emperor will bring to it an entirely different spirit from the one that he would have brought to it if, as a reward for the crown of Italy which he offers to Your Majesty, you would have granted him the hand of your daughter for his closest relative. If there is one characteristic which distinguishes the Emperor, it is the constancy of his friendships and of his antipathies. He never forgets a service rendered, just as he never forgives an offense. But there is no denying that a refusal, to which he has exposed himself, would be a deeply wounding offense.— Such a refusal would be inconvenient in another way: it would place an implacable enemy in the councils of the Emperor. Prince Napoleon, even more Corsican than his cousin, would conceive a mortal hatred against us, and the position which he occupies, the one to which he can aspire, the affection, I will almost say the weakness, which the Emperor has for him, will give him numerous opportunities to satisfy it.

There is no denying it: in accepting the alliance which is being proposed to you, Your Majesty and your nation bind themselves in an indissoluble manner to the Emperor and to France. If the outcome of the war which will result therefrom is fortunate, the dynasty of Napoleon will be consolidated for one or two generations; if it is unfortunate, Your Majesty and your family run as grave dangers as your powerful neighbor. But what is certain is that the success of the war, the glorious consequences which must result from it for Your

Majesty and your people, depend in large measure upon the good will of the Emperor, upon his friendship toward Your Majesty. If, on the contrary, he develops in his heart a real grudge against you, the most deplorable consequences could result. I do not hesitate to declare with the most profound conviction that to accept the alliance and to refuse the marriage would be an immense political mistake, which could bring down great misfortunes upon Your Majesty and upon our country.

But, I know, Your Majesty is father as well as King; . . . .

. . . .

If Your Majesty will be pleased to reflect upon the considerations which I have just had the honor of submitting to you, I dare hope that you will recognize that you can consent as father to a marriage which the supreme interest of the state, the future of your family, of Piedmont, of all of Italy, counsel you to contract.

I beg Your Majesty to forgive my frankness and the length of my recital. I did not know how to be more reserved or more concise in such a grave question. The feelings which inspire me, the motives which guide my actions, are, I trust Your Majesty will agree, sufficient excuse.

Having had to write this eternal epistle on the corner of a table at the hotel, without having had the time to copy it or even to read it over, I beg Your Majesty to want to judge it with indulgence and to excuse whatever disorder in ideas and incorrectness in style it may contain. Despite these faults to which I have just drawn attention, this letter, containing the true and exact expression of the communications made to me by the Emperor, I dare to beg Your Majesty to want to keep it so that, upon my return to Turin, I can extract notes which will serve in the course of the negotiations which will take place.

I have the honor to be, etc.

C. CAVOUR.

No. 41   Summary of the Agreement Reached at Plombieres——
August 1858[1]

Cavour to Napoleon III.[2]

(*3 August 1858.*)

1.

With the objective of freeing Italy from Austria's yoke and of consecrating the great principle of Italian nationality, an offensive and defensive treaty of alliance shall be concluded between the Emperor of the French and the King of Sardinia.

2.

As soon as war shall have been declared between Sardinia and Austria,—France would immediately intervene by sending an army corps to Spezia and one or two divisions to Genoa, which, together with the Sardinian Army, would advance against the Austrian forces concentrated along the Po and the Ticino.

The military forces of the allies in Italy should be rapidly increased to 300,000 men, that is to say, 200,000 French and 100,000. Sardinian and Italian.

A naval fleet in the Adriatic would support the operations of the armies on land.

3.

The preparations to be made, the immediate action to be taken, shall be concerted in advance between France and Sardinia.

To this effect, the Emperor shall decide if he wants to send an officer who enjoys his entire confidence to Turin, or if he believes it preferable that General La Marmora go to Paris.

4.

The military convention, to be signed following these preliminary agreements, shall regulate the manner in which the two Nations shall meet the expenses of the war and the use of resources which the successively occupied countries could furnish.

5.

France shall assist Sardinia in obtaining a loan at Paris.

6.

The successively occupied Italian provinces shall be declared in a state of siege and submitted to military authority. The administration shall be entrusted to employees nominated by the King of Sardinia. An immediate attempt shall be made either through recruitment or through an appeal to volunteers, to enlist all the active forces in the country.

The recruits and the volunteers shall be incorporated in the Sardinian Army.

7.

The purpose of the war being the complete deliverance of Italy, it shall be pursued until this purpose should be achieved.

8.

At the peace, the Kingdom of Upper Italy shall be created. It shall include, in addition to the areas already a part of the Kingdom of Sardinia:

The Austrian provinces in Italy;

The Duchies of Parma and of Modena;

The Papal States this side of the Appennines.

9.

The conduct of the Grand Duke of Tuscany and of the King of Naples toward the allies and the political events caused by the war shall determine the fate of these States at the peace.

It is, however, established in principle that the Holy See shall remain in Rome, and that the Pope shall continue to exercise sovereign authority therein, as well as in the territory which shall be annexed thereto; and that the portion of Italy not included in the Kingdom of Upper Italy shall be divided into two states.

10.

The diverse Italian States shall constitute a confederation.

11.

It shall remain to be seen if, in the event that the throne of Tuscany should become vacant, it could not be disposed of in favor of the Duke of Parma.

12.

Since the war is being fought in defense of the great principle of nationalities, the populations of Savoy could be reunited with France. Sardinia shall retain, however, the fortress of Esseillon, located at the foot of Mount Cenis.

The nationality of the inhabitants of the County of Nice being in doubt, the question as regards them is reserved.

SEPARATE ARTICLE.

If between now and the coming spring no occasion arises which leads to war with Austria, the Government of Sardinia shall not further oppose an appeal to it by the populations of Massa and of Carrara, who have long been subjected to the most oppressive regime, to obtain aid and protection. It shall permit the inhabitants of these districts to demand, in a formal petition, the annexation of these two small Duchies to Sardinia.

King Victor Emmanuel, without granting this wish, will place them under his protection by addressing a forceful and menacing remonstrance to the Duke of Modena.

The question thus precipitated, not only with Modena, but also with Austria, her natural protector, would necessarily lead to a declaration of war. If need be, Sardinia could occupy Massa and Carrara.

Nigra[3] *to Cavour.*[4]

Paris, Hotel du Louvre, 31 August 1858.

My dear Count,

.   .   .   .

At 9:30 a.m., I was presented to His Majesty, ...

The Emperor first looked over the summary of what had been agreed to at Plombières, which Your Excellency had sent to him.

.   .   .   .

The Emperor then said to me that, since these were not formal treaty stipulations, the comments he had made were not to the point, and he charged me with writing to Your Excellency to assure you that, for his part, the summary which he held in his hand was an exact and complete expression of the agreements reached at Plombières.

.   .   .   .

No. 42   The Franco-Sardinian Alliance——January 1859[1]

Secret Treaty, and which Must Always Remain Secret, between Their Majesties the King of Sardinia and the Emperor of the French.

[*Turin, 24 January 1859.*][2]

The critical state of Italy being of such a nature as to foresee complications which could give Piedmont legitimate reasons to invoke the support of France, the Emperor of the French and the King of Sardinia have resolved to consult together in advance in anticipation of the said eventualities, and, after having deliberated upon them, have agreed to the following articles:

ARTICLE 1.

In the event that, as the result of an aggressive act by Austria, war should break out between His Majesty the King of Sardinia and His Majesty the Emperor of Austria, an Offensive and Defensive Alliance shall be concluded between His Majesty the Emperor of the French and His Majesty the King of Sardinia.

ARTICLE 2.

The purpose of the Alliance shall be to free Italy from the Austrian occupation, to satisfy the wishes of the populations, and to prevent the return of the complications which shall have caused the war and which constantly endanger the peace of Europe, by constituting, if the outcome of the war permits it, a Kingdom of Upper Italy of about eleven million inhabitants.

ARTICLE 3.

In the name of the same principle, the Duchy of Savoy and the Province of Nice shall be reunited with France.

ARTICLE 4.

Whatever the course of events caused by the war may be, it is expressly stipulated, in the interest of the Catholic Religion, that the Sovereignty of the Pope shall be maintained.

ARTICLE 5.

The costs of the War shall be met by the Kingdom of Upper Italy.

ARTICLE 6.

The High Contracting Parties place themselves under the obligation not to accept any overture nor any proposal tending to bring hostilities to an end without having previously deliberated upon them together.[3]

No. 43   Cavour Prepares for War——29 January 1859[1]

Cavour to Villamarina.[2]

29 January [*1859*].

My dear Marquis,

Since the Prince [Napoleon] should only arrive in Marseille[s] on Wednesday, I think that you should await in Paris the return of Mme. de Villamarina, who has kindly agreed to bring you this letter.

The Prince will leave Turin tomorrow

at one o'clock, taking his charming wife[3] with him. He leaves us, in compensation, the offensive and defensive treaty of alliance, signed not by him, but by the Emperor himself. The treaty has been carried to Paris by an aide-de-camp of the Prince; leaving here Monday,[4] he was back yesterday morning with the Emperor's signature. You can see that it is impossible to be more prompt or more gracious about it. Since the officer had no inkling of the mission with which he was charged, I could, therefore, inquire about the Emperor's frame of mind without arousing his suspicion. I was charmed by his reply—"Never," he said to me, "have I seen the Emperor in such good humor, he looked delighted." If the Emperor has acted so well in the matter in spite of the absence of the Prince, who left the field free to Walewski,[5] it seems to me that we now have nothing more to fear.

I am not frightened for our Princess by the nasty temper of the *vile slanderers* at the Imperial Court. Her charm, her perfect deportment, her precocious judgment, place her above the intrigues of insipid courtiers. The Emperor will appreciate her, I am certain of it, and she will exercise a benevolent influence over him.

Now that the wedding has taken place, we shall think only of the war. Upon our return, we shall submit to the Chambers a bill enabling us to contract a loan of 40,000,000, and we shall vigorously push on with our armaments. Our language, however, shall be most moderate, and we shall pose as the victims of Austria's menaces. It is essential that the treaty remain ignored. We are the only ones who can say that we know for certain that, as long as right is on our side, the Emperor shall not abandon us.

While we are preparing to make the Austrians dance to our tune in Italy, we are arranging another kind of festival for them closer to the heart of the Empire. I have made contact with General Klapka who, with the support of France, is preparing a vast movement[6] in Hungary. I am sending you a letter for him, which I would like you to transmit to him.

I am asking him to get in touch with you, being, however, very cautious and prudent, so that the Anglo-Austrian spies, with which Paris must abound, do not give the alarm to our enemies about our projects.

Klapka is to send me agents who are to contact the Hungarian troops stationed in Italy. If it is necessary, you are to furnish him[7] with passports.

I am, etc.

P.S.—It is possible that General Klapka may not be in Paris at the moment when you shall receive this letter, you shall await his return to make certain that it is transmitted only to him.

No. 44   Minutes of the Conferences of the Austrian Council of Ministers——5 January to 27 April 1859[1]

· · · · · · · · ·

The original protocols of the conferences held by the Council of Ministers on the subject are to be found in the archives of the "Central Military Chancellery." These protocols reveal:

The first conference[2] to deal with the conditions in the Italian crown-lands and in the adjoining areas, particularly regarding the aggressive activity of Piedmont, took place on *5 January 1859*. Napoleon's New Year's speech probably concentrated attention upon these questions.

Grünne's motion, to strengthen the army in Italy by transferring the III Army Corps there in its present state of readiness, "is carried unanimously." *Buol*, especially, "denotes this as necessary; he anticipates that it will make a good impression," . . .

On *19 February*, the conference of ministers[3] decides upon the most needed increases in the state of the 2nd Army and of the II [III?] Army Corps destined for Italy, also the accumulation of food-stores. The debate on this subject contains a number of noteworthy comments: *Buol* thinks that there can be no doubt about the necessity for these preparations, although "the crisis appears to him the more dangerous the closer spring approaches, at the moment war appears less threatening;" he also adds that "Louis Napoleon has not yet determined upon war under the prevailing circumstances." The *Emperor* asks "whether the German governments can be persuaded to conclude active alliances?" *Buol* answers in the affirmative, "only in regard to Prussia is he incapable of giving such an assurance." *Hess* requests that the Austrian army be increased to the same level as the eventually united forces of France and Sardinia. . . .

On *6 April*, the conference[4] takes up Russia's proposal for a Congress and England's attempts at mediation, as well as the question of disarmament connected therewith.

Buol explains the circumstances, and comes to the conclusion: ". . . considering Piedmont's continuously increasing threats, Austria must undertake its disarmament herself and peremptorily demand this of Sardinia; in case it should refuse, adequate grounds exist for Austria to consider herself released from her conditional promise not to want to attack and to proceed with every right to the forceful disarmament of Piedmont. A decisive, firm resolution concerning this has to be formed now. The opinion of all the German princes and their governments

—perhaps with the exception of Prussia—are on our side, England and Prussia not against us. France shall have to carefully weigh that other Powers could support Austria, therefore either urge Piedmont to comply with our request for disarmament, or she is already so strongly committed that she has to enter the war on Piedmont's side, but then all of Germany would fully mobilize and welcome our troops. In any case, even if war should break out with Piedmont, this would not yet mean a general war. France could then still act as she pleased, and our present position should be judged in accordance with these viewpoints." *Grünne* wishes that the possibility "of a general war be constantly kept in mind, and he would like to see all preparations for it completed before a categorical demand is made for Sardinia's disarmament and a probable refusal is interpreted as a reason for going to war.—Furthermore, considering the present political and military combinations, the important factors of 'Russia' and the 'Rajah' have to be carefully weighed." *Hess* is of the opinion that "the ultimatum suggested by the Foreign Minister (. . .)[5] could confront Austria with a serious dilemma. If it should occur, then one had to be ready for all eventualities and the whole Austrian army be placed on a war footing, for which we need three months, whereas France, within three weeks, could place 160,000—after completion of its cadres, 200,000 men in the theater of operations; (. . .) but from a political viewpoint, too, it must be considered if aggressive action could not cost us alliances; finally, it would be well to take into consideration if, in the case of an eventual extension of the theater of operations to the Rhine, we are in a financial condition to place adequate military forces there (. . . .)" *Buol* "declares that the case in which Prussia would not be on our side in a general war against France is entirely inconceivable." *Bach* sums up his lengthy exposition with the words: to yield any further "would not be an act of moderation, but already one of weakness which would cause deep sorrow throughout the Empire, even in Germany, too, and which could rob us of the support of public opinion which is so fickle." *Grünne* does not cast a doubt over any of this; however, "he wishes the general war be kept in mind and the preparations for it completed." *Bruck* is opposed to yielding any further. "However, it must be carefully considered that, from a military viewpoint, an attack on Piedmont will, in all probability, unleash a war against France as well, and that, after the first cannonball has roared away, it cannot be foreseen when the last one will be fired (. . .)"—*Result*: Unanimous opinion "that the safety and dignity of the Empire do not permit the continuation of the present conduct of the Sardinian government any longer, that, in anticipation of the general war, our preparations be continued, and, finally, also that the II Army Corps, stationed in Vienna fully equipped, should be transferred to Italy (. . . .)"

In the conference of ministers[6] on *19 April*, the Emperor asked the Foreign Minister "if the time had come to present" the ultimatum "to the Turin Cabinet (. . . .), finally, if, in case of an unsatisfactory reply to the dispatch on the part of Piedmont, the Commanding General, Count Gyulai (. . .) is to take the offensive immediately after considering only military circumstances."

Buol "hereupon declares that the presentation of the ultimatum, which has already been prepared, should not be delayed a moment longer because otherwise Austria may possibly not be in a position at all to still take this step against Piedmont since, according to the most recent stand of the diplomatic negotiation, France—obviously concerned over the alliances which are gradually building up for Austria—is already seeking to find ways of withdrawing from the policy which it has pursued until now, consequently the possibility also suggests itself that Piedmont will lend a willing ear to the advice which, accordingly, can be expected from France that it yield to Austria's demands (. . .)." "As to the determination of the proper moment for the eventual offensive by the army, Buol believes that its commander could start immediately with the preparations for such a plan by concentrating combat forces in advanced positions, a measure which, apart from its military usefulness, can also only have a beneficial effect upon the diplomatic step mentioned above. But directly after the arrival of the reply from Turin, Count Gyulai must first communicate to us here by telegraph its most essential points or the possible failure to reply within the designated space of time, and thus in either case,—for it must be presumed beyond any doubt that an agreement will have been reached within the three days between Sardinia and France—the diplomatic decision will have been made with certainty of the question: whether Sardinia's possible resistance against our demands will be supported by France, or whether the latter, yielding to the pressure of Europe, has also been able to persuade Sardinia to submit to the Austrian ultimatum. *Buol*, who, moreover, believes he may assume the latter result as the more likely one, accordingly does not see the necessity for denying His Majesty the Emperor the previous right of the highest decision to determine the moment of the eventual opening of hostilities." *Hess* and *Kempen* examine the situation which would result if Sardinia were eventually to yield; whereupon *Grünne* comments "that, for the time being, what is involved is less an examination of the case of Sardinia's submission than really what was to be done in case of its resistance, eventually supported by France." *Hess* "replies that in this case Austria's foremost task must be the mobilization of 600,000 men and the shifting of the general war to the Rhine in order, through a direct attack upon France, to prevent her from according energetic support to Sardinia and to the revolution in Italy which will spread simultaneously with the outbreak of the war." . . . *Buol* denotes the eventual separation of the enemy's forces[7] as facilitating our operations, and "now takes up his repeated, emphatic declaration that the execution of the above-mentioned step of a categorical demand to Sardinia for disarmament, regardless of any possible military considerations, should also not be delayed one minute longer. The presentation of the ultimatum to the Turin Cabinet is, as a political measure, of such urgency because only Sardinia's pretention of wanting to participate in the Congress as an equal with the Great Powers is left to us as the sole cause upon which it can be based today." *Bach*, too, "speaks for the greatest urgency of the measure, whose quick execution is even being demanded by public opinion." *Grünne, with the concurrence of all the participants in the conference,* expresses regret "over the delay, too protracted until now, of the said step, which will finally bring about a decision." *Grünne* and the *military participants* move "the immediate mobilization of the entire army, a decision which is all the more urgent since fully 3 months will be required to achieve it completely." *Buol* "believes such an important measure should be delayed until France shall have made a definite pronouncement, a decision which must occur in a few days in connection with the demand for disarmament addressed by Austria to Sardinia. At the present moment, we are really only concerned with Piedmont—but as to its ally, France, we are dealing with an opponent who, to all appearances, has already yielded. If, however, the opposite were to be the case and France's hostile action definitely confirmed, then the moment would thereby have arrived for the development of Austria's full power and, at the same time, for the motion to be made at the Diet in Frankfurt am Main, in common with Prussia as already agreed upon in this way, for the

mobilization of the German confederate contingents." *Bruck* agrees, and wishes a full clarification, the sooner the better, "since the present uncertain state of affairs is more dangerous and more insufferable than even a war." The *Emperor* hereupon decrees, "that the demand be dispatched to the Turin Cabinet by courier this very day."[8]

On *27 April,* at 3 p.m., the conference of ministers[9] took place which was to decide on war or peace.[10]

Buol "reads aloud the dispatch by the Sardinian Minister-President, Count Cavour, dated 26 April 1859,[11] whose main contents had been communicated by Count Gyulai by telegraph, and *His Majesty, together with all the participants in the conference,* are unanimously of the opinion that its contents are completely unsatisfactory since they evade Austria's demands." "*His Majesty* is pleased to remark, in particular, that the Note, even though not really expressing a refusal, does not change anything in the previous declarations of the Turin Court, either, therefore, in reality, must be regarded as no answer at all." *Buol* "designates the comments of the Piedmontese dispatch . . . as excuses, inserted in order to gain time for the completion of Sardinian and French military preparations during repeated diplomatic negotiations. . . ." . . . Thereupon *Bach* comments: ". . . Sardinia has been preparing the reasons for a final break for ten years, and, counting on the patience which, as all the world knows, we have always exhibited and on our position, which forces us to want to maintain the peace, the said Power and her ally apparently only agreed to the attempts at mediation and to the disarmament negotiations, which have already dragged on for three months, for the purpose of gaining time for their military preparations. Therefore, the question at issue now is not any more whether diplomatic negotiations would still be possible at all, and every reflection on this subject must yield to the heart of the problem. To be in doubt over what to do now would be the worst possible position. After Austria presented the ultimatum to Sardinia, honor and absolute necessity demand that we bear its consequences. There can be no other question any more, not even that England and Prussia would view it with satisfaction if we stopped short of war and once again entered into new negotiations." . . . The *Emperor* "thereupon remarks that, if no result can really be expected from a continuation of diplomatic efforts to preserve the peace, then, to be sure, the quickest attack, in a military sense, would offer the greatest advantages, and every day of continued hesitation would be a loss." In this conviction *Hess* insists "that a decision has to be reached without waiting a moment longer. After Austria (. . .) sent the ultimatum to Sardinia, informed the Powers of its contents, and has now received an answer to it which is thoroughly unsatisfactory, it appears completely inconceivable to retain any doubts over our next task, and it would be no less irresponsible to hesitate in the least with its execution and thereby to give France, which, in the meantime, has already begun to move

120,000 men against us, the leisure of throwing even larger combat forces into the theater of operations in Italy before we can do so." At this point *Buol* admits the fact "that France, which, as he believed he could assume at the conference of 19 April, appeared to be out of countenance at that time, has used the fortuitous delay of the past 8 days in order to strengthen her combat forces stationed along the frontiers, . . ." *The Emperor, together with all the participants in the conference,* "immediately agree, with vigorous unanimity, to launch an offensive at once." The *Emperor,* . . . "No doubt exists," declares His Majesty, "concerning the decision to be reached today. Apart from our present and future relations with the other Powers, honor and duty demand the war against Sardinia and its ally. We undertake it in the clear conviction of our lawful right, forced to do so, and trusting in God's support."—*His Majesty* immediately orders that the following telegraphic dispatch be forwarded at once to the commander of the 2nd Army, Count Gyulai: 'You are to launch an offensive against Sardinia and its French allies.' "[12]

.   .   .   .

No. 45   The Austrian Ultimatum to Sardinia——19 April 1859[1]

Buol to Cavour.

Vienna, 19th April, 1859.[2]

The Imperial Government, as your Excellency is aware, has hastened to accede to the proposal of the Cabinet of St. Petersburg to assemble a Congress of the 5 Powers with the view to remove the complications which have arisen in Italy.[3]

Convinced, however, of the impossibility to enter, with any chance of success, upon pacific deliberations in the midst of the noise of arms, and of preparations for War carried on in a neighbouring Country,

we have demanded the placing on a Peace Footing of the Sardinian Army, and the disbanding of the Free Corps, or Italian Volunteers, previously to the meeting of the Congress.

Her Britannic Majesty's Government finds this condition so just, and so consonant with the exigencies of the situation, that it did not hesitate to adopt it, at the same time declaring itself to be ready, in conjunction with France, to insist on the immediate disarmament of Sardinia, and to offer her in return a Collective Guarantee against any attack on our part, to which, of course, Austria would have done honour.

The Cabinet of Turin seems only to have answered by a categorical refusal to the invitation to put her Army on a Peace Footing, and to accept the Collective Guarantee which was offered her. This refusal inspires us with regrets, so much the more deep, that if the Sardinian Government had consented to the testimony of pacific sentiments which was demanded of her, we should have accepted it as a first symptom of her intention to assist, on her side, in bringing about an improvement in the relations between the two countries which have unfortunately been in such a state of tension for some years past. In that case it would have been permitted us to furnish, by the breaking up of the Imperial troops stationed in the Lombardo-Venetian kingdom, another proof that they were not assembled for the purpose of aggression against Sardinia.

Our hope having been hitherto deceived, the Emperor, my august master, has ordered me to make directly a last effort to cause the Sardinian Government to reconsider the decision which it seems to have resolved on. Such is the object of this letter.

I have the honour to entreat your Excellency to take its contents into your most serious consideration, and to let me know if the Royal Government consents, yes or no, to put its Army on a Peace Footing without delay, and to disband the Italian Volunteers.

The bearer of this letter, to whom, M. le Comte, you will be so good as to give your answer, is ordered to hold himself at your disposition to this effect for 3 days.

Should he receive no answer at the expiration of this term, or should this answer not be completely satisfactory, the responsibility of the grave events which this refusal would entail would fall entirely on His Sardinian Majesty's Government.

After having exhausted in vain all conciliatory means to procure for these populations the guarantee of Peace, on which the Emperor has a right to insist, His Majesty will be obliged, to his great regret, to have recourse to the force of Arms to obtain it.

In the hope that the answer which I solicit of your Excellency will be congenial to our wishes for the maintenance of Peace, I seize, &c.,

BUOL.

No. 46   The Sardinian Reply——26 April 1859[1]

Cavour to Buol.

26 April, 1859.[2]

The question of the Disarmament of Sardinia, which constitutes the basis of the demand which your Excellency addresses to me, has been the subject of numerous negotiations between the Great Powers and the Government of the King. These negotiations led to a proposition drawn up by England, to which France, Prussia, and Russia adhered. Sardinia, in a spirit of conciliation, accepted it without reserve or afterthought. Since your Excellency can neither be ignorant either of the proposition of England nor the answer, I could add nothing in order to make known the intentions of the Government of the King with regard to the difficulties which were opposed to the assembling of the Congress.

The decided conduct of Sardinia has been appreciated by Europe. Whatever may be the consequences which it entails, the King, my august master, is convinced that the responsibility will devolve upon them who first armed, who have refused the propositions made by a great Power, and recognised as just and reasonable by the others, and who now substitute a menacing summons in its stead.

No. 47   The Austrian Manifesto and Declaration of War Against
Sardinia——28 April 1859[1]

TO MY PEOPLE

I HAVE ordered my faithful and gallant Army to put a stop to the inimical acts which, for a series of years, have been committed by the neighbouring State of Sardinia against the indisputable rights of my Crown, and against the integrity of the realm placed by God under my care, which acts have lately attained the very highest point. By so doing I have fulfilled the painful but unavoidable duty of a Sovereign. My conscience being at rest, I can look up to an omnipotent God, and patiently await His award. With confidence I leave my decision to the impartial judgment of contemporaneous and future generations. Of the approbation of my faithful subjects I am sure. When more than 10 years ago the same enemy, violating international law and the usages of war, and without any cause being given, invaded the Lombardo-Venetian territory with an army, with the intention of seizing upon it, although he was twice totally defeated by my gallant army, and at the mercy of the victor, I behaved generously, and held out my hand to a reconciliation. I did not appropriate to myself one inch of his territory; I encroached on no right which belongs to the Crown of Sardinia, as one of the members of the European family of nations. I insisted on no guarantees against the recurrence of similar events. The hand of peace which I, in all sincerity, extended, and which was taken, appeared to me to be a sufficient guarantee. The blood which my army shed for the honour and right of Austria I sacrificed on the altar of peace. The answer to this forbearance, which has hardly had an example in history, was a resumption of hostility, and an agitation carried on by all the expedients of perfidy, increasing from year to year, against the peace and welfare of my Lombardo-Venetian Kingdom. Well knowing how much I ought to value the priceless boon of peace for my people and for Europe, I patiently bore with these new hostilities. My patience was not exhausted when the more extensive measures which recently I was forced to take, in consequence of the revolutionary agitation on the frontiers of my Italian Provinces, and within the same, were made an excuse for a higher degree of hostility. Willingly accepting the well-meant Mediation of friendly Powers for the maintenance of Peace, I consented to become a party to a Congress of the 5 great Powers. The 4 points proposed by the Royal Government of Great Britain as a basis for the deliberations of the Congress, were forwarded to my Government, and I accepted them, with the conditions which alone were calculated to bring about a true, sincere, and durable peace. But in the consciousness that no step on the part of my Government could, even in the most remote degree, lead to a disturbance of the peace, I required at the same time that the Power which was the cause of the complication, and had brought about the danger of war, should, as a preliminary measure, disarm. Being pressed thereto by friendly Powers, I at length accepted the proposal for a general disarmament. The Mediation failed in consequence of the inadmissible nature of the conditions on which Sardinia made her consent dependent. Only one means of maintaining peace remained. I addressed myself directly to the Sardinian Government, and summoned it to place its army on a peace footing, and to disband the free corps. Sardinia did not accede to my demand: therefore, the moment for deciding the matter by an appeal to arms has arrived.

I have ordered my army to enter Sardinia.

I am aware of the vast importance of the measure, and if ever my duties as a monarch weighed heavily on me it is at this moment. War is the scourge of mankind. I see with emotion that the lives and property of thousands of my subjects are imperilled, and deeply feel what a severe trial war is for my realm, which, being occupied with its internal development, greatly requires the continuance of peace. But the heart of the monarch must be silent at the command of honour and duty. On the frontiers the enemy stands in arms, in alliance with the revolutionary party, openly announcing his intention to seize upon the possessions of Austria in Italy. To support him, the Ruler over France, who, under futile pretexts, interferes in the legally established relations of the Italian Peninsula, has set his troops in movement. Detachments of them have already crossed the frontiers of Sardinia. The Crown which I received without spot or blemish from my forefathers has already seen trying times. The glorious history of our country gives evidence that Providence, when the shadows of a revolution, menacing to the highest good of humanity, appear about to spread over this quarter of the world, has frequently used the sword of Austria in order to dispel those shadows with its lightning. We are again on the eve of a period when the world is threatened with an overthrow of everything subsisting, and that not by parties only, but from thrones downwards. If I draw the sword, that sword receives a con-secration, as a defence for the honour and the good right of Austria, for the rights of all peoples and States, and for all that is held most dear by humanity.

To you, My People, whose devotion to the hereditary reigning family may serve as a model for all the nations of the earth, I now address myself. In the conflict which has commenced you will stand by me with your oft-proved fidelity, devotion, and self-sacrifice. To your sons, whom I have taken into the ranks of the army, I their commander, send my martial greeting. With pride you may regard them, for the eagle of Austria will, with their support, soar high in honour.

Our struggle is a just one, and we begin it with courage and confidence. We hope we shall not stand alone in it. The soil on which we have to do battle was made fruitful by the blood lost by our German brethren when they won those bulwarks which they have maintained up to the present day. There the crafty enemies of Germany have generally begun their game when they have wished to break her internal power. The feeling that such a danger is now imminent prevails in all parts of Germany, from the hut to the throne, from one frontier to the other. I speak as a Sovereign member of the Germanic Confederation when I call attention to the common danger, and recall to memory the glorious times in which Europe had to thank the general and fervent enthusiasm for its liberation.

For God and Fatherland!

Given at my residence and metropolis of Vienna, on this 28th day of April, 1859.

FRANCIS JOSEPH.

No. 48   The Sardinian Proclamation of War with Austria—— 29 April 1859[1]

PEOPLE OF THE KINGDOM!

Austria attacks us with a powerful army, which, while professing a love of peace, she has assembled to assault us in the unhappy provinces subject to her domination.

Unable to support the example of our civil order, and unwilling to submit to the judgment of an European Congress, on the evils and dangers of which she alone is the cause in Italy, Austria violates her promise to England, and makes a case of War out of a law of honour.

Austria dares to demand the diminution of our troops; that that brave youth, which from all parts of Italy has thronged to her standard of national independence, be disarmed, and handed over to her.

A jealous guardian of the ancestral common patrimony of honour and glory, I have handed over to my beloved cousin Prince Eugène the Government of the State, while I myself again draw the sword.

The brave soldiers of the Emperor Napoleon, my generous Ally, will fight the fight of liberty and justice with my soldiers.

PEOPLE OF ITALY!

Austria attacks Piedmont because I have advocated the cause of our common country in the Councils of Europe, and because I have not been insensible to your cry of anguish. Thus she has violently broken those Treaties which she never respected; thus now all right is on the side of the nation, and I can conscientiously perform the vow made on the tomb of my illustrious parent. Taking up Arms in the defence of my Throne, of the liberty of my people, and of the honour of the Italian name, I fight for the rights of the whole nation.

We trust in God and in our concord; in the valour of the soldiers of Italy, and in the alliance of the noble French nation, and we trust in the justice of public opinion.

My only ambition is to be the first soldier of Italian Independence.

Turin, 29th April, 1859.

Viva l'Italia!

VICTOR EMMANUEL.

No. 49   The French Proclamation of War with Austria—— 3 May 1859[1]

The Emperor to the French People.

FRENCHMEN!

Austria, in causing her Army to enter the territory of the King of Sardinia, our Ally, declares War against us. She thus violates Treaties and justice, and menaces our Frontiers. All the Great Powers have protested against this aggression. Piedmont having accepted the conditions which should have insured peace, one asks, what can be the reason of this sudden Invasion? It is that Austria has brought matters to this extremity, that her dominion must either extend to the Alps, or Italy must be free to the Adriatic; for in this country every corner of territory which remains independent endangers her power.

Hitherto moderation has been the rule of my conduct; now energy becomes my first duty.

Let France arm, and say resolutely to Europe, "I desire no conquest, but I desire firmly to maintain my national and traditional policy. I observe the Treaties on condition that no one shall violate them against me. I respect the Territory and Rights of Neutral Powers, but I boldly avow my sympathy for a people whose history is mingled with our own, and who groan beneath foreign oppression."

France has shown her hatred against anarchy; she has been pleased to give me a power strong enough to reduce to helplessness the abettors of disorder and the incorrigible members of those old factions whom one perpetually sees plotting with our enemies: but she has not, therefore, abdicated her task of civilization. Her natural allies have always been those who desire the improvement of the human race, and when she draws the sword it is not in order to dominate, but to liberate.

The object of this War, then, is to restore Italy to herself, not to make her change masters, and we shall then have next our frontiers a friendly people, who will owe to us their Independence.

We are not going into Italy to foment disorder or to shake the Power of the Holy Father, whom we have replaced upon his throne, but to free him from this foreign pressure, which weighs upon the whole Peninsula, and to help to establish there order upon legitimate satisfied interests.

We are going, in fine, to seek upon this classic ground, illustrated by so many victories, the footsteps of our fathers. God grant that we may be worthy of them!

I am going soon to place myself at the head of the army. I leave in France the Empress and my son. Seconded by the experience and the enlightenment of the last surviving brother of the Emperor, she will understand how to show herself equal to the grandeur of her mission.

I confide them to the valour of the army which remains in France to watch over our frontiers as well as to protect our homes; I confide them to the loyalty of the National Guard; I confide them, in a word, to the whole people, who will encircle them with that affection and devotion of which I daily receive so many proofs.

Courage, then, and Union! Our country is going once more to show the world that she has not degenerated. Providence will bless our efforts, for the cause which rests on justice, humanity, love of country, and independence, is holy in the eyes of God.

NAPOLEON.

Paris, 3rd May, 1859.

No. 50 Great Britain Opts for Neutrality——4 May 1859[1]

Circular to Her Majesty's Ministers Abroad.

Foreign Office, 4th May, 1859.

Sir,

The apprehensions which, as I stated to you at the close of my despatch of the 7th ultimo, Her Majesty's Government at that time entertained lest all their efforts to prevent Peace from being interrupted should prove unavailing, have unfortunately been realised. It is, therefore, unnecessary for me to enter into a detailed account of the various transactions which intervened between the date of my last despatch and the breaking out of War between France and Sardinia, on the one side, and Austria, on the other, although it is right that you should have a general idea of what has occurred in that interval.

The negotiations turned generally on two points, the one relating to Disarmament, the other to the admission of the Italian States, in some form or other, to the proposed Congress.

The Cabinet of Vienna insisted, at first, as an indispensable condition to its entry into the Congress, that Sardinia should, in the first instance, disarm and disband the free corps which she had enrolled; but it finally acquiesced, with some modification, in a proposal made by Her Majesty's Government, and declared it would be contented if a general disarmament were carried out by Austria, France, and Sardinia, previously to the meeting of the Congress.

The Government of France was prevailed upon to admit, for itself, the principle of a General Disarmament; but it hesitated for a long time before it consented to press the acceptance of it on Sardinia, and at length only agreed to do so on condition that the Italian States should be admitted to send Representatives to the Congress, not simply as Advocates, but as Plenipotentiaries, having an equal position and voice with the Plenipotentiaries of the Great Powers in the deliberations that might ensue.

On reviewing the state of the negotiation, His Majesty's Government conceived that there was still a chance of affecting such an understanding between the parties as would ensure the meeting of the Congress, and for this purpose they proposed, on the 18th of last month,—

1st. That there should be a previous, immediate, effective, and simultaneous Disarmament, on the part of Austria, France, and Sardinia;

2ndly. That the details of that Disarmament should be settled by 6 Military or Civil Commissioners, to be named severally by the Great Powers and by Sardinia;

3rdly. That those Commissioners having met and entered upon their duties, the Congress should forthwith be convened; and,

4thly. That the Congress, when convened, should invite the Italian States to send Representatives, who would be admitted to, and take part in the deliberations of, the Congress, in the same manner and on the same footing as they were admitted to, and took part in the deliberations of, the Congress of Laybach.

This proposal was accepted in the main by the Governments of France, Prussia, and Russia, and partially by the Cabinet of Vienna. The latter however, absolutely refused to agree to the admission of the Representatives of the Italian States to the Congress, or to the participation of Sardinia in that Assembly, under any conditions whatever.

This decision on the part of the Austrian Government put an end to all hope of any Congress being brought together; for, though the point was not again raised, I may as well mention to you that, in an earlier stage of the negotiations, Her Majesty's Government and that of Prussia refused to entertain a suggestion made by the Cabinet of St. Petersburgh, that,—in consequence of the hesitation at that time shown by Austria,—England, France, Prussia, and Russia should hold a Congress on the affairs of Italy, without her participation.

The refusal of Austria to accept the last proposal of Her Majesty's Government, was accompanied, on her part, by a peremptory summons to Sardinia to disarm, and to disband the free corps. Her Majesty's Government, on receiving this intelligence, addressed to the Cabinet of Vienna the strongest remonstrances on the impolicy of this proceeding, and directed Her Majesty's Minister at that Court to place on record a formal Protest against it. This precipitate measure was the more to be regretted inasmuch as the Cabinet of Turin, which had previously declined to comply with the combined representations of England and Prussia, on the subject of disarmament, had announced, on the very day that the summons was dispatched from Vienna, though the Austrian Government were unacquainted with the fact when the summons was dispatched, that as France had united with England in demanding the previous disarmament of Sardinia, the Cabinet of Turin, although foreseeing that such a measure might entail disagreeable consequences for the tranquillity of Italy, was disposed to submit to it.

In this state of things, all hopes of accommodation seemed to be at an end: nevertheless, Her Majesty's Government resolved to make one more attempt to stay hostilities, and they accordingly formally tendered the Mediation of England between Austria and France, for the settlement of the Italian question, on bases corresponding with the understanding arrived at between Lord Cowley and Count Buol at Vienna.

But this too failed: and Her Majesty's Government have only to lament the little success which has attended all their efforts, jointly with other Powers or singly, to avert the interruption of the general Peace. In the present position of the contending parties, it would obviously be to no purpose to attempt to restrain them from engaging in a deadly struggle. Her Majesty's Government will, however, watch the progress of the War with the most anxious attention, and will be ready to avail themselves of any opportunity that may arise for the exercise of their Good Offices in the cause of Peace.

It is their earnest desire and firm intention to observe the most scrupulous Neutrality between the contending parties.

MALMESBURY.[2]

On the following day the Earl of Malmesbury addressed a further Dispatch to Her Majesty's Ambassador in Paris, in which the following passage occurs:—

"The British Government have always recognised as a sacred rule of international obligation, that no country has a right authoritatively to interfere in the Internal Affairs of a Foreign State, or, with a sound policy, long withhold its acknowledgment of any new form of government which may be adapted and established, without territorial usurpation or absorption, by the spontaneous wish of its people.

"The British Government have shown, for a long series of years, how steadily they have observed these principles, and they certainly cannot depart from them on the present occasion, however earnest may be their desire to secure the freedom of the Italian people, and to maintain the Treaties which confirmed the Independence of their respective States."

(Great Britain proclaimed its Neutrality in this War on the 13th May, 1859.–Ed.)

No. 51   The Preliminary Peace of Villafranca— 11 July 1859[1,2]

Between His Majesty the Emperor of Austria and His Majesty the Emperor of the French, it has been agreed as follows:—

Creation of Italian Confederation under Presidency of the Holy Father.

The two Sovereigns favour the creation of an Italian Confederation. This Confederation shall be under the honorary Presidency of the Holy Father.

Cession of Lombardy, except Fortresses of Mantua and Peschiera, to France.

The Emperor of Austria cedes to the Emperor of the French his rights over Lombardy, with the exception of the

Fortresses of Mantua and Peschiera, so that the Frontier of the Austrian Possessions shall start from the extremity of the rayon of the Fortress of Peschiera, and extend in a straight line along the Mincio as far as Legrazia, thence to Szarzarola, and Lugano on the Po, whence the existing Frontiers continue to form the Boundaries of Austria.

*Ceded Territory to be presented
to King of Sardinia.*

The Emperor of the French shall present the ceded Territory to the King of Sardinia.

Venetia to form part of Italian Confederation, subject to Crown of Austria.

Venetia shall form part of the Italian Confederation, remaining, however, subject to the Crown of the Emperor of Austria.

*Restoration of Grand Duke of Tuscany
and Duke of Modena. Amnesty.*

The Grand Duke of Tuscany and the Duke of Modena return to their States, granting a General Amnesty.

Reforms in States of the Church.

The two Emperors shall request the Holy Father to introduce in his States some indispensable reforms.

*Full and complete Amnesty
by France and Austria.*

Full and complete Amnesty is granted on both sides to persons compromised on the occasion of the recent events in the territories of the belligerents.

Done at Villafranca, 11th July, 1859.

FRANCIS JOSEPH.[3]

No. 52 Sardinia Annexes Emilia and Tuscany——
18 and 22 March 1860[1]

Decree.

VICTOR EMANUEL II, King of Sardinia, of Cyprus, and of Jerusalem, &c., Duke of Savoy and of Genoa, &c., Prince of Piedmont, &c.;

Considering the result of the Universal Suffrage of the Emilian Provinces,[2] proving their unanimous desire to be united to our State:

Having consulted our Ministers, we now decree:

ART. I. The Provinces of Emilia shall make an integral part of the State from the day of the date of the present Decree.

ART. II. The present Decree shall be presented to Parliament to be converted into law.

Our Ministers are charged with the execution of the present Decree, which, furnished with the Seal of State, shall be inserted in the collection of Government Acts, and be published in the Provinces of Tuscany.

Given at Turin, 18th March, 1860.

VICTOR EMANUEL.[3]

No. 53   Savoy and Nice Are Ceded to France——
24 March 1860[1]

His Majesty the Emperor of the French having explained the considerations which, in consequence of the changes which have arisen in the Territorial relations between France and Sardinia, caused him to desire the Annexation of Savoy and the Arrondissement of Nice to France, and His Majesty the King of Sardinia having shown himself disposed to acquiesce in it, their said Majesties have decided to conclude a Treaty for that purpose, and have named as their Plenipotentiaries:

His Majesty the Emperor of the French, Baron de Talleyrand-Périgord, &c.; and M. Vincent Benedetti, &c.; and His Majesty the King of Sardinia, His Excellency Count Camille Benso de Cavour, &c.; and His Excellency the Chevalier Charles Louis Farini, &c.;

Who after having exchanged their Full Powers found to be in good and due form, have agreed upon the following Articles:

Union of Savoy and Nice to France.

ART. I. His Majesty the King of Sardinia consents to the Annexation of Savoy and the Arrondissement of Nice to France, and renounces for himself, and all his Descendants and Successors, in favour of His Majesty the Emperor of the French, his Rights and Titles over the said Territories. It is understood between their Majesties that this Annexation shall be effected without any constraint of the wishes of the Populations, and that the Governments of the Emperor of the French and of the King of Sardinia will concert as soon as possible upon the best means of appreciating and verifying the manifestations of those wishes.

Appointment of Mixed Boundary Commission.

ART. III. A Mixed Commission shall determine, in a spirit of equity, the Frontiers of the two States, taking into account the configuration of the Mountains and the requirements of defence.

Nationality of Subjects of Savoy and Nice.

ART. VI. Sardinian Subjects natives of Savoy and the Arrondissement of Nice, at present domiciled in those Provinces, who shall desire to preserve their Sardinian Nationality, shall enjoy, during the space of one year from the date of the exchange of the Ratifications, and provided that they make a previous Declaration before the competent authority, the right of transporting their domicile into Italy, and of fixing it there; in which case, the character of Sardinian Citizen shall be continued to them.

Preservation of Immoveable Property in ceded Territories.

They shall be free to retain their Immoveable Property situated in the Territory annexed to France.

Execution of Treaty by Sardinia.

ART. VII. As concerns Sardinia, the present Treaty shall be in force as soon as the necessary Legislative Sanction shall have been given by Parliament.

Ratifications.[2]

ART. VIII. The present Treaty shall be ratified, and the Ratifications of it shall be exchanged at Turin within 10 days, or sooner if possible.

In faith of which the respective Plenipotentiaries have signed it, and have affixed to it their Armorial Seals.

Done in Duplicate, at Turin, the 24th day of the month of March, of the year of Grace, 1860.

(L.S.) TALLEYRAND.   (L.S.) CAVOUR.
(L.S.) BENEDETTI.   (L.S.) FARINI.

No. 54   Garibaldi and His Redshirts, by a British Eyewitness ——April to November 1860[1]

. . . .

On the 14th [of April, 1860], thirteen insurgents, taken with arms in their hands at the Guancia Convent, were shot by sentence of court-martial at Palermo. By this act the Neapolitan Government blew away every prospect of reconciliation, for it determined Garibaldi to come to the rescue. With difficulty restrained by his friends from a last visit to his Nizzard home,[2] which might have been attended with untoward results, he now decided upon organising a Southern expedition; for, though he had never counselled the insurrection in Sicily, he had promised to help all Italians that would assist themselves; and no longer able to remain a passive spectator of their sacrifices, he summoned his followers of the old Cacciatori[3] once more; at the same time sending word to the Sicilians to confine themselves to the mountainous portions of the island until his arrival.

To Italians he appealed in the following

"PROCLAMATION.

"Italians!—The Sicilians are fighting against the enemies of Italy and for Italy. To help them with money, arms, and especially men, is the duty of every Italian.

"The chief cause of the misfortunes of Italy has been disunion, and the indifference one province showed for the fate of another.

"The salvation of Italy dates from the day when the sons of the same soil hastened to the support of their brothers in danger.

"If we abandon the brave sons of Sicily to themselves, they will have to fight the mercenaries of the Bourbon, as well as those of Austria and of the priest who rules at Rome.

"Let the people of the free provinces raise their voices in favour of their brethren who are fighting—let them send their generous youth to where men are fighting for their country.

"Let the Marches, Umbria, Sabine, the Roman Campagna, and the Neapolitan territory rise, so as to divide the enemy's forces.

"If the cities do not offer a sufficient basis for insurrection, let the more resolute throw themselves into the open country.

"A brave man can always find a weapon. In the name of Heaven, hearken not to the voice of those who cram themselves at well-served tables.

"Let us arm. Let us fight for our brothers; to-morrow we can fight for ourselves.

"A handful of brave men, who have followed me in battles for our country, are advancing with me to the rescue. Italy knows them; they always appear at the hour of danger. Brave and generous companions, they have devoted their lives to their country; they will shed their last drop of blood for it, seeking no other reward than that of a pure conscience.

" 'Italy and Victor Emmanuel!' that was our battle cry when we crossed the Ticino;

it will resound into the very depths of Ætna.

"As this prophetic battle-cry re-echoes from the hills of Italy to the Tarpeian Mount, the tottering throne of tyranny will fall to pieces, and the whole country will rise like one man.

"To arms, then! Let us by one blow put an end to our chronic misfortunes. Let us show the world that this is truly the land once trodden by the great Roman race.
"G. GARIBALDI."

It is not wholly impossible but that the bitter cup he had swallowed regarding Savoy and Nice may have influenced him in espousing this most congenial distraction.

No sooner had Garbaldi unpacked his red shirt, than the whole of North Italy responded: it was the one thing needful to give direction to an impulse which was panting for a leader. Subscriptions were opened all over Italy; men came forward by thousands; transport was the only hitch. And it was wisely determined that the first expedition should be composed only of tried men, leaving the others to come after as transport might become available.

On the 5th of May Garibaldi and his followers embarked, to the number of 1067, on board two steamers, the "Lombardo" and "Piemonte," a little to the eastward of Genoa, ...

The order of assault was, with equal misfortune, changed. It was intended that the Cacciatori should lead the way, but the Squadri[4] claimed the honour of entering first under La Maza, merely preceded by the guides and three men from each company of the Cacciatori, under the Hungarian major, Tükori, as an advance-guard. After the Squadri, about 1300 strong, followed the Genoese carbineers, and the two battalions of Cacciatori. The rearguard was composed of a cloud of very irregular Sicilians.

At ten o'clock the column cheerfully advanced to the capture of Palermo, where the committee were expecting them—not so the Neapolitans. During the evening runners had arrived from Bosco, and the commandant at Monreale, announcing the retreat and dispersement of the Garibaldians, Lanza[5] ordered out the band on the Marina, and gave a supper in honour of the success; sending off a steamer to Naples to impart the joyful news. At midnight he dismissed his *convives*, the *élite* of the garrison, congratulating them on the happy despatch of their antagonists, who were at that time floundering amid the almost impassable defiles of Mezzagna, which the Sicilians had chosen for them. To add to the confusion, the guides mistook the track, which was happily discovered in time; but dawn had broken before the advance-guard entered the extensive suburbs around the gate of Termini; and instead of surprising the bridge of the Ammiragliato, which spans a watercourse on that side the town, not only were the leading files received with a sharp fire, but time was given to the Neapolitans to advance reinforcements; thanks to the "evivaing" of the Squadri, coupled with a most profligate expenditure of ammunition. As for the Squadri, they retired very sensibly and made way for the Cacciatori; but had the original plan been adhered to, Garibaldi would have been in the town without firing a shot. Meantime, the first intimation which Lanza received of his not being in full retreat on Corleone, was his aide-de-camp rushing into his bedroom—"Sir!" "What?" "Garibaldi is in the town!"

In spite of the cross-fire from the gate of St. Antonio and the troops on the Marina, the wide strategic "stradoni" or road was crossed, and the gate and barricade at the Porta di Termini carried. But it was only by a copious application of flats of swords, and every species of threat, that the Squadri could be induced to follow. A young Genoese of the carbineers, to encourage those wayward warriors, coolly took a chair and sat himself down in the centre of the street, under the cross-fire, and it had the desired effect; for when the Picciotti[6] saw that every shot did not kill, they ran the gauntlet, and even assisted in throwing up a barricade. To Tükori and the guides belong the honour of being first over the Neapolitan breastwork, but the gallant leader had his left leg shattered; otherwise the loss was wonderfully small, considering the cross-fire of guns and musketry. As the Garibaldians advanced the Squadri plucked up and followed and the Palermitans began to move wherever the Regi were driven back. It was now three o'clock, and the Castello and men-of-war commenced bombarding the lower portions of the town, which were rapidly passing into the hands of Garibaldi. At five o'clock he had almost undisputed possession of the lower half of the town, but the fire of the shipping and fort was not without great effect. Fires burst out in every direction. No spot was safe from their shells, and the wretched inhabitants began almost to repent the advent of their liberator.

Forcing his way up to the Piazza del Pretorio, in the centre of the town, where the committee were sitting, Garibaldi established his headquarters there, and, before night, had possession of the entire town, with the exception of the royal palace and its environs, and the line of communication between it and the Mole. . . .

.　.　.　.　.　.　.　.　.　.

On the 25th [of July], Count Litta Modignani arrived from Turin, bearing a letter from the King to Garibaldi, begging him to confine his operations to the island of Sicily. This was the result of an autograph letter from Napoleon III, urging the King to use all his interest to prevent Garibaldi's crossing to the main, as the King of Naples had promised Baron Brenier to grant a constitution, carry out reforms, and adopt a national Italian policy, based on a Piedmontese alliance, which the Neapolitan Cabinet, finding themselves *in extremis*,

were endeavouring to form at Turin with an ardour only equal to that with which they rejected a similar proposition made by Piedmont in last December. Piedmont, however, was already too far compromised with the revolution to recede; her own preservation had now become the first object.

Garibaldi replied, in a letter full of devotedness and affection to the King, that he could not now think of sheathing his sword until he had carried out his programme, and made him King of Italy. Count Trecchi, who is the chief confidential and oral medium between the King and Garibaldi, was likewise sent off with explanations.

.　.　.　.　.　.　.　.　.

The attitude of Piedmont is that of expectancy. Cavour has, at least for the moment, ceased to push for immediate annexation, and a thoroughly cordial understanding exists between the King and the Dictator;[7] whilst the royal squadron under Persano takes a singular interest in his movements. The expedition for the Papal States has been merely turned from its projected route, and ordered to proceed with its chief by way of Calabria, instead of breaking fresh ground, which might possibly give causes of solicitude to the eldest son of the Church;[8] and, besides, Piedmont will herself operate in that direction, and has verbally intimated that she may be at Ancona in the middle of September.

From the cheerful city of Paris, Türr, who had been invited there by Prince Napoleon, brought assurances that, whatever course the Emperor might diplomatically be obliged to pursue, he wished Italy well; and that all the Dictator had to do was to outstrip diplomacy by the theory of accomplished facts. Austria, true to her traditions, waters this her last branch of despotic influence in Southern Italy with withering counsels, and has mirrored her own apparently not far-distant disruption, so intimately blended with Italian nationality. That Austria should counsel stolid stupidity in dealing with the masses, or that Napoleon, wishing to retain the Italian question in his grasp, holding as he does all possible diplomatic threads in hand, should occasionally pull the Italian checkstring, none can be astonished; but that the paladin of non-intervention[9] should interfere, by offering gratuitous advice to the Cabinet of Turin as to what course they ought to pursue in Italian politics, must have considerably surprised the Italians, who, ere long, our diplomacy permitting, will become our stanchest modern allies.

. . . .

. . . As for Garibaldi, he was nearly devoured by the population as he advanced. Salerno was gone mad; its inhabitants could hardly realise the dream. A few short hours before, Afant de Rivera[10] were [was] lording it over them with 12,000 men, and here was their deliverer entering with half-a-dozen of his staff in a couple of open carriages, his nearest troops being sixty or seventy miles behind him.

It is almost impossible to paint with a pen this magic scene, the romantic beauty of the well-known bay, the town illuminated, *à giorno*, throngs of armed men and excited women in the streets; bands in every direction: in short, a population who had been deprived of speech from its infancy, hailing their deliverer; while he who had consecrated a life to the achievement of his sublime task, was with difficulty forcing his way through the dense masses which crowded round to obtain a glimpse of the idol of their country. Garibaldi immediately retired to rest, ordering his staff to be ready at two in the morning: of their destination there could be no doubt.

The 7th of September ought never to be erased from Neapolitan memory. A deputation of the National Guard having arrived from Naples during the night, as well as an energetic appeal from the Azione Committee—who, almost overpowered by the Cavourian party, were compelled to threaten violent measures if any further attempt was made to form a government prior to the Dictator's arrival—Garibaldi determined to enter the capital, which the King [of Naples] had left but a few hours before, in spite of its fortresses being still in the hands of the royal troops. We started in a special train (of four carriages) at half-past nine, for the capital—Garibaldi, Cosenz, and thirteen of the staff representing the national army, a few English amateurs and National Guards occupying the remaining seats. At every station the enthusiasm increased, and the roofs of the carriages became crowded with National Guards, with flags, and evergreens. The vast populations of Torre del Greco, Resina, and Portici, took complete possession of the line, and we were obliged to halt at each station, and proceed at a snail's pace, to avoid destroying those masses of human beings, in which women and children, bands, and National Guards surged to and fro in ecstatic confusion.

At Naples order was maintained in the interior of the station, but outside, the scene baffled description—horses and carriages, lazzaroni and ladies, National Guards and gendarmerie, rival committees and royalist partisans, were alike heaped together, and rendered egress apparently impossible. Sir Richard Mayne would have been distracted; however, Missori, Nullo, and two other favourite Guides led the way on rather lively horses, and Garibaldi followed in an open carriage with Cosenz, Stanietti, and Gusmarola, amid an everlasting chorus of vivas, which was kept up without intermission, until he drove into the courtyard of the Queen-mother's palace, at the foot of the Toledo.

Though nothing could have been more enthusiastic than the reception, and though houses were bedecked with the tricolor and cross of Savoy to the seventh story, the aspect of the [Neapolitan] troops, with few exceptions, in the various barracks, and especially in the Castello Nuovo, was sullen, and anything but reassuring; and more than once, as this handful of men passed under the very muzzles of the guns bearing up the different streets, I could not help thinking that Garibaldi was tempting Providence in too audacious a manner, for one wanton shot from the crowd would have brought on a general conflagration; not that it would not have been a healthy thing for the Neapolitans, who have bought their liberty so cheaply that they hardly appreciate it; but one chance ball might have condemned Italy to another decade of servitude, as with Garibaldi would, in all probability, have perished the hopes of the present generation. As fate would have it, he escaped, and was addressing the populace from the palace window before one-half of the town knew of his arrival.

.   .   .   .

In short, the game at Turin is becoming more and more apparent; the Piedmontese would create anarchy in the South in order to have a plausible pretext for action, for it has long become evident that those who aim at governing the Italians must lead, or be led by, the revolution, the system of judicious compromise fast becoming untenable. Though the Emperor Napoleon was fettered, unable to escape the consequences of that master-stroke of Italian policy, the vendition of Savoy and Nice, which alone prevented Austria's reoccupying Lombardy for the thirteenth time, there were other powers to be considered. And in order to justify in the eyes of constitutional and despotic governments the bold and righteous step Piedmont is about to make—Republicanism, the dread of every well-balanced European mind, must be introduced into this comedy. Though committing an act of revolution, Piedmont must step in as a conservative power to stay anarchy and stifle republicanism; and if they do not exist, the world must be made

to believe so. Papers relative to a mock Mazzinian movement are found in circulation at Genoa, and in the Marches. Because the high priest of republicanism has sought an asylum at Naples, to be near his old and cherished friend the Dictator, he is represented to have gone there for the purpose of fomenting republican councils, as if he and his party had not given a faithful adherence to monarchy through Garibaldi as the only possible means of accomplishing nationality. They were, doubtless, republicans still, but, like Garibaldi, they sacrifice their political convictions to the expediency of securing, before all things, Italy to the Italians. "What does it matter under what form of government we create Italy—whether under a monarchy, despotism, or a republic? Our first object is to emancipate ourselves from foreign dominion; that accomplished, if we are dissatisfied, it will then be quite time enough to elect what form of government we choose to live under."

Such are the open declarations of the republican party which is now headed by Bertani, not Mazzini, whose declining years and energies disqualify him for the post, and who, whatever doctrines he may have at times advocated, and which cannot for a moment be defended, has done more for Italy than any living man save Garibaldi. To his ceaseless and restless activity, from the day on which he enlisted Garibaldi in the cause of "Giovane Italia" at Genoa, he has kept up an agitation throughout the country, the fruits of which are this day being reaped at Naples. Of course I know you will say I am fast becoming an enthusiast. I decline this honour with thanks, well remembering the source of all information in England relative to Mazzini, at the same time declining to kick a poor devil when he is down; for where is there to be found a virtuous man without some failing, or one so wicked as to have no good quality? And though there may have been blots in his career which cannot for a moment be defended, for a principle he has remained a pauper; the last 30,000 francs Mazzini had in the world he sent the other day to Stocco to help to bring the Calabrians to Naples. I may be wrong, but I confess the pecuniary test is, in my idea, the greatest of any; and when I see a man foregoing money, and denying himself the common necessaries of life, however much I may differ from him politically or religiously, I cannot help respecting, though I may not admire him.

.   .   .   .

Owing to the interruption of the telegraph between this town [Naples] and Rome, we are generally several days behind European events; consequently, it was not until the 13th [of September] that Garibaldi heard of the reception given by the King to the deputations from Umbria and the Marches on the 11th, and of the commencement of the long-looked-for movement of the Piedmontese.

Victor Emmanuel's spirited proclamation to his soldiers, together with the memorandum addressed to foreign courts, announced to Europe his determination to assume henceforward the responsibilities of an Italian Prince, and to place himself at the head of the struggle for nationality.

On and after this memorable day the Pope's temporal power ceased to exist; . . . .

.   .   .   .

. . . the European Sphinx[11] has allowed his cardinal friends to imagine that he will never permit an heretical flow from the north—and yet here is an irruption which was to have been dammed by the army of France. To check it is hopeless, unless by appeal to its master, but he is in Algeria.

"What you do," as he said to Cialdini[12] at Chambery, before he set out, "do quickly."

Accomplished facts must be accepted; and this opportune visit to Algeria relieves the Emperor of a very difficult question, and the Pope of his temporal power. The comedy is, however, to be maintained by the withdrawal of the French minister from Turin. France being satisfied, Europe is to remain passive; though Sardinia has been the power first to transgress the glorious doctrine of non-intervention, a term which does not seem expressive of the "idea" intended to be conveyed, which means non-interference in the *internal* affairs of other powers, unless invited by the will of the people. England will be titillated with the downfall of the Papacy; Austria cannot move—she has Hungary and Venetia on her hands; Russia will be diplomatically shocked, but, at the same time, her "faith" flattered. What the other powers think does not much matter.

.   .   .   .

What with the intrigues of partisans, place-hunters, and itinerant politicos, who have the effrontery to imagine they are competent to advise him, Garibaldi has to endure what would break down any intellect, save his; his unswerving integrity alone enables him to carry out "sa tâche sublime."

And in his downright honesty, we have the secret of his unparalleled successes.

He cannot lie; and if he could, why should he?

From the hour when he dreamt "Italian Unity," he declared war to every obstacle in his path, whether priestly or princely. When he saw a Mastai Ferretti in the Papal Chair, he hailed him from the banks of the Plata; when he saw an Italian prince lead on against the Austrians, he hastened to join him. Though Europe dared not oppose a French occupation of Rome, he did. By his uncompromising hostility to oppressors, whether foreign or domestic, he revivified the nation, and inaugurated that spirit which has emancipated sixteen millions of his countrymen. Three millions more are yearning in Rome and Venetia, and because he is bold enough to avow his determination to finish his task, haggard diplomacy desires him to be more circumspect. What, in the name of heaven, has diplomacy ever done for Italy, since it condemned her to half a century of misrule at the treaty of Vienna?

Garibaldi has nothing to conceal; he declared himself, twenty-seven years since, at Genoa. He feels the anguish of Venice, and says, "Be patient—I come!"

He sees the Rome of the Popes made the hotbed of intrigue against the rising liberties of his country, and though she is bristling with French bayonets, he declares she shall be the Italian capital.

Having nothing to be ashamed of, he knocks boldly at the door, and says, what are you doing in *casa nostra*? Not that he need, or would, attack the French garrison, for their position has become, if not irksome, impossible; he only wishes them to clear out on the first opportunity. In a word, he would, and will, see the dream of his life completed in an Italy of the Italians. But there is another man working for the same end, who is conventionally prevented by the public law, as it is termed, of Europe, from telling the truth. He must work in the diplomatic groove. That man is Louis Napoleon.

Whether he is acting in his own interest or in that of Italy matters not; it is impossible to deny that he removed that Austrian incubus, from which Italy could never have emancipated herself; and when Savoy and Nice are forgotten, and the old world is eclipsed by the rising empires of the new, Napoleon will be read of as the man who quickened the national idea. Not only in Italy, but in other countries, he will be spoken of as the prime cause of that vast upheaving of nationalities which will soon obliterate many of the ancient landmarks of Europe.

.   .   .   .

On the 9th [of October] Victor Emmanuel issued his first proclamation to his future subjects, and on the 11th placed his foot on his new territory—the very day on which Garibaldi issued his decree directing the annexation vote by universal suffrage to be taken throughout the Two Sicilies, on the 21st of the month. . . .

.   .   .   .

On the 4th [of November] Garibaldi distributed the medals to the remnant of the "Glorious Thousand" who landed with him at Marsala, and the Largo del Palazzo was again chosen for this simple but thrilling ceremony. Six months since they embarked at Genoa 1067 strong, and 1007 landed in Sicily in the face of a squadron of 900 guns, and an army of 120,000 men. How they fought I have endeavoured to depict in the preceding pages; but what can speak so forcibly as the fact, that to-day but a scant half are alive to answer the muster-roll, many of them honourably scarred—their comrades are sleeping on the hard-earned fields of Calatafimi, Palermo, Melazzo, and Volturno—and their efforts were crowned yesterday when the "Plebiscite" determined by 1,303,064 votes to 10,312, that the Bourbon should be banished from these realms for ever. The national Italian idea, so much scoffed at, had swept all before it, thanks to the self-sacrifice of these immortal men, who are as worthy of their Chief as he is of the cause he represents. He rendered homage to those through whom he accomplished his mission in the following laconic terms: "It is because I knew you that I undertook with you an enterprise thought impossible by every one. I knew that with men like you I might attempt everything. This impossible work you have accomplished. But many of those who went with us are now absent—their bones are bleaching on the fields of Calatafimi and Palermo—the Montanaras, the Schiaffinis, the Tücköris: they will not, however, be forgotten. Let their families keep this testimonial of their valour as an heirloom; and you, young veterans, who have survived to receive it with your own hands, remember that all is not done yet, and that I trust and reckon on you whenever your services shall be again required. Let us begin the distribution with those who have fallen in our sacred cause."

.   .   .   .

At eleven on the 8th of November, Garibaldi waited on the King, attended by the two pro-Dictators, Pallavicini and Mordini, and formally made over the Two Sicilies—. . . .

The King, whose manner, to do him justice, is invariably kind, cordial, and affectionate to Garibaldi himself, vainly endeavoured to induce him to remain, and offered him almost unconditional powers to reorganise the army of Southern Italy. This he declined, feeling that it would bring him into constant collision with the civil and military authorities of Piedmont, and only

tend to widen that breach which it was his greatest desire to heal. . . .

In spite of his loyalty to the King, a longer residence at Naples, under the circumstances, was too much to expect from him; besides, he felt that he had yet much to do for Italy, and that it could best be accomplished by his preserving complete liberty of action, and by seeking his island repose at Caprera. As for the titles and rewards proffered by the King, they were refused, not from any want of respect to the crown, but because patriotism and honour alike counselled it.

Before daybreak the following morning he embarked in the "Washington," completely unmanned by the severance from his most faithful followers. For the British Admiral was reserved the high honour of his farewell visit in Naples; and the king-maker steamed out of the bay for his island home as morning salutes greeted the elect of the Italians. . . .

No. 55   Naples, Sicily, Umbria and the Marches Are United with Italy——17 December 1860[1]

Decree.

VICTOR EMANUEL II, King of Sardinia, of Cyprus, and of Jerusalem, &c., Duke of Savoy, and of Genoa, &c., Prince of Piedmont, &c.;

Whereas the "Plebiscito" submitted to universal suffrage in the Neapolitan Provinces convoked in the Comitia on the 21st October last;

Whereas the declaration of presentation and acknowledgment of such 'Plebiscito" ensued in Naples the 8th November last;

Whereas the law of the 3rd instant, by which the Government of the King is authorised to accept and establish by Royal Decrees the Annexation to the State of those Provinces of Central and Southern

Italy in which is manifest, by universal suffrage direct, the will to become an integral part of our Constitutional Monarchy;

Upon hearing the Council of Ministers, We have decreed and do Decree:

ART. I. That the Neapolitan Provinces shall form an integral part of the Italian State, from the date of the present Decree.

ART. II. Article LXXXII of the Statute, whereby it is established that, until the first meeting of Parliament, the public service shall be provided for by the sovereign regulations, will also be applied to the above-named Provinces until the meeting of the National Parliament; the full powers which were conferred upon our Lieutenant-General of the Neapolitan Provinces continuing in force.

We ordain that the present Decree, bearing the Seal of State, shall be inserted in the Collection of the Acts of the Government, and published in the aforesaid Provinces; commanding all whom it may concern to observe it and have it observed.

Given at Naples, 17th December, 1860.

VICTOR EMANUEL.[2]

No. 56   Victor Emmanuel II Is Proclaimed King of Italy—— 17 March 1861[1]

VICTOR EMANUEL II, King of Sardinia, Cyprus, Jerusalem, &c. The Senate and the Chamber of Deputies have approved, We have sanctioned and published as follows:

Sole Article.

King Victor Emanuel II assumes for himself and his successors the Title of King of Italy.

We order that the present, sealed with the Seal of the State, be inserted in the Collection of the Acts of Government, ordering all whom it may concern to observe it and to cause it to be observed as a Law of the State.

Done at Turin, 17th March, 1861.

VICTOR EMANUEL.

On the 30th March, 1861, the British Government recognised this Title, "acting on the principle of respecting the Independence of the Nations of Europe."

In March and April, 1861, the Grand Duke of Tuscany, the Dukes of Modena and Parma, and the Pope of Rome, protested against the Assumption of this Title by King Victor Emanuel.—Ed.

Notes

No. 37, pp. 101-106

[1] *Brit. Parliam. Papers* (1856), LXI, 97-105.
[2] In the preceeding part of his speech, Walewski had discussed "the abnormal state of things in Greece."—HNW.
[3] Should probably read "unreasonable."—HNW.
[4] This protocol was read and approved at the meeting of 14 April 1856.—HNW.

No. 38, pp. 106-110

[1] Napoleon III, Emperor of the French, *Oeuvres,* 5 vols. (Paris, 1854-69); the title of the essay, the date of its composition or publication, and page references are indicated at the end of the quotations from each essay. Translated by Herman N. Weill.
[2] "Rêveries politiques" (1832), I, 380-381, 387.
[3] "Des idées napoléoniennes" (1839), ch. v: "But où tendait l'Empereur," and ch. vii; "Con-clusion," I, 153-158, 162-163, and 169, 172.
[4] "Opinion de l'Empereur sur les rapports de la France avec les puissances de l'Europe" (1843), I, 467-470.
[5] "Des gouvernements et de leurs soutiens" (1843), II, 59-60.
[6] "La paix" (1844), II, 43-44, 46-47, 49.

No. 39, pp. 110-115

[1] *The* [London] *Times,* Friday, January 15, 1858, p. 7.
[2] This is an error (compare the last paragraph). The telegram was sent *after* midnight. See *The* [London] *Times,* January 18, 1858, p. 7.—HNW.
[3] *The* [London] *Times,* Monday, January 18, 1858, p. 7.
[4] *The* [London] *Times,* Saturday, February 27, 1858, p. 9.

5 Napoleon commuted Rudio's sentence to penal servitude for life. See *The* [London] *Times*, March 15, 1858, p. 9.–HNW.
6 *The* [London] *Times*, Wednesday, March 3, 1858, p. 9.
7 Orsini's defense counsel and a political opponent of Napoleon's.–HNW.
8 *The* [London] *Times*, Monday, March 15, 1858, p. 9.
9 "To Die for My Country."–HNW.

No. 40, pp. 116-120
1 Conte Camillo Benso di Cavour, *Il Carteggio Cavour-Nigra*, 4 vols. (Bologna, 1926-29), I, 103-114. Hereafter cited as *Il Carteggio Cavour-Nigra*. Translated by Herman N. Weill.
2 See *No. 37*, above.–HNW.

No. 41, pp. 121-123
1 *Il Carteggio Cavour-Nigra*, I, 121-124 and 135-137. Translated by Herman N. Weill.
2 This summary was enclosed with a letter from Cavour to Napoleon III, dated 2 August 1858; *ibid.*, I, 117-121.–HNW.
3 Count Nigra, Cavour's private secretary, was the principal intermediary in the secret negotiations with Napoleon III.–HNW.
4 *Il Carteggio Cavour-Nigra*, I, 135-137.

No. 42, p. 123
1 *Il Carteggio Cavour-Nigra*, I, 312-313. Translated by Herman N. Weill.
2 This treaty was predated to show that it had been signed at Turin on 12 December 1858 and at Paris on 16 December 1858. The correct dates are Turin, 24 January 1859, and Paris, 26 January 1859. See, a.o., Cavour to Nigra, (23 January [1859]), *ibid.*, I, 307, and Cavour to Villamarina, 29 January [1859], *No. 43*, below.–HNW.
3 A military and a financial convention, to become a part of the treaty of alliance, were signed on the same day (see *ibid.*, I, 313-315). They follow, in the main, the guidelines established in *Nos. 40* and *41*, above.–HNW.

No. 43, pp. 123-124
1 *Il Carteggio Cavour-Nigra*, I, 308-309. Translated by Herman N. Weill.
2 Sardinian Ambassador at Paris.–HNW.
3 Princess Clotilda.–HNW.
4 29 January 1859 fell on a Saturday. Thus the Monday here mentioned was 24 January 1859. See the note on the correct dates for

the signing of the Franco-Sardinian Alliance, *No. 42*, above.–HNW.
5 French Foreign Minister, and known to be opposed to the Franco-Sardinian Alliance.–HNW.
6 *I.e.*, an insurrection. See also Cavour to General Klapka, Turin, 29 January [1859], *ibid.*, I, 307-308.–HNW.
7 Probably should be "them" or "for them."–HNW.

No. 44, pp. 124-128
1 Josef von Paić, "Zur politischen Vorgeschichte des Feldzuges 1859. Nach offiziellen österreichischen Quellen," *Institut für Österreichische Geschichtsforschung, Wien-Mitteilungen*, XLIII (1929), 377-386, 390. Translated by Herman N. Weill.
2 Present were: the Emperor, presiding; Count Buol-Schauenstein, Foreign Minister; Baron von Bach, Minister of the Interior; Baron von Bruck, Minister of Finance; Count Grünne, first Adjutant-General; Count Nádasdy, Minister of Justice.
3 Present were: the Emperor, presiding; Buol, Bach, Bruck, Grünne, also Baron von Hess, Quartermaster-General.
4 Present were: the same as on 19 February.
5 Omissions occuring in the original text are indicated by parentheses–HNW.
6 Present were: the same as on 19 February, also: Baron von Kempen, Minister of Police, and Baron von Schlitter.
7 The possibility of a French naval attack upon Austria's Adriatic coast had been discussed in the preceding section.–HNW.
8 For the Austrian ultimatum to Sardinia, see *No. 45*, below.–HNW.
9 Present were: the Emperor, presiding; Buol, Bach, Bruck, Grünne, Hess, Schlitter.
10 The last part of this sentence is apparently a comment by Paić. However, to judge from the minutes of the preceding conferences, it would seem to me that the decision had already been reached, whether consciously or not, and that it was for war.–HNW.
11 See *No. 46*, below.–HNW.
12 The minutes end here. There follows a very short, and rather harsh, judgment of Buol by Paić.–HNW.

No. 45, pp. 128-129
1 Hertslet (ed.), *Map of Europe*, II, 1359-1360.

2 This Ultimatum was received by Sardinia on the 23rd April, 1859.–Ed.

3 For details concerning this proposed Congress, see *No. 50*, below.–HNW.

No. 46, p. 129

1 Hertslet (ed.), *Map of Europe*, II, 1361.

2 An Austrian Army crossed the Ticino on the same day (26th April), and entered Sardinian Territory.–Ed. [If the minutes reprinted in *No. 44*, above, are accurate, then the date should be 27th April.–HNW.]

No. 47, pp. 130-131

1 Hertslet (ed.), *Map of Europe*, II, 1362-1364.

No. 48, p. 132

1 Hertslet (ed.), *Map of Europe*, II, 1365-1366.

No. 49, pp. 132-133

1 Hertslet (ed.), *Map of Europe*, II, 1368-1369.

No. 50, pp. 133-135

1 Hertslet (ed.), *Map of Europe*, II, 1370-1373.

2 On 18 June 1859, Palmerston succeeded Derby as Prime Minister, and Russell succeeded Malmesbury as Foreign Secretary. Officially, British neutrality continued, but it was a benevolent neutrality favoring the Italians. See, e.g., the assistance rendered by British naval commanders to Garibaldi mentioned in *No. 54*, below.–HNW.

No. 51, pp. 135-136

1 Hertslet (ed.), *Map of Europe*, II, 1374-1375.

2 A Convention of Armistice was signed on the 8th July, 1859.–Ed.

3 Almost all the provisions of this preliminary peace were rendered obsolete by subsequent events. The major exceptions were the cessation of hostilities and the cession of Lombardy to Sardinia. For the Peace of Zürich, signed on 10 November 1859, see Hertslet (ed.), *Map of Europe*, II, 1380-1413.–HNW.

No. 52, p. 136

1 Hertslet (ed.), *Map of Europe*, II, 1416.

2 Included were: Bologna, Ferrara, Forli, Massa and Carrara, Modena, Parma, Placentia, Ravenna, and Reggio.–Ed.

3 By an identical decree, dated 22 March 1860, Tuscany was united with Sardinia. See *ibid.*, II, 1417.–HNW.

No. 53, pp. 137-138

1 Hertslet (ed.), *Map of Europe*, II, 1429-1431.

2 Ratifications exchanged at Turin, 30th March, 1860.–Ed.

No. 54, pp. 138-145

1 Commander Charles Stuart Forbes, *The Campaign of Garibaldi in the Two Sicilies: A Personal Narrative* (Edinburgh and London, 1861), pp. 15-18, 44-46, 110, 137-138, 231-234, 242-244, 259-264, 322, 336-337, 344-345.

2 Garibaldi was born in Nice, and deeply resented its cession to France.–HNW.

3 "Band of Companions-in-arms."–HNW.

4 Locally recruited followers of Garibaldi.–HNW.

5 The commander of the Neapolitan troops.–HNW.

6 *Picciotti*–youngsters composing the mass of the Squadri.

7 Garibaldi's official title.–HNW.

8 France.–HNW.

9 England.–HNW.

10 The Neapolitan commander.–HNW.

11 Napoleon III.–HNW.

12 Sardinian commander.–HNW.

No. 55, pp. 145-146

1 Hertslet (ed.), *Map of Europe*, II, 1458.

2 Sicily, Umbria, and the Marches were united with Italy by almost identical decrees of the same date. See *ibid.*, II, 1459-1461.–HNW.

No. 56, p. 146

1 Hertslet (ed.), *Map of Europe*, II, 1468.

The Unification of Germany

4

INTRODUCTION

THE UNIFICATION of Germany has sometimes been depicted as a three-act drama: Act I, the Danish War, leads inexorably to Act II, the Austro-Prussian War, which, in its turn, prepares the way for the stirring climax of Act III, the Franco-Prussian War. The playwright, producer, director, stage manager, and principal actor were, of course, all one and the same person, Otto von Bismarck. The historical reality is not quite that simple. There was drama aplenty in the unification movement, and Bismarck played an important, perhaps even an indispensable, role in it, but the analogy breaks down on at least two points: First, when the curtain rose in 1863, no one knew that this was supposed to be Act I. At the time, there was no script for the drama of unification. The only reason Bismarck took an interest in the quarrel over the Duchies was that there appeared to be the possibility that Prussia might benefit from it. His primary objective, from beginning to end, was the expansion of Prussian power and influence, and not the unification of Germany. Secondly, in its neat, causal progression from Act I to Act III, such an interpretation presupposes a prescience and a degree of control over persons and events which Bismarck would have been the first to ridicule as unrealistic and absurd. Frederick VII, Hall, Napoleon III, Gramont, Francis Joseph, Rechberg, and a host of other leading figures of the time were not marionettes dancing at the end of strings which he manipulated. No one was more keenly aware than Bismarck of the unpredictability of human reaction, of the dizzying number of alternate combinations that always exist in a complex situation, or of the sudden, sometimes completely irrational, twists and turns that events are capable of taking. His genius as a diplomat consisted precisely in being aware of these many imponderables, and, because of them, in refusing to draw up, much less follow, any master plan. The hallmark of his diplomacy was flexibility, timing, and an acute sense of the limitations of his power.

The genesis of the quarrel over the Duchies of Schleswig, Holstein, and Lauenburg was an exceedingly complex one, but it becomes more manageable if we concentrate on three major contributing factors: nationalism, the political relationship of Denmark to the Duchies, and the right of succession. The population of Holstein and Lauenburg was German, that of large parts of Schleswig, Danish. Holstein and Lauenburg were members of the German Confederation, but Schleswig was not. The Duchies were joined to Denmark only in a loose personal union through the King of Denmark. Frederick VII, who ruled in 1863, was childless. Upon his death, a dispute was bound to arise over the right of succession in the Duchies among several claimants, of whom the German Duke of Augustenburg was the most prominent one.

During the Revolutions of 1848, Danish nationalists had tried to make the Duchies an integral part of the Kingdom. This resulted in a war with members of the German Confederation. The Great Powers finally intervened, and in 1851-52, Denmark agreed to the loose personal union already mentioned. Ten years later, the wave of Danish nationalism crested once more, and the cry for the integration of the Duchies was raised again. Frederick yielded to this clamor. His March Patent of 1863 (*No. 57*) closely joined Holstein and Lauenburg to Denmark. He then ordered a new Constitution drawn up which would not only achieve the same result with regard to Schleswig, but would also settle the right of succession in his favor. Frederick died on 15 November 1863, two days after the Danish Royal Assembly had approved the new Constitution. His successor, Christian IX, had some apprehensions about signing it, but Danish nationalistic fervor had become so intense that Christian feared for his throne if he withheld his signature. On 18 November 1863, he signed the document (*No. 58*).

The March Patent had already caused an uproar in the Duchies and in Germany, but this was intensified by the November Constitution. Holstein and Lauenburg appealed to the German Diet for assistance, and on 24 December 1863, Confederate troops entered these two Duchies. The Duke of Augustenburg, who had proclaimed himself the rightful successor upon the death of Frederick, arrived in their wake one week later. The March Patent also concerned Prussia and Austria directly because it violated the Agreements of 1851-52, an interpretation in which Sir Paget, the British ambassador at Copenhagen, concurred (*No. 59*). This would have given Bismarck a

ready excuse to intervene, but he was not in the habit of acting precipitously. He spent the next several months ascertaining the attitude of the other Powers. It was only after he had persuaded Austria to join Prussia in a common front and had become convinced that neither Russia, France, nor Great Britain was likely to intervene on Denmark's side that he was ready to act. On 16 January 1864, the Austrian and Prussian ambassadors in Copenhagen presented an ultimatum to Denmark, giving her 48 hours to annul the November Constitution (*No. 60*). When the ultimatum was rejected (*No. 61*), Austro-Prussian troops, rudely jostling aside the German Confederate forces in Holstein and Lauenburg, crossed the Eider River into Schleswig (*No. 62*).

The Danes resisted stoutly, but were greatly outnumbered and forced to fall back. After the great victory at Düppel, achieved primarily by the newly reorganized Prussian army led by the brilliant strategist, Helmuth von Moltke, it was only a question of time until all of Denmark would be overrun. The war was briefly interrupted by the London Conference, but no solution to the problem of the Duchies could be found that was acceptable to all three belligerents. Shortly after hostilities were resumed, Denmark sued for peace, and, in the Treaty of Vienna (*No. 63*), ceded her rights in the Duchies to Austria and Prussia.

The victors now began to wrangle over the spoils. Bismarck had advocated Prussia's annexation of the Duchies as early as November, 1863, but William I had refused to take him seriously (*No. 64*). It took Bismarck several months to overcome his monarch's scruples. His task was greatly facilitated by Austria's inept diplomacy. Ill will between the two erstwhile allies steadily mounted. By the spring of 1865, Prussia's leading ministers and generals were so angered by what they thought was Austria's willful obstreperousness that they were ready to wrest the Duchies from Austria by force (*Nos. 65* and *66*). But Bismarck put on the brakes. A war against Austria would be considerably more hazardous than the war against Denmark had been. If he had first taken all possible diplomatic precautions then, it was even more imperative that he take them now. The dispute with Austria was temporarily patched up in the Gastein Convention (*No. 67*). Assessing the military strength of the two countries, Moltke was confident of Prussia's superiority. The task would be more difficult if the small German states were to join Austria, for this would compel Moltke to divide his forces. But the logical countermove was to have Italy join Prussia in return for Venetia, thus compelling the Austrians to divide their forces, too. However, the odds against Prussia would increase considerably if Austria were able to ally herself with any of the Great Powers.

Bismarck had nothing to fear from Russia. Although Gortschakow (see Chapter Two, above) was having some second thoughts about Austro-Russian relations, an alliance with Austria was still unthinkable. Considering the weak and indecisive role which England had played only a short time before in the Danish War, the likelihood of its armed intervention was almost as small. This left the enigmatic Emperor of the French as the major unknown factor in Bismarck's diplomatic equation. To sound out Napoleon III, Bismarck journeyed to Biarritz, in southern France. On the way, he stopped off in Paris and made a courtesy call on Drouyn de Lhuys, who was again Foreign Minister. In Biarritz, he had several interviews with Napoleon, and another conversation with the Emperor in Paris on his way back to Berlin.

What exactly transpired between the two men at these interviews is still the subject of much debate among historians. Napoleon, as usual, left no memoranda or reports. There are two key documents from Bismarck's hand, a lengthy report from Biarritz (*No. 68*) and a short telegram from Paris (*No. 69*), both sent to William I. The telegram was obviously designed to increase the Prussian monarch's ire against Austria, and, to judge from William's marginal exclamation points, it had the desired effect. In his report from Biarritz, Bismarck first summarized the conversation with Drouyn in Paris. The Foreign Minister had broached the subject of French territorial compensations in return for Prussia's annexation of the Duchies, but Bismarck had given him a noncommittal reply. At Biarritz, Napoleon, undoubtedly informed of the substance of Bismarck's conversation with Drouyn, did not press the matter. Instead, the two men talked about such vital concerns to their countries as the prevention of the spread of cholera.

This has seemed so unlikely to some historians that they have accused Bismarck of having concealed the truth. But given Bismarck's evasive reply to Drouyn, his report to William was, in all probability, accurate. The real puzzler in the affair is why Bismarck refused to negotiate on French compensations. Drouyn's question could not have taken him by surprise, for this was not the first time that the subject had been mentioned. One of Napoleon's major diplomatic objectives was a rearrangement of the territories along the left bank of the Rhine. Some of these territories belonged to Prussia and to members of the German Confederation, while there was a large French-speaking population in such areas as Luxemburg and Belgium. Napoleon's plans for these areas were rather indefinite and subject to frequent changes. He spoke vaguely of restoring the frontiers of the First Napoleonic Empire, or of France's "natural" frontiers, but if this meant the Rhine, the German territories would present a problem. Not only would it be difficult for France to acquire them, but their acquisition would also violate Napoleon's principle of nationalities. Napoleon therefore veered increasingly toward a scheme in which, following the precedent of Savoy and Nice, he would concentrate on acquiring Luxemburg and Belgium, and the German territories, together with the other small German states, would constitute a French-dominated counterweight to Prussian expansion.

Bismarck was well aware of these plans. As early as December, 1863, while he was still preparing for the Danish War, he had tried to obtain French support by hinting at Prussian acquiescence to such a territorial rearrangement (*No. 70*). By the spring of 1865, the subject had been mentioned so often that the Prussian ambassadors in London, St. Petersburg, and Paris reported that it was commonly assumed in diplomatic circles that France would agree to the Prussian annexation of the Duchies in return for Belgium (*No. 71*). Most peculiar of all, however, is that on the eve of his departure for Biarritz, Bismarck had several interviews with Béhaine, the French *chargé d'affaires* in Berlin, in which he not only freely discussed the subject of French compensations but made it unmistakably clear that he was willing to negotiate with France in the matter (*No. 72*). As a matter of fact, it was these interviews that caused Drouyn to broach the subject in the first place, for they had left the impression that such negotiations was the major purpose of Bismarck's trip. Some German historians have tried to explain this sudden about-face by insisting that Bismarck, as a good, patriotic German, would never have agreed to ceding a square inch of German territory. This thesis has been proven untenable by Professor Pflanze in the first volume of his excellent Bismarck biography, but even if it were valid, what prevented Bismarck from discussing Belgium and Luxemburg? These were not German territories, and as the case of Venetia was to prove, Bismarck had no scruples in giving away other countries' territory.

Whatever Bismarck's reasons, his trip to Biarritz must be considered a failure, for he did not obtain France's assurance that she would not intervene in the coming showdown in Germany. The threat of French intervention hung over his head like a sword of Damocles from the moment the Austro-Prussian War started. It helped to build up so much tension that it pushed him to the very brink of a nervous breakdown, and, as he himself admitted, was a significant factor in his insistence at Nikolsburg on an immediate peace with Austria (*No. 81*). It would seem that it also provides an important clue to his savage and almost irrational attitude toward the French during the Franco-Prussian War.

What about Napoleon? If he was serious about his Rhineland scheme, why did he dally with it until the outbreak of the Austro-Prussian War? The large number of diplomatic dispatches devoted to the subject leave no doubt that he was serious, but he could not force Bismarck's hand, for if he exerted too much pressure prematurely, he ran the danger that Bismarck would form an Austro-Prussian-German coalition against him. Timing was of the essence, and the best time to acquire Rhine territory was when an Austro-Prussian War was imminent or after it had started. Empress Eugénie revealed this train of thought when she remarked, somewhat indiscreetly, to Prince Metternich, son of the famous Foreign Minister and the Austrian ambassador at Paris: "A Power which can mobilize 700,000 men can always do better after or during than before a war" (*No. 75*).

There was another reason why Napoleon did not press Bismarck for compensations. His advisers, including, for instance, most military experts (*No. 73*), Drouyn (*No. 74*), and Eugénie (*No. 75*), were so strongly convinced of Austria's military superiority over Prussia that as late as 29 June 1866, four days before the Battle of Königgrätz/Sadowa, Napoleon was confidently expecting an Austrian victory (*No. 76*). In that event, the country to negotiate with over Rhine territories was Austria and not Prussia. Such negotiations were started in the spring of 1866, and their first fruit was the secret Austro-French Convention of 12 June 1866 (*No. 77*). Although its major subject was Austria's cession of Venice, point (7) of the "Additional Stipulations" referred to "territorial rearrangements," an admittedly vague phrase which was to be made more precise in later negotiations.

Bismarck's sensitive diplomatic antennae picked up the drift of this policy soon enough. Napoleon and Drouyn continued to assure the Prussian ambassador that, in case of an Austro-Prussian War, France would observe a strict neutrality (*No. 78*), but Bismarck correctly interpreted these assurances to mean that France would remain neutral only until the war had begun. Nevertheless, the decision to prepare for war with Austria was made. It was still an enormous gamble, but when you play for high stakes you must be willing to take great risks. The Italo-Prussian Alliance was signed (*No. 79*). Austria, still as proud, stubborn, and unrealistic as she had been in 1853 and 1859, then obligingly precipitated the crisis. Ignoring the Gastein Convention and insisting that Holstein was still a member of the German Confederation, she placed a motion before the Diet in Frankfurt which condemned Prussian actions in Holstein and demanded the mobilization of Confederate troops. Most of the small German states voted with Austria, and the motion was passed. The Prussian delegate thereupon announced that this was equivalent to a declaration of war, and, because it violated the Confederate Constitution, that his government considered the Confederation dissolved (*No. 80*).

The War of 1866 is one of the shortest major wars ever fought. On 3 July 1866, less than three weeks after it began, the Austrians suffered a disastrous defeat at the Battle of Königgrätz/Sadowa, and shortly thereafter, they sued for peace. Bismarck was anxious to bring the war to a speedy conclusion, but William, backed by the Prussian generals, refused to agree. A

stormy scene ensued between the King and his Minister-President, and it was only after the Crown Prince intervened on Bismarck's side that William yielded reluctantly (*No. 81*). In the preliminary Peace of Nikolsburg (*No. 82*), Austria accepted Bismarck's relatively lenient terms: she ceded Venice to Italy and her rights in the Duchies to Prussia, and agreed to the payment of an indemnity. Indemnities were also imposed upon the South German States, and they had to sign defensive alliances with Prussia (*No. 83*). It was the German states north of the Main River who had to bear the brunt of the war. Prussia annexed Hanover, Hesse-Kassel, Nassau, the city of Frankfurt, and parts of Hesse-Darmstadt outright. The remaining states were forced to join the North German Confederation, which was completely dominated by Prussia.

The astounding Prussian victory had knocked Napoleon's calculations into a cocked hat. He desperately tried to retrieve the situation by demanding some form of Rhineland compensation as a reward for French neutrality. If Bismarck is to be believed, Count Benedetti, the French ambassador, made his way through the Prussian lines and appeared beside his bed in the middle of the night of 11/12 July 1866 to open negotiations (*No. 81*). They culminated on 23 August 1866, when Benedetti handed Bismarck the draft of a treaty in which France offered to recognize Prussia's conquests in Germany in return for Prussia's assistance in the French acquisition of Belgium and Luxemburg. These territorial rearrangements were to be safeguarded by a Franco-Prussian Alliance (*No. 84*). But Napoleon had missed his opportunity, although it should be added in his defense that he was playing from a rather weak hand. For several reasons, most notably strong pacific French public opinion and unsettled internal economic and social conditions, the French army had not been mobilized. Without an army to back up Napoleon's demands, Bismarck could afford to procrastinate. Thus the only practical result of the French proposal was the abortive Luxemburg affair of 1867, another diplomatic defeat for Napoleon. Shortly after the outbreak of the Franco-Prussian War, The [London] Times published Benedetti's draft treaty, which it had obtained from Bismarck (the two versions are combined in No. 84). Its publication did not have the impact on British opinion that Bismarck thought it would, but it did help to sow suspicion against France, and thus contributed toward England's decision to remain neutral during that war.

The ostensible cause of the Franco-Prussian War was the Hohenzollern Candidacy. Spain was seeking a new king, and, in late February 1870, offered the crown to Prince Leopold of Hohenzollern-Sigmaringen, a distant relative of the King of Prussia. Bismarck claimed in his memoirs that he did not become involved in the candidacy until July, but we now have documentary evidence which shows that he not only was involved from the beginning, but played a major role in it. On 9 March 1870, he wrote a lengthy memorandum to William in which he strongly advocated Leopold's acceptance (No. 85). William was not convinced. A Hohenzollern on the Spanish throne was bound to acerbate Franco-Prussian relations, it might even lead to war. Such a risk far outweighed the benefits to Prussia. However, he was not going to pull rank on the young Prince. The decision was Leopold's alone to make. By the end of April, Leopold decided to refuse the offer, and William thought the issue was settled. But Bismarck revived it. In a letter to Charles Anthony, Leopold's father, he urged them to reconsider the matter (No. 86). Charles Anthony, apparently more ambitious than his son, persuaded Leopold to accept.

The news of Leopold's acceptance was to have been kept secret until the Spanish Cortes, waiting in hot Madrid, could elect him King of Spain, and thus present France with a fait accompli. But through an error by a code clerk in Madrid, the Cortes was adjourned prematurely, before an election could take place. When the news reached Paris, the reaction was violent (No. 87). Since 1859, the French had suffered a series of diplomatic defeats. There was the Mexican misadventure, the Polish imbroglio, the Luxemburg humiliation. Prussia, that new colossus on their frontier, was now threatening to encircle them. This was too much. On 6 July 1870, the Duke of Gramont, the newly appointed Foreign Minister, made a bellicose speech in the Chamber in which he threatened war unless the Hohenzollern Candidacy were withdrawn (No. 88). Gramont also instructed Benedetti to go to Bad Ems, where William was on vacation, and to urge the King to exert his influence on Leopold to withdraw. William agreed to do so, but Leopold was mountain-climbing somewhere in the Alps and could not be reached. Efforts were therefore concentrated on Leopold's father, and on 12 July, Charles Anthony withdrew his son's candidacy (No. 89). But the French were not satisfied with this diplomatic victory. On the evening of the 12th, Gramont sent Benedetti what came to be known as the "à tout jamais" demand (No. 90). On the morning of the 13th, Benedetti presented this demand to William while the King was taking his usual morning stroll in the park at Bad Ems, but William refused to accede to it (No. 91). On the afternoon of the 13th, Abeken, the representative of the Foreign Ministry at Ems, sent a dispatch to Bismarck in Berlin giving him an account of William's interview with Benedetti (No. 92).

Bismarck had been following these events with increasing irritation. He considered Gramont's bellicose speech of 6 July as an insult to Prussian honor, yet William, acting as his own Foreign Minister, had made matters worse by giving France the satisfaction of Leopold's withdrawal. Bismarck was in danger of losing control over Prussia's foreign policy. Abeken's dispatch from Ems gave him the unexpected opportunity to regain the initiative. As he tells the story in a famous passage in his memoirs, it reached him on the evening of the 13th in Berlin, while he was at dinner with Moltke and Roon. Professor Langer has thrown considerable doubt on the authenticity of Bismarck's dramatic account of that dinner meeting, but there can be no doubt that Bismarck revised Abeken's dispatch. By crossing out a few words here and rearranging a few sentences there, his revised version made it sound as if William had insulted Benedetti. He then ordered copies of the revised dispatch sent to the Prussian missions abroad and released to the newspapers (the two versions are given in *No. 92*). When the text of the revised Ems Dispatch became known in Paris on the 14th, the uproar was tremendous (*No. 93*), and five days later, France declared war against Prussia (*No. 94*).

After the initial battles of the Franco-Prussian War—more accurately, the Franco-German War, since all the German states joined Prussia against France—it began to appear as if this war would be as short as the War of 1866 had been. On 2 September 1870, a large French army was forced to surrender at Sedan. The most prominent prisoner was Napoleon himself (*No. 95*). Although this led to the fall of the Empire and the proclamation of the Third Republic, the French continued to resist. During the siege of Paris, the Second German Empire was founded at Versailles (*No. 96*). Ten days later, Paris capitulated. In the peace negotiations, Bismarck, who had advocated some territorial compensation along the Rhine almost from the beginning of the war (*No. 97*), insisted on the French cession of Alsace and parts of Lorraine. The preliminary peace of Versailles (*No. 98*) included these cessions, as well as an indemnity of five billion francs. When these terms were submitted to the newly elected National Assembly, some members preferred to continue the war, even against hopeless odds, rather than to pay such a price for peace, but the great majority of the representatives voted for acceptance. It is interesting to compare these terms with the conditions for peace which Gramont had in mind if France should win the war (*No. 99*).

No. 57   Frederick VII's March Patent of 1863[1]

Royal Decree.

WE, Frederick VII, etc., hereby make known. When in our gracious Patent of January 28, 1852, we expressed the intention, by a common Constitution, to unite the different portions of our Monarchy in a well-regulated whole, we were fully aware, as proved by the negotiations which preceded, that such a common Constitution would only be practicable on condition that our sovereignty in both our German Duchies, should not be more confined or

limited than by the already existing, and by us approved, Federal laws, and that the population of these Duchies would sincerely attach itself to the new administration of the State.

This expectation has not been fulfilled. ....

.   .   .   .

We have therefore graciously decided and hereby command as follows:

ART. 1. Of the soldiers called out in the Duchies of Holstein and Lauenburg, with the exception of those destined for our body-guard, an independent division of our army shall be established under the orders of our Minister for War. This corps shall be supplied with all "materiel" for complete equipment, and shall, with due regard to the military law of the German Confederation, furnish our Federal contingent. All expenses connected with the Holstein division of the army shall be defrayed from the separate finances of the Duchy of Holstein, which shall for such purpose receive a contribution from the revenue of the Duchy of Lauenburg.

ART. 2. The Duchy of Holstein shall also in future take part in those common expenses of the Monarchy which, under the heads 1-6 and 6-11, are entered in the provisional Normal Budget of February 28, 1856, for a financial period of two years, namely—

	Rix-dollars.
1. Our Civil List	1,600,000
2. Appanage of the Royal Family	706,000
3. Privy Council	106,600
4. Interest on and Reduction of the common State Debt	12,290,000

. . . .

ART. 4. The administration of the separate finances of the Duchy of Holstein shall be transferred to our ministry for the Duchy of Holstein and Lauenburg.

ART. 5. The legislative power in all common affairs, as far as regards our Duchy of Holstein, shall be exercised by us in common with the Holstein States. When such a law shall be issued by us for Holstein with the consent of the States, while a similar law cannot be, simultaneously, issued for the other portions of the Monarchy, then such measures shall be adopted as may be a necessary consequence thereof, provided the law concerns matters in which a different legislation is incompatible with the maintenance of the hitherto existing fellowship ("Falledskab") or union.

ART. 6. The provision made in Article 5 comes into operation immediately; the others only after the close of the financial year, on the 1st of April, 1864.

The detailed instructions regarding the position of the Duchy of Holstein, and of its representation to the common affairs of the Monarchy shall be laid before the Assembly of States for resolution thereon.

In the Draft of the law, which will have to be prepared, not only will the wishes expressed with respect to greater religious and civil liberty, but the necessary regulations will also be inserted with regard to extension of the right of voting, and of being elected, as also with respect to a resolving co-operation of the representation of Holstein concerning the separate finances of Holstein.

Done at our Palace of Fredensborg the 30th March, 1863, under our Royal sign-manual and arms.

(Signed)   FREDERICK R.
(*Arms.*)
(Countersigned)   C. HALL.[2]

No. 58   The Danish Constitution of 18 November 1863[1]

We, Christian the Ninth, etc.—Hereby proclaim: The Royal Assembly has resolved upon, and We, by our assent, have sanctioned, the following Constitution for the common affairs of the Kingdom of Denmark and the Duchy of Schleswig:

SEC. 1. The form of government is that of a limited monarchy. The crown is hereditary. The succession is the one established for the entire Danish Monarchy in the law of the royal succession of 31 July 1853.[2]

SEC. 9. The King has, with the limitations

noted below, supreme authority in the common affairs of the Realm, and exercises it through his ministers.

SEC. 11. The King appoints and dismisses his ministers. He determines their number and assigns them their responsibilities. Resolutions concerning legislation and government are legally validated by the King's signature and if they are countersigned by one or by several ministers. Every minister is responsible for the resolution which he has countersigned.

SEC. 15. The King declares war and concludes peace, contracts alliances and commercial treaties and dissolves them. However, he cannot cede a part of the Realm or contract an obligation which changes the existing constitutional relations without approval by the Royal Assembly.

SEC. 18. The legislative power in the common affairs of the Kingdom of Denmark and of the Duchy of Schleswig is exercised by the King together with the Royal Assembly.

The effectiveness in the Kingdom and in Schleswig of a law passed by the Royal Assembly and confirmed by the King can only be made dependent upon the acceptance of a corresponding law for another area of the law or for a single part of the country if such a provision is expressly contained in the law passed [by the Royal Assembly].[3]

SEC. 19. Common affairs are all those which are not expressly designated as separate ones for the individual parts of the country.

If a dispute should arise between the Royal Assembly and the Assembly of a part of the country as to whether an affair should be considered as a common one or as a separate one, the matter shall be taken up first by the Council of Ministers. Every minister has to there record his vote in the protocol. This shall then be submitted in a secret Council of State to the King who decides the matter. The King's decision shall be countersigned by those ministers who agree with it.

SEC. 20. The Royal Assembly consists of a *Volksthing* [Popular Assembly] and of a *Landesthing* [National Assembly].

The *Volksthing* has 130 members, of whom 101 are elected by the Kingdom and 29 by Schleswig.

The *Landesthing* consists of 83 members, of whom 52 are elected by the Kingdom, 13 by Schleswig, and 18 are appointed by the King.

SEC. 40. The resolutions of the Royal Assembly shall be composed in Danish. In the course of the debates, those members who wish to do so may use German. The protocol shall be written in both languages.

SEC. 55. The sum by which the common expenditures for the Kingdom and for Schleswig exceed the common revenues for these parts of the country shall be paid from their separate revenues, and in such a way that the Kingdom shall contribute 79.61 per cent and Schleswig 20.39 per cent. Any change in this proportional quota shall be made by law.

SEC. 65. The Royal Assembly can accept changes in this Constitution only if more than one-half of all the members of each *Thing* vote for them.

SEC. 66. This Constitution becomes effective on 1 January 1864.

Interim Provisions.

.   .   .   .

Given at our Castle of Christiansborg, 18 November 1863. By our royal signature and seal.

CHRISTIAN R.

(countersigned)

C. Hall and 7 others.

No. 59   Sir Paget's Opinion on the Legality of the March Patent—29 April 1863[1]

Sir A. Paget[2] to Earl Russell.
(Received May 4.)

Copenhagen, April 29, 1863.

My Lord,

AS the Proclamation of the King of Denmark, regulating the constitutional position of the Duchy of Holstein in the Danish monarchy, has been productive of communications from the Austrian and Prussian Governments to the Cabinet of Copenhagen, of a character which leads to the impression that the relations of peace between those Powers and Denmark may, ere long, be seriously compromised, your Lordship may, perhaps, expect from me some expression of opinion on the subject of the measures it enacts. I shall endeavour to state my views in as concise a manner as possible.

The Proclamation in question appears to me to admit of being considered in a two-fold light:

First, in what manner does it affect the material interests of the Duchy of Holstein? and

Secondly, What is its bearing upon the engagements entered into by Denmark with Austria and Prussia, in the course of the negotiations of 1851 and 1852?

In regard to the first point, ...

. . . .

In regard to the bearing of the Royal Patent of the 30th of March on the engagements of the Danish Government with Austria and Prussia, I fear that the verdict must be less favourable to the Danish Government, however much the force of circumstances may plead in favour of the necessity of having recourse to it.

It is not that the measure itself, as before stated, is a hardship upon the Duchy of Holstein, but it is impossible to deny that as a definitive arrangement, it is contrary to the stipulations entered into by the Danish Government with Austria and Prussia in 1851-52. In the course of those negotiations the Danish Government undoubtedly undertook to unite the different portions of the monarchy under one common constitution, and it is, to say the least, bad policy on the part of the Danish Government to issue a Proclamation setting forth that that basis is no longer to be adhered to. It is, as it were, throwing down the gauntlet to those two great Powers, and, as was to be expected, they have not failed to take it up.

No argument *ab inconveniente*, as your Lordship justly observes in your despatch to me of the 20th of November, "can be allowed to prevail against positive stipulations and honourable engagements," and the Danish Government was therefore bound to persist against every discouragement, and in spite of every obstacle, in its endeavours to bring about the realization of the common Constitution which had been promised. Such has been the advice which has frequently been given to the Danish Government, but it has always been met by the objection that the affairs of the country could not remain at a standstill until such time as a solution, agreeable to Holstein and to Germany, had been found. This is the argument *ab inconveniente*, but the remedy was at hand. The measures which have now been adopted by the Danish Government are, with the exception of the separation of the army, those which were collectively urged by the Representatives of England, France, Russia, and Sweden, in the month of March, 1861, as a provisional arrangement, and there is little doubt that, if the advice had then been loyally acted on, a breathing-time would have occurred in this most vexatious question, during which the Danish Government would have had ample leisure to negotiate respecting the common Constitution, either with a successful result or with that of proving to the satisfaction of Europe that success in that direction was impossible.

The first fault, therefore, committed by the Danish Government was in not following the advice of the Great Powers on the occasion alluded to, and it has certainly not been wiped out by the wisdom of their policy since that time. They have consistently rejected the counsels which have on various occasions been offered to them, and which, if they had accepted them, would at all events, have gone far to secure them the support of the non-German Powers. The proposals which they have made to the Holstein States on the basis of a common Constitution have been of so flimsy and uncircumstantial a nature that they could hardly be considered as being offered with a serious intent; and, to wind up all, they have now promulgated measures of a definitive character which, however good in themselves, go directly in the face of their previous engagements. If the same measures, with the exception of the separation of the army, had been adopted as a provisorium, they would have been in accordance with the Federal Decrees. But, promulgated as they now are, in a definitive form, they can only be considered as a decided step in the policy of separation; and, therefore, the two Great German Powers are, no doubt, fully entitled to protest, as they have already done, against the step thus taken.

.   .   .   .

I have, etc.
(Signed)   A. PAGET.

No. 60   The Austro-Prussian Ultimatum to Denmark——16 January 1864[1]

*Baron Brenner and M. de Balan
to M. Quaade.*

Copenhagen, January 16, 1864.

THE Governments of Austria and Prussia had cherished the hope that the common Constitution for Denmark and Schleswig, which was sanctioned by King Christian IX on the 18th of November last year,[2] and which it was resolved to bring into force on the 1st of January, 1864, would have been withdrawn before the present period.

This hope has not been fulfilled. On the 1st of January of this year the Constitution acquired legal force, and the incorporation of Schleswig was completed. The Danish Government has thereby broken in the most distinct manner the obligations which it contracted in the year 1852 towards the German Diet, and especially to the two German Powers, and has called into existence a state of things which cannot justly be regarded as in accordance with Treaty engagements.

The two Powers, in consequence of the position which they assumed in those negotiations, the result of which was on their recommendation accepted by the German Diet, owe it to themselves and to the Diet not to permit such a state of things.

They therefore address once more to the Danish Government the express demand to withdraw the Constitution of November 18,

1863, which is based on no principle of right, and at least to establish the *status quo ante* as the necessary preliminary condition to further negotiation.

Should the Danish Government not meet this demand the two Powers will find themselves compelled to employ such means as may be in their power for the establishment of the *status quo ante,* and the security of Schleswig from unjust incorporation with the Kingdom of Denmark.

The Undersigned, former Ministers of the two Powers, who although not formally accredited, negotiate in this case on the special commands of their Governments, are ordered to demand the withdrawal of the Constitution of November 18, last year, and if the declaration that this has been done does not reach them in the course of the 18th of this month, to quit Copenhagen.

The Undersigned, &c.

(Signed) BRENNER.
BALAN.

No. 61   Denmark Rejects the Austro-Prussian Ultimatum—— 18 January 1864[1]

M. Quaade to Baron Brenner and M. de Balan.

Copenhagen, January 18, 1864.

IN a collective note which has been delivered to the Undersigned, His Danish Majesty's Minister for Foreign Affairs, the former Ministers of Austria and Prussia have, at the special direction of their respective Courts, addressed a summons, dated the 16th instant, to His Majesty's Government to withdraw the Constitutional Law of the 18th of November, both Powers, in case of a refusal, reserving to themselves the right of employing the means at their command for re-establishing the *status quo ante.* Should the announcement on the part of His Majesty's Government that the required withdrawal has been effected not be made to the Ministers in the course of the 18th instant, the latter are directed to leave Copenhagen.

The Undersigned has felt it his duty to lay the contents of this communication before the King his most gracious Sovereign, and he is now commanded by His Majesty to make the following reply to the Ministers:—

While, on the one hand, His Majesty's Government are unwilling to enter here into any further discussion on the motive of the note, which the presumed object of the Constitution of November 18 and its incompatibility with the negotiations of 1851-52 have called forth, on the other hand they cannot, in face of the judgment thus delivered and the assertions by which it is accompanied, refrain in passing from maintaining their opposite view of the case.

As to what more immediately concerns the summons itself which has been addressed to His Majesty's Government, His Majesty the King finds himself at once unable to comply with it, since the delay fixed has not even admitted of his making the necessary preparations for effecting in a legal manner the withdrawal of the Constitution which has been objected to. Since His Majesty's Government are thus under the impossibility of complying with the summons contained in the note of the 16th instant, they must also decline all and every responsibility which may on this occasion ensue from the initiative taken by the two Great German Powers.

The Undersigned, &c.

(Signed)   G. QUAADE.

No. 62   The Beginning of the Danish War——30 January to 1 February 1864[1]

The Commander-in-Chief of the Allied Army to The Commanding General of the Royal Danish Army.

Headquarters Bordesholm. 30 January 1864.

The undersigned Royal Prussian General-Fieldmarshal and Commander-in-Chief of the united Prusso-Austrian army, Baron von Wrangel, has the honor to respectfully submit the following communication to the Commanding General of the Royal Danish troops in the Duchy of Schleswig, etc.:

Through a Note presented by the ambassadors of Prussia and Austria on 16th January 1863,[2] a copy of which the undersigned has the honor of enclosing, these two governments have called upon the Royal Danish government to annul the common constitution for the Kingdom of Denmark and the Duchy of Schleswig of 18 November 1863,[3] and thereby to re-establish the previous *status quo*.

Because this demand was rejected by the Royal Danish Minister for Foreign Affairs in the Note of 18 January,[4] and because the constitution has not been annulled in the meantime, the situation mentioned in the said Note has now occurred and the two German Powers are obliged to use the means at their disposal to re-establish the *status quo* and to ensure the rights of the Duchy of Schleswig guaranteed by treaty.

Accordingly, the undersigned has been ordered to occupy the Duchy of Schleswig with the Prussian and Austrian troops united under his command and to assume its provisional administration.

While the undersigned has the honor of respectfully submitting this information to the Commanding General, he adds the request to be informed at once whether the Commanding General has received orders to vacate the Duchy of Schleswig and to withdraw the Royal Danish troops from its territory.

He remains, etc.

(Signed)   v. WRANGEL.

The Commanding General of the Royal Danish Troops in Schleswig to General-Fieldmarshal von Wrangel.

The undersigned, who can neither acknowledge the right of the Prussian and Austrian troops to occupy any part of the Danish Empire nor the logical consequence of the content of the document enclosed with your Excellency's letter of 30 January, who, furthermore, has received instructions from his government which are the exact opposite of your Excellency's expectations, is prepared to resist any assault with the force of arms.

Schleswig, 31 January 1864.

(Signed)   CH. JULIUS DE MEZA,

Lieutanant-General.

Proclamation to the Inhabitants of the Duchy of Schleswig.

Inhabitants of the Duchy of Schleswig! Charged by His Majesty the King of Prussia, my gracious Sovereign, with the occupation of the Duchy by Prussian troops and those which His Majesty the Emperor of Austria has also been pleased to entrust to my command for this purpose, I call upon you to extend a hospitable and friendly welcome to these troops.

We are coming to protect your rights.

These rights have been injured by the common constitution for Denmark and

Schleswig, which His Majesty the King of Denmark had approved on 18 November 1863, and through which, contrary to the agreements of 1852, the Duchy has been made an integral part of the Kingdom.

The demand addressed to His Majesty the King of Denmark to dissolve this relationship was fruitless. Consequently, the governments of Prussia and of Austria have decided, for their part, to use the means at their disposal to annul the incorporation in fact and to ensure for the Duchy the rights guaranteed it by treaty by occupying it with their united forces and by assuming its provisional administration.

This administration will be exercised by civilian commissioners of the two German Powers. I call upon you to obey their decrees and to support them in their efforts to maintain law and order. The laws of the land remain in force, insofar as the safety of the troops does not make momentary and temporary exceptions inevitable.

I expect of the sense of lawfulness and circumspection of the inhabitants of the Duchy that they will refrain from all demonstrations, regardless of their political persuasion. You will convince yourselves that political agitations can only injure your legal rights, and that, in your own interest, I cannot permit them.

Our troops come as friends—you shall welcome them as friends.

(Signed)   V. WRANGEL.

No. 63   The Treaty of Vienna——30 October 1864[1]

*Reference to Preliminaries of
Peace of 1st August, 1864.*[2]

In the Name of the Most Holy and Indivisible Trinity.

HIS Majesty the King of Prussia, His Majesty the Emperor of Austria, and His Majesty the King of Denmark, have resolved to convert the Preliminaries signed on the 1st of August last into a Definitive Treaty of Peace.

To that effect, their Majesties have appointed as their Plenipotentiaries, namely:

His Majesty the King of Prussia, the Sieur Charles, Baron de Werther, Envoy Extraordinary and Minister Plenipotentiary to the Court of Austria, &c.; and

The Sieur Armand Louis de Balan, Member of the Council of State, Envoy Extraordinary and Minister Plenipotentiary, &c.;

His Majesty the Emperor of Austria, the Sieur Jean Bernard, Comte de Rechberg-Rothenlöwen, Chamberlain and Intimate Councillor, &c.; and

The Sieur Adolphe Marie, Baron de Brenner-Felsach, Envoy Extraordinary and Minister Plenipotentiary, &c.;

His Majesty the King of Denmark, the Sieur George Joaquim de Quaade, Chamberlain and Minister without Portfolio, &c.; and

The Sieur Henrik Auguste Theodore de Kauffman, Chamberlain and Colonel of the Staff, &c.;

Who have assembled at Vienna, and after having exchanged their Full Powers, found to be in good and due form, have agreed upon the following Articles:

Perpetual Peace and Friendship.

ART. I. There shall be for the future Perpetual Peace and Friendship between their Majesties the King of Prussia, and the Emperor of Austria, and His Majesty the King of Denmark, as well as between their Heirs and Successors, their States, and their respective Subjects.

Renewal of Treaties.

ART. II. All Treaties and Conventions concluded before the War between the High Contracting Parties are re-established in their vigour, in so far as they are not abrogated or modified by the tenor of the present Treaty.

Renunciation by Denmark of Rights over Duchies of Schleswig, Holstein, and Lauenburg.

ART. III. His Majesty the King of Denmark renounces all his Rights over the Duchies of Schleswig, Holstein, and Lauenburg in favour of their Majesties the King of Prussia and the Emperor of Austria, engaging to recognise the dispositions which their said Majesties shall make with reference to those Duchies.

Cession of Islands and Territories of Schleswig.

ART. IV. The Cession of the Duchy of Schleswig includes all the Islands belonging to that Duchy, as well as the Territory situated on *terra firma*.

.   .   .   .

Evacuation of Jutland.

ART. XXII. The Evacuation of Jutland by the Allied Troops shall be effected within the shortest possible delay, at latest within 3 weeks after the exchange of the Ratifications of the present Treaty.

Ratifications.

ART. XXIII. The present Treaty shall be ratified, and the Ratifications thereof shall be exchanged at Vienna within 3 weeks, or sooner if possible.

In testimony whereof the respective Plenipotentiaries have signed it, and have affixed thereto the Seal of their Arms.

Done at Vienna, the 30th day of October, in the year of Our Lord, 1864.

(L.S.) QUAADE.   (L.S.) WERTHER.
(L.S.) KAUFFMAN.   (L.S.) BALAN.
                        (L.S.) RECHBERG.
                        (L.S.) BRENNER.

Annex. Protocol relative to the Evacuation of Jutland by the Allied Troops.

[A Protocol, dated 1st April, 1865, was signed between Austria and Prussia, relative to the Indemnities, &c., to the Duke of Augustenburg.—Ed.]

No. 64   Bismarck Advocates Prussia's Annexation of the Duchies——November 1863[1]

The gradations which appeared attainable in the Danish question, every one of them meaning for the Duchies an advance to something better than the existing conditions, culminated, in my judgment, in the acquisition of the Duchies by Prussia, a view which I expressed in a council held immediately after the death of Frederick VII.[2] I reminded the King that every one of his immediate ancestors, not even excepting his brother, had won an increment of territory for the state; Frederick William IV had acquired Hohenzollern and the Jahde district; Frederick William III the Rhine province; Frederick William II, Poland; Frederick II, Silesia; Frederick William I, old Hither Pomerania; the Great Elector, Further Pomerania and Magdeburg, Minden, &c.; and I encouraged him to do likewise. This pronouncement of mine did not appear in the protocol. As Geheimrath Costenoble, who had drawn up the protocol, explained to me, when I asked him the reason of this, the King had opined that I should prefer what I blurted out not to be embedded in protocols. His Majesty seems to have imagined that I had spoken under the Bacchic influences of a *déjeuner,* and would be glad to hear no more of it. I insisted, however, upon the words being put in, and they were. While I was speaking, the Crown Prince raised his hands to heaven as if he doubted my sanity; my colleagues remained silent.

. . . .

No. 65   Minutes of the Prussian Crown Council of 29 May 1865[1]

Berlin, 29 May 1865.

In today's Crown Council, attended, by order of His Majesty, by His Royal Majesty the Crown Prince, all the ministers of state, the Chief of the General Staff of the Army, Lieutenant-General Baron von Moltke, and the Adjutant-Generals, Lieutenant-Generals Baron von Manteuffel and von Alvensleben, which convened in the local royal palace, the following was discussed:

His Majesty the King was pleased to draw attention to the general political situation resulting from the negotiations conducted until now over the future of the Elbe-Duchies, and to the serious consequences which could ensue if they took a different turn. His Majesty remarked that, from the very beginning, the Schleswig-Holstein question had only been considered from the *German,* not from the *Prussian,* viewpoint, but that, even before the Eider was crossed, in a dispatch discussed at a Crown Council and sent to Vienna on 31 January 1864, the possibility of a change in this viewpoint and in this concept was hinted at, and that the extent of the final demands to be made by Prussia as a result of the actual war would depend upon the size of Prussia's sacrifices. These sacrifices in treasure and men had far exceeded what had been anticipated at the beginning of the war. But because of them, and of the glorious days of Düppel and Alsen, the Schleswig-Holstein question had taken a turn which justified its consideration as primarily a *Prussian* question. A profound change had also occurred in public opinion, in the attitude of the nation, since those martial deeds, particularly since the victory at Alsen.

Although one had previously supported the claims of the hereditary Prince of Augustenburg, the annexation of the Duchies by Prussia was now being demanded almost unanimously by the nation, ... Now that these Prussian demands were being opposed, at least to a large degree, by envy in a large part of the small German states and by a recurrence of the old anti-Prussian Austrian policy, the question was what Prussia should demand for the future of the Duchies, whether annexation *or* only consent to the demands made so far and formulated in the published dispatch of 22 February 1865 and its enclosure—and whether even the danger of a war should not be shunned to accomplish the one or the other?

His Majesty the King wished to hear the opinion of the assembled councillors upon these questions.

The Minister-President [Bismarck] was the first to speak, and remarked:

The least that Prussia was entitled to in the Schleswig-Holstein question was the guarantee that it would not be worse off after having freed the Duchies from Danish sovereignty than it had been before, when Denmark was friendly. . . .

. . . .

Public opinion demanded complete annexation, ... If one wanted to satisfy public opinion, then one had to undertake annexation upon the danger of war on a major scale. One could think of *three* means of realizing annexation, *three* ways of accomplishing it. *First,* in case the minimal Prussian conditions were granted and a separate Schleswig-Holstein state were created. The imposition upon it of new public debts amounting to the capital sum of at least 70 to 80 million talers, the bearing of Prussian sovereignty to the population, the dichotomy between the relationships of the country with its own government and with that of Prussia and the distrust of Prussia which this would cause, would create unavoidable friction and conflict which would ultimately have to lead to actual annexation. A *second* road to annexation would exist if Prussia were to compensate the other pretenders peacefully with rich donations and thereby perhaps obtain Austria's consent to the incorporation of the Duchies. In this case, Prussia could not ask the latter to compensate it for the costs of the war, furthermore, it would have to indemnify Austria at least for the costs of the war and thus make a monetary sacrifice of almost 70 to 80 million talers, and even then only the *difference* would have been paid between *annexation* and fulfillment of the minimal conditions posed by us which, in their political value, are not worth much less. A *third* road to reach annexation would consist in the Prussian government's holding fast to the conditions it had made without allowing any changes and that it await an opportunity for martial conflict with Austria. Such a war would confront the Austrian cabinet with a serious dilemma considering Austria's political position in Italy and because it could not expect support either from Russia or from France. On the other hand, the present moment would offer Prussia better chances for a war against Austria which, in view of the Vienna Cabinet's traditional anti-Prussian policies, surely could hardly be avoided sooner or later.

But regardless of any of these considerations, as His Majesty's minister he could merely advise that the attempt be made to obtain what he had just designated as the indispensable minimal conditions and to consider a higher objective only if this attempt should fail completely. Whether His Majesty the King would not be satisfied with those conditions but would rather insist on the complete incorporation of the Duchies was a decision which His Majesty alone could make. He was convinced that none of the crown councillors would regret such a royal decision, but would rather be cheerfully prepared to assist in its execution with all their might.

Most of the other ministers of state indicated their complete agreement with the advice which the Minister-President had given to His Majesty the King. . . .

. . . .

No. 66   Moltke's Notes on the Prussian Crown Council of 29 May 1865[1]

Berlin, 29 May 1865.

Minister-President von Bismarck: there are 3 ways:

1. The minimal demands can probably be achieved peacefully, with some modifications, if the military oath of allegiance [to Prussia] is dropped.—Impose 80 to 100 millions upon the Duchies, will be considered a retreat by public opinion in Prussia.

2. Compensation to Austria and payments to the pretenders by Prussia. His Majesty does not wish territorial cessions—hence not to be followed up.

3. Outright annexation, which will probably result in war against Austria. In such a case France and Russia would presumably maintain a benevolent neutrality. Presumably war with Austria cannot be avoided sooner or later, where the policy of Prussia's suppression has already been resumed.

. . . .

The Crown Prince expresses an opposite point of view. Annexation will lead to civil war in Germany and intervention by foreign Powers. The hereditary prince's sympathies are thoroughly pro-Prussian, and he is ready to accept the Prussian conditions.

Von Bismarck protests against the assumption that a war against Austria is a civil war. If war against Austria in alliance with France is to be erased from the dictionary of diplomacy, then no Prussian policy is possible any more. Only through a war against Austria can Prussia gain something. Austria has always sought a French alliance, and even now would accept it the moment France agreed.

Count Eulenburg emphasizes the ambiguity of Augustenburg's agreements. Every single paragraph contains an escape clause.

His Majesty finally asked me, "What is the opinion of the army?"

"Personally, I am convinced that annexation is the only salutary solution for the Duchies as well as for Prussia.

"The gain is so great that one must be prepared to make considerable sacrifices for it as well as to accept the chance of war. Austria's completely justified claims should be satisfied if at all possible.[2] If that does not succeed, then the prospect of war must be held out, which one must be irrevocably determined to conduct.

"I have not ascertained the opinion of the army, but from what I know of it and from what I have heard, it is for annexation.

"I have had to ask myself, can Prussia enter into combat with Austria. It would take much too long to present all the details here, but as a result of my inquiries I can assert that, in addition to the excellence of our army, numerical superiority can also be attained at the decisive point if that part of our secondary reserves which is not [required][3] for the occupation of the fortresses which will be threatened first can also be moved into the field—otherwise not."

. . . .

Result of the conference: The unchanged retention of the once formulated demands.[4]

No. 67   The Gastein Convention——14 August 1865[1]

Reference to Treaty of 30th October, 1864.

THEIR Majesties the Emperor of Austria and the King of Prussia have become convinced that the Co-Sovereignty which has hitherto existed in the Territories ceded by Denmark in the Treaty of Peace of 30th October, 1864,[2] leads to untoward results, which at the same time endanger both the good understanding between their Governments and the Interests of the Duchies.

Their Majesties have therefore resolved for the future not to exercise in common the Rights which have accrued to them by Article III of the above-mentioned Treaty, but to divide the exercise thereof geographically until a further agreement may be made.

For this purpose His Majesty the Emperor of Austria, &c., has appointed as his Plenipotentiary, Count von Blome; the King of Prussia, &c., has appointed as his Plenipotentiary, M. von Bismarck-Schönhausen;

who, after having communicated to each other their respective Full Powers, which were found in good and due form, have agreed upon the following Articles:

Austria to administer the Duchy of Holstein, and Prussia the Duchy of Schleswig.

ART. I. The exercise of the Rights acquired in common by the High Contracting Parties, in virtue of Article III of the Vienna Treaty of Peace of 30th October, 1864, shall, without prejudice to the continuance of those rights of both Powers to the whole of both Duchies, pass to His Majesty the Emperor of Austria as regards the Duchy of Holstein, and to His Majesty the King of Prussia as regards the Duchy of Schleswig.

Proposal to be made to Diet to establish a German Fleet in Harbour of Kiel.

ART. II The High Contracting Parties will propose to the Diet the establishment of a German Fleet, and will fix upon the Harbour of Kiel as a Federal Harbour for the said Fleet.

Harbour of Kiel to be under command, &c., of Prussia.

Until the resolutions of the Diet with respect to this proposal have been carried into effect, the Ships of War of both Powers shall use this Harbour, and the Command and the Police Duties within it shall be exercised by Prussia. Prussia is entitled both to establish the necessary Fortifications opposite Friedrichsort for the protection of the entrance, and also to fit up along the Holstein bank of the inlet the Naval Establishments that are requisite in a Military Port. These Fortifications and Establishments remain likewise under Prussian command, and the Prussian marines and troops required for their Garrison and Protection may be quartered in Kiel and the neighbourhood.

Canal between the North Sea and the Baltic, through Holstein.

ART. VII. Prussia is entitled to make the Canal that is to be cut between the North Sea and the Baltic, through the Territory of Holstein, according to the result of the professional investigations undertaken by the Prussian Government.

Rights of Prussia over Construction, &c., of Canal.

In so far as this shall be the case, Prussia shall have the right to determine the direction and the dimensions of the Canal; to acquire possession of the Land necessary for carrying out the work by means of expropriation, with an indemnification to the amount of the value; to conduct the construction of the Canal; to superintend the inspection and conservation of the Canal; and to give her assent to all regulations respecting the said Canal.

.   .   .   .

Cession by Austria to Prussia of Right over Lauenburg. Indemnity to Austria for Lauenburg.

ART. IX. His Majesty the Emperor of Austria cedes to His Majesty the King of Prussia the Rights acquired in the aforementioned Vienna Treaty of Peace with respect to the Duchy of Lauenburg; and in return the Royal Prussian Government binds itself to pay to the Austrian Government the sum of 2,500,000 Danish rix-dollars, payable at Berlin in Prussian silver, 4 weeks after confirmation of the present Convention by their Majesties the Emperor of Austria and the King of Prussia.

Division of Co-Sovereignty over Holstein and Schleswig.

ART. X. The carrying into effect of the foregoing division of the Co-Sovereignty, which has been agreed upon, shall begin as soon as possible after the approval of this Convention by their Majesties the Emperor of Austria and the King of Prussia, and shall be accomplished at the latest by the 15th September.

Cessation of Joint Command.

The joint Command-in-Chief, hitherto existing, shall be dissolved on the complete Evacuation of Holstein by the Prussian troops and of Schleswig by the Austrian troops, by the 15th September, at the latest.

Exchange of Declarations.

ART. XI. The present Convention shall be approved by their Majesties the Emperor of Austria and the King of Prussia by exchanging written Declarations at their next meeting.[3]

In witness whereof both the Plenipotentiaries named at the beginning have on this day set their signatures and seals to this Convention in duplicate copy.

Done at Gastein, 14th August, 1865.

(L.S.)   G. BLOME.

(L.S.)   VON BISMARCK.

No. 68   Bismarck's Report to William I from Biarritz—— 11 October 1865[1]

Biarritz, 11th October 1865.

Since I have had no other opportunity than the mails until now, I take advantage of Count Goltz's[2] departure to respectfully report to Your Majesty on my political observations in Paris and here.

In Paris, I first paid a visit to Minister of State Rouher and found him thoroughly well disposed toward our interests, which I consider to be of particular importance because M. Rouher seems to possess the personal confidence of the Emperor to a larger degree than Drouyn de Lhuys[3] and, in any case, is more candid than the latter. He had heard that it was doubtful, since I would remain in Paris only for one day, whether I would visit with the Foreign Minister. He warmly encouraged me to do so, otherwise a personal offense given to M. Drouyn de Lhuys would make it more difficult to overcome the ill will caused by the circular of 29 August.[4] Since I had already decided to make the visit in question, I let M. Rouher, who is a personal and political opponent of Drouyn de Lhuys, take the credit for having persuaded me to do so. It seemed to me all the more

necessary to consign the incident of 29 August to oblivion after M. Rouher had left no doubt that the Emperor himself had seen and approved the circular before it was sent out.

The courtesy with which M. Drouyn de Lhuys received me shortly afterward was designed to remove any irritability over the circular. The Imperial Minister explained that the origin of this hostile declaration rested in the fear that Prussia would acquire the Duchies without incurring any obligation to France, and, strengthened by means of this new acquisition, would shortly afterward pursue a Francophobe policy. He said that Prussia derived considerable gains from France's benevolent attitude, whereas the advantages which could accrue to France from her good relations with Prussia depended upon an uncertain future. In response to my request, he sketched in greater detail the advantages which France was hoping for along the same lines as had *chargé d'affaires* Lefèbvre in comments which I reported to Your Majesty shortly before my departure from Berlin.[5] He emphatically denied having any designs upon

Prussian or German territories. I replied that we could not determine in advance the course which future history would take nor could we invent it at our pleasure, but only wait and exploit its development; we, on our part, hoped and desired that this shall occur in such a way that the naturally good relations between Prussia and France would be preserved and advanced.

In spite of the assiduous, I might say exaggerated, friendliness with which the Minister attempted to expunge the bad impression of his dispatch, I am still not fully convinced of the sincerity of his goodwill toward us, but believe the demonstration of the latter to be only the result of certain imperial instructions.

On the day after my arrival in Biarritz,[6] I was granted a special audience by the Emperor. I have already respectfully sent a telegram to Your Majesty containing the gist of the imperial remarks.[7] It was obvious that the Emperor himself sincerely wished to have been able to undo the circular of 29 August. He did not appear to know that I was aware of his previous approval of it; for he emphasized that, although he personally directed foreign policy in any situation of importance, he could not be bothered with the details of ordinary daily routine as long as he did not recognize its significance. He repeatedly rebuked the publication of the document and the precipitation with which it had been composed without previous consultation with Your Majesty's representative. It was in this way that the impact of the Gastein Convention upon Prussia's total policy had been overrated in Paris, particularly since no one could believe that a result so favorable to Prussia had not been bought with any secret concessions to Austria. The Emperor hinted, what Drouyn de Lhuys had distinctly intimated to me, that the Austrian communications, which had reached him through highly confidential channels (apparently through Her Majesty

the Empress), had strengthened the supposition of a secret coalitional understanding between the German Powers directed against France. His Majesty again asked me, with some solemnity, as a question of conscience, whether we had given Austria any guarantee concerning Venetia. I denied it with the assurance that the Emperor could be all the more certain of my sincerity since such agreements, if they were reached, would hardly remain secret for long, and I felt the necessity to retain his faith in the trustworthiness of my assurances; furthermore, I also considered an agreement impossible in the future through which we would enable Austria to start a war whenever she chose to do so and which Prussia then would be forced to join without any advantage to itself. Next, the Emperor asserted that he did not intend to launch any plans by which the European peace could be disturbed, and that M. Lefèbvre, whose reports concerning our conversations he had received, had gone farther in his disclosures than in his instructions. He said, in almost the same words in which I had expressed a similar idea to Minister Drouyn de Lhuys and which the latter had doubtlessly reported in the meantime: one must not try to create events, but let them ripen; they will not fail to occur, and then they will furnish proof that Prussia and France are the two states in Europe whose interests make them most mutually dependent, and that he would then always be ready to implement the friendship and sympathy for Prussia which animated him.—Here the Emperor continued with the question, in what way we believed we could settle the Holstein question with Austria. I replied frankly that we hoped to acquire and to retain Holstein through monetary compensation. His Majesty made no objection to this and expressly declared his agreement with the motives with which I had refuted the concern of Minister Drouyn de Lhuys over the growth of Prussian power without an equivalent for France, as I emphasized that the acquisition of the Elbe Duchies in itself would not yet be an increase in Prussia's power but, on the contrary, would tax the energies of our Fatherland in more than one direction, for the purpose of the development of our navy and of our defensive position toward the north, to a degree which would not be counterbalanced by the accession of one million inhabitants. The acquisition of the Duchies would only be earnest-money (arrhes) for the fulfilment of the task which history had imposed upon the Prussian state, and for whose further progress we would need continual friendly relations with France. It seemed to me to be in the interest of French policy to encourage Prussia's ambition in the fulfilment of national tasks; for an aspiring Prussia would always place a high value upon France's friendship, whereas a discouraged one would seek its protection in defensive alliances against France. The Emperor designated this line of reasoning as one which was completely obvious to him and with which he sympathized.

This essential content of the conversation with His Majesty was repeated in different versions during the first audience and during even lengthier talks which I later had after breakfast with the Emperor. On the latter occasion, he inquired with eager interest about the course which Your Majesty's government intends to pursue in view of the disorders in the Danubian Principalities. The prospect that these countries could some day serve to compensate Austria for Venetia was discernible in the background, particularly in view of the more precise hints which *chargé d'affaires* Lefebvre had previously given to me. I replied that so far our direct interest in the fate of the Danubian Principalities did not go beyond the safety of German trade in them, and that our participation in the possible reconstruction of those countries' future would be circumscribed by the necessity not to become involved in complications with Russia over a question of relatively little importance to us. The de-

pendability of our friendly relations with Russia and the importance of our neighborly circumstances made it our duty not to undermine the mutual confidence which has long existed between the two Courts. The Emperor appeared to do justice to the truth of these remarks.

He developed further, as Your Majesty has probably since read in the newspapers, that it is in Europe's interest to bottle up the source of contagious diseases which, as is presently the case with cholera, have their origin in pilgrimages to Mecca and which are spread to the West by returning pilgrims. His Majesty believed that dangers of this sort could be considerably reduced through common actions by the European Powers, and he expressed the hope that Prussia would be inclined to cooperate in this respect. Although the danger cannot be overlooked that, through interference in pilgrimage matters, the fanaticism of the Mohammedans could be incited and, intentionally or unintentionally, an uproar could be caused in the Middle East, I still believed that I should express the conviction, in a general way, that Your Majesty would gladly participate in any work of civilization in that direction, insofar as Prussia might be in a position to exert some influence in these distant regions. I assume that France will address an official communication on this subject to the other governments.

In accordance with my general observations, I believe that I may characterize the present mood of the local Court as one which is extremely favorable toward us. Count Goltz and Mr. von Radowitz, who begin their return-journey to Paris tomorrow, enjoy the special favor of the Empress, and are the only foreigners who are invited daily to the more intimate circles of the Imperial Court. The health of the Emperor and of the Prince Imperial is all that can be desired, except for the well-known difficulty with which the Emperor moves on foot.

No. 69   Bismarck's Telegram to William I from Paris——
3 November 1865[1]

Telegram to the Ministry of Foreign Affairs.
[deciphered]

Paris, 3 November 1865.

To be reported to His Majesty:
Audience in St. Cloud very satisfactory. No uncomfortable expectations.[a]* Repeated agreement by the Emperor with the acquisition of the Duchies through compensation to Austria. Only useful to have the annexation afterward sanctioned by some offical organ of the country. The question of possible cessions to Denmark to be left to the future depending upon events.[b] The Emperor declared, without being prodded to do so, that, in the event of conflicts in Germany, it would be impossible for him to conclude an alliance with Austria. Attempt by Prince Metternich in this direction, made prior to[c] Gastein, has been declined by him. Tomorrow dinner in my honor by Drouyn de Lhuys, for which I believe I ought to remain here. Is my return urgent to the day and hour?[d] Otherwise I would like to stay here until Sunday, in any case half a day in Hanover on the return-journey in order to see the King if possible, in any case Count Platen. Music by the 34th is having a brilliant success at every concert.

---

*Such lettered reference marks indicate marginal comments, at the end of the document.– HNW.
Marginal comments by King William I on the deciphered copy:
[a] ?
[b] ??
[c] !
[d] No, I don't think so, since F [rankfurt a.] M. stands adjourned. W. 11/3/65.–Ed.

No. 70   French Rhineland Compensations: Bismarck's
Interview with General Fleury——24 December 1863[1]

Fleury[2] to Napoleon III.
(telegram)

Berlin, 24 December 1863.

First very long interview with Mr. von Bismarck. He is satisfied with the assurances which I gave to him concerning Denmark's dispositions, but it is important that the French Cabinet emphasize the point I made in my dispatch from Copenhagen, that is to say, withdrawal of the Constitution before the 1st of January. Only under this condition will Prussia be strong enough to impose moderation upon the German Confederation, prevent a compromising conflict, even war, which now has to be avoided at any price. There must well be a subject for negotiations if one wants a congress[3] to take place.

Now to the most important part of the question. Mr. von Bismarck says that the congress must be solely confined to the affair of the Duchies. The congress, even restricted, but having to deal with general affairs, impossible. Prussia and Russia would not attend any more than Engalnd and Austria. Rather to die, says Mr. von Bismarck, than to let our possessions in

Posen be discussed. I would rather cede our Rhenish provinces! But the Minister will make an effort to have all the interested signatory[4] Powers attend this special Congress: England, Russia, Austria, etc. The reunion would take place in Paris, to please the Emperor.

This would be the first stage, the bridge over which the King could be made to cross, who is very timorous with respect to his family of princes and princesses, very sentimental with respect to Austria over the German question, still very alarmed over the question of Poland and over French opinion on this subject. Mr. von Bismarck, himself, would lose all his influence with respect to Germany if he were to separate himself from Austria in the German question.

Thus, nothing is ultimately possible if one does not first proceed with the Danish affair. Everything will depend upon this, and the situations will become visible.

As to projects of aggrandizement, of preponderance at the expense of Austria, that's understood. As to the Rhine frontiers, the word has been given. Must it be underlined?

But, to come to an agreement with the King, to form an alliance in short, there is no other way than the Danish congress.

We will yet see each other again tomorrow at 6 o'clock.

As to Russia, nothing can be done with a lot of noise, as the Emperor had thought. The reconciliation should take place of itself, by sending another ambassador to take the place of Montebello, who has lost his authority.[5]

No. 71   French Rhineland Compensations: Reports by Three Prussian Ambassadors on Belgium——9 May to 14 June 1865[1]

Count Bernstorff to King William I.

London, 9 May [1865].

In my very humble report No. 79 of the 6th of this month, I took the liberty of briefly mentioning the designs which the Emperor of the French is said to have upon several parts of Belgium. Since then, I have seen the Austrian ambassador, after his return from Paris where he spent a dozen days or so on vacation; he told me that in Paris it was believed that France had reached an understanding with Holland to divide Belgium upon King Leopold's death, and that Holland would receive the Scheldt and Antwerp, whereas France would take the Walloon part of the Kingdom. When I observed to Count Apponyi that the rumor of a similar understanding between the Courts of Paris and The Hague

had circulated before, a couple of years ago, and that, if my memory served me, a Frankfurt newspaper had given some rather curious details in revealing this secret, he replied that he had not heard anyone talk about it until now, but that in Paris the plan was considered as a new one. He added, however, that he failed to see how such a project could be executed without bringing about a general war once the Duke de Brabant, who has now returned to Brussels, should have mounted the throne and have been recognized by the other Powers.

Those who believe in these fancies on the Emperor Napoleon's part think though that it would not be by a sudden declaration or a taking of possession without any other pretext that the thing would be done, but that, when the wise and firm hand which has ruled Belgium until now shall some day be missing, disorders will be fomented and a cell of malcontents and revolutionaries will be organized in Brussels who would end up demanding annexation to France. It is claimed that there is no dearth of such people, and that it is only the attachment full of respect which the country in general harbors for the person of King Leopold which still holds them back and which prevents them from risking revolutionary attempts while His Majesty is still alive.[2]

Baron von Magnus to Count Bismarck.

St. Petersburg, 24 May 1865.

. . . that the opinion has also recently been expressed to me in local official circles that the Emperor of the French, in view of the apparently shortly to be expected demise of King Leopold, is preparing to take possession of all or part of the Belgian inheritance.

It is believed here that these French projects are connected with the future solution of the Schleswig-Holstein question, and it is hinted that Belgium would be the price for which France would let the annexation of the Elbe Duchies to Prussia take place.

I have heard this view expressed by a person whose political arguments usually reflect the opinions of Prince Gortschakoff.[3] But I have not been able to ascertain whether it is based upon possible diplomatic reports.

Even though Your Excellency has probably been informed by a competent source of the opinion which is attributed to King Leopold in this regard, I still consider it my duty to very obediently indicate to Your Lordship that, already some time ago, communications were forwarded to me from a very competent Belgian source, but in a very confidential and private manner, according to whose content the royal Belgian Court carries the conviction that the idea of an expansion of France at Belgium's expense, as an equivalent for the

definitive annexation to be effected of the Elbe Duchies to Prussia, had already been the subject of discussions in the autumn of last year, at the time of Your Excellency's presence in Paris, and that on this occasion Your Lordship had not shown himself averse to those French plans.

Count Goltz to Count Bismarck.

Paris, 14 June 1865.

. . . I had the impression that an old rumor had been resurrected and placed in circulation on the part of Austrian diplomacy with the intention of drawing the Royal government's attention to the dangers of a separation from Austria. . . .

Considering the delicate nature of the subject, I have refrained from making any inquiries, particularly with Prince Metternich[4] and have confined myself to remarking jokingly to the ambassador of the Netherlands that the story is being told that France and Holland wanted to divide Belgium between them. Mr. Lightenvelt commented that the Dutch were glad they had nothing more in common with the Belgians, but he remarked, however, in the course of the conversation, that the Flemish language, which predominates in northern Belgium, is almost identical with the Dutch language. The Dutch Ambassador's remarks gave me the impression that an idea of the indicated kind had been expressed years ago, perhaps during the visit here by the Queen of Holland, that even Mr. Lightenvelt himself would consider the combination in question as natural, but that the project has not recently been the subject of diplomatic negotiations, even less that it should have led the latter to an agreement.

If now, according to the report by Mr. von Magnus, that project is connected with the eventuality of an annexation of the Elbe Duchies to Prussia, then this convinces me all the more of the accuracy of my previous conjecture concerning the origin and the tendency of the rumor.

As Your Excellency will kindly recall, I have already been assured repeatedly here for some time that France would demand no compensation whatsoever for the annexation of the Elbe Duchies by Prussia as long as it took place under certain conditions, and that even if, in view of possibly more extensive acquisitions by Prussia, compensations were mentioned, then hints were made about the Bavarian Palatinate, about Saarbrücken, about a part of Luxemburg, about the secession of the Dutch part of Limburg from the German Confederation, but the name of Belgium was never pronounced.

This does not preclude that one would welcome here the eventuality of an internal movement in Belgium and of a voluntary union of the population of a part of the country taking place as a consequence, and that perhaps one considers the annexation of the Elbe Duchies by Prussia useful to facilitate such a result. But I am convinced that an agreement with Holland to this effect does not exist, and also believe that such an eventuality has become more remote since the French government does not any more possess, to the same degree as it did earlier, the sympathy of the clerical parties which so substantially facilitated its annexation of Savoy.

No. 72   French Rhineland Compensations: Bismarck's Interviews with Behaine——12 to 30 September 1865[1]

Lefèbvre de Béhaine[2] *to Drouyn de Lhuys.*[3]

Berlin, 12 September 1865.

The Minister-President [Bismarck] kindly consented to give me information about the new state of affairs inaugurated by the Gastein Convention in Germany and in the Duchies which differs in a very marked fashion from that furnished to Your Excellency by Count von Goltz.[4] . . .

As for himself, he is fully aware that the Gastein Convention is only a first step, a very important one, taken by Prussia on a road which must lead it not only to the complete annexation of the two Duchies, but also to the triumph of his projects of hegemony. He is confident that Kiel will never become a Confederate port; . . . As to several other points, characterized even now by an obscurity which he does not seek to dissemble, the Minister-President expresses the hope that they will be regulated at an opportune moment, to the exclusive satisfaction of Prussia: he even went so far as to say that the ambiguity of certain stipulations had been, on his part, the result of calculation. I have already had the honor to point out to Your Excellency how easily the wording of the articles concerning the postal system, the telegraph, could give rise to serious difficulties: they hardly frighten the Cabinet of Berlin, which holds them in reserve to complete and to emphasize the success which it has won over Austria.

.   .   .   .

In developing for me the ideas whose general effect I have just summarized, Mr. von Bismark's purpose was to demonstrate to me the facility with which he could create new causes of conflict with Austria at such a time as the general state of affairs in Europe would permit Prussia to follow an even more decisive foreign policy.

.   .   .   .

Lefèbvre de Béhaine to Drouyn de Lhuys.

Berlin, 14 September 1865.

I have given Your Excellency an account

in another dispatch[5] of the information which I have received from Mr. von Bismarck concerning the consequences which the Gastein Convention must have for Germany; it remains for me to acquaint you, in their approximate textual sense, with the ideas which the Minister-President expressed to me on the position which Prussia wishes to take in relation to France.

According to him, we were absolutely mistaken both over the significance and over the real import of the arrangements ratified on 21 August at Salzburg. He sees therein a success for the government of the Emperor; the Cabinet of Berlin does not forget, will never forget, that the revenge gained so fortunately for the defeat suffered at Olmütz fourteen years ago can only inaugurate a fruitful policy for Prussia under the condition that the royal government shall be authorized to count, on the part of the Cabinet of the Tuileries, upon a good will without which one would soon sink here into impotence.

I replied that nothing had prepared us for a development in which great astonishment replaced in our minds the sentiment of calmness and of benevolent confidence which had animated us for the past six months.

Furthermore, what would be the consequences, from the point of view of the general interest of Europe, of the new successes which the Minister-President himself was disclosing at this time? Obtained by means of transactions which Austria would not be in a position to repel, could these successes not affect the equilibrium of the continent at the same time that they must profoundly disturb the conditions of existence of the Germanic Confederation? Repeating, then, what Count von Eulenburg[6] had told me, Mr. von Bismarck assured me that Prussia did not aspire to extend itself beyond the line of the Main River, that neither he nor the King thought of attacking the independence of southern Germany, and that they could not see anything of a

nature to disturb us. I reminded him that, if this important transformation took place at our doorstep with the agreement of Austria, we would have reason to fear that it would lead to a solidarity between the Cabinets of Vienna and of Berlin which would prejudice our moral influence, and the legitimate tendencies of governments whose destinies are more closely tied to those of France.

The Minister-President then declared, with a distinctness which left no room for doubt, that Prussia could not, it is true, go to war against Austria in spite of her, but that the concessions which the Cabinet of Berlin would obtain would never be paid for by him at the price of such a compromising solidarity.

He added that he admitted, moreover, that he even wished, that we, on our part, would want to give our policy a better impetus by seeking increases in territory and in influence in the sphere of action which the similarity of language and of race assigns to us; Prussia would take no umbrage whatsoever thereat, it would proceed in the same way in relation to Italy, and, as anxious as he is to maintain the integrity of Federal territory, King William would not consider himself personally responsible for the consequences of a war into which the states of southern Germany would let themselves be led in Austria's wake.

I asked the minister if I should transmit these words to you, and he did not manifest any desire that I attenuate their impact in any way.

Would Your Excellency permit me to sum up before finishing my account of the impression which this interview with Mr. von Bismarck had upon me? He is rather well aware of the extreme attention with which we must envisage the more or less imminent realization of his audacious projects. He would be prepared, not to offer us, but to let us take, compensations; in any event, he is too prudent, too adroit, to sacrifice the eventual concurrence of our alliance to a Platonic cult for reactionary principles from which he knows we are far removed, but which he is satisfied to see prevail in the interior. Finally, he is constantly pre-occupied with the prospect of a grave crisis occurring in Europe; he desires it, seeing in it a means of assuring his country a benefit which he does not believe would be too dearly bought by facilitating, within certain limits, considerable advantages and compensations to Italy and to France.

Mr. von Bismarck will accompany the King to Merseburg, and will attend, at the same time as His Majesty, the fall maneuvers. He will return to Berlin on the 23rd, and intends to travel to Biarritz at the end of this month. He wishes to be received by the Emperor, and to talk with Your Excellency on his passage through Paris.

Lefebvre de Béhaine to Drouyn de Lhuys.

Berlin, 27 September 1865.

. . . .

With great affability and a good grace, Mr. von Bismarck undertook to satisfy my curiosity. After having been careful to tell me that our conversation would henceforth be of an exclusively academic nature, he conceded that, if he risked a crisis in order to obtain the aggrandizements of territory and of influence which he earnestly desires for his country, France could not withdraw into an absolute neutrality without compromising the rank which she intended to maintain. . . .

Count von Bismarck then opened an atlas which was lying on his desk, and he began by studying with me the map of Schleswig; with a pencil, he drew for me a line with which Prussia would be satisfied as a frontier. . . .

The Minister-President continued to turn the pages of his atlas, and, after having thrown a rapid glance at Wallachia, towards which Austria should, he added, let herself

be carried with the drift of the current of the Danube, he examined with particular care the configuration of the Italian peninsula. . . .

These were some of the combinations whose accomplishment France and Prussia could, if such should be the case, seek to pursue. The Cabinet of Berlin, however, would be liable, in proceeding in this manner, to displease Russia, which is always concerned about its interests along the Danube; it was necessary, therefore, that France's friendship should rest upon a solid foundation, and that the government of the Emperor, to whom Prussia would voluntarily recognize the right to extend itself eventually "wheresoever French is spoken in the world," should consent to guarantee Prussia with a constant good will against the dangers which would menace it from another side.

. . . .

Lefèbvre de Béhaine to Drouyn de Lhuys.

Berlin, 30 September 1865.

As I have just informed Your Excellency by telegraph, Count von Bismarck leaves today for Biarritz. I took leave of him yesterday evening. He told me that, pressed by a lack of time, he could stay in Paris only for one day, Monday, but that he would not fail to call upon Your Excellency; . . . .

I told him that I was pleased to think that he would soon, in conversing with Your Excellency, enable the government of the Emperor to acquaint itself even more completely with his views concerning all the questions about which he had spoken to me since his return from Baden; I added that I had given Your Excellency an exact account of everything he had said, and that I did not even believe it necessary for me to abstain from transmitting to you an analysis of that one of our conversations which had been of a purely academic nature. Count von Bismarck is not the kind of man to recoil from the responsibility which he assumes in expressing certain ideas, and my declaration did not startle him at all. He merely replied that there were some subjects which were fascinating, that he

made no pretense of acting "in the name of God," and that he was always of the opinion that one had to await "the hour of the tide," but that one had to know how to profit from it. . . .

.   .   .   .

No. 73   French Opinion on Austrian vs. Prussian Military Strength: Military Opinion

Marshal Canrobert.[1]

.   .   .   .

Facing a war which was becoming inevitable, public opinion wished above all that France should not become involved in it; in the second place, it was—in spite of almost all the newspapers and reviews, bought by Prussia and by Italy—rather favorable to Austria.

Besides, there was a general belief in the victory of the latter Power. Except for General Bourbaki, who had attended the military maneuvers at Spandau two years earlier, and a few officers, like Colonels de Berckheim, Février, and Commander de Clermont-Tonnerre, the military *attaché* at Berlin, military circles were not aware of the organization and the excellence of the Prussian army.

At the general headquarters of the camp at Châlons, where the Guards were assembled, the respective chances of the two adversaries were discussed, and *fun* was made of Prussia's national-guard army: "Yes, yes, make fun of it," repeated General Bourbaki, "this army of notaries and of opticians, well, it will march right to Vienna without any trouble at all."

The Emperor, as inscrutable as ever, did not reveal his opinion about the valor of the future belligerents any more than his projects; it is probable, however, that at this

moment (May 1866) he believed in the victory of the Prussian army, which he had studied in his prison cell at Ham and for which he professed great admiration.

A fortuitous circumstance, however, came to change his conviction. General Desvaux, who had just traveled through Moravia, Bohemia, and Venetia, who had encountered the principal Austrian generals and had witnessed, at Ollmütz, the first concentric movements of the Austrian troops, returned to Paris.

Everybody wanted to have his opinion. Having known him for many years, Marshal Canrobert invited him several times to dinner at his townhouse on Place Vendôme, and each time the traveller praised the Austrian army highly. It was an entirely different army from the one he had seen in 1859. The officers were now energetic and well instructed, and the soldiers had absolute confidence in them.

This evaluation, coming from a man known for his lack of passion and his reserve, made an impression upon all those present, [although] the Marshal could not help but ask him: "Why is it that, after having been in Austria, you did not also go to Prussia, you would have then known the two adversaries and you would have been able to compare them?"

General Desvaux's remarks, passed from mouth to mouth, finally reached the ear of the Emperor, who asked for him. Three times General Desvaux was so affirmative in his account that he upset Napoleon III, caused him to doubt a Prussian victory, and led him to believe in any case in a prolonged struggle—six months, perhaps a year!

The Emperor then negotiated secretly with Austria to assure Venice to Italy, even in case of defeat; but, in return, he demanded nothing for France.

Despite the fears of war, the balls and parties did not discontinue at all in the spring of 1866. The Emperor and Empress held great receptions every week at the Tuileries, and intimate parties on Mondays where, as usual, one saw many beautiful women, especially foreigners; among the latter were two recent arrivals in Paris, to whom the Emperor payed particular attention: . . . .

. . . .

Marshal Randon.[2, 3]

. . . the reputation of the Austrian troops was such, and the tenacity, of which they had, in the past, given so many memorable proofs, was so well established, that diplomats and generals did not foresee, however vigorous the struggle would be, a defeat like Sadowa, followed by a peace treaty resembling the one of Prague.

. . . .

No. 74   French Opinion on Austrian vs. Prussian Military Strength: Drouyn[1]

Count Goltz[2] *to Bismarck.*

CONFIDENTIAL.

Paris, 18 May 1866.

(Hostile attitude of *La France* toward Prussian foreign policy. The Emperor is said to have disapproved of this attitude, and thereupon Drouyn de Lhuys is said to have asked Senator Viscount de la Gueronnière, the editor of *La France,* to see him and to have told him the following):

. . . The objective of French foreign policy had been, not exactly a war, but certainly a rupture of the alliance between Prussia and Austria. Events now threatened to push matters beyond that. The Emperor formerly strove for war, he (the Minister) only for a rupture. Their positions were now reversed, he (Drouyn de Lhuys) more warlike than the Emperor, perhaps the most warlike man in France. For a war holds out the prospect of great, perhaps greater, advantages for the latter than a mere rupture. In any event, it would lead to the weakening of Germany. . . . France would not tolerate the centralization of Germany under Prussian leadership. Moreover, the news from Berlin about the mood there sounded very gloomy; there were many symptoms throughout the land of an approaching revolution; according to all military information, the Prussian army would be defeated by the Austrian army as it had never been defeated before (this opinion prevails here generally, even in military circles, therefore its utterance by Drouyn de Lhuys does not deserve any special attention). . . .

No. 75   French Opinion on Austrian vs. Prussian Military
Strength: Empress Eugenie[1]

Prince Metternich[2] to Count Mensdorff.[3]

Paris, 16 May 1866.

The Empress seems to me to have lifted a corner of the veil which covers the plans of her august husband;—if what she has been kind enough to reveal in my presence, of the knowledge that she has of the Emperor's intentions, is true—we should hardly have to fear them. What I believe I am certain of is that, if the Emperor intended the humiliation of Austria and if the Empress knew about it, she would not take it upon herself to receive me and to talk openly with me, as she continues to do.

Our conversations reveal, on her part, such confidence in the success of our arms and such abandon on the subject of even the most delicate points that I could never believe that, if this be a double or triple game, it would be directed exclusively against us.

I told her in the evening of the day before yesterday:

"I have the feeling, Madame, of a man who, involved by duty and by patriotism in the events of the day, understands nothing, but nothing at all, about the situation.

How could Mr. von Bismarck have gone as far as he has without being certain of your support?

How could Italy think for an instant of risking to lose forever the hope of obtaining Venetia by attacking us without the certainty of seeing you come to her aid?

Finally, how could France, which today admires the patriotic attitude of our people and which keeps an exact count of the brave regiments that we shall place on the line, let us go to war without seeking to ally herself with us in future questions of such importance?

If I did not see that, among the French public, in the army, and even at the Tuileries the chances of our success were being predicted, I would understand your indifference, but in admitting that we could defeat our enemies, why do you not seek to make sure of us and to avert probabilities contrary to your interests in Germany and in Italy which our successes could bring about!"

The Empress, not wanting to admit the unquestionable justice of my arguments, replied:

"A Power which can mobilize 700,000 men can always do better after or during than before a war."

I did not quite understand what she was trying to say, ...

.   .   .   .

No. 76   French Opinion on Austrian vs. Prussian Military Strength: Napoleon III[1]

Baron Wendland[2] to Ludwig II.[3]

[*Paris*], *17 August 1866.*

. . . That Emperor Napoleon expected Austria's victory over Prussia is evident from a conversation which he had on June 10th with the resident Russian ambassador, on the occasion of the publication of his letter to Mr. Drouyn de Lhuys. His Majesty explained to Baron Budberg in great detail the reasons why the Austrian army must, in all probability, defeat the Prussian army, and when the ambassador emphasized the excellence of the Prussian artillery in particular, the Emperor replied: "But cannon hardly fire by themselves, they need soldiers, and what I said about the difference of the latter in the two armies also must have an effect upon the result which the artillery will be capable of achieving." . . .

Prince Metternich to Count Mensdorff.

SECRET.

Paris, 29 June 1866.

I gave Emperor Napoleon the letter which our august master addressed to him on the 24th of this month.

.   .   .   .

After this conversation, the Emperor led me over to his large map of Germany which was covered with pins colored for Austria and Prussia.

.   .   .   .

His Majesty then talked to me about General Benedek,[4] and told me that the confidence which our army had in him was shared by the French army. "Thus," the Emperor said to me, "during the war in Italy, every time we knew that we were facing Benedek, we took cover and the greatest precautions as at Melegnano.

If he knows how to maneuver with 200,000 men as well as he did with 30,000, he is the greatest general of the moment."

.   .   .   .

Prince Metternich to Count Mensdorff.

Paris, 29 June 1866.

My most recent conversations with the Emperor and Drouyn de Lhuys have proven to me that, in spite of the efforts of Prince Napoleon[5] and of the Prusso-Italians,[6] no demonstration at all will be made in favor of the one or the other. . . .

I have the Emperor's word that he does not intend to form an observation corps in the south, that he will not stop our advance, that he will not intervene diplomatically, and that he will give us timely notice of everything that will be necessary to our government.

No. 77 The Austro-French Convention of 12 June 1866[1]

Their Majesties, the Emperor of Austria, King of Hungary and of Bohemia, and the Emperor of the French, having judged it appropriate to conclude a secret convention in view of the events which could arise in Europe, have named as their plenipotentiaries for this purpose:

His Majesty, the Emperor of Austria, etc., Count von Mensdorff-Pouilly, etc.,

and His Majesty, the Emperor of the French, Duke de Gramont, etc.,

Who, after having exchanged their full powers found to be in good and due form, have agreed upon the following articles:

ARTICLE I

If war breaks out in Germany, the French government pledges to the Austrian government to preserve an absolute neutrality and to bend every effort to obtain the same attitude on the part of Italy.

ARTICLE II

If the fortunes of war favor Austria in Germany, she pledges to cede Venetia to the French government at the moment when she shall conclude peace. If the fortunes of war favor [her] in Italy, she pledges not to change the *status quo ante bellum* in this kingdom, unless an understanding [exists] with France.

ARTICLE III

If the events of the war should change the relations of the German Powers among themselves, the Austrian government pledges to reach an understanding with the French government before sanctioning territorial re-arrangements which would be of a nature to upset the European equilibrium.

ARTICLE IV

The present convention shall be ratified, and the ratifications of it exchanged at Vienna, with the shortest delay possible.[2]

In faith of which the respective plenipotentiaries have signed it and have affixed to it their armorial seals.

Done in duplicate at Vienna on the 12th day of June, 1866.

(s.) MENSDORFF.   (s.) GRAMONT.

ADDITIONAL NOTE

annexed to the Secret Convention between Austria and France signed on 12 June 1866.

In deciding, with a common accord, the terms of the secret convention, signed on the 12th of this month, the undersigned have summed up, in an additional note, certain explications destined to state precisely the scope of the obligations contracted on both sides and to regulate partly the method of their execution. This additional note, whose text follows, constitutes one of the essential elements of the negotiation and of the convention mentioned above, with several of its clauses designed to become a part of the treaty regulating the eventual cession of Venetia.

(1)[3]

.   .   .   .

(6) If the fortunes of war favor Austria in Germany, the French government shall sanction all increases of territory conquered by Austria, provided that they should not be of a nature to upset the equilibrium of Europe by establishing an Austrian hegemony which would unite Germany under a single authority.

(7) In case of territorial re-arrangements, the Austrian government, reserving the

rights of sovereignty of the princes of the
Imperial House who have been dispossessed,
shall be able to demand compensations for
them everywhere else but in Italy.

Done in duplicate at Vienna on the 12th
day of June, 1866.

(s.)   MENSDORFF.   (s.)   GRAMONT.

No. 78   France Assures Prussia of Her Neutrality in the Coming Austro-Prussian War——17 February 1866[1]

Count Goltz to Bismarck.

CONFIDENTIAL

Paris, 17 February 1866.

Before my departure for Berlin, I thought
it incumbent upon me to ascertain repeatedly the posture which France would assume in the event of an armed conflict
between the two major German Powers.

The result of my confidential inquiries is
quite satisfactory.

Only the day before yesterday, Mr.
Drouyn de Lhuys told me that the attitude
of the Imperial government had not changed
since the month of August. France would
remain neutral in the event indicated. She
did not object to the annexation of the
Duchies by the Prussian monarchy. If,
thereby, more or less of an allowance could
be made at the same time for what he called
"our philosophical principles," then the
French government would demonstrate its
sympathetic posture all the more clearly.
French interests were not directly concerned in the question of the Elbe Duchies.
If the struggle should take on larger dimensions and develop in a direction which
would touch upon those interests, then the
Emperor would always be ready to reach an
understanding with us. "We would," said
the Minister, "accept your confidential communications, and treat them with the greatest discretion; we would reply to them, and
we would rely upon an equal discretion on
your part; and I do not doubt that we
would reach an agreement."

Even more candid was the language of
the Emperor, who received me yesterday
afternoon. . . .

"I beg you to tell the King that he can
always count upon my friendship. In the
event of an armed conflict between Prussia
and Austria, I shall maintain the most absolute neutrality. But I do not need to say
toward which side my sympathies shall lean.
I desire the reunion of the Duchies with
Prussia. This is, I believe, in conformance
with the tendencies of the times in which
we live, and it is always useful that military
movements should be supported by public
opinion. If, by this solution, you could, at
the same time, make allowance for certain
principles, I would applaud it twice as
much. Even if the struggle should take on
dimensions which there is no way of foreseeing today, I am convinced that I could
always reach an understanding with Prussia, whose interests are, in a great number
of questions, identical with those of France,
whereas I do not see any ground which I
could ever share in common with Austria.
If you read in some newspapers, even semi-
official ones, about projects of an Austro-
French understanding, do not pay any attention to them. One cannot prevent these
people from talking politics. Even though
this one or that one of my ministers should
express himself in this sense, this would not
mean anything. I am the only one who
knows what the foreign policy of France
shall be,—I and, of course, my Minister of
Foreign Affairs."

.   .   .   .

No. 79   The Prussian Alliance with Italy——8 April 1866[1]

. . . .

The document was worded as follows:[2]—

"Their Majesties, the King of Prussia and the King of Italy, inspired by the desire to strengthen the guaranties of general peace, and in consideration of the needs and justifiable aspirations of their respective nations, have appointed as their plenipotentiaries, and provided with instructions concerning the wording of the Articles of an Offensive and Defensive Alliance, the following persons. [The names are given here.]

ART. I. Friendship and alliance are to be maintained between His Majesty the King of Prussia, and His Majesty the King of Italy.

ART. II. If the negotiations His Majesty the King of Prussia has opened with the other German Governments concerning certain reforms of the Confederate Constitution, which are demanded by the needs of the German Nation, shall fail, and in consequence thereof His Majesty be forced to take up arms in order to give effect to his proposals, then His Majesty the King of Italy, after Prussia has taken the initiative, and so soon as he is made aware of that fact, shall, in virtue of this Treaty, immediately declare war against Austria.

ART. III. From that moment the war shall be carried on by both their Majesties with all the powers that Providence has placed at their disposal; and neither Italy nor Prussia shall conclude either peace or armistice without consent of the other.

ART. IV. This consent may not be withheld, when Austria shall have expressed her willingness to cede to Italy the Lombardo-Venetian kingdom and to Prussia Austrian territory that shall be equivalent in population to the above-mentioned kingdom. [Concerning this point, it was orally explained, that, instead of such territorial acquisitions, Prussia intended to require certain corresponding concessions in the German Question.][3]

ART. V. This treaty loses its validity three months after being signed, unless the conditions mentioned in Article II shall have been fulfilled, namely, that Prussia shall have declared war upon Austria.

ART. VI. If the Austrian fleet, which is now being equipped, shall have quitted the Adriatic Sea before the declaration of war, then shall His Majesty the King of Italy send a sufficient number of ships to the Baltic Sea, which shall take up their station there in order to be ready to unite with the Prussian fleet at the outbreak of hostilities."

Then followed the signatures, and also a protocol in which both Powers pledged themselves to keep secret both the contents and the existence of this treaty.

. . . .

No. 80 Prussian Declaration on the Causes of War with Austria and the Dissolution of the German Confederation——14 June 1866[1]

Frankfort, 14th June, 1866.

ALTHOUGH the Envoy had, in the name of his exalted Government, protested against the Austrian motion, the Federal Assembly has nevertheless proceeded to a Vote contrary to that Protest.

The Envoy has now to fulfill the serious duty of making known to the High Assembly the resolutions which his exalted Government, after the Vote which has just taken place, considers imposed upon it for the safety of the rights and interests of the Prussian Monarchy, and of its position in Germany.

The presentation of the motion of the Austrian Government constitutes of itself, in the firm conviction of the Royal Government, an act indubitably in manifest contradiction with the Federal Constitution, an act which Prussia must, in consequence, consider as a dissolution of the Confederation.

The Federal Law only recognises for the Confederated States measures of execution for which forms and conditions previously determined upon are prescribed; the movement of a Federal Army against a Confederate State is as foreign to the Military Federal Constitution as any measure decreed by the Diet against a Confederate State beyond the means of execution.

The position of Austria in Holstein especially is not placed under the protection of Federal Treaties, and His Majesty the Emperor of Austria cannot be considered as a Member of the Confederation for the Duchy of Holstein.

.   .   .   .

The Motion, in contravention of the Treaties, drawn up by Austria, and the adoption of that Motion by a part of the Confederated States, no doubt after a previous understanding, could only confirm and strengthen the views of the Royal Government.

By virtue of the Federal Law, no Declaration of War can be made against any Member of the Confederation. The Austrian motion, therefore, and the vote of the States adhering to it, being a Declaration of War against Prussia, the Royal Government considers the Dissolution of the Federal Pact as accomplished.

In the name, and by the august order of His Majesty the King, his gracious master, the Envoy therefore declares that Prussia considers the Federal Pact in force up to the present time as dissolved; that so far from considering it henceforth obligatory, it will consider it as having expired, and will act accordingly.

.   .   .   .

[On the 12th June, 1866, the Austrian Ambassador at Berlin had demanded his Passports "in consequence of the forcible occupation of Holstein by the Prussian Troops, and in defiance of Treaties."—Ed.]

No. 81   Bismarck's Stormy Interview with William I at
Nikolsburg——24 July 1866[1]

.   .   .   .

After the battle of Königgrätz the situation was such that a favourable response on our part to the first advances of Austria with a view to peace negotiations, was not only possible, but seemed demanded by the interference of France. The latter dates from the telegram, addressed to his Majesty, which arrived at Horricz[2] between July 4 and 5, in which Louis Napoleon informed the King that the Emperor Francis Joseph had ceded Venetia to him, and had invited his intervention. . . .

.   .   .   .

It was my object, in view of our subsequent relations with Austria, as far as possible to avoid cause for mortifying reminiscences, if it could be managed without prejudice to our German policy. A triumphant entry of the Prussian army into the hostile capital would naturally have been a gratifying recollection for our soldiers, but it was not necessary to our policy. It would have left behind it, as also any surrender of ancient possessions to us must have done, a wound to the pride of Austria, which, without being a pressing necessity for us, would have unnecessarily increased the difficulty of our future mutual relations. It was already quite clear to me that we should have to defend the conquests of the campaign in further wars, just as Frederick the Great had to defend the results of his two first Silesian wars in the fiercer fire of the Seven Years' War. . . . . Moved by this consideration, I had a political motive for avoiding, rather than bringing about, a triumphal entry into Vienna in the Napo-

leonic style. In positions such as ours was then, it is a political maxim after a victory not to enquire how much you can squeeze out of your opponent, but only to consider what is politically necessary. The ill-feeling which my attitude earned for me in military circles I considered was the result of a military departmental policy to which I could not concede a decisive influence on the policy of the state and its future.

When it came to the point of dealing with Napoleon's telegram of July 4, the King had sketched out the conditions of peace as follows: a reform of the Federation under the headship of Prussia; the acquisition of Schleswig-Holstein, Austrian Silesia, a strip on the frontier of Bohemia, and East Friesland; the substitution of the respective heirs-apparent for the hostile sovereigns of Hanover, Electoral Hesse, Meiningen, and Nassau. Subsequently other demands were advanced, which partly originated with the King himself, and were partly due to external influences. The King wished to annex parts of Saxony, Hanover, Hesse, and especially to bring Anspach and Baireuth again into the possession of his house. The reacquisition of the Franconian principalities touched his strong and justifiable family sentiment very nearly.

.   .   .   .

Meanwhile in my conferences with Karolyi and with Benedetti,[3] who, thanks to the clumsiness of our military police in the rear of the army, had succeeded in reaching Zwittau on the night of July 11 to 12, and there suddenly appeared beside my bed, I had found out the conditions on which we could procure peace. Benedetti declared as the basis of Napoleon's policy, that an augmentation of Prussia to the extent of four million souls in North Germany at the utmost, with the retention of the line of the Main as the frontier on the south, would not entail French intervention.[4] He hoped, I suppose, to form a South German confederation affiliated to France. Austria withdrew from the German confederation, and was ready to recognise all the arrangements that the King might make in North Germany, reserving however the integrity of Saxony. These conditions contained all we wanted; that is to say, a free hand in Germany.

I was firmly resolved, in consequence of the above considerations, to make a cabinet question of the acceptance of the peace offered by Austria. The position was difficult. All the generals shared the disinclination to break off the uninterrupted course of victory; and during these days the King was more often and more readily accessible to military influences than to mine. . . .

On July 23, under the presidency of the King, a council of war was held, in which the question to be decided was whether we should make peace under the conditions offered or continue the war. A painful illness from which I was suffering made it necessary that the council should be held in my room. On this occasion I was the only civilian in uniform. I declare it to be my conviction that peace must be concluded on the Austrian terms, but remained alone in my opinion; the King supported the military majority. My nerves could not stand the strain which had been put upon them day and night; I got up in silence, walked into my adjoining bedchamber and was there overcome by a violent paroxysm of tears. Meanwhile, I heard the council dispersing in the next room. I thereupon set to work to commit to paper the reasons which in my opinion spoke for the conclusion of peace; and begged the King, in the event of his not accepting the advice for which I was responsible, to relieve me of my functions as minister if the war were continued. . . . Armed with my document[5]

I unfolded to the King the political and military reasons which opposed the continuation of the war.

We had to avoid wounding Austria too severely; we had to avoid leaving behind in her any unnecessary bitterness of feeling or desire for revenge; we ought rather to reserve the possibility of becoming friends again with our adversary of the moment, and in any case to regard the Austrian state as a piece on the European chessboard and the renewal of friendly relations with her as a move open to us. If Austria were severely injured, she would become the ally of France and of every other opponent of ours; she would even sacrifice her anti-Russian interests for the sake of revenge on Prussia.

On the other hand, I could not see any guarantee for us in the future of the countries constituting the Austrian monarchy, in case the latter were split up by risings of the Hungarians and Slavs or made permanently dependent on those peoples. What would be put in *that* portion of Europe which the Austrian state from Tyrol to the Bukowina had hitherto occupied? Fresh formations on this surface could only be of a permanently revolutionary nature. German Austria we could neither wholly nor partly make use of. The acquisition of provinces like Austrian Silesia and portions of Bohemia could not strengthen the Prussian state; it would not lead to an amalgamation of German Austria with Prussia, and Vienna could not be governed from Berlin as a mere dependency.

If the war continued, the probable theatre would be Hungary. The Austrian army which, if we crossed the Danube at Pressburg, would not be able to hold Vienna, would scarcely retreat southwards, where it would be caught between the Prussian and Italian armies, and, by its approach to Italy, once more revive the military ardour of the Italians which, already depressed, had been restricted by Louis Napoleon; it would retreat towards the east, and continue its defence in Hungary—if only in the expectation of the prospective intervention of France and the weakening of Italy's interest in the matter, through France's agency. Moreover I held, even from a purely military standpoint, and according to my knowledge of Hungarian territory, that a prosecution of the war there would not repay us, and that the successes to be won there would be out of all proportion to the victories we had hitherto gained, and consequently be calculated to diminish our prestige—quite apart from the fact that the prolongation of the war would pave the way for a French intervention. We must finish off rapidly before France won time to bring further diplomatic action to bear upon Austria.

To all this the King raised no objection, but declared the actual terms as inadequate, without, however, definitely formulating his own demands. Only so much was clear, that his claims had grown considerably since July 4. He said that the chief culprit could not be allowed to escape unpunished, and that justice once satisfied, we could let the misled backsliders off more easily, and he insisted on the cessions of territory from Austria which I have already mentioned. I replied that we were not there to sit in judgment, but to pursue the German policy. Austria's conflict in rivalry with us was no more culpable than ours with her; *our task was the establishment or initiation of a German national unity under the leadership of the King of Prussia.*

Passing on to German states, he spoke of various acquisitions by cutting down the territories of all our opponents. I repeated that we were not there to administer retributive justice, but to pursue a policy; that I wished to avoid, in the German federation of the future, the sight of mutilated territories, whose princes and peoples might very easily (such is human weakness) retain a lively wish to recover their former possessions by means of foreign help; such allies would be very unreliable. The same would be the case if, for the purpose of compensating Saxony, Würtzburg or Nu-

remburg were demanded of Bavaria, a plan, moreover, which would interfere with the dynastic prejudice of his Majesty in favour of Anspach. I had also to resist plans which were aimed at an enlargement of the Grand Duchy of Baden, the annexation of the Bavarian Palatinate, and an extension in the region of the lower Main. The Aschaffenburg district of Bavaria was at the same time regarded as a fit compensation to Hesse-Darmstadt for the loss of Upper Hesse, which would result from the projected Main frontier. Later, at Berlin, the only part of this plan still under negotiation was the cession of that portion of Bavarian territory which lay on the right bank of the Main, inclusive of the town of Baireuth, to Prussia; the question then arose whether the boundary should run on the Northern or Red Main or the Southern or White Main. What seemed to me to be paramount with his Majesty was the aversion of the military party to interrupt the victorious course of the army. The resistance which I was obliged, in accordance with my convictions, to offer to the King's views with regard to following up the military successes, and to his inclination to continue the victorious advance, excited him to such a degree that a prolongation of the discussion became impossible; and, under the impression that my opinion was rejected, I left the room with the idea of begging the King to allow me, in my capacity of officer, to join my regiment. On returning to my room I was in the mood that the thought occurred to me whether it would not be better to fall out of the open window, which was four storeys high; and I did not look round when I heard the door open, although I suspected that the person entering was the Crown Prince, whose room in the same corridor I had just passed. I felt his hand on my shoulder, whilst he said: 'You know that I was against this war. You considered it necessary, and the responsibility for it lies on you. If you are now persuaded that our end is attained, and peace must now be concluded, I am ready to support you and defend your opinion with my father.' He then repaired to the King, and came back after a short half-hour, in the same calm, friendly mood, but with the words: 'It has been a very difficult business, but my father has consented.'[6] This consent found expression in a note written with lead pencil on the margin of one of my last memoranda, something to this effect: 'Inasmuch as my Minister-President has left me in the lurch in the face of the enemy, and here I am not in a position to supply his place, I have discussed the question with my son; and as he has associated himself with the Minister-President's opinion, I find myself reluctantly compelled, after such brilliant victories on the part of the army, to bite the sour apple and accept so disgraceful a peace.' I do not think I am mistaken as to the exact words, although the document is not accessible to me at present. In any case I have given the sense of it; and, despite its bitterness of expression, it was to me a joyful release from a tension that was becoming unbearable. I gladly accepted the Royal assent to what I regarded as politically necessary without taking offence at its ungracious form. At this time military impressions were dominant in the King's mind; and the strong need he felt of pursuing the hitherto dazzling course of victory perhaps influenced him more than political and diplomatic considerations.

·   ·   ·   ·   ·   ·   ·   ·   ·   ·

No. 82   The Preliminary Peace of Nikolsburg——26 July 1866[1]

THEIR Majesties the Emperor of Austria and the King of Prussia, animated with the desire of restoring the benefits of Peace to their Countries, have for that purpose, and in order to settle the Preliminaries of Peace, appointed Plenipotentiaries, that is to say:

His Majesty the Emperor of Austria, the Count Aloisius Karolyi, and the Baron Adolphus von Brenner-Felsach;

And His Majesty the King of Prussia, Otho, Count von Bismarck-Schönhausen, his President of the Council and Minister for Foreign Affairs;

Who, after exchanging their Full Powers, which were found in good and due form, have agreed upon the following fundamental points as the basis of the Peace to be concluded without delay.

Austrian Territory to remain intact,
with the exception of the
Lombardo-Venetian Kingdom.
Withdrawal of Prussian Troops.

ART. I. With the Exception of the Lombardo-Venetian Kingdom,[2] the Territory of the Austrian Monarchy remains intact. His Majesty the King of Prussia engages to withdraw his Troops from the Austrian Territories occupied by them as soon as the Peace shall be concluded, under reservation of the arrangements to be made upon the definite conclusion of the Peace for guaranteeing the payment of the War Indemnity.

Dissolution of the Germanic Confederation.
Formation of North German
Confederation and a South German Union.

ART. II. His Majesty the Emperor of Austria recognises the Dissolution of the Germanic Confederation as it has existed hitherto, and consents to a new organisation of Germany without the participation of the Empire of Austria. His Majesty likewise promises to recognise the closer Union which will be founded by His Majesty the King of Prussia, to the north of the line of the Main, and he declares that he consents to the German States south of that line entering into a Union, the national relations of which, with the North German Confederation, are to be the subject of an ulterior agreement between the two Parties.

Schleswig and Holstein to be transferred to Prussia except Northern part to be retroceded to Denmark on certain Conditions.

ART. III. His Majesty the Emperor of Austria transfers to His Majesty the King of Prussia all the Rights which the Treaty of Vienna of 30th October, 1864,[3] recognised as belonging to him over the Duchies of Schleswig and Holstein, with this reservation, that the people of the Northern Districts of Schleswig shall be again united to Denmark if they express a desire to be so by a vote freely given.[4]

Austria to pay War Expenses of Prussia.

ART. IV. His Majesty the Emperor of Austria undertakes to pay His Majesty the King of Prussia the sum of 40,000,000 thalers to cover a part of the Expenses which Prussia has been put to by the War. But from this sum may be deducted the amount of the Indemnity for the costs of War which His Majesty the Emperor of Austria still has the right of exacting from the Duchies of Schleswig and Holstein, by virtue of Article XII of the Treaty of Peace of 30th October, 1864 before cited, say 15,000,000 thalers, with 5,000,000 in addition, as the equivalent of the cost of providing for the Prussian army, maintained by the Austrian Countries occupied by that army until the time of the conclusion of the Peace.

Territorial State of the Kingdom of Saxony.

ART. V. In conformity with the wish expressed by His Majesty the Emperor of Austria, His Majesty the King of Prussia declares his willingness to let the Territorial State of the Kingdom of Saxony continue in its present extent, when the modifications are made which are to take place in Germany; reserving to himself, however, to regulate in detail, by a special Peace with His Majesty the King of Saxony, the questions as to Saxony's part in the expenses of the War, as well as the future position of the Kingdom of Saxony in the North German Confederation.

Austria to recognise New Organisation of North Germany.

On the other hand, His Majesty the Emperor of Austria promises to recognise the New Organisation which the King of Prussia will establish in the North of Germany, including the Territorial modifications consequent thereon.

Preliminaries of Peace and Armistice to be recognised by King of Italy.

ART. VI. His Majesty the King of Prussia undertakes to prevail upon His Majesty the King of Italy, his Ally, to give his approval to the Preliminaries of Peace and to the Armistice based on those Preliminaries, so soon as the Venetian Kingdom shall have been put at the disposal of His Majesty the King of Italy by a Declaration of His Majesty the Emperor of the French.

Ratifications.

ART. VII. The Ratifications of the present Convention shall be exchanged at Nikolsburg in the space of two days at the latest.

Peace to be concluded on Basis of Preliminary Treaty.

ART. VIII. Immediately after the Ratification of the present Convention shall have been effected and exchanged, their Majesties the Emperor of Austria and the King of Prussia will appoint Plenipotentiaries, who will meet at a place to be hereafter named, to conclude the Peace upon the Basis of the present Preliminary Treaty, and to agree upon the details of the conditions.[5]

Armistice to be concluded between Austria and Saxony and Prussia.

ART. IX. For that purpose the Contracting States, after having decided upon these Preliminaries, will conclude an Armistice for the Austrian and Saxon armies on the one part, and for the Prussian army on the other part, of which the detailed conditions, from the military point of view, are to be immediately determined. That Armistice shall date from the 2nd of August, the day to which the present Suspension of Arms shall be prolonged.

Conclusion of Armistice with other States.

The Armistice shall, at the same time, be concluded with Bavaria, and General the Baron von Manteuffel will be instructed to conclude with the Kingdom of Wurtemberg and the Grand Duchies of Baden and Hesse-Darmstadt, as soon as those States shall propose it, an Armistice beginning on the 2nd August, and founded on the state of military possession at the time.

In faith whereof the respective Plenipotentiaries have signed the present Convention, and to it have affixed the Seals of their Arms.

Done at Nikolsburg, 26th July, 1866.

[(L.S.) BISMARCK.][6]   (L.S.) KAROLYI.
                             (L.S.) BRENNER.

Accessories.

Baden	13th August, 1866
Bavaria	17th August, 1866
Hesse-Darmstadt	22nd August, 1866
Saxe-Meiningen	8th October, 1866
Saxony	21st October, 1866
Wurtemberg	13th August, 1866

[A Convention of Armistice was concluded between Austria and Prussia at Vienna on the 26th July, 1866; and another Convention between the Austrian and Italian Military Commissioners on the 12th August, 1866.—Ed.]

No. 83   The Prussian Alliance with the South German States ——13 to 22 August 1866[1]

Treaty of Alliance between Prussia and Württemberg.[2]

His Majesty, the King of Prussia, and His Majesty, the King of Württemberg, animated by the desire to make the future relationship of the sovereigns and their states as cordial as possible, have decided, in corroboration of the treaty of peace signed by them on 13 August 1866, to continue negotiations, and have appointed for this purpose:

His Majesty, the King of Prussia:
    Count Otto von Bismarck-Schönhausen, etc.,

and Carl Friedrich von Savigny, etc.;
His Majesty, the King of Württemberg:
    Baron Carl von Varnbüler, etc.,
    and Lieutenant-General Oscar von Hardegg, etc.;
who, after having exchanged their full powers found to be in good and due form, have agreed upon the following treaty articles:

ART. I. His Majesty, the King of Prussia, and His Majesty, the King of Württemberg, hereby conclude a treaty of alliance and of friendship.

The high contracting Parties guarantee

to each other the territorial integrity of their respective countries, and bind themselves, in the event of war, to place all of their armed forces at each others' disposal for this purpose.

ART. 2. His Majesty, the King of Württemberg, shall transfer, in this event, the supreme command of his troops to His Majesty, the King of Prussia.

ART. 3. The high contracting Parties pledge to keep this treaty secret for the time being.

ART. 4. The ratification of the present treaty shall take place at the same time as the ratification of the treaty of peace signed today, that is, not later than 21 August of this year.

In faith of which the plenipotentiaries named above have signed this treaty today in duplicate, and have affixed to it their armorial seals.

Done at Berlin on 13 August 1866.

(L.S.) BISMARCK.   (L.S.) VARNBÜLER.
(L.S.) SAVIGNY.   (L.S.) HARDEGG.

The exchange of ratifications has taken place.

(Preussischer Staatsanzeiger.)

No. 84   Benedetti's Draft of a Franco-Prussian Treaty—— 23 August 1866[1]

Benedetti[2] *to Rouher.*[3]
Berlin, 23 August 1866.

ENCLOSURE.

(His Majesty, the Emperor of the French, and His Majesty, the King of Prussia,)[4] deeming it useful (to consult together in order)[5] to draw closer the bonds of friendship which unite them and to consolidate the relations of good neighbourliness which fortunately exist between the two countries, convinced, moreover, that, to obtain this (twin)[5a] result, proper, too, to assure the maintenance of the general peace, it is important for them to reach an understanding over questions which concern their future relations, have resolved to conclude a treaty to this effect, and therefore have named as their plenipotentiaries:

His Majesty,—

His Majesty,—

Who, after having exchanged their full powers found to be in good and due form, have agreed upon the following articles:

ART. I.—His Majesty, the Emperor of the French, admits and recognizes the acquisitions which Prussia has made as a result of the recent war which it has fought against Austria and her allies, (as well as the arrangements made or to be made for the constitution of a Confederation in northern Germany, at the same time taking it upon himself to lend his complete support to the conservation of this work.)[6]

ART. II.—His Majesty, the King of Prussia, promises to facilitate the acquisition of Luxemburg by France. For this purpose, the said Majesty shall enter into negotiations with His Majesty, the King of the Netherlands, in order to persuade him to cede to the Emperor of the French his sovereign rights in this Duchy, in return for such compensation as shall be judged sufficient or otherwise. For his part, the Emperor of the French pledges to assume the pecuniary charges which this transaction may require.

ART. III.—His Majesty, the Emperor of the French, shall not oppose a federal union of the northern Confederation with the states of southern Germany, with the exception of Austria, which union could be based upon a common parliament while still respecting, to a proper degree, the sovereignty of the said states.

ART. IV.—For his part, His Majesty, the King of Prussia, in the event that His Majesty, the Emperor of the French, should be led by circumstances to have his troops march into Belgium or to conquer it, shall grant France the assistance of his armies, and (he)[6] shall support her, with all of his army and navy, against any Power which, in this eventuality, should declare war against her.

ART. V.—To assure the complete execution of the preceding arrangements, (His Majesty, the Emperor of the French, and His Majesty, the King of Prussia,)[4] contract, through the present treaty, an offensive and defensive alliance, which they solemnly pledge to maintain. Their Majesties bind themselves, more particularly, to fulfil it whenever their respective states, whose integrity they mutually guarantee to each other, should be threatened by aggression, holding themselves under an obligation in such circumstances, to take, without delay and not to decline under any pretext, those military dispositions which their common interest would demand, in conformity with the clauses and provisions expressed above.

No. 85   Bismarck's Memorandum to William I on the Hohenzollern Candidacy——9 March 1870[1]

Berlin, 9 March 1870.

May Your Royal Majesty permit me to most humbly summarize herewith in writing the motives which, according to my modest interpretation, speak for the acceptance of the Spanish crown by His Highness, the Hereditary Prince of Hohenzollern, after I had already respectfully indicated them orally.

I am of the opinion that it would bring direct and indirect advantages to the Prussian and German state interest if the acceptance occurs, and that, in the opposite case, disadvantages and dangers must be feared.

The acceptance of the Spanish royal crown by a prince of Your Majesty's illustrious House would strengthen the existing sympathies between two nations who are, by way of exception, in the fortunate position of having no conflicting interests because they are not neighbors, and whose friendly relations seem capable of considerable development. The Spaniards would have a feeling of gratitude toward Germany if they were rescued from the anarchical conditions into which a predominantly monarchical people threatens to sink because it lacks a king.

It is desirable for Germany to have on France's other side a country upon whose sympathies we can rely and whose sensibilities France is forced to take into account. If, in the course of a war between Germany and France, conditions exist as they had under Queen Isabella, where there was the prospect of an alliance between the Latin Catholic Powers, and if, on the other hand, one imagines, in such a case, a government in Spain which sympathizes with Germany, then the difference in the two situations relative to the armed forces available to France against Germany may amount to at least one to two French army corps. For, in the first case, it would even become possible to make French troops available because they would be relieved by Spanish troops, in the second case, it would be necessary to station at least one French army corps at the Spanish border. France's pacific intentions towards Germany would always increase or decrease in proportion to the danger of a war with Germany. In the long run, we cannot expect peace to be maintained by the benevolence of France, but only by the impression of our position of power.

Spain's prosperity, and German trade with this country, would experience a mighty increase under Hohenzollern rule. . . . The esteem for the Hohenzollern dynasty, the justified pride with which not only Prussia views its royal House, but Germany, too, gets more and more into the habit of being proud of this name as a common national possession, as a symbol of German fame and German esteem abroad, to increase and to strengthen this important element of political self-consciousness, this would be useful for an invigoration of national feeling in general, and in a monarchical direction at that. It is, therefore, in Germany's political interest that the Hohenzollern House acquire the esteem and occupy the high position in the world for which an analogy can only be found in the Habsburg antecedents since Charles V. This element of pride in the dynasty is a factor for the contentment of our people and the consolidation of our circumstances which should not be taken lightly. Just as in Spain shame for the not very dignified position of the dynasty has paralyzed the strength of the nation for decades, so with us pride in an illustrious dynasty was an immense moral impetus for Prussia's German development of power. This impetus will grow mightily if the need of the Germans for recognition abroad, so little satisfied before, is met by an incomparable world position of the dynasty.

The rejection of the offered crown would, in all probability, have undesirable consequences.

To begin with, it could not but highly offend the Spaniards that one rejects a crown which has always occupied a high rank in history, and repulses a nation of 16 million people, which begs to be saved from the anarchy into which it feels itself sinking, by denying it the king of its choice.

In the case of a rejection, the wishes of the Spaniards would probably turn first to Bavaria. If the line of Prince Adalbert or that of the Duke there accepted the offer, then one would have a dynasty in Spain which would seek its support in France and Rome, which would maintain contact with the anti-national elements in Germany and offer them a secure, even though distant, rallying point. Under Carlist rule, Spain would succumb in the same direction of leaning upon Rome, France, and Austria, while favoring ultramontane reaction in the interior. We could then also be sure of finding it consistently in the ranks of our opponents.

If the Bavarian and the Carlist eventualities do not occur, Spain may well succumb to a republic at first. The repercussions of a Spanish republic would be felt most directly in France and Italy. How easily revolutionary movements spread from Spain to Italy may be remembered from the beginning of the twenties.[2] . . .

. . . .

A safe development of the Spanish question would be brought about by an acceptance. It would be of great value for France if the Orleanist candidacy as well as a republic in Spain were to appear to be definitely eliminated.

According to information received, the Cortes would elect the Hereditary Prince with a majority of more than ¾th of all the votes.

That a great nation like the Spanish appoints its ruler with such a majority, bordering on unanimity, has occurred only twice in history for centuries: in England, at the election of the presently ruling House in place of the expelled Stuarts, and in Russia, at the election of the Romanov dynasty. . . .

No danger whatsoever can be foreseen for the person of the Hereditary Prince. In all the revolutions which have convulsed Spain, the idea of a deed of violence against the highest person in the land has never arisen, a threat never even been uttered. . . .

Therefore, I can only respectfully recommend to Your Royal Majesty to graciously prevent the Spanish crown from being rejected, unless the Hereditary Prince feels an insurmountable aversion for it.

.   .   .   .

I feel it as a personal necessity to state, by the present respectful memorandum, that the responsibility for the rejection, if it occurs, cannot be placed on my shoulders, especially not then when, in a near or more distant future, historians and public opinion should search for the reasons which brought about the rejection.

No. 86   Bismarck Revives the Hohenzollern Candidacy——— 28 May 1870[1]

Bismarck to Prince Charles Anthony of Hohenzollern.

Berlin, 28 May 1870.

Upon resuming the burdens of office,[2] I have been informed of the most recent negotiations over the candidacy for the Spanish throne, and I cannot avoid the impression that in their course German interests have not received their due. The reports received in the meantime show that the temporary rulers have endeavored, with great earnestness and not without success, to bring order into the finances, the armed forces, and throughout the administration, and that this nation of 17 million, dependent, as we are, upon the preservation of peace in Europe, is already now capable, in case of European complications, of throwing a weight into the scales which would not be without practical significance for us. Today as before, I have no doubt that Germany has a fundamental interest therein, and that, in critical moments, whether the scales will come down on one side or the other will depend on us having friends or enemies in Madrid. I have asked His Majesty, the King, to weigh the question once more in this sense, and I have received the reply that, as soon as one of the Princes of the Hohenzollern House

showed an inclination to accept the crown, the King would not at all oppose such an inclination. I consider this as the most favorable reply which can really be expected from His Majesty under the present circumstances, for the King will certainly never decide to order a member of the royal House to undertake a mission whose guarantee for success consists above all in the *vocation* which the individual undertaking it personally feels for it. I believe that public opinion and history will render the same judgment when the details of these events become known. One cannot, in my opinion, expect the King to assume a personal responsibility in a matter which would not involve his own decision, but an order to other members of the royal House to assume their own responsibility.

I do not doubt that His Royal Highness, the Crown Prince, is in complete agreement with this view. If His Highness, the Hereditary Prince, or one of the younger sons of Your Royal Highness, were inclined to render this service to *both* countries and to earn the gratitude of Spain and Germany, then I believe that a telegram, addressed to me by Marshal Prim[3] *after* the latest refusal and which I have not yet answered, presents me with the possibility of reopening the question.

No. 87   The Reaction in the Parisian Press to the Hohenzollern Candidacy——5 to 13 July 1870[1]

. . . .

If the press is really the voice of a nation, then a nation never expressed more clearly how it felt. The first to speak up, and the most vehement, was, of course, the war-baiting newspaper *Le Pays*, edited by Granier de Cassagnac and his son Paul: "This Spanish affair, which would have been unimportant ten years ago, is the drop of water which causes our cup, already filled to the brim with bitterness, to overflow. The deceitful promises of 1866, the Schleswig affair, the failure to carry out the treaty of Prague, the spoliation of Hanover, the disguised annexation of Baden and of all of Germany, the insolent conduct in the Luxemburg events, the Italian alliance, the Saint Gotthard pass, all this followed in rapid succession, was heaped together, in defiance of our security, of our rights, of the European equilibrium. And now, one would try to force a Prussian king in Madrid upon us? No, we shall not permit it." Ordinarily, the furious sallies of *Le Pays* provoked a smile rather than excitement, except, perhaps, among a small circle of readers. It was to be different this time. Almost everyone appropriated and echoed them. *Le Soir*, newspaper of the disappointed or impatient ambitious, represented by the brilliant About, did it with virulence: "In the midst of the tergiversations of personal diplomacy, it is announced that General Prim creates a king of Spain all by himself. It is another Hohenzollern, another Prussian colonel catalogued in Mr. von Bismarck's repertory. It is not enough that Prussia should extend and fortify itself on our eastern frontier; it is a trifle that it has acquired, through our fault, a faithful and devoted ally on our southeastern frontier; it shall now be permitted to install a proconsul in the southwest, on our Spanish frontier. But we are thirty-eight million prisoners, if the news is not false. It absolutely must be false; it shall be, if one is determined; but is the French government still capable of being determined? Is all its energy limited to rebuffing the candidacy of the Duke de Montpensier?" *Le Gaulois*, an independent organ, and edited by a writer with a charming and refined mind, Pessard, is hardly more resigned: "If the authoritarian Empire has been pleased to accept Sadowa and to console itself over the Luxemburg affair, France, restored partly to herself, shall not be willing to tolerate that one challenges and provokes her with impunity. . . . War! no one hates it more than liberal France, devoted to right and justice. No one knows better than liberal democracy how dangerous a victorious war may be to liberty. No one shudders more than we others at the thought of the misfortunes which a defeat could bring down upon us. But if a choice must be made once more between a diminished, a reduced fatherland and war, we do not hesitate! . . . We believe that the French government could not tolerate these Prussian agitations for one more day without treason against France. The Cabinet could be forgiven for having failed to keep its promises, for having aroused our wrath, it could not be forgiven for not having known how to be French."

. . . *Le Français,* also an Orleanist newspaper, edited by François Beslay and Thureau-Dangin, two young writers of talent, very well informed on the true national tradition, does not hesitate, either:

"French patriotism will not be able to accept, without alarm, a combination which would place Spain under the domination of Prussia, already allied with Italy. To have created two powerful unities on our flanks is too much; to go beyond this would be to revive at will the formidable preponderance against which our fathers have fought during two centuries." . . . Then there comes the series of republican newspapers . . . who battle among themselves as to who will flagellate with greater sarcasm and scorn a government surprised by the Bismarckian plot. Le Siècle: "The Empire has favored the preponderance of Prussia in Germany; it has been unable either to forsee Sadowa or to guard against its consequences; it has let Mr. von Bismarck make a fool of it; it has alienated Italy, it has thrown this Power, our natural ally, into the arms of Prussia; and, to top off the blundering, it is to have allowed Prussian Germany to create a new client state in Spain! France, entwined on all sides by Prussia or by nations submitting to its influence, would find herself reduced to an isolation comparable to the one which formerly motivated the long struggles of our ancient monarchy against the House of Austria. The situation would be, in many respects, more serious than on the morrow of the treaties of 1815. Such a result, occurring after nineteen years of a regime which had chosen as its mission to restore French influence abroad, would constitute, to the detriment of the Empire, an argument which the most clamorous plebiscite[2] majorities would fail miserably to gainsay."—Le Charivari: "Prussia already has Rumania devoted to it;[3] it has one foot in Italy through its alliances, the other foot in Switzerland through the Saint Gotthard pass, and now it's the turn of Spain. During this time, France, embarrassed, hesitant, isolated,

looks on without being able to act. Do you believe that there is really anything about this which would make you proud of being a Frenchman, even in regarding the column?—VÉRON." — Paris-Journal: "This time, it's too much, the present government itself cannot silently tolerate such an affront. Bismarck is wrong, this is not 1866 any more . . . Republican France would not tolerate it, monarchical France should not tolerate it either.—ALFRED ASSOLANT."—. . . François-Victor Hugo, with the insistence of an implacable hatred, sums up public sentiment in Le Rappel: "Finally, today, here it is hatching an intrigue with the Cabinet of Madrid to offer the crown of Charles V to Prince Leopold of Hohenzollern, Lieutenant in the [Prussian] First Regiment of the Guards. Thus, Prussia extends its outposts to all points of the Continent, to the north, the south, the east, the west, to the mouth of the Danube, to the mouth of the Scheldt, beyond the Pyrenees, beyond the Alps. Proud of having realized, for the benefit of their dynastic ambition, this patriotic and generous idea—German unity,—the Hohenzollern have now reached the point of audacity that they dare to contemplate this monstrous project of universal domination which Charles V, Louis XIV, and Napoleon have dreamed of in vain. They are not satisfied any more with having conquered Germany. They aspire to dominate Europe! It will be an eternal humiliation for our times that such a project should have been, we do not say undertaken, but even conceived. The Prussian monarchy's inordinate presumption is the logical and fatal punishment for all the mistakes committed during several years by the personal government which rules us. Never, since the reign of Pompadour, never, since Rossbach, has France atoned more harshly for the incapacity of her masters." (13 July.)

No. 88   Gramont's Speech of 6 July 1870[1]

On the morning of the 6th, at a Council of Ministers, Gramont[2] explained what had occurred. The discussion began. We inquired, at first, about our military and diplomatic situation. . . .

. . . .

We left Saint Cloud at half past noon. Gramont, returning to the Ministry of Foreign Affairs, dictated the declaration to two secretaries. At 2 o'clock, when the *Corps législatif* opened, he was not ready yet, and the session was suspended until his arrival. I was the first to enter; . . . My colleagues arrived one after the other, and, finally, Gramont appeared. He went directly to the speaker's stand, and read, without changing a word, the text[3] agreed upon that morning:

"I have come here to reply to the question which was addressed to the government yesterday by the Honorable Mr. Cochery.

It is true that Marshal Prim has offered the crown of Spain to Prince Leopold of Hohenzollern, and that the latter has accepted it. But the Spanish people have not expressed an opinion in the matter yet, and we still do not know the true details of a negotiation which has been hidden from us. Furthermore, a discussion would not lead now to any practical result at all. We ask you, gentlemen, to postpone it.

We have not ceased to demonstrate our sympathy for the Spanish nation, and to avoid anything which could have had the appearance of any interference whatsoever in the internal affairs of a noble and great nation in the plain exercise of its sovereignty. We have not departed, in regard to the diverse pretendants to the throne, from the strictest neutrality, and we have never demonstrated either a preference or an aversion for any of them.

We shall[4] persist in this conduct.

But we do not believe that respect for the rights of a neighboring people compels us to permit that a foreign Power, by placing one of its princes upon the throne of Charles V, should upset the present equilibrium of forces in Europe to our detriment, and imperil the interests and the honor of France. (*Loud applause.*)

This eventuality, we firmly hope, will not be realized.

To prevent it, we count both upon the wisdom of the German people and upon the friendship of the Spanish people.

If it should be otherwise, strengthened by your support, gentlemen, and by that of the nation, we would know how to do our duty without hesitation and without weakness." (*Long applause.—Repeated acclamations.*) The acclamations accompanied Gramont all the way to his bench.

This declaration is beyond reproach, and I read it again, after so many years, with satisfaction. . . .

No. 89   The Hohenzollern Candidacy Is Withdrawn——12 July 1870[1]

France.

Paris, July 12, 4 P.M.
The Spanish Ambassador here has received a despatch, signed by Prince Antoine [Charles Anthony] of Hohenzollern, informing him that he had telegraphed to General Prim that, in consequence of the opposition his son appears to meet with, he has withdrawn his nomination in the name of Prince Leopold. Prince Antoine adds that late events having created a state of things in which Spain could only be guided by the sentiment of her independence, the vote of the Cortes, therefore, could not be considered as sincere and spontaneous, as it should be for the election of a Monarch.

.   .   .   .

EXTRA EDITION[2]

Kölnische Zeitung

Telegraphic Dispatches

Sigmaringen, 12 July.
It is reported with certainty: Prince Leopold[3] renounces his candidacy for the Spanish throne, following his feelings, which make it impossible for him as a Prussian and German officer to plunge Germany into war because of him and, at the same time, to bring to Spain a sanguinary struggle as dowry.

Paris, 12 July, 3 p.m.
Prices rise on the Exchange. Bonds 69.75. Peace is considered as assured.

No. 90   The French "a tout jamais" Demand: Gramont's Dispatch to Benedetti——12 July 1870[1]

[Paris] 12 July 1870, 6:15 p.m.
We have received, from the hands of the Ambassador of Spain, the renunciation by Prince Antoine, in the name of his son Leopold, of his candidacy for the throne of Spain. In order for this renunciation by Prince Antoine to produce the maximum effect, it appears necessary that the King of Prussia associate himself with it, and that he give us the assurance that he would not authorize this candidacy again.

Would you immediately wait upon the King to demand this declaration from him, which he should be unable to refuse if, indeed, he does not entertain any mental reservations. In spite of the renunciation, which is now common knowledge, public opinion is so excited that we do not know if we can control it.

Paraphrase this telegram when communicating its contents to the King.

Reply as promptly as possible.

No. 91   The French "a tout jamais" Demand: William I's Own Account of His Interview with Benedetti at Ems—— 13 July 1870[1]

Memorandum by King William.[2]
Composed on the evening of July 13th or on the following day.

The 13th of July in Ems.

While I was taking my fountain promenade as usual from 8-10 o'clock, 1st. Lt. Prince Radziwill[3] brought me a telegram from Paris, which Ct. Benedetti had just forwarded to him, with the news from Madrid that the Prince v. Hohenzollern had officially notified the Spanish government of his son's withdrawal of his acceptance of the Spanish crown. Since I had not yet received this news, I let Ct. Benedetti be informed of this, and let him be sincerely thanked for the communication since it was of such great importance. When I had completed my promenade and was on my way home, Ct. B. met me near the director's building; I walked over to him and, shaking his hand, I said: I am delighted to encounter you so that I can thank you orally for the important communication which you have just sent me; you can see that you are better and earlier informed at this moment than I am, myself, for I have still not received this good news directly. I have only received a personal telegram which says that it appears that Prince Leopold renounces the crown. So that brings the affair to an end which could have led to trouble between us considering the way you were looking at it.

Benedetti: Certainly, Sire, this is very good news, and we are more than pleased with the decision which Prince Hohenzollern has just taken. But since it is only the Prince, father of the Hereditary Prince, who, in the name of the latter, has made the communication of the Prince, his son, we must still wait for the latter to confirm his renunciation.

I replied that this last demand appeared to me to give offense to Prince Hohenzollern, for he most certainly could only have rendered such an important decision officially with the full knowledge and consent of his son. Besides, I was not yet in possession of any direct official communications from the Prince, which I would probably receive in the course of the day and then communicate to him.

B.: But the deficiency in Pr. Leopold's declaration could well be made up if Your Majesty would inform us that you would take it upon yourself never to permit Pr. Leopold to accept the crown again in case it were offered to him anew.

I (not concealing my astonishment at such an unreasonable request, replied): You are demanding a declaration from me which it would be impossible for me to make. In circumstances as grave as these, one can never tie one's hands in advance; such questions always present themselves again in different forms, conjectures, etc., they must be studied anew and thoroughly before making as important decisions as these. Besides, I am convinced that Pr. L. would not think of embarking a second time upon such an enterprise, considering what political complications it gives rise to.

B.: Indeed, it is not probable that, after the experience he has made, the Prince thinks of taking up again a question which he seems to have abandoned; but we cannot be certain of this; if Y.M. gives us the declaration which I have just submitted to you, the question is settled once and for all.

I must repeat that it would be impossible for me to make such a binding declaration, and no one would do so in my place. Let me give an example: You as head of the family, you had given your consent to the marriage of someone in your family; after a certain time, the fiancés wish to break their engagement; a third person, opposed to this marriage, persuades you to give him your word not to give your consent again in case the young people, after mature consideration and convinced that their happiness depends upon it, desire to renew their engagement; in what position would you find yourself then in relation to the third person if you, yourself, were convinced that your relative's happiness depends upon this union?

B.: Ah! that would only be a private affair; that is not as grave as a question of high politics which is on the point of bringing down upon us the most disastrous complications.

I: But what if, at some future date, Emp. Napoleon himself finds that the Prince von Hzl. is the best candidate for the throne of Spain; what would I do in that case if I had given him the solemn promises which you are demanding of me?

B.: But that would never happen; with public opinion so strongly opposed to this candidacy, the Emp. could never think of seeing it revived; the agitation in Paris and in my country increases from hour to hour, and all is to be feared if Y.M. does not give us the declaration which I am soliciting.

I: With the same right with which you assert that the Emp. will never take up the Hohenzollern candidacy, I could assert, in my turn, that the communication made by the Prince's father has settled the question of that candidacy forever.

After a momentary pause,

B. said: Well! Sire, I can write to my government that Y.M. has consented to declare that you will never permit Pr. Leopold to take up the candidacy in question again?

At these words, I stepped back a few paces and, in a very stern tone, said:

It seems to me, Mr. Ambassador, that I have expressed myself so clearly and so distinctly that I could never make such a declaration that I have nothing further to add. With that, I tipped my hat and went on my way.

W.

Pr. Radziwill's Notes contain additional information.[4]

No. 92 The Two Versions of the Ems Dispatch——— 13 July 1870[1]

Text of the Dispatch from Ems.	*Text of Bismarck's Version.*
Abeken[2] to Bismarck.	

Ems, 13 July 1870, 3:50 p.m.
Received 6:09 p.m.

DECIPHERED   URGENT

His Majesty, the King writes me:
"Count Benedetti intercepted me on the promenade in order to demand of me, at the end in a very importunate manner, that I should authorize him to telegraph immediately that I promised, for all time to come, never again to give my consent if the Hohenzollern should take up their candidacy once more. I refused his request, at the end somewhat sternly, because one neither should nor could assume such obligations *à tout jamais.* I told him, of course, that I had not received anything as yet, and, since he was more quickly informed via Paris and Madrid than I, he would surely understand that my government was once again not involved in the matter."

His Majesty has since then received a letter from the Prince. Inasmuch as His Majesty had told Count Benedetti that he expected a communication from the Prince, His Majesty decided, in view of the unreasonable expectation mentioned above, upon the advice of Count Eulenburg[3] and myself, not to grant Count Benedetti another audience, but only to let him be told through an adjutant:[4] that His Majesty had now obtained from the Prince confirmation of the news which Benedetti had already received from Paris, and had nothing further to say to the Ambassador.

His Majesty leaves it to Your Excellency's discretion whether Benedetti's new demand, together with its rejection, should not be communicated to our ambassadors as well as to the press.

After the news of the renunciation by the Hereditary Prince von Hohenzollern had been officially communicated to the Imperial French government by the Royal Spanish government, the French Ambassador made the additional demand of H. Maj., the King, in Ems, that he be authorized to telegraph to Paris that H. Maj., the King, promises, for all time to come, never again to give his consent if the Hohenzollern should again take up their candidacy once more.

His Maj., the King, thereupon declined to grant the French Ambassador another audience, and let him be told through the adjutant on duty that H. Majesty had nothing further to communicate to the Ambassador.

No. 93   The Uproar in Paris——14 July 1870

Ollivier's Memoirs.[1]

On the morning of the 14th, finally quiet after so much anguish, I started to compose the declaration which I intended to submit that evening to the Council of Ministers at Saint-Cloud. . . .

I was about to continue by mentioning the rôle of Olozaga[2] and of Spain, when the door opens and the usher announces: His Excellency, the Minister of Foreign Affairs. Hardly through the door, even before having reached the center of the room, Gramont cries out: "My friend, you are looking at a man who has just been slapped in the face!" I stand up: "I don't understand you, what do you mean?" He then gives me a small sheet of yellow paper, which I shall see forever before my eyes. It was a telegram from Lesourd,[3] sent from Berlin on the 13th, after midnight, which stated: "An extra edition of the *Norddeutsche Zeitung,* which appeared at 10 o'clock in the evening, contains, in brief, the following: 'The Ambassador of France, having demanded in Ems that H.M., the King, authorize him to telegraph to Paris that he would promise for the future not to give his consent to the Hohenzollern candidacy if it should arise again, the King has refused to receive the Ambassador, and let him be told through the aide-de-Camp on duty that he had nothing further to communicate to him.' This news, published by the semi-official newspaper, has created a great stir in the city."

—"Then Benedetti had not warned you?," I said to Gramont.—"Here," he replied, "is what he telegraphed me in the afternoon. I received these four telegrams in succession in the evening, and I had not thought it urgent to add them to my two notes." After having read the telegrams from Benedetti, I read the one from Lesourd again. I understood Gramont's exclamation. Never had a ship foundered closer to a safe harbor. I remained silent and dejected for several moments. "We cannot delude ourselves any longer," I said; "they want to force us to declare war." We agreed that I would assemble my colleagues at once to inform them of this unforeseen blow, while Gramont would return to the Foreign Ministry, where Werther[4] had announced his arrival. . . .

* * * * * * * * * *

The boulevards looked as they do on public holidays: "the same crowds, the same curiosity, the same high spirits; it was impossible for vehicles to move on the streets, and the busses had to change their routes. On all sides one heard the cries: 'Hurrah for war! To Berlin!' As much as the possibility of an arrangement had produced deception, the rupture of negotiations was welcomed with feverish animation. Everybody breathed freely again, as if delivered from an oppressive uncertainty." A large crowd, increasing and decreasing in size as it went along, coming from the Bastille, marched up the boulevard, with a flag up front, to the cries of: "Long live France!," singing the *Song of the Girondins* and the *Marseillaise.* Cries of: "Long live the Emperor! Long live the army! Long live France!" blended with these songs. Applause from the cafés and private houses accompanied them. A few individuals, having wanted to protest, were roughed up. . . .

* * * * * * * * * *

*Report by the Police Prefect.*⁵

Report by the Police Prefect.[5]

Paris, 15 July 1870.

There was great agitation yesterday evening, and war-like manifestations occurred in various parts of Paris. Without awaiting the general account of these demonstrations, we believe it our duty to report immediately the one which took place, towards midnight, in the vicinity of the Prussian Embassy. Various groups, numbering from 600 to 1,200 individuals, approached Mr. von Werther's residence, shouting: "Long live France! Hurrah for War! Down with Prussia! To Berlin!"

Some of them even tried to climb over the gates.

The policeman on duty, who had taken some precautions, restrained them, and made them understand that they were in the wrong. He was listened to. Count Daru and the Marquis de Villeneuve joined their efforts to his, and Mr. von Werther let him be sent for in order to thank him.

The policeman replied that he was under orders to protect the Embassy, and that a detail had been organized for this purpose.

During these incidents, the entire staff of the Prussian Embassy was standing in the courtyard of the residence, a prey to vivid emotions.

No. 94   The French Declaration of War Against Prussia—— 19 July 1870[1]

. . . .

Le Sourd to Bismarck.

Berlin, 19th July, 1870.

THE Undersigned, French *Chargé d'Affaires,* in pursuance of instructions received from his Government, has the honour to make to his Excellency the Minister for Foreign Affairs of His Majesty the King of Prussia the following comunication:—

The Government of His Majesty the Emperor of the French, being unable to consider the proposal to raise a Prussian Prince[2] to the Throne of Spain otherwise than as an attempt against the Territorial security of France, was compelled to ask the King of Prussia for an assurance that such an arrangement could not be carried out with his consent.

His Majesty the King of Prussia having refused to give this assurance, and having, on the contrary, given the Ambassador of His Majesty the Emperor of the French to understand that he intended to reserve for this eventuality, and for every other, the power of acting according to circumstances, the Imperial Government could not but see in the King's declaration a reservation threatening to France and to the general Balance of Power in Europe. This Declaration was further aggravated by the notification made to the Cabinets of the refusal to receive the Emperor's Ambassador and to enter into any new explanation with him.

The Government of His Imperial Majesty has consequently thought itself obliged to provide immediately for the defence of its honour and its compromised interests; and being resolved to take for this purpose all the measures enjoined by the position in which it has been placed, considers itself from henceforth in a state of War with Prussia.

The Undersigned, &c.

LE SOURD.

No. 95   Napoleon III Surrenders at Sedan——
2 September 1870[1]

. . . .

Then Count Reille[2] appeared, accompanied by Captain von Winterfeld of the General Staff and a trumpeter of the Prussian Lancers. As soon as he saw the King, he dismounted, first straightened out something about his riding-breeches, then took off his red cap and, a large stick in his hand, with downcast eyes, to be sure, but yet not at all without dignity, approached His Majesty and, with a few words, handed him Napoleon's letter.

The King opened it and read the short message written by the Emperor himself: "My dear Brother, not having been able to die amidst my troops, nothing remains for me but to surrender my sword into Your Majesty's hands. I remain, Your Majesty's good Brother, Napoleon. Sedan, 1 Sept. 1870." Thereupon the King immediately told Count Reille that, unless the whole French army laid down its arms, he would not enter into any negotiations, but at the same time declared himself willing to answer Emperor Napoleon's letter at once.

Then the King first discussed with Count Bismarck, General Moltke, and myself the content of the letter which he wished to send to Napoleon; thereupon a draft of it was first dictated to, and written down by, Councillor of Legation Count Paul Hatzfeld. The letter, then written by His Majesty himself, ran as follows: "My dear Brother. While regretting the circumstances in which we meet, I accept Your Majesty's sword, and I ask that you would kindly appoint one of your officers, provided with your full powers, to negotiate the conditions for the capitulation of the army which has fought so bravely under your orders. For my part,

I have designated General von Moltke for this purpose. I remain, Your Majesty's good Brother, William.–In front of Sedan, 1 September 1870."

. . . .

The King had announced that today [2 September], from eight o'clock on, he would await the day's further developments on the hill from which I had directed the battle yesterday; however, His Majesty appeared much later, and while I was waiting on the road at the foot of the hill, suddenly General von Moltke drove up from the direction of Donchéry. From him I learned the following: the negotiations with the French General Wimpffen, who had come out from Sedan, had as yet been unsuccessful because he had shown no inclination at all to capitulate and had returned to Sedan for further orders. But the whole situation had really entered a new stage through the fact that suddenly, at five o'clock in the morning, Emperor Napoleon had left Sedan in a carriage, accompanied only by his adjutant, and then had stopped in a potato field not far from Donchéry to wait until Count Bismarck[3] and General von Moltke had been informed of his presence. Both hurried at once to meet him, and offered him their lodgings in Donchéry, which the Emperor, however, declined; it seemed as if he wanted to avoid the cities altogether, and therefore preferred to alight at a peasant cottage nearby. Napoleon then said that he had appeared in person in order to obtain more favorable terms than the laying down of arms, and suggested the withdrawal of the army, with all of its equipment, into Belgium, where it would then be interned; furthermore, he had requested both gentlemen to ask the King to grant him an audience. All of this gave Moltke the impression that these were only pretended reasons, that in reality Emperor Napoleon had feared for his life in Sedan, and, after some unpleasant incidents, had been forced to flee from his own soldiers. It was said that groups of soldiers had assembled in front of his house at night, shouting "down with the pig" and similar invectives. His household staff was rather worried about getting the carriages and baggage wagons out of Sedan, and they all breathed a sigh of relief when the news arrived that they were safely out of the fortress. . . .

At last the King appeared, and, upon General von Moltke's advice, ordered that the unconditional laying down of arms be demanded; the officers, however, were to be placed on their word of honor. If this condition were not accepted, then the bombardment was to start again immediately. General von Moltke returned with this order, which he himself had urgently advocated, and the result of it was that, about at noon, the capitulation was agreed to unconditionally and signed by the Generals von Moltke and Wimpffen. . . .

.   .   .   .

. . . In a quarter of an hour, we arrived at the pretty little country manor of Bellevue, where our Royal Cuirassiers and Bavarian infantry were standing guard. . . . The King and I dismounted, and were received by General Castelnau, who wore a dejected look. Emperor Napoleon, in full uniform, wearing the Star of the Legion of Honor and several smaller decorations, appeared at the entrance to the reception hall and led the King into the drawing room, whose glass doors I then closed and in front of which I remained, while the French staff went out into the garden. . . .

The interview may have lasted for a good quarter of an hour, after which the King and Napoleon by his side stepped back into the reception hall, where the tall, commanding figure of our King appeared wonderfully exalted beside the small, very thick-set figure of the Emperor. When Napoleon saw me, he shook hands with me; heavy tears ran down his cheeks, which he wiped away with his hand, as he mentioned, with the utmost gratitude for both the words and the manner, the way in which His Majesty had just expressed himself. I told him that it was only natural to meet the unfortunate above all with compassion. Upon my question whether he had been able to find something of a night's rest, he replied that worry about his family, in the midst of the miseries of war, had left him with little sleep. When I then remarked that the present war had assumed a formidable and very sanguinary character, Napoleon replied, yes, that could not be denied, but it was all the more terrible if one had not wanted war ("above all, when one did not want war"). At this, I was silent for a moment because I did not want to give an answer and was more than a little surprised to hear such a statement expressed by Napoleon himself, the originator of this war. Then I inquired after the Empress and the Prince Imperial, but he had received no news of them for more than eight days. Upon his question how my wife and my children were, I could only give him exactly the same answer.

Napoleon asked the King for permission to send a coded telegram to the Empress, which was granted. Thereupon His Majesty and Napoleon shook hands and said goodby, and I did the same; then the Emperor accompanied our King to the top of the steps, but he had already disappeared by the time we were back in the saddle. . . .

No. 96   The Founding of the Second German Empire at
Versailles——18 January 1871[1]

By 11:30 a.m., there were assembled in the large Hall of Mirrors of the palace [of Versailles] the Protestant and Catholic military chaplains, the commanding generals of the army corps of the Third Army and the Army of the Meuse, every one of the division and brigade generals; all the regimental commanders, all the military staffs, the Great General Staff, the Ministry of War, the office of the Quartermaster General, the office of the Adjutant General of the Army, and the officials of the various administrative branches, the office of the Chancellor of the Confederation, the Ministry for the Royal Household. Finally, the flags of the entire Third Army and those of its non-commissioned officers and soldiers decorated with the Iron Cross. This assembly numbered well over 2,000 persons.

In the first three adjoining halls were placed two guards of honor composed of infantrymen and one of cavalrymen, and individual honor guards from all the branches of the service were stationed at all the doors. In the fourth hall were assembled the retinues of the nobles, and in the fifth hall all the nobles and princes, led by the Crown Prince and the Prussian princes.

. . . A few minutes later, one heard commands being given, the guards presented arms, the serried ranks opened, and the King entered. He was dressed in the uniform of the 1st. Guards Infantry Regiment, as he usually is for great occasions; he wore all the military decorations and insignia of Europe. I have rarely yet seen the King so affected that he gave the impression of being deeply depressed. He had climbed the great marble stairway quickly, and entered the hall where the princes were so out of breath that, combined with his inward agitation, he had difficulty in delivering a short speech to us in which [he] briefly described the importance of the approaching ceremony.

. . . We now walked through the splendid halls mentioned before to the great Hall of Louis XIV, in which the following arrangement had been made. An altar had been set up in front of the middle window of the Hall, around which the clergy assembled. To the right and left of the altar, along the row of large windows, were placed the non-commissioned officers and soldiers of the Third Army decorated with the Iron Cross in 4-5 ranks, and, closest to the altar, a military band and choir. Facing this arrangement were the already mentioned officers and officials, arrayed in dense groups by army corps.

The King now took up a position facing the altar, and we assembled in a semi-circle behind him. The band played a psalm, which was sung by the choir: Shout with Joy, etc. Then the assemblage sang the song: Praise and Honor to the Highest, etc. There followed the Creed and the Lord's Prayer. Next, Division Chaplain Rogge gave a sermon appropriate to the ceremony, at the end of which he offered a prayer and said the Lord's Prayer. Then the assemblage began to sing very vigorously and sonorously the song: Thank Ye All God, of which three stanzas were sung. The benediction ended the religious ceremony, which may be said to have been just as simple as it was dignified, and thereby also stirring. A platform had been built at the western end of the Hall, upon which stood non-commissioned officers with the flags of all the regiments of the Third Army; Prussian and Bavarian flags formed the venerable background for the position now taken up by the King. . . .

When the nobles had gathered around the King and the entire assembly had turned toward this end of the Hall, the King took out a sheet of paper, turned toward the nobles, and read something like the following speech. Since the German nobles and free cities had offered him the imperial dignity and a formal declaration on the subject had now been given him, he declares his willingness, while expressing his thanks, to accept the Imperial crown for himself and his heirs, and sets this forth in a proclamation which he addresses to the German people and which he herewith instructs the Imperial Chancellor to read aloud.—We bowed before the King, who now took up his position in our midst and turned toward the assembly.—The Chancellor of the Confederation stepped in front of the King, bowed before him, then stood to his left below and next to him, and read, in an audible, but very agitated, voice, the proclamation to the German people, wherein the confirmation of what was said is expressed. The text of this document is too important to give only an excerpt of it here.[2]—After reading the proclamation, the Chancellor of the Confederation again approached, bowed, and took up his former position to the left of the platform.—Now it was my turn—I approached the Emperor, bowed, and asked for permission to be allowed to lead the assembly in a cheer for him. The Emperor nodded approval, and I shouted as loudly as possible to the expectant, but hushed, assembly: Long live His Imperial and Royal Majesty, Emperor William,[3] long may he live, long may he live!—There now began jubilant cheering, repeated six times, which one had to have heard but cannot describe. Thereupon the Emperor shook my hand in a very cordial way and turned next to the Crown Prince, who was so moved by the ceremony that he fell to one knee in front of his father and beseeched his blessing hand. The Emperor raised him up with a fervent embrace and in the deepest affection, which had a visible effect upon all those present. Then the Emperor greeted each and every one of the nobles, and accepted the greetings of the numerous assembly by letting those present approach him in groups and make a bow. After this greeting ceremony, the Emperor went over to the flags and talked to their bearers; then he descended from the platform, spoke with many generals and noblemen, and, to the sound of a festival march, walked down the long row of decorated soldiers, saying a friendly word to many of these brave veterans. The Emperor had now regained his customary brisk, strong bearing, and it could be clearly observed that he felt elated at the highly important ceremony of this hour. He looked serious, to be sure, but satisfied, and his remarks corresponded to this look.

In the last part of the Hall were drawn up a rather large number of newly promoted officers, whose salute the Emperor returned, and he then began to make his way back through the four halls already mentioned. As the Emperor left the Hall of Mirrors, the band struck up the Hohenfriedberger March composed by Frederick the Great, and from the halls where the guards of honor stood endless hurrahs rang out.

.   .   .   .

No. 97   Bismarck and Alsace-Lorraine——
11 August to 17 September 1870[1]

Bismarck to Henry VII Prince Reuss.[2]

Saarbrücken, 11 August 1870.

.   .   .   .

. . . It is not only Napoleon, it is France herself which, in her lust for power, constitutes a continuous danger to her neighbors, with or without a Napoleon to rule her. A change of dynasty would only be a decorative change; the essentials of the drama, which is based upon the combination of French national character with France's concentrated development of power, would continue to unfold whether the name of her ruler is Orleans or Bonaparte.

.   .   .   .

. . . We do not have to take any other consideration towards France than our own and the general political interest.

.   .   .   .

Bismarck to Count von Bernstorff.[3]

Pont-à-Mousson, 21 August 1870.
I have already briefly informed Yr. Exc. by telegraph that I agree with the intention expressed in your kind report No. 242 of the 17th inst. to already prepare public opinion now, through, at first, a more academic discussion in the most important English newspapers, for the peace terms which we would have to demand of France in case of the continued fortunate success of our arms. I find this to be all the more correct because here, considering the healthy common sense of the English people, we can perhaps more readily count upon some

understanding than with the statesmen grown up during the last few years of prevailing French sympathies. Public opinion in England will comprehend that we must prevent, if possible, a repetition in the near future of the immense sacrifices which this war is costing our people, from the palaces to the cottages a[nd] that we must protect southern Germany in particular better than we have until now against the danger of its open geographical position where, coming from Strassburg, under skillful a[nd] energetic leadership, not only Baden, but Württemburg and Bavaria, can be invaded at any time. We are fighting today against the 12th. or 15th. invasion a[nd] war of conquest which France has conducted against Germany during the past 200 years. In 1814 and 1815, assurances against a repetition of these breaches of the peace were sought by treating France with forbearance. But the danger lies in the incurable lust for power a[nd] arrogance which is peculiar to the French national character and which can be misused by every ruler of the country to attack peaceful neighboring states. Our protection against this evil does not lie in the fruitless attempt to momentarily attenuate the sensitivity of the French, but in our acquisition of well fortified frontiers. We must bring to an end the pressure which France has exerted for two centuries against a southern Germany abandoned to her without protection, and which has become a crucial lever for the shattering of German conditions. Through the consistently pursued annexation of German territory and of all of its natural protective barriers, France has placed herself in the position of being able to penetrate at any time with a relatively small army into the heart of southern Germany before ready assistance can be there. Since Louis XIV, under him, under the Republic, under the First Empire, these incursions have been repeated again and again; and the feeling of insecurity which they leave behind, and the fear of a repetition of this horror, forces the South German states to constantly keep an eye upon France. We cannot always count upon such an extraordinary groundswell of popular sentiment, nor can we expect the nation to repeatedly bear the burden of such heavy armaments. If the disarmament theory has honest adherents in England, then they must want France's closest neighbors to be better protected than they have been until now against this sole disturber of the peace in Europe. That this would arouse *bitterness* in the French can be of no moment in comparison. Such bitterness will develop to exactly the same degree if they emerge from this war *without* cessions of territory. This was one of the main reasons why we did not demand any cessions of land from Austria; have we received any thanks at all for it? Our victory at *Sadowa* has already aroused bitterness in the *French;* how much more will result from our victory over the French themselves! Even without cessions of territory, revenge for Metz, for Wörth, will remain a battlecry for a longer time than revenge for Sadowa or Waterloo! The only correct policy under such circumstances is to at least render an enemy, whom one *cannot* convert into a sincere friend, somewhat less harmful and to protect ourselves better against him, for which purpose we cannot be satisfied with the demolition of those of his fortresses which threaten us, but only with the cession of a few of them.

I trust that I may humbly leave it to Yr. Exc.'s discretion that these viewpoints influence as much as possible the discussion in the English press in a manner commensurate with local circumstances.

Bismarck to Baron von Werthern.[4]

Reims, 6 September 1870.

We hear that foreign gov[ernmen]ts have made declarations against cessions of territory by France. You are not to leave any doubts that we will insist, whatever the danger, upon a better regulation of the frontier in the interest of safeguarding southern Germany, without dynastic interests. In Paris, provisional government of Republican composition proclaimed.

Bismarck to Henry VII Prince Reuss.[5]

CONFIDENTIAL.

Reims, 6 September 1870.

. . . .

Yr. Exc. knows that His Majesty, the King, is free of any personal or dynastic ambition which would prompt his desire to enlarge Prussia by annexing parts of France. The demands which we shall make have as their sole purpose the protection and safety of Germany, and we shall, therefore, strive for their realization only in the name, and for the benefit, of all of Germany.

I have already indicated to Yr. Exc. before that the objective of His Majesty's decisions is the strategic safety of Germany, particularly of southern Germany. . . . Until now, France has been aware that she has emerged from every war started arbitrarily by her without any penalty and without a diminution of her territory which had been increased at Germany's expense. To leave her in this certainty, and to reinforce it by a new concession, would be to place a premium upon arrogance and a thirst for war. Under Germany's control, the position which we must strive to gain for its strategic protection will always be only a defensive one and will never endanger the peace and tranquillity of Europe.

We are, therefore, determined not to accept any peace which would not ensure the strategic safety of Germany's southwestern frontier. Everyone in Germany agrees on this point; and no German ruler would be able to oppose this national demand without danger to himself.[6]

. . . .

Circular Dispatch to All Missions Abroad.
Reims, 13 September 1870.

. . . .

. . . We must not deceive ourselves on the point that, as a result of this war, we must expect a renewed attack by France soon and not a lasting peace, and this wholly irrespective of the conditions which we could possibly impose upon France. It is the defeat itself, it is our victorious defense against her outrageous attack, which the French nation shall never forgive us. If we now were to withdraw from France without any cessions of territory, without any indemnity, without any other advantage than the glory of our arms, there would still remain in the French nation the same hatred, the same thirst for revenge because of her injured vanity and arrogance, and she would only live for the day when she could hope to successfully transform these feelings into action. . . .

. . . .

Bismarck to Count von Bernstorff.[7]

Meaux, 17 September 1870.
Reply to telegram no. 241.
We have no intention of interfering in the internal affairs of the French, particularly of imposing a government upon them. We could not care less who rules France, Napoleon or white or red Republic. Our sole objective is the strategic safety of our southwestern frontier against [the] *doubtlessly imminent* next attack by France upon Germany; until this objective is close to being reached through [the] cession of Alsace and Lorraine, we are determined to continue the war, a[nd], remaining at war, to wait not only for the Constituent [Assembly], but one year and several years. We are not interested in supporting the present government against its possible red successor, or the latter against the former, unless the former or the latter is ready and able to conclude a treaty with us on the above basis. The improved safety of Germany's western frontier has become, as a result of this war, such an overriding necessity for us that to achieve it we do not shrink back either from a war of extermination around or in Paris, or from 10 years of war, or from the most daring appeal to Germany's national power against neutral intervention, or from an alliance with Napoleon.

Lord Granville himself has, unfortunately, contributed to the prolongation of an uncertain situation by transmitting French proposals; we would be closer to the goal of peace if he had left it to the government in Paris to communicate directly with us.

You are to discuss the content of this dispatch in private with Lord Granville.

No. 98   The Preliminary Peace of Versailles——26 February 1871[1]

BETWEEN the Chancellor of the Germanic Empire, Count Otto de Bismarck-Schönhausen, furnished with Full Powers from His Majesty the Emperor of Germany, King of Prussia; the Minister of State and of Foreign Affairs of His Majesty the King of Bavaria, Count Otto de Bray-Steinburg; the Minister for Foreign Affairs of His Majesty the King of Würtemberg, Baron Auguste de Wächter; the Minister of State, President of the Council of Ministers of His Royal Highness the Grand Duke of Baden, Monsieur Jules Jolly, representing the Germanic Empire, on the one part; and on the other part, the Chief of the Executive Power of the French Republic, Monsieur Thiers, and the Minister for Foreign Affairs, Monsieur Jules Favre, representing France; the Full Powers of the two Contracting Parties having been found in good and due form, the following has been agreed upon, to serve as a Preliminary Basis to the Definitive Peace to be concluded hereafter.[2]

Renunciations by France in favour of Germany.

ART. I. France renounces in favour of the German Empire all her Rights and Titles over the Territories situated on the East of the Frontier hereafter described.

Line of new Frontier between France and Germany.

The Line of Demarcation begins at the North-west Frontier of the Canton of Cattenom, towards the Grand Duchy of Luxemburg, follows on the South the Western Frontiers of the Cantons of Cattenom and Thionville, passes by the Canton of Briey, along the Western Frontiers of the Communes of Montjois-la-Montagne and Roncourt, as well as the Eastern Frontiers of the Communes of Marie-aux-Chênes, St. Ail, Habonville, reaches the Frontier of the Canton de Gooze, which it crosses along the Communal Frontiers of Vionville, Bouxières, and Onville, follows the South-west Frontier, south of the District of Metz, the Western Frontier of the District of Chateau-Salins, as far as the Commune of Pettoncourt, taking in the Western and Southern Frontiers thereof to follow the Crest of the Mountains between Seille and Moncel, as far as the Frontier of the District of Sarreburg, to the South of Garde. The demarca-

tion afterwards coincides with the Frontier of that District as far as the Commune of Tanconville, reaching the Frontier to the North thereof, from thence it follows the Crest of the Mountains between the Sources of the White Sarre and Vezouze, as far as the Frontier of that Canton of Schirmeck, skirts the Western Frontier of that Canton, includes the Communes of Saales, Bourg-Bruche, Colroy-la-Roche, Plaine, Ranrupt, Saulxures, and St. Blaise-la-Roche of the Canton of Saales, and coincides with the Western Frontier of the Departments of the Lower Rhine and the Upper Rhine as far as the Cantons of Belfort, the Southern Frontier of which it leaves not far from Vourvenans, to cross the Canton of Delle at the Southern Limits of the Communes of Bourogne and Froide Fontaine, and to reach the Swiss Frontier skirting the Eastern Frontiers of the Communes of Jonchery and Delle.

International Boundary Commission to be appointed.

The German Empire shall possess these Territories in perpetuity in all Sovereignty and Property. An International Commission, composed of an equal number of Representatives of the two High Contracting Parties, shall be appointed immediately after the exchange of the Ratifications of the present Treaty, to trace on the spot the new Frontier, in conformity with the preceding stipulations.

· · · · · · · · · ·

Indemnity to be paid by France.

ART. II. France shall pay to His Majesty the Emperor of Germany the sum of 5,000,000,000 Francs (5 milliards).

Time of Payment of Indemnity.

The Payment of at least 1,000,000,000 (one milliard) Francs shall be effected within the year 1871, and the whole of the remainder of the Debt in the space of 3 years, dating from the Ratification of the present.

Evacuation of French Territory by German Troops.

ART. III. The Evacuation of the French Territory occupied by German Troops shall begin after the Ratification of the present Treaty by the National Assembly sitting at Bordeaux. . . .

Gradual Evacuation according to Payments made.

The Evacuation of the Departments between the Right Bank of the Seine and the Eastern Frontier by German Troops shall take place gradually after the Ratification of the Definitive Treaty of Peace and the payment of the first 500,000,000 (half milliard) of the contribution stipulated by Article II, beginning with the Departments nearest to Paris, and shall continue gradually, according to the proportion of the Payments made on account of the Contribution; after the first Payment of a 500,000,000 (half milliard) that Evacuation shall take place in the following Departments: Somme, Oise, and the parts of the Departments of the Seine Inférieure, Seine et Oise, Seine et Marne, situated on the Right Bank of the Seine, as well as the part of the Department of the Seine, and the Forts situated on the Right Bank.

Conditions for Payment of the last 3,000,000,000 (3 milliards) of Indemnity.

After the payment of 2,000,000,000 (two milliards), the German occupation shall only include the Departments of the Marne, Ardennes, Haut Marne, Meuse, Vosges, Meurthe, as well as the Fortress of Belfort, with its Territory, which shall serve as a pledge for the remaining 3,000,000,000 (3 milliards), and in which the number of

the German Troops shall not exceed 50,000 men. His Majesty the Emperor will be willing to substitute for the Territorial Guarantee, consisting in partial occupation of the French Territory, a Financial Guarantee, should it be offered by the French Government under conditions considered sufficient by His Majesty the Emperor and King for the interests of Germany. The 3,000,000,000 (3 milliards), the payment of which shall have been deferred, shall bear Interest at the rate of 5 per cent, beginning from the Ratification of the present Convention.

Maintenance of German Troops of Occupation.

ART. IV. The German Troops shall abstain from levying contributions either in money or in kind in the occupied Departments. On the other hand, the maintenance of the German Troops remaining in France shall be at the expense of the French Government in the manner decided upon by an Agreement with the German Military Administration.

RATIFICATIONS.

ART. X. The present Preliminary Treaty shall be immediately submitted to the Ratification of His Majesty the Emperor of Germany and to the French National Assembly sitting at Bordeaux.[3]

In testimony whereof the Undersigned have signed the present Preliminary Treaty, and sealed it with the Seal of their Arms.

Done at Versailles, 26th February, 1871.

(L.S.) BISMARCK   (L.S.) A. THIERS.

(L.S.) JULES FAVRE.

Accession of Baden, Bavaria, and Würtemberg.

The Kingdoms of Bavaria and Würtemberg, and the Grand Duchy of Baden, having taken part in the actual War as Allies of Prussia, and now forming part of the

Germanic Empire, the Undersigned adhere to the present Convention in the name of their respective Sovereigns.

Versailles, 26th February, 1871.

CTE. DE BRAY-STEINBURG.   MITTNACHT.
BN. DE WACHTER.   JOLLY.

[Conventions were concluded between France and Germany on the 21st May, and 12th October, 1871, on the 29th June, 1872, and on the 15th May, 1873, with reference to the payment of the War Indemnity of 3 Milliards = 5,000,000,000 Francs or £200,000,000. The last Instalment was paid by France on the 5th September, 1873, and the last German Troops passed the French Frontier on the 16th of the same Month.—Ed.]

No. 99   Summary of Gramont's Conditions for Peace—— 3 August 1870[1]

Bismarck to Count von Bernstorff.[2]

General Headquarters.
Pont-à-Mousson, 22 August 1870.

. . . .

1. Reduction of Prussia to its frontiers of 1866.

2. Cession of the Saar coal region to France.

3. Payment of the costs of war to France, and restitution of the costs of war [of 1866] to Austria.

4. Restoration of the dispossessed.

5. Increase of the [German] middle states at the expense of Prussian territory.

6. The creation of groups of states in Germany which would permanently destroy Prussian supremacy.

In addition, he [Gramont] mentioned that, once French troops had reached Berlin, Danzig could be offered to Russia as the price for its neutrality.

. . . .

Notes

No. 57, pp. 155-156
[1] *Brit. Parliam. Papers* (1864), LXIV, 28-29.
[2] Danish Prime Minister.—HNW.

No. 58, pp. 156-157
[1] From the official German text as reprinted in *Das Staatsarchiv, Sammlung der officiellen Actenstücke zur Geschichte der Gegenwart,* VI (1864), 78-86. Hereafter cited as *Staatsarchiv.* Translated by Herman N. Weill.
[2] The order of succession in the Duchies was one of the important points at issue between Denmark and the members of the German Confederation.—HNW.
[3] In addition to the Royal Assembly, there were local Assemblies or Estates. This provision was apparently designed to prevent these local Assemblies, particularly the ones in the Duchies, from annulling a law passed by the Royal Assembly.—HNW.

No. 59, pp. 158-159
[1] *Brit. Parliam. Papers* (1864), LXIV, 59-61.
[2] British Ambassador at Copenhagen.—HNW.

No. 60, pp. 159-160
[1] *Brit. Parliam. Papers* (1864), LXIV, 585.
[2] See *No. 58,* above.—HNW.

No. 61, p. 160
[1] *Brit. Parliam. Papers* (1864), LXIV, 585-586.

No. 62, pp. 161-162
[1] *Staatsarchiv*, VI (1864), 613-614. Translated by Herman N. Weill.
[2] See *No. 60*, above.–HNW.
[3] See *No. 58*, above.–HNW.
[4] See *No. 61*, above.–HNW.

No. 63, pp. 162-163
[1] Hertslet (ed.), *Map of Europe*, III, 1630-1633.
[2] An Armstice was concluded on the 18th July, 1864, and Preliminaries of Peace were signed at Vienna on the 1st August, 1864.–Ed.

No. 64, pp. 163-164
[1] Otto von Bismarck, *The Man and the Statesman, Being the Reflections and Reminiscences of Otto, Prince von Bismarck, Written and Dictated by Himself after His Retirement from Office*, trans. A. J. Butler, 2 vols. (New York and London, 1898-99), II, 9-10. Hereafter cited as Bismarck, *Man and Statesman*.
[2] Frederick VII died on 15 November 1863.–HNW.

No. 65, pp. 164-165
[1] Prussia. Historische Reichskommission. *Die auswärtige Politik Preussens, 1858-1871: Diplomatische Aktenstücke*, eds. Erich Brandenburg, *et al.*, 10 vols. in 11 (Oldenburg, 1933-39), Vol. 6, No. 100, pp. 174-179. Hereafter cited as *Ausw. Politik Preussens*. Translated by Herman N. Weill.

No. 66, pp. 165-166
[1] *Ausw. Politik Preussens*, Vol. 6, No. 100, pp. 179-180. Translated by Herman N. Weill.
[2] The following marginal comment appears here: "His Majesty himself had already remarked that we would have conquered the Duchies even without Austria, but that Austria had prevented a European war."–Ed.
[3] Added by Ed.
[4] Moltke's marginal comment: "An important point, which was not discussed, is how to satisfy Austria's justified claims."–Ed.

No. 67, pp. 166-168
[1] Hertslet (ed.), *Map of Europe*, III, 1638-1642.
[2] See *No. 63*, above.–HNW.
[3] Approved at Salzburg, 20th August, 1865.–Ed.

No. 68, pp. 168-170
[1] Hermann Oncken (ed.), *Die Rheinpolitik Kaiser Napoleons III. von 1863 bis 1870 und der Ursprung des Krieges von 1870/71*, 3 vols. (Stuttgart and Berlin, 1926), I, 69-73. Hereafter cited as Oncken (ed.), *Rheinpolitik Napoleons III*. Translated by Herman N. Weill.
[2] Prussian Ambassador at Paris.–HNW.
[3] French Foreign Minister.–HNW.
[4] In this circular—the ostensible cause of Bismarck's visit—Drouyn had sharply protested against the Gastein Convention which, he maintained, was inimical to French interests.–HNW.
[5] For extracts from the reports by Lefebvre de Béhaine, French *chargé d'affaires* in Berlin, on his conversations with Bismarck, see *No. 72*, below. Oncken states that Bismarck's report to William I appears to have been given orally, for there is no written report in the archives; see Oncken (ed.), *Rheinpolitik Napoleons III.*, I, 70, n. 2.–HNW.
[6] Bismarck, accompanied by his wife and daughter, arrived in Paris on 1 October 1865. He reached Biarritz on 3 October, and thus had his first interview with Napoleon on 4 October; see Otto von Bismarck, *Die gesammelten Werke*, eds. Herman von Petersdorff, *et al.*, 15 vols. in 19 (Berlin, 1924-1933), V, 306—hereafter cited as Bismarck, *Gesammelte Werke*.–HNW.
[7] The text of the telegram was as follows:
"Biarritz, 5 October, 1865.
"Yesterday lengthy interview with the Emperor. Repeats sincere regret over circular of 29 August. Assurances of unchanged friendship and sympathy. Did not take offense at the thought of our peaceful agreement with Austria over Holstein through money. No expectation for the future which would have embarrassed me. However ready to join with us in taking advantage of events which arise unsought. His Majesty looks better than I have ever seen him before."
In Bismarck, *Gesammelte Werke*, V, 306-307; translated by Herman N. Weill.

No. 69, p. 171
[1] Bismarck, *Gesammelte Werke*, V, 316. Translated by Herman N. Weill.

No. 70, pp. 171-172
[1] France, Ministère des Affaires Etrangères, *Les origines diplomatiques de la guerre de 1870-*

1871, 29 vols. (Paris, 1910-1932), I, 2-4. Hereafter cited as France, *Origines diplomatiques 1870/1871*. Translated by Herman. N. Weill.

2 General Count Fleury, aide-de-camp to Napoleon, had been appointed ambassador extraordinary to convey the Emperor's felicitations to Christian IX, the new King of Denmark. He was also instructed to join with the British and Russian representatives at Copenhagen in their attempt to persuade Christian to withdraw the November Constitution (see *No. 58*, above), and to try to convince Bismarck that the German-Danish conflict over the Duchies should not be solved by recourse to war.—HNW.

3 Great Britain had taken the lead in pressing for a European Congress to settle the dispute over the Duchies.—HNW.

4 The signatory Powers of the protocol of 8 May 1852: England, France, Austria, Prussia, Russia, Sweden, Denmark.—Ed.

5 The Duke de Montebello had left St. Petersburg on October 20th, and had accredited Count de Massignac as *chargé d'affaires* with Prince Gortchakoff.—Ed.

No. 71, pp. 172-174

1 Oncken (ed.), *Rheinpolitik Napoleons III.*, I, 45-47. Translated by Herman N. Weill.

2 Bismarck sent copies of this dispatch to the Prussian ambassadors in St. Petersburg and in Paris. He asked them to make confidential inquiries on the subject, and to report back to him. The following two documents are from their replies.—HNW.

3 Russian Foreign Minister.—HNW.

4 Austrian Ambassador at Paris.—HNW.

No. 72, pp. 174-177

1 France, *Origines diplomatiques 1870/71*, VII, 57-59, 63-65, 88-91, 100-102. Translated by Herman N. Weill.

2 French *chargé d'affaires* at Berlin.—HNW.

3 French Foreign Minister.—HNW.

4 Prussian ambassador at Paris.—HNW.

5 See the preceding dispatch of 12 September 1865.—HNW.

6 Prussian Minister of the Interior.—HNW.

No. 73, pp. 177-178

1 Germain Bapst (ed.), *Le Maréchal Canrobert: Souvenirs d'un siècle* (6 vols., Paris, 1898-1913), IV, 34-36. Translated by Herman N. Weill.

2 [Jacques Louis] Randon, *Mémoires du Maréchal Randon* (2 vols., Paris, 1875-77), II, 206. Translated by Herman N. Weill.

3 French Minister of War.—HNW.

No. 74, p. 178

1 Oncken (ed.), *Rheinpolitik Napoleons III.*, I, 212-213. Translated by Herman N. Weill.

2 Prussian Ambassador at Paris.—HNW.

No. 75, p. 179

1 Oncken (ed.), *Rheinpolitik Napoleons III.*, I, 204-205. Translated by Herman N. Weill.

2 Austrian Ambassador at Paris.—HNW.

3 Austrian Foreign Minister.—HNW.

No. 76, p. 180

1 Oncken (ed.) *Rheinpolitik Napoleons III.*, I, 284-286. Translated by Herman N. Weill.

2 Bavarian Ambassador at Paris.—HNW.

3 King of Bavaria.—HNW.

4 Austrian commander on the northern front.—HNW.

5 The Emperor's cousin and a known opponent of Austria.—HNW.

6 That is, those advocating French intervention on the side of the Prusso-Italian alliance.—HNW.

No. 77, pp. 181-182

1 Oncken (ed.), *Rheinpolitik Napoleons III.*, I, 265-267. Translated by Herman N. Weill.

2 The secret convention and the Additional Note were ratified in Paris on June 16th. The copy in the Vienna Imperial Archives carries Napoleon's own signature and the countersignature of Drouyn de Lhuys.—Ed.

3 Points (1) through (4) contain details of the cession of Venetia to Italy, Point (5) an agreement that, in the event of an internal upheaval in Italy, neither France nor any other foreign Power would intervene.—HNW.

No. 78, p. 182

1 Oncken (ed.), *Rheinpolitik Napoleons III.*, I, 89-91. Translated by Herman N. Weill.

No. 79, p. 183

1 Heinrich von Sybel, *The Founding of the German Empire by William I*, trans. Marshall L. Perrin and Gamaliel Bradford, Jr., 7 vols. (New York, 1890-98), IV, 354-356.

2 For the original French text, see *Origines diplomatiques*, VIII, 462-463, and particularly

Friedrich Thimme's foreword to No. 310 in Bismarck, *Gesammelte Werke*, V, 462.–HNW.
3 The sentence in brackets is an editorial addition made by Sybel. Thimme, in the foreword mentioned above, comments: "There is no supporting evidence in the archives for this comment by Sybel; it is probably based upon a later communication made by Bismarck to Sybel."–HNW.

No. 80, p. 184
1 Hertslet (ed.), *Map of Europe*, III, 1652-1654.

No. 81, pp. 185-188
1 Bismarck, *Man and Statesman*, II, 36-37, 42-43, 47-54.
2 So written by the general staff. It is pronounced Horsitz.
3 The Austrian and French ambassadors, respectively.–HNW.
4 Negotiations on the specific French demands continued for the next 7 weeks and culminated in Benedetti's draft treaty of 23 August 1866, given in *No. 84*, below.–HNW.
5 The memorandum, with the King's marginal comments, is reprinted in Bismarck, *Gesammelte Werke*, VI, 78-81.–HNW.
6 This scene has been corroborated by the Crown Prince. See Friedrich III, German Emperor, *Tagebücher von 1848-1866*, ed. Heinrich O. Meissner (Leipzig, 1929), pp. 471-475. –HNW.

No. 82, pp. 188-190
1 Hertslet (ed.) *Map of Europe*, III, 1698-1701.
2 The Lombardo-Venetian Kingdom was ceded by Austria to Italy by the Treaty of Prague of 23rd August, 1866.–Ed.
3 See *No. 63*, above.–HNW.
4 This provision was evaded by Prussia, and later by the German Empire. It was only in the wake of World War I that plebiscites were held in this region. The great majority of the inhabitants then voted for reunion with Denmark.–HNW.
5 The provisions in this preliminary peace are almost identical with the final peace treaty signed at Prague on 23 August 1866. The latter is given in Hertslet (ed.), *Map of Europe*, III, 1720-1728.–HNW.
6 Hertslet omits Bismarck's signature.–HNW.

No. 83, pp. 190-191
1 *Archiv des Norddeutschen Bundes*, ed. Glaser,

Vol. I (1867), No. 3, p. 39. Translated by Herman N. Weill.
2 Identical treaties between Prussia and Baden, and Prussia and Bavaria, signed on 17 and 22 August 1866, respectively, are reprinted *ibid.*, pp. 40-42.–HNW.

No. 84, pp. 191-192
1 France, *Origines diplomatiques 1870/71*, XII, 173-175. Translated by Herman N. Weill. Bismarck released a copy of this draft to *The* [London] *Times*, which published it, in French, on 25 July 1870 (p. 9), shortly after the outbreak of the Franco-Prussian War. The two versions are similar, but not identical. I have indicated the differences by the use of parenthesis.–HNW.
2 French Ambassador at Berlin.–HNW.
3 Bypassing Drouyn de Lhuys, who was to resign as Foreign Minister one week later, Napoleon had designated Rouher, Minister of State, as his go-between in these secret negotiations. For additional dispatches concerning this proposed alliance, see France, *Origines diplomatiques 1870/71*, XII, 116-117, 170-173, 175-176, 192-196, 213-216.–HNW.
4 In *The* [London] *Times* version, the King of Prussia is named first.–HNW.
5,5a Omitted in *The* [London] *Times* version.–HNW.
6 *Ibid.*–HNW.

No. 85, pp. 192-194
1 Bismarck, *Gesammelte Werke*, Vol. 6-B, pp. 271-274. Translated by Herman N. Weill.
2 See *No. 4*, above.–HNW.

No. 86, p. 194
1 Bismarck, *Gesammelte Werke*, Vol. 6-B, pp. 324-325. Translated by Herman N. Weill.
2 Bismarck had been sick with jaundice for several weeks, and had just returned to Berlin one week earlier.–HNW.
3 Spanish Minister-President.–HNW.

No. 87, pp. 195-196
1 Émile Ollivier, *L'Empire libéral: Études, récits, souvenirs* (18 vols., Paris, 1895-[1918]), XIV, 40-47. Hereafter cited as Ollivier, *L'Empire libéral*. Translated by Herman N. Weill.
2 The result of a plebiscite held on 8 May 1870, technically on a constitutional issue, was

generally interpreted as a resounding triumph for Napoleon and the Empire.–HNW.

3 Charles of Hohenzollern-Sigmaringen–a brother of Leopold, the candidate for the Spanish crown–had become Prince of Rumania in 1866 (as Carol I, he became King of Rumania in 1881).–HNW.

No. 88, p. 197

1 Ollivier, *L'Empire libéral*, XIV, 96, 108-110. Translated by Herman N. Weill.

Ollivier headed the French Cabinet at this time, and thus is writing from personal experience.–HNW.

2 French Foreign Minister.–HNW.

3 There has been some dispute about the accuracy of several passages in Ollivier's work, including the text of Gramont's speech given here. I have, therefore, compared Ollivier's version with the one given by Lord Lyons, the British Ambassador at Paris (Lyons to Granville, dated Paris, 6 July 1870, Inclosure, in *British and Foreign State Papers*, Vol. 60: *1869-1870*, pp. 788-789,) and by Gramont himself (in *La France et la Prusse avant la guerre*, pp. 40-41). With the exception of the tense of one verb, indicated below, a few punctuation marks, and the absence of paragraphs in Ollivier (where the whole speech is run together in one paragraph), the three versions are identical. For reasons of clarity, I have followed the paragraph arrangement of Lyons and Gramont.–HNW.

4 Present tense in Ollivier, future tense in both Lyons and Gramont.–HNW.

No. 89, p. 198

1 *The* [London] *Times*, Wednesday, July 13, 1870, p. 5.

2 Ernst Walder (ed.), *Die Emser Depesche* (Bern, Switzerland, 1959), p. 49. Hereafter cited as Walder, *Emser Depesche*. Translated by Herman N. Weill.

This extra edition is of some interest because a copy of it was handed to William I in Bad Ems on the morning of 13 July 1870, prior to his interview with Benedetti; see *ibid.*, pp. 49-50, and *No. 91*, below.–HNW.

3 This is inaccurate, as *The* [London] *Times* dispatch indicates.–HNW.

No. 90, p. 198

1 France, *Origines diplomatiques 1870/71*,

XXVIII, 255. Translated by Herman N. Weill.

No. 91, pp. 199-200

1 Walder, *Emser Depesche*, pp. 52-54. Translated by Herman N. Weill.

2 William also wrote two letters to his wife, Queen Augusta, both dated Ems, 13 July 1870, on the day's events, which are given *ibid.*, pp. 49-51. Benedetti sent Gramont a short telegram and a report, both dated 13 July 1870, on his interview with William and on the day's subsequent events; they are printed in France, *Origines diplomatiques 1870/71*, XXVIII, 293-294 and 314-318, respectively.– HNW.

3 William's aide-de-camp.–HNW.

4 These notes, given in Walder, *Emser Depesche*, p. 55, describe those events of the afternoon in which Radziwill acted as a messenger between William and Benedetti.–HNW.

No. 92, p. 201

1 Both texts in Walder, *Emser Depesche*, pp. 15 and 25, respectively. Translated by Herman N. Weill.

2 Representative of the Foreign Ministry at Ems.–HNW.

3 Prussian Minister of the Interior, and Bismarck's emissary, who had just arrived in Ems from Berlin.–HNW.

4 This was Prince Radziwill; see *No. 91*, above. –HNW.

No. 93, pp. 202-203

1 Ollivier, *L'Empire libéral*, pp. 354-356, 384. Translated by Herman N. Weill.

2 Spanish Ambassador at Paris.–HNW.

3 French *chargé d'affaires* at Berlin.–HNW.

4 Prussian Ambassador at Paris.–HNW.

5 France, *Origines diplomatiques 1870/71*, XXVIII, 385-386. Translated by Herman N. Weill.

No. 94, p. 203

1 Hertslet (ed.), *Map of Europe*, III, 1880.

2 Prince Leopold of Hohenzollern-Sigmaringen. –Ed.

No. 95, pp. 204-205

1 Friedrich III, German Emperor, *Das Kriegstagebuch von 1870/71*, ed. Heinrich O. Meisner (Berlin and Leipzig), pp. 94-101. Translated by Herman N. Weill.

2 Napoleon's aide-de-camp.–HNW.

[3] Bismarck's well-known report to William I of this meeting is printed in Bismarck, *Gesammelte Werke*, Vol. 6-B, pp. 467-470. Bismarck also described the event in a letter to his wife, dated 3 September 1870. The letter, it is interesting to note, was captured by the French and first published in Paris. It is given in Rothfels (ed.), *Bismarck-Briefe*, pp. 359-360.—HNW.

No. 96, pp. 206-207

[1] Friedrich I, Grand Duke of Baden, *Grossherzog Friedrich I. von Baden und die deutsche Politik von 1854-1871: Briefwechsel, Denkschriften, Tagebücher*, ed. Hermann Oncken (2 vols., Stuttgart, 1927), II, 322-325. Translated by Herman N. Weill.

[2] The proclamation is reprinted in Bismarck, *Gesammelte Werke*, Vol. 6-B, pp. 671-672.—HNW.

[3] A heated argument, reminiscent of the stormy interview at Nikolsburg, had erupted on the previous day between Bismarck and William over the exact form of William's new title, with the former insisting on "German Emperor" and the latter demanding that it be "Emperor of Germany." Thus, the wording of Grand Duke Frederick's cheer was an ingenious compromise on his part. For details of the argument, see Friedrich III, German Emperor, *Kriegstagebuch 1870/71*, pp. 334-344, and Bismarck, *Man and Statesman*, II, 129-134. —HNW.

No. 97, pp. 208-210

[1] Bismarck, *Gesammelte Werke*, Vol. 6-B, pp. 443-444, 454-455, 476, 477-478, 493-494, 504. Translated by Herman N. Weill.

[2] Prussian ambassador in St. Petersburg. In this dispatch, Bismarck commented on a report that the Duke of Orléans intended to proclaim himself the new ruler of France, and that, in such an event, Germany would be willing to end the war on more favorable terms since it was fighting primarily against Napoleon III and not against France.—HNW.

[3] Prussian Ambassador at London.—HNW.

[4] Prussian Ambassador at Munich.—HNW.

[5] This dispatch was a reply to the urging of the Russian Czar, Alexander II, not to demand territorial cessions from France, for he feared that to do so would sow the seeds of constant future conflict.—HNW.

[6] This view is also completely shared by King William I. In his letter to the Queen of 7 September (W. Oncken, *Unser Heldenkaiser*, p. 215), he writes, regarding the necessity of the cession of Alsace and German Lorraine: "This is also the general attitude in all of Germany, and if the rulers were to attempt to stand firmly against it, they would risk their thrones."—Ed.

[7] Lord Granville, British Foreign Secretary, had expressed some concern about a report that Bismarck intended to help Napoleon III back into power; he had also offered to act as intermediary between Bismarck and the provisional government in Paris. Bismarck, obviously annoyed, sent this dispatch in reply.—HNW.

No. 98, pp. 210-213

[1] Hertslet (ed.), *Map of Europe*, III, 1912-1918.

[2] The Treaty of Frankfurt, incorporating the provisions of this preliminary peace treaty, was signed on 10 May 1871. It is reprinted *ibid.*, III, 1954-1962.—HNW.

[3] Ratifications exchanged at Versailles 2nd March, 1871.—Ed.

No. 99, p. 213

[1] In Kurt Rheindorf, *England und der deutsch-französische Krieg 1870/71* (Leipzig, 1923), p. 134. Translated by Herman N. Weill.

Gramont had listed these conditions in an interview with the Russian *chargé d'affaires* in Paris, who communicated them to St. Petersburg. Bismarck learned of them when the Czar mentioned them to Colonel von Werder, the Prussian military attaché in St. Petersburg. See Rheindorf, *ibid.*, p. 134 and n. 21.—HNW.

[2] Prussian Ambassador at London. Bismarck forwarded this information to Bernstorff with the obvious intention of prejudicing British policy against France; his release of Benedetti's draft treaty to *The* [London] *Times* (see *No. 84,* above) had served the same purpose.—HNW.

Origins of World War I

INTRODUCTION

THE SINGLE, most important event of European diplomatic history in the period from 1871 to 1914 occurred at the very beginning: the creation of the Second German Empire. The simple existence of this new colossus in the center of Europe would have been enough to upset the old European balance of power, but added to its size and geographical position was a steadily increasing military and economic power. Germany, defeating its Austrian and French foes with incredible speed, emerged from the Wars of Unification with the most powerful army in Europe. During the next forty years, it not only maintained, but widened, this lead. It was able to do so largely because it reaped enormous economic benefits from the industrial and commercial integration made possible by unification. Its productivity increased by leaps and bounds, until by 1913 it was second only to the United States as the world's leading industrial nation.

As a result of this combination of size, position, and power, Berlin became the diplomatic capital of Europe. While Germany did not dominate every important development which occurred during this period, its reaction to any international event, even if its interests were not directly involved, was now of vital importance to every European nation. If, as Metternich had remarked during an earlier era, Europe caught cold when Paris sneezed, now Europe trembled when Berlin barked, for it knew that if the bite followed, it would be painful indeed.

Perhaps the Germans had acquired this great power too quickly; perhaps it was only natural for them to want to get even for centuries of domination and exploitation by their stronger neighbors; whatever the reasons, they did not use their power wisely. They displayed an arrogance of power which caused consternation and fear throughout Europe. They singlemindedly pursued their own national interests while ignoring Europe's interests, and failed to see that the former could not be achieved without destroying the latter. This is not to exonerate the other nations of Europe, but Germany had the greater power and thus the greater responsibility. When the guns of August boomed, the curtain went up on the final act of a profound tragedy: a great nation brought down by its own *hubris*.

Bismarck continued to direct German diplomacy until his dismissal from office in 1890. After 1871, the primary objective of his foreign policy was to prevent aggression against Germany. To the German Ambassador in St. Petersburg he wrote: ". . . we do not pursue power-politics, but safety-

219

politics." In the Reichstag, he declared that Germany was a "saturated" state. It had no further territorial ambitions, all it wanted was peace so that it could concentrate its attention and energy on the innumerable urgent internal problems that were awaiting a solution. The two major means he used to achieve this objective were a strong army and diplomacy. He knew that a weak Germany would invite aggression, but the German Army's sole purpose was defensive, and, much as the generals chafed at this restriction, Bismarck never used it for aggressive purposes. As to his diplomacy, there was always the threat of a French war of revenge, but he was confident that Germany could repulse a French attack if France was not aided by one or more allies. The real danger was, therefore, as he himself put it, a repetition of the Kaunitz coalition between France, Austria, and Russia, which had come so close to crushing Frederick the Great in the Seven Years' War. To prevent such a coalition from forming again, it was essential that Germany maintain friendly relations with both Austria and Russia. An exchange of visits among the Emperors and their Ministers was arranged, and, in 1873, the Three Emperors' League was formed, a rather loose agreement to preserve the peace.

As events were soon to prove, however, Bismarck's most vexing problem was not in keeping the peace between Germany on the one hand and Austria and Russia on the other, but in preventing a clash between Austria and Russia. The bone of contention between them was again the Balkans. It will be recalled that only twenty years earlier, Russia's expansionary policy in this area had been temporarily blocked by the Crimean War (see Chapter Two, above). Russia welcomed the opportunity to resume the offensive when the Slavs, whose revolt against the Turks had been brutally crushed (the occasion of the infamous "Bulgarian Massacres"), called upon their fellow-Slavs for help. Russia entered the war against Turkey, defeated its armies, and forced it to sign the Treaty of San Stefano (*No. 100*).

When the terms of this Treaty became known, they caused shocked dismay in several capitals, notably in Vienna and London. Austria protested vehemently against Russia's intrusion into what it considered its own backyard. England made it clear that it was not about to accept a Russian expansion which it had so determinedly opposed in the Crimean War. Disraeli had just fortified the British position in the Eastern Mediterranean by buying a controlling interest in the Suez Canal. Another wave of war hysteria swept over the British Isles, where sundry Englishmen were singing a ditty from a musical which added the word "jingoism" to the language:

We don't want to fight, but by jingo if we do,
We've got the men, we've got the ships,
We've got the money, too.

War seemed imminent when Bismarck offered to act as an "honest broker," and issued invitations to discuss the matter at the Congress of Berlin. He did so reluctantly, knowing full well that even with his consummate diplomatic skill he would be unable to devise a solution which would please everyone, yet knowing, too, that Germany had to avoid a war if at all possible.

The result of the deliberations of the most glittering Congress since Vienna was the Treaty of Berlin (*No. 101*). Its terms infuriated the Russians, who claimed that the spoils of victory had been literally snatched out of their hands. Their rage was directed primarily against Austria and England, but they reserved a generous share for Bismarck. Sullen and defiant, they now threatened to conclude an alliance with France. Under these circumstances, Bismarck made a fateful decision: on 7 October 1879, he concluded the Dual Alliance with Austria (*No. 103*).

Bismarck's critics often point to the Dual Alliance as the first link in that chain of permanent peacetime alliances which was to divide Europe into two armed camps and which was to play such a crucial role in the outbreak of World War I. Yet a study of the document itself, as well as of a memorandum written only two weeks before in which he spelled out his reasons for the alliance (*No. 102*), will show that this was certainly not his intention. In keeping with Bismarck's basic diplomatic principles, the Dual Alliance was devised to attain a specific, limited objective: to prevent Russia's threat against Austria, and, through France, against Germany, from escalating into war. Its sole purpose was defensive. The farthest thing from Bismarck's mind was to present Austria with a 'blank check." On the contrary, if Austria labored under the delusion that the Dual Alliance was an irrevocable promise of German support for its aggressive, expansionary policies in the Balkans, a rude awakening was in store for it as long as Bismarck remained Chancellor. In the 1880's, there were renewed tensions between Austria and Russia. Leading military circles in Vienna, soon joined by those in Berlin, began to advocate a preventive war against Russia, citing the Dual Alliance as justification for common action. Bismarck, in a sharply worded dispatch to the German Ambassador in Vienna, left no doubt that this was, in his opinion, a complete misinterpretation of the alliance, and that under no circumstances would he ever consent to Germany's participation in such a war (*No. 104*).

The Dual Alliance was successful. It was an important factor in preventing Russia's anger at the terms of the Treaty of Berlin from leading it to a rapprochement with France. Yet its main weakness, so far as Russo-German relations were concerned, was that it was essentially negative. It failed to strengthen these relations. Bismarck pondered the problem, and finally came up with the Reinsurance Treaty (*No. 106*).

There are those who point to this Treaty as an excellent example of Bismarck's duplicity, for they insist that the Reinsurance Treaty was incompatible with the Dual Alliance. The student can compare the two texts for himself, and form his own opinion.

Prior to the Reinsurance Treaty, Italy, Austria, and Germany had formed the Triple Alliance (*No. 105*). It was Italy which, alarmed over French advances in North Africa, initiated negotiations for this alliance. Austria, wanting to secure its Italian frontier in case of complications in the Balkans, was willing to cooperate. Bismarck was rather disdainful of the Italians —"They have a large appetite and such poor teeth!" he is reported to have said—and he considered them unreliable, but William I remembered their contribution in the War of 1866. Without the diversion of 130,000 Austrian troops in Italy, the Emperor remarked, Prussia might not have won the Battle of Königgrätz, and he thought that they could fulfill the same function if Germany were at war with France. In 1914, these hopes were not to be realized, but that, of course, could not be foreseen then.

In March, 1890, William II dropped the pilot who had guided the German ship of state so successfully for twenty years. That the young Emperor should have chafed under Bismarck's tight-reined tutelage, that he should be anxious to exchange the trappings for the reality of power, is understandable. What is considerably more puzzling, however, is why he and his advisers should have proceeded to dismantle, and eventually to completely wreck, Bismarck's foreign policy. Was that policy really so complex that, as Caprivi, Bismarck's immediate successor, claimed, only a man of Bismarck's stature could have continued to make it work? Was it too modest a policy for a Germany not satisfied with dominating the Continent and determined to make a "grab for world power"? Or was the wrecking job the result, not of any deliberate plan, but of saber-rattling braggadocio, of threats which boomeranged, of lack of foresight, in short, of diplomatic blunders and miscalculations? Since the question deals with motives, we will never know the definitive answer. What we do know is that, within eighteen years of Bismarck's dismissal, Austria, whose aggressive and reckless ambitions in the Balkans he had thwarted, had gained Germany's unquestioned support for those same ambitions; that France had broken out of its diplomatic isolation; and that the encirclement of Germany by the Triple Entente, which had given him nightmares when he only dreamed about it, had become a reality.

The first step on the road towards this Second Diplomatic Revolution was taken within days of Bismarck's forced retirement when Germany refused to renew the Reinsurance Treaty (*No. 107*). The arguments adduced against the Treaty seem rather weak and unconvincing. The major objection was directed against the Straits clause, which was held to be incompatible with the Dual Alliance, but when Giers offered to change the offending passage or even to omit it entirely, the Germans still persisted in their refusal. Nor were they impressed by his threat to "seek support elsewhere." They should have been, for Giers now initiated discussions with France, and two years later, the Russian and French military representatives signed the Dual Entente (*No. 108*).

Although the Dual Entente took Berlin by surprise, it was not considered a cause for alarm. The Central Powers would feel threatened only if England were to join the Entente, but they were convinced that such an eventuality was rather remote. As late as 1901, when the British suggested that it might occur, Holstein contemptuously called the idea "a total fraud" (*No. 111*). There was, it is true, considerable evidence for this view. Anglo-Russian relations were marked by almost constant tension as a result of numerous clashes of interest in areas extending from Constantinople to Vladivostok. Anglo-French relations were not much better; on several occasions—see, for instance, the crisis over Fashoda (*No. 109*)—the two nations were on the brink of going to war. By the end of the nineteenth century, when England was mired in the morass of the Boer War, it discovered that its isolation was far from "splendid" and almost complete.

England's plight presented Germany with a unique opportunity to effect a rapprochement. Its task was made much easier when several prominent Englishmen, most notably Joseph Chamberlain and Lloyd George, publicly advocated closer ties with Germany (*Nos. 111* and *118*). But instead of eagerly grasping the proffered hand, the Germans rudely knocked it aside. The Kaiser, in particular, seemed to go out of his way to antagonize the British. There was, for example, the yachting rivalry between the German Emperor and the Prince of Wales. Edward considered the sport a pleasant diversion, but William II, determined to best his uncle at all costs, took the fun out of it by turning it into a ferocious competition. There was the thoughtless Kruger Telegram, and William II's galling, unsolicited advice on how the British should conduct the Boer War (*No. 110*). There was the provocative *Daily Telegraph* interview (*No. 119*). Worst of all, however, was the huge naval construction program begun by Germany at the turn of the century (*No. 112*). William II was undoubtedly correct when he argued that Britannia had no Divine Right to rule the Seven Seas, and that if England were conceded the right to restrict the German Navy, then France or Russia would have an equal right to restrict the German Army (*No. 118*). But the issue involved here was not one of legal rights. The question, which William II and Tirpitz failed to ponder with sufficient care, was whether the advantages Germany would derive from a large navy would not be far outweighed by the disadvantages. A clearly foreseeable liability, and one unmatched by any possible compensatory advantages, was the worsening of Anglo-German relations, for the British were bound to conclude that a navy of such size could be destined only for offensive purposes against them and their Empire. This is precisely the conclusion they did reach, with Lloyd George remarking to the German Ambassador that this single issue had sown more discord between the two nations than any other. The damage was further compounded when William II brusquely refused to even discuss the British suggestion of placing some limitations on what was becoming an increasingly costly and dangerous Naval Race.

Faced with this mounting evidence of German intransigence, the British statesmen were forced to reassess England's foreign policy. This was a slow and painful process; they had haughtily gone their own way for so long that they were reluctant to admit the need for cooperation with other Powers. The first indication that the era of "splendid isolation" was drawing to a close came with the signing of the Anglo-Japanese Treaty (*No. 113*). This was followed by the Anglo-French Agreement (*No. 115*), and then by the Anglo-Russian Agreement (*No. 117*). These two Agreements were rapprochements, not alliances. They were designed to improve England's relations with France and with Russia by solving specific, mostly territorial, problems. Yet once again, German and Austrian blunders hammered them into much stronger links than they were originally intended to be.

The Germans reacted to the Anglo-French Agreement by precipitating the First Moroccan Crisis (*No. 116*). The Kaiser's bombastic speech in Tangier was obviously designed to intimidate the French, and to drive a wedge between England and France. German pressure succeeded in forcing Delcassé's resignation,

but it only angered the British. Edward VII wrote to Lord Lansdowne: "The Tangier incident was the most mischievous and uncalled for event which the German Emperor has ever been engaged in since he came to the Throne. It was also a political theatrical fiasco, and if he thinks he has done himself good in the eyes of the world, he is very much mistaken. He is no more nor less than a political *enfant terrible*, and one can have no faith in any of his assurances." The result was not only that England backed up France during the crisis, but that the first steps were taken to make their association even closer by the initiation of joint military planning by the French and British Staffs.

Hardly had the excitement over the First Moroccan Crisis died down when the Bosnian Crisis erupted (*No. 120*). The immediate cause of this imbroglio, often called the dress rehearsal for World War I, was Austria's annexation of Bosnia and Herzegovina. These two provinces had been placed under Austrian administration by the Congress of Berlin. To change their status thus would have required the approval of the signatory Powers of the Treaty of Berlin. But Aehrenthal was afraid that if another Congress were convened for this purpose, it would stir up a hornet's nest of claims and counterclaims by the other Balkan states, especially by Serbia, which had coveted these provinces itself. The decision was therefore taken to proceed with the annexation unilaterally, after having cleared the matter first with Germany and Russia, the two Powers most likely to help or hinder Austria (*No. 120-3*).

Bülow readily granted Germany's support (*Nos. 120-1, 120-2, 120-7, 120-8*). As a matter of fact, he expressed that support in such sweeping terms that the Dual Alliance was completely transformed: instead of the defensive alliance envisaged by Bismarck, designed to serve Germany's foreign policy objectives and not Austria's (*Nos. 102, 104*), it now became an offensive alliance, in which Germany promised to support Austria's Balkan schemes sight unseen. The negotiations with Russia were more complex. After some preliminary correspondence, Aehrenthal met Izvolsky at Buchlau, where the Russian Minister apparently agreed to the annexation in return for Austria's support of the opening of the Straits to Russian warships (*Nos. 120-5, 120-6*). Izvolsky later cried "Foul!" and claimed that he had been duped by Aehrenthal, yet the evidence strongly suggests that it was Izvolsky who had tried to pull a fast one on the Balkan Slavs by gaining passage of the Straits at their expense. The reason he could not obtain his part of the questionable bargain was not Aehrenthal's duplicity, but his failure to anticipate the wave of Pan-Slavic sympathy which swept over Russia after the annexation was proclaimed, and Serbia's furious reaction which led it to mobilize against Austria.

This Serbian threat hardly fazed Aehrenthal, for we now know that he had initially planned to use the occasion to settle accounts with Serbia by invading it (*No. 120-4*). However, considering the agitated state of Russian public opinion, there was some danger that an Austrian attack against Serbia would bring Russia into the war on Serbia's side. Conrad was therefore instructed to initiate discussions with Moltke in order to ascertain whether, in such an event, Austria could count on Germany's military support against Russia (*No. 120-9*). In his reply, which had been approved by William II and Bülow, Moltke assured Conrad that Germany would stand loyally by its ally's side even if Austria were to provoke Russia's intervention by invading Serbia. He also discussed France's role in the war which would ensue. William II seemed to believe that France could be pressured into remaining neutral (*No. 120-11*), but Moltke obviously took it for granted that France would join Russia, and faced with equanimity the almost certain prospect that an Austrian attack against

Serbia would thus unleash an European war. This letter takes on particular significance when we realize that both Moltke and Conrad still occupied their high military positions on the eve of World War I, and that neither William II nor Bethmann, Bülow's successor, made any effort in the intervening years to withdraw the rash promises made therein to Austria.

With Austria backed up by Germany, and Serbia by Russia, the four nations were steaming on a collision course and rapidly closing when Russia suddenly veered off. In March, 1909, the German Ambassador in St. Petersburg presented what Izvolsky later called an "ultimatum": Russia must recognize the annexation without any reservations or Germany would "withdraw and let matters take their course" (*No. 120-12*). Izvolsky, well aware that Russia was ill prepared to fight both Germany and Austria, capitulated (*No. 120-13*). Russia recognized the annexation, and Serbia was forced to do the same.

In Russia and in Serbia, the Bosnian Crisis left a legacy of bitter hatred and a thirst for revenge against the Central Powers (*Nos. 120-15, 120-16, 120-18, 120-19*). In England, it reinforced the growing conviction that Germany was engaged in a determined bid for power which only resolute opposition could thwart (*Nos. 120-14, 120-17*). The leaders of the Central Powers rejoiced over their great diplomatic victory. It confirmed their belief in the efficacy of a policy of threats and intimidation. Their only regret was that they had not seized the opportunity to crush Serbia (*No. 120-20*), and they probably resolved not to miss a second opportunity if it should present itself.

They got their chance in the summer of 1914 when they learned of the murders at Sarajewo. Even with insufficient evidence, there was no doubt in Vienna about Serbia's responsibility for the crime. Yet Austria's determination to destroy this "incubator of criminal agitation" was not solely based on a primitive urge to avenge the Archduke's death. With more than half of the Austrian Empire's polyglot population consisting of Slavs, there was a genuine fear that if Serbia's ruthless drive for hegemony in the Balkans were allowed to succeed, it would lead to the disintegration of the Empire. But Berchtold was as aware as Aehrenthal had been that Russia might back up Serbia, and he therefore first requested German support (No. 121-1).

William II and Bethmann did not hesitate to proffer Germany's support, with the Kaiser adding, in his usual blustering fashion, that the pledge would be redeemed even if it came to a war against Russia (Nos. 121-2, 121-3). Not that either one of them really expected such a war. They were convinced that Russia was too weak to intervene. She was still suffering from widespread internal turmoil, with over one million workers out on strike by June, 1914. There was also the precedent of the Bosnian Crisis when the Central Powers had won a brilliant diplomatic victory because Austria had acted quickly, facing the Entente with a *fait accompli,* and because German threats had been sufficient to prevent Entente intervention. If this script were followed again, it should lead to equally satisfactory results. Germany therefore urged Austria to attack Serbia at once (Nos. 121-2, 121-3, 121-15). It also insisted in St. Petersburg, Paris, and London on the localisation of the Austro-Serbian conflict (No. 121-6), clearly implying that intervention by any of the Entent Powers would be followed immediately by German intervention.

Germany's assurances left no doubt in Vienna about its support (No. 121-4), yet Austria was slow to take action against Serbia. Berchtold, to his great surprise, discovered that there was internal opposition to such action. It was led by Count Tisza, Prime Minister of Hungary, who strenuously objected to any plan which would incorporate more Slavs into the Empire. Berchtold at last overcame these scruples by promising that the Austrian occupation of Serbian territory would only be temporary, a promise he could make all the more readily since he had no intention of keeping it. Another reason for the delay was the ponderousness of Austria's mobilization, and the deliberations concerning its expense. Finally, there was the fortuitous circumstance of the state visit to Russia by the leaders of the French Government at just this time. Poincaré and Viviani set sail from Le Havre on July 15th, were in St. Petersburg from July 20th to July 23rd, and did not return to Paris until July 27th. Berchtold feared that if the news of Austria's attack against Serbia reached the Russian capital during the state visit, France and Russia would immediately concert on intervention. He therefore decided to postpone action until the French leaders had left St. Petersburg.

After ascertaining their departure on the 23rd, Giesl was ordered to deliver the Austrian ultimatum to Serbia that same evening (No. 121-9). Its terms had deliberately been made harsh enough to be rejected. When the rumor reached Vienna on July 24th that Serbia would accept them nevertheless, the Viennese were keenly disappointed at the prospect of being denied their revenge (No. 121-17). They need not have worried. Although the Serbian reply (No. 121-16) was very conciliatory—"A brilliant achievement for a time limit of only 48 hours!" William II exclaimed when he read it—Giesl and his staff had already packed their luggage. After a cursory glance at the reply, Giesl pulled out a previously prepared Note declaring it to be unsatisfactory, and at once broke off diplomatic relations. That same evening, Francis Joseph I ordered partial mobilization against Serbia (No. 121-18). Three days later, Austria declared war against Serbia (No. 121-23), and on July 29th, Austrian artillery bombarded Belgrade (No. 121-27).

While matters were thus proceeding according to plan in Belgrade, there were increasing signs that Russia would not play its assigned role. Sazonov perceived early that the Austro-German thrust was directed as much at Russia as it was at Serbia (*Nos. 121-12, 121-14*). But threats could be matched with threats. He first warned the Central Powers that 1914 was not 1908, and that Russia would not stand idly by while Austria crushed Serbia (*Nos. 121-7, 121-12, 121-21*). To back up his words, he then persuaded Nicholas II to approve preparations for partial mobilization against Austria (*No. 121-13*), and on July 28th, after learning of Austria's declaration of war against Serbia, to issue the order for partial mobilization (*No. 121-25*).

Was partial mobilization such a hostile act that it would inevitably lead to war? Moltke thought so (*No. 121-28*), but Sazonov apparently did not. He not only believed it possible for Russia to partially mobilize against Austria and to continue to remain at peace with Germany (*Nos. 121-20, 121-25*), but when he announced Russia's partial mobilization against Austria he added that the Russian Ambassador in Vienna would not be recalled (*No. 121-25*). Thus, negotiations could continue, and he urged Germany to mediate the dispute. The best that Germany could offer, however, was William II's "Halt in Belgrade" proposal: that Austria should be allowed to occupy Belgrade as a guarantee of Serbia's future good behavior (*No. 121-22*). If the German Emperor had studied diplomatic history more carefully, he would have known that, sixty years earlier, Nicholas I had occupied the Danubian Principalities as a guarantee of Turkey's future good behavior (see Chapter Two, above). Such action was considered intolerable in international relations then, and led to war; it was still considered intolerable now, and would have the same result.

Giving Russia the benefit of the doubt, her partial mobilization could still be viewed as merely a threat. But on July 29th, Russia crossed the thin line dividing threat from aggression when the Tsar ordered general mobilization (*No. 121-30*). The order was revoked the same evening (*No. 121-33*), primarily because of Bethmann's warning (*No. 121-31*), but, under Sazonov's urging, it was reinstated the following day (*No. 121-36*). If Nicholas II was, or pretended to be, under the impression that even general mobilization did not mean war (*No. 121-48*), Sazonov had no such illusions, for by now he was convinced that war was probably inevitable (*No. 121-32*). Several factors led him to this conviction. To judge from his violent reaction when he learned of it, the bombardment of Belgrade seems to have been the catalyst (*No. 121-29*). It furnished convincing proof that Austria was determined to crush Serbia. But Russia could not allow this to happen; public opinion would not tolerate it (*No. 121-26*). The bombardment also implicated Germany for neither Sazonov nor the Russian military leaders could believe that Austria would act so aggressively if it had not first obtained Germany's backing. In that case, Russia had to proceed with general mobilization at once since her army was not nearly as efficient as Germany's, and unless it started to mobilize earlier, it would be at a hopeless disadvantage. Finally, the French—Poincaré during his state visit (*Nos. 121-8, 121-11*), and especially Paléologue (*Nos. 121-11, 121-14, 121-24*)—had repeatedly assured Russia of their full support. England, it was assumed, was likely to join the Entente Powers, which would greatly enhance their prospects for winning the war.

July 29th was the day of fateful decision in Berlin as well as in St. Petersburg. Russia, with her partial mobilization, had clearly called Germany's bluff. This was Germany's last chance to turn back at the edge of the precipice by cancelling the reckless promises she had made to Austria. Germany did not turn back. In his warning to Russia of

July 26th (*No. 121-19*), Bethmann had still made the distinction between a Russian partial mobilization directed against Austria and one directed against Germany, indicating that only the latter would lead to German intervention. But on July 29th he received a memorandum from Moltke (*No. 121-28*) in which the Chief of the German General Staff maintained that even a Russian partial mobilization directed only against Austria would "inevitably" lead to an Austro-Russian War, which, according to his interpretation of the Dual Alliance, Germany would have to join on Austria's side. Even though Moltke was aware that such a war "will destroy the culture of almost all of Europe for decades to come," he did not make a single suggestion for avoiding it. Instead, he focused his attention on the necessity of Germany's faithful support of its Austrian ally.

Bethmann fully shared this aggressive interpretation of the Dual Alliance. Haunted, as bullies are apt to be haunted, by a deep-seated sense of insecurity, he could not bear the thought of Germany's standing alone. Nor did he protest either against Moltke's fatalistic assumption that war was inevitable or, more importantly, against this unwarranted interference by the military in Germany's foreign policy. On the contrary, he diligently began preparations for a two-front war. The ultimatum to Belgium, originally drafted by Moltke, was accepted by Bethmann and sent to Below for safekeeping on July 29th (*No. 121-52*). At 12:50 P.M. he dispatched the warning to Russia (*No. 121-31*) which, by failing to make the distinction he had made on July 26th, helped to persuade Sazonov that war against Germany was probably inevitable. That same evening, he made a bid for British neutrality (*No. 121-34*) which left the same impression in London, and is also remarkable for the incredible cynicism and obtuseness which it displayed. When Sir Eyre Crowe, the Assistant Under-Secretary of State for Foreign Affairs, read it the

next day, he minuted: "The only comment that need be made on these astounding proposals is that they reflect discredit on the statesman who makes them." He then added: "It is clear that Germany is practically determined to go to war."

In the face of this evidence, there are those who still insist that Bethmann was strenuously exerting himself until the very last moment to save the peace, and that it was Moltke who sabotaged these efforts. In support of this thesis, they cite the series of telegrams sent by Bethmann to Vienna during the night of July 29/30, in which he sought to bring "pressure" on Austria to negotiate with Russia on the basis of the "Halt in Belgrade" proposal. Bethmann must have known that this proposal was unacceptable to Russia. In his circular dispatch of July 21st (*No. 121-6*), he had defended Austria's attack against Serbia on the grounds that, if Austria did not act decisively, it would have to renounce forever its position as a Great Power. Yet it did not take a Herculean stretch of the imagination to recognize that this was also true for Russia: if Russia abandoned Serbia, she, too, would suffer a disastrous setback. Nor did Bethmann's proposal constitute any real pressure on Austria. It would have been happy to negotiate on such a basis, for once its troops were in possession of Belgrade, how were they to be dislodged by Russia or by anyone else without recourse to arms? If Bethmann had been genuinely concerned with saving the peace, he would have suggested, and forced Austria to accept, less Draconian measures than the invasion and occupation of the Serbian capital and its surrounding territory.

As for Moltke, the case against him rests primarily on his telegram to Conrad (*No. 121-37*), which, it should be noted, the latter received on the morning of July 31st, long after Austria had taken the decision for general mobilization (*Nos. 121-35, 121-39*). It was this telegram which supposedly caused Berchtold's famous outcry:

"That's really something! Who is in charge: Moltke or Bethmann?" This reaction is rather puzzling, for it is based on the assumption that Bethmann disagreed with the contents of this telegram. Yet none of the communications made by Bethmann to Berchtold substantiates this view. As already pointed out, the generals were in charge by now, and not only in Berlin, but, as Berchtold failed to see, in Vienna as well.

The die having been cast, it took only two more days for Mars to begin to fill it with a stream of white-hot, death-dealing metal. On July 31st, when Bethmann learned of Russia's general mobilization (No. 121-38), he immediately proclaimed a "threatening danger of war" (No. 121-40). That same afternoon, he ignored the Tsar's appeal (No. 121-41) and dispatched an ultimatum simultaneously to Russia (No. 121-42) and to France (No. 121-43). On August 1st, having received no reply from Russia, Germany declared war against her (Nos. 121-46, 121-49). France curtly rejected the German ultimatum (No. 121-47), but before declaring war against her on the obviously trumped up charge of French aggression (No. 121-54), Bethmann had to deal with Belgium. The Schlieffen Plan, that monument to the dire consequences which result when military strategists ignore the political impact of their battle plans, called for German troops to attack France by advancing across Belgium. Therefore, in spite of Lichnowsky's warning (No. 121-51), Below was instructed to present the German ultimatum in Brussels (No. 121-52). The Belgians, in a rare display of courage and integrity, rejected the ultimatum (No. 121-53), and on the morning of August 4th, German troops crossed the Belgian frontier.

It was this violation of the treaty guaranteeing Belgian neutrality—of a "scrap of paper," to quote Bethmann, a phrase only too accurately revealing his degenerate concept of diplomacy—which brought England into the war (Nos. 121-56 to 121-59). Does Grey, as his critics claim, bear a heavy burden of responsibility for that war because he did not warn Germany in time of British intervention? This criticism is only valid if it can be shown that a majority of Cabinet, Parliament, and country would have supported intervention at an earlier stage of the crisis. Perhaps the most startling evidence pointing in the opposite direction are the two interviews which Grey had with Cambon on July 31st (No. 121-44) and on August 1st (No. 121-50). The Entente Cordiale notwithstanding, Grey emphatically refused to give France any assurance of British support even if France were to be attacked by Germany! The poor French Ambassador, seeing his efforts of many years going up in smoke, nearly collapsed from helpless rage and disappointment. However, we should note that in both instances the Cabinet had met prior to the interviews, and that Grey's replies represented a consensus among his colleagues. Whatever the reasons for this consensus— internal political turmoil, ignorance of how far Anglo-French military planning had committed British forces, the conviction that no British interests were involved and that the whole crisis was essentially a Continental quarrel—it first had to be changed before England could intervene. It would have been irresponsible folly for Grey to have ignored it, and to have attempted to push England into such a life-and-death struggle without the united support of Parliament and people. Much as we may deplore England's lack of foresight, particularly its failure to recognize that the defense of Serbia's independence was as vital to the peace of Europe as the defense of Belgium's, the fact of the matter is that only Germany's violation of Belgian neutrality provided Grey with that united support.

Italy was the only one of the Big Six to proclaim its neutrality. The official reason for its refusal to join its allies was the correct contention that Austria was pursuing an aggressive policy towards Serbia, and that therefore the *casus foederis* of the Triple Alliance did not apply (*No. 121-45*). Unofficially, however, it soon became apparent that a more important reason was Italy's desire for territorial compensation. San Giuliano became convinced that Austria, if victorious, intended to expand its Empire in the Balkans, and he wanted something in return. After much hemming and hawing, he designated the Trentino as suitable compensation. When this was brusquely rejected by Berchtold, who refused to cede a square inch of Austrian territory, Italy initiated discussions with the Entente Powers (*No. 121-55*). It was this hypocritical combination of high principle and base greed which brought down scorn and contempt upon the Italians. But perhaps we should be more charitable. Flawed as their motives were, they did not plunge heedlessly into war. If the other Powers had followed their example, the guns might have remained silent in that tragic August of 1914.

No. 100   The Treaty of San Stefano——3 March 1878[1]

His Majesty the Emperor of Russia and His Majesty the Emperor of the Ottomans, inspired with the wish of restoring and securing the blessings of peace to their countries and people, as well as of preventing any fresh complication which might imperil the same, have named as their Plenipotentiaries, with a view to draw up, conclude, and sign the Preliminaries of Peace:—

His Majesty the Emperor of Russia on the one side, the Count Nicolas Ignatiew, Aide-de-Camp General of His Imperial Majesty, etc.; and Le Sieur Alexander Nelidow, Chamberlain of the Imperial Court. etc.;

And His Majesty the Emperor of the Ottomans on the other side, Safvet Pasha, Minister for Foreign Affairs, etc.; and Sadoullah Bey, His Majesty's Ambassador at the Imperial Court of Germany, etc.;

Who, after having exchanged their full powers, which were found to be in good and proper form, have agreed to the following Articles:—

ART. I. In order to put an end to the perpetual conflicts between Turkey and Montenegro, the frontier which separates the two countries will be rectified conformably to the Map hereto annexed, subject to the reserve hereinafter mentioned, in the following manner:—

From the mountain of Dobrostitza the frontier will follow. . . .

.   .   .   .

ART. II. The Sublime Porte recognizes definitively the Independence of the Principality of Montenegro.

ART. III. Servia is recognized as independent. Its frontier, marked on the annexed Map, will follow. . . .

.   .   .   .

ART. V. The Sublime Porte recognizes the Independence of Roumania, which will establish its right to an indemnity, to be discussed between the two countries.

.   .   .   .

ART. VI. Bulgaria is constituted an autonomous tributary Principality, with a Christian government and a national militia.

The definitive frontiers of the Bulgarian Principality will be traced by a special Russo-Turkish Commission before the evacuation of Roumelia by the Imperial Russian Army.

.   .   .   .

ART. VII. The Prince of Bulgaria shall be freely elected by the population and confirmed by the Sublime Porte, with the assent of the Powers. No member of the reigning dynasties of the great European Powers shall be capable of being elected Prince of Bulgaria. . . .

Before the election of the Prince, an assembly of Bulgarian Notables, to be convoked at Philippopolis (Plowdiw) or Tyrnowo, shall draw up, under the superintendence of an Imperial Russian commissioner, and in the presence of an Ottoman Commissioner, the organization of the future administration, ...

The introduction of the new system into Bulgaria, and the superintendence of its working, will be entrusted for two years to an Imperial Russian Commissioner. . . .

ART. VIII. The Ottoman army will no longer remain in Bulgaria, and all the ancient fortresses will be razed at the expense of the local government. . . .

Until the complete formation of a native militia sufficient to preserve order, security, and tranquillity, and the strength of which will be fixed later on by an understanding between the Ottoman Government and the Imperial Russian Cabinet, Russian troops will occupy the country, and will give armed assistance to the Commissioner in case of need. This occupation will also be limited to a term approximating to two years.

. . . .

ART. XIX. The war indemnity and the losses imposed on Russia which His Majesty the Emperor of Russia claims, and which the Sublime Porte has bound itself to reimburse to him, consist of—

(a.) 900,000,000 roubles for war expenses (maintenance of the army, replacing of war material, and war contracts).

(b.) 400,000,000 roubles on account of damage done to the south coast of Russia, to her export commerce, to her industries, and to her railways.

(c.) 100,000,000 roubles for injuries inflicted on the Caucasus by the invasion. and,

(d.) 10,000,000 roubles for costs and damages of Russian subjects and establishments in Turkey.

Total 1,410,000,000 roubles.

Taking into consideration the financial embarrassments of Turkey, and in accordance with the wishes of His Majesty the Sultan, the Emperor of Russia consents to substitute for the payment of the greater part of the moneys enumerated in the above paragraph, the following territorial cessions:—

(a.) The Sandjak of Toultcha, ...

Not wishing, however, to annex this territory and the Delta Islands, Russia reserves the right of exchanging them for the part of Bessarabia detached from her by the Treaty of 1856,[2] and which is bounded on the south by the thalweg of the Kilia branch and the mouth of the Stary-Stamboul. . . .

(b.) Ardahan, Kars, Batoum, Bayazet, and the territory as far as the Saganlough. .

(c.) The territories mentioned in paragraphs (a) and (b) are ceded to Russia as an equivalent for the sum of one milliard and one hundred million (1,100,000,000) roubles. As for the rest of the indemnity, apart from the 10,000,000 of roubles intended to indemnify Russian interests and establishments in Turkey—namely, 300,000,-000 of roubles—the mode of payment and guarantee of that sum shall be settled by an understanding between the Imperial Government of Russia and that of His Majesty the Sultan.

. . . .

ART. XXIX. The present Act shall be ratified by their Imperial Majesties the Emperor of Russia and the Emperor of the Ottomans, and the ratifications shall be exchanged in fifteen days, or sooner if possible, at St. Petersburgh. . . .[3]

In witness whereof the respective Plenipotentiaries have appended their signatures and seals to the present Act.

Done at San Stefano, the nineteenth February/third March, one thousand eight hundred and seventy-eight.

(L.S.) CTE. N. IGNATIEW. (L.S.) SAFVET.
(L.S.) NELIDOW. (L.S.) SADOULLAH.

No. 101   The Treaty of Berlin——13 July 1878[1]

In the name of Almighty God.

Her Majesty the Queen of the United Kingdom of Great Britain and Ireland, Empress of India, His Majesty the Emperor of Germany, King of Prussia, His Majesty the Emperor of Austria, King of Bohemia, etc., and King Apostolic of Hungary, the President of the French Republic, His Majesty the King of Italy, His Majesty the Emperor of all the Russias, and His Majesty the Emperor of the Ottomans, being desirous to regulate, with a view to European order, conformably to the stipulations of the Treaty of Paris of 30 March 1856, the questions raised in the East by the events of late years and by the war terminated by the Preliminary Treaty of San Stefano, have been unanimously of opinion that the meeting of a Congress would offer the best means of facilitating an understanding.

Their said Majesties and the President of the French Republic have, in consequence, appointed as their Plenipotentiaries, that is to say:[2]

Her Majesty the Queen of Great Britain, Benjamin Disraeli, Earl of Beaconsfield, Prime Minister of England; Robert Cecil, Earl of Salisbury, Secretary of State for Foreign Affairs; and Lord Odo Russell, Ambassador in Berlin;

His Majesty the Emperor of Germany, Otto Prince Bismarck, Chancellor of the Empire; Bernard de Bülow, Minister of State; and Chlodwig Prince of Hohenlohe-Schillingsfürst, Ambassador in Paris;

His Majesty the Emperor of Austria, Jule Count Andrássy, Minister for Foreign Af-

fairs; Louis Count Károlyi, Ambassador in Berlin; and Henri Baron de Haymerle, Ambassador in Rome;

The President of the French Republic, William Waddington, Minister for Foreign Affairs; Charles Count de Saint-Vallier, Ambassador in Berlin; and Hippolyte Desprez, Councillor of State;

His Majesty the King of Italy, Louis Count Corti, Minister for Foreign Affairs; and Edward Count de Launay, Ambassador in Berlin.

His Majesty the Emperor of all the Russias, Alexander Prince Gortchakow, Chancellor of the Empire; Peter Count de Schouvaloff, Ambassador in London; and Paul d'Oubril, Ambassador in Berlin;

And His Majesty the Emperor of the Ottomans, Alexander Carathéodory Pasha, Minister of Public Works; Mehemed Ali Pasha, Mushir of the Armies; and Sadoullah Bey, Ambassador in Berlin;

Who, in accordance with the proposal of the Court of Austria-Hungary, and on the invitation of the Court of Germany, have met at Berlin furnished with full powers, which have been found in good and due form.

An understanding having been happily established between them, they have agreed to the following stipulations:—

ART. I. Bulgaria is constituted an autonomous and tributary Principality under the suzerainty of His Imperial Majesty the Sultan; it will have a Christian Government and a national militia.

. . . .

ART. III. The Prince of Bulgaria shall

be freely elected by the population and confirmed by the Sublime Porte, with the assent of the Powers. No member of the Reigning Dynasties of the Great European Powers may be elected Prince of Bulgaria. . . .

ART. IV. An Assembly of Notables of Bulgaria, convoked at Tirnovo, shall, before the election of the Prince, draw up the Organic Law of the Principality. . . .

ART. VI. The provisional administration of Bulgaria shall be under the direction of an Imperial Russian Commissary until the completion of the Organic Law. An Imperial Turkish Commissary, as well as the Consuls delegated *ad hoc* by the other Powers, signatory of the present Treaty, shall be called to assist him so as to control the working of this provisional *régime*. . . .

ART. VII. The provisional *régime* shall not be prolonged beyond a period of nine months from the exchange of the ratifications of the present Treaty. . . .

. . . .

ART. XIII. A province is formed south of the Balkans which will take the name of "Eastern Roumelia," and will remain under the direct political and military authority of His Imperial Majesty the Sultan, under conditions of administrative autonomy. It shall have a Christian Governor-General.

. . . .

ART. XVII. The Governor-General of Eastern Roumelia shall be nominated by the Sublime Porte, with the assent of the Powers, for a term of five years.

. . . .

ART. XXII. The strength of the Russian corps of occupation in Bulgaria and Eastern Roumelia, which shall be composed of six divisions of infantry and two divisions of cavalry, shall not exceed 50,000 men. It shall be maintained at the expense of the country occupied. . . .

The period of the occupation of Eastern Roumelia and Bulgaria by the Imperial Russian troops is fixed at nine months from the date of the exchange of the ratifications of the present Treaty. . . .

. . . .

ART. XXV. The Provinces of Bosnia and Herzegovina shall be occupied and administered by Austria-Hungary. The Government of Austria-Hungary, not desiring to undertake the administration of the Sandjak of Novi-Bazar, which extends between Servia and Montenegro in a south-easterly direction to the other side of Mitrviotza, the Ottoman Administration will continue to exercise its functions there. Nevertheless, in order to assure the maintenance of the new political state of affairs, as well as freedom and security of communications, Austria-Hungary reserves the right of keeping garrisons and having military and commercial roads in the whole of this part of the ancient Vilayet of Bosnia. To this end the government of Austria-Hungary and Turkey reserve to themselves to come to an understanding on the details.

ART. XXVI. The independence of Montenegro is recognized by the Sublime Porte and by all those of the High Contracting Parties who had not hitherto admitted it.

. . . .

ART. XXXIV. The High Contracting Parties recognise the independence of the Principality of Servia, subject to the conditions set forth in the following Article.

ART. XXXV. In Servia the difference of religious creeds and confessions shall not be alleged against any person as a ground for exclusion or incapacity in matters relating to the enjoyment of civil and political rights, admission to public employments, functions, and honours, or the exercise of the various professions and industries, in any locality whatsoever.

The freedom and outward exercise of all forms of worship shall be assured to all persons belonging to Servia, as well as to foreigners, and no hindrance shall be offered either to the hierarchical organization of the different communions, or to their relations with their spiritual chiefs.

.   .   .   .

ART. XLIII. The High Contracting Parties recognize the independence of Roumania. . . .

.   .   .   .

ART. XLV. The Principality of Roumania restores to His Majesty the Emperor of Russia that portion of the Bessarabian territory detached from Russia by the Treaty of Paris of 1856, bounded on the west by the mid-channel of the Pruth, and on the south by the mid-channel of the Kilia Branch and the Stary-Stamboul mouth.

ART. XLVI. The islands forming the Delta of the Danube, as well as the Isle of Serpents, the Sandjak of Toultcha, comprising . . . , are added to Roumania. The Principality receives in addition the territory situated to the south of the Dobroutcha as far as a line starting from the east of Silistria and terminating on the Black Sea, south of Mangalia.

.   .   .   .

ART. LII. In order to increase the guarantees which assure the freedom of navigation on the Danube which is recognized as of European interest, the High Contracting Parties determine that all the fortresses and fortifications existing on the course of the river from the Iron Gates to its mouths shall be razed, and no new ones erected. No vessel of war shall navigate the Danube

below the Iron Gates with the exception of vessels of light tonnage in the service of the river police and customs. . . .

.   .   .   .

ART. LVIII. The Sublime Porte cedes to the Russian Empire in Asia the territories of Ardahan, Kars, and Batoum, together with the latter port, as well as all the territories comprised between the former Russo-Turkish frontier and the following line:—

.   .   .   .

ART. LX. The valley of Alaschkerd and the town of Bayazid, ceded to Russia by Article XIX. of the Treaty of San Stefano, are restored to Turkey.

.   .   .   .

ART. LXIV. The present Treaty shall be ratified, and the Ratifications exchanged at Berlin within three weeks, or sooner if possible.[3]

In faith whereof the respective Plenipotentiaries have signed it, and affixed to it the seal of their arms.

Done at Berlin, the thirteenth day of the month of July, one thousand eight hundred and seventy-eight.

(L.S.) BEACONFIELD.   (L.S.) L. CORTI.
(L.S.) SALISBURY.   (L.S.) LAUNAY.
(L.S.) ODO RUSSELL. (L.S.) GORTCHAKOW.
(L.S.) V. BISMARCK. (L.S.) SCHOUVALOFF.
(L.S.) BÜLOW.   (L.S.) P. D'OUBRIL.
(L.S.) HOHENLOHE.   (L.S.) SADOULLAH.
(L.S.) ANDRASSY. (L.S.) AL. CARATHÉODORY.
(L.S.) KAROLYI.   (L.S.) HAYMERLE.
(L.S.) WADDINGTON. (L.S.) MEHEMED ALI.
(L.S.) H. DESPREZ. (L.S.) SAINT-VALLIER.

No. 102   Bismarck's Reasons for the Dual Alliance——24 September 1879[1]

Bismarck to William I.

Vienna, 24 September 1879.

I most humbly report to Your Majesty that I arrived here on the evening of the 21st, on the following day was ordered by His Majesty the Emperor to an audience and dinner, and for the rest devoted my remaining time to discussions with Count Andrássy[2] and Baron Haymerle.[3] . . .

. . . .

Concerning Your Majesty's demand that any arrangement to be made must be of an exclusively defensive nature, and that any consent to aggressive enterprises remain *absolutely* excluded, His Majesty the Emperor as well as Count Andrássy declared the most categorical agreement. The Emperor said that he himself would never give his consent to the conduct of an aggressive war, and least of all to such an unproductive and dangerous war as one against Russia. Even if he should emerge victoriously from such a war, he could not at all imagine of what use such a victory would be for the Austro-Hungarian monarchy. Particularly if Austria should let itself be pushed by England and France into an attack upon Russia, it would surely be obvious to everyone that in such a war Austria would run the danger and bear the main burden all by itself, since England and France were inaccessible to the Russian armed forces.

. . . .

The ends, with which we must be concerned, and which we shall achieve through the proposed treaty, are, in my respectful opinion, the following:

1. To prevent that the Triple Alliance: "Russia, France, Austria," could be formed against us.

2. To prevent that Austria conclude an alliance *either* with Russia *or* with France to Germany's detriment.

3. In case of a French attack upon us, to at least ensure Austria's benevolent neutrality.

4. If that danger should occur which at present is the most threatening, the danger of a Russo-French alliance, to know that we can count with Austria's active support immediately upon the outbreak of war.

5. To prevent, in all probability, any attack at all by Russia *without* France upon us or upon Austria, since Russia will hardly attack one of the two German Powers as soon as it knows for certain that, in such an event, it will be opposed by both of them.

The German-Austrian Alliance is, in my view, the only safe means of inducing Russian policy to be more peacefully disposed and of providing Emperor Alexander with some support against the influence of the belligerent and revolutionary Pan-Slavists and particularly of Minister Miljutin[4] and his adherents. I have insisted, therefore, that, contrary to the Austrian demand for keeping the treaty absolutely secret, there be added to Article IV of Count Andrássy's treaty draft a clause according to which, for reasons of loyalty, it would have to be announced to Emperor Alexander, as soon as warlike dispositions could be discerned in Russia's policy, that an attack upon *one* of the two German Powers would be defended by both of them together.

I take the liberty of stressing several additional advantages which, in my respectful opinion, the enclosed Austrian proposal will have for Germany's interests in preference to a general alliance against any attacking Power.

1. The attack to which Austria seems to be most exposed at the moment is by Italy, as soon as the poorly consolidated monarchical power in this country should succumb to the domination of revolutionary elements. In this case, the statesmanlike considerations of the Italians would probably be unable to cope with the agitation of *Italia irredenta* against Trieste and Trent. According to the enclosed draft, Austria would have to fight out this quarrel alone, but would also be capable of doing so alone. If a general alliance should force Germany to participate in the struggle, then the danger arises that an Austro-Italian war would develop from a local into an European one.

2. According to the Austrian draft, we would still not be obligated to participate even if France in alliance with Italy, or, what is not very probable, without Italy, should become involved in a quarrel with Austria.

3. If the relations between Austria and Turkey in Novi-bazar or through the Albanians should develop into open strife, then this, too, would not involve us yet. Only a war against the opponent whose intervention would also endanger Germany's safety, against Russia, would constitute a *casus foederis*.

4. The difference in the policy of Russia and of France in their relation to Germany, which prevents the union of the two Powers until now, remains unchanged according to the proposal of Count Andrássy, whereas a treaty with Austria which, from the very beginning, is also directed against France would create a common bond between French and Russian policy which has not hitherto existed.

As a result, in my political judgment I cannot but consider the alliance in the form proposed by Count Andrássy as more appropriate to German interests than would be the case in a general alliance applicable against any Power.

.   .   .   .

No. 103   The Dual Alliance——7 October 1879[1]

Considering that Their Majesties the German Emperor, King of Prussia, and the Emperor of Austria, King of Hungary, must regard it as their imperative royal duty to provide for the safety of their Empires and the repose of their peoples in all eventualities;

Considering that both Monarchs will be in a position to fulfill this duty more easily and more effectively through the firm coöperation of both Empires, similar to the federal relations which formerly existed between them;

Considering, finally, that the intimate collaboration of Germany and Austria-Hungary can threaten no one, but is, indeed, more likely to consolidate the peace of Europe created by the stipulations of Berlin.

Their Majesties the Emperor of Germany and the Emperor of Austria, King of Hungary,

while solemnly promising each other that they never intend to give their purely defensive agreement an aggressive tendency in any direction, have decided to conclude an alliance of peace and of mutual defense.

For this purpose, Their Most Exalted Majesties have appointed as their Plenipotentiaries:

His Majesty the German Emperor, Prince

Henry VII Reuss, Ambassador in Vienna, etc.,

His Majesty the Emperor of Austria, King of Hungary, Julius Count Andrássy, Minister for Foreign Affairs, etc.,

who have met on this day at Vienna, and, after the exchange of their full powers, found to be in good and due form, have agreed as follows:

ARTICLE I.

Should, contrary to the hopes and against the sincere desire of the two High Contracting Parties one of the two Empires be attacked on the part of Russia, then the High Contracting Parties are obligated to assist each other with the entire armed forces of their Empires, and, accordingly, to conclude peace only in common and after mutual agreement.

ARTICLE II.

Were one of the High Contracting Parties to be attacked by another Power, then the other High Contracting Party herewith binds himself not only not to assist the aggressor against his High Ally, but to observe at least a benevolent neutrality towards the allied High Contracting Party.

If, however, in such a case the attacking Power should be supported on the part of Russia, either in the form of an active coöperation or by military measures which threaten the attacked Party, then the obligation of mutual assistance with the entire armed forces stipulated in Article I. of this treaty is immediately applicable in this case too, and the conduct of the war by the two High Contracting Parties shall then also be in common until the common conclusion of peace.

ARTICLE III.

The duration of this treaty shall be fixed for the time being at five years from the day of its ratification. One year before the expiration of this term, the two High Contracting Parties shall enter into negotiations concerning the question whether the conditions which gave rise to this treaty still prevail, and shall agree upon the further continuation or the eventual modification of individual modalities. If in the course of the first month of the last year of the treaty neither side has extended an invitation to open these negotiations, then the treaty is to be considered as renewed for the further duration of three years.

ARTICLE IV.

This treaty shall, in conformity with its peaceful character and in order to exclude any misinterpretation, be kept secret by both High Contracting Parties and shall be communicated to a third Power only after the consent of both Parties and according to a special agreement.

Both High Contracting Parties cherish the hope that, after the convictions expressed by Emperor Alexander at the meeting in Alexandrowo, Russia's armaments shall not, in fact, prove to be a threat to them, and for this reason have at present no cause for a communication,—but should this hope, contrary to expectation, prove to be erroneous, then the two High Contracting Parties would consider it as a duty of loyalty to at least confidentially inform Emperor Alexander of the fact that they would have to consider an attack upon one of them as being directed against both.

ARTICLE V.

This treaty shall derive its validity from the approval of the two High Sovereigns and shall be ratified within fourteen days after Their Most Exalted Majesties have given their approval.[2]

In witness whereof the Plenipotentiaries have signed this treaty in person and have affixed the seal of their arms.

Done at Vienna on the 7th of October 1879.

(L.S.) ANDRÁSSY. (L.S.) H. VII v. Reuss.

No. 104 Bismarck Stresses the Defensive Character of the Dual Alliance——15 December 1887[1]

Bismarck to Prince Henry VII Reuss.[2]

SECRET.

Friedrichsruh, 15 December 1887.
I have received Your Excellency's telegram no. 126 and report no. 508 of the 11th. inst.

Your Excellency thereby seems to assume that the military views of the General Staff, which have been communicated to you in memorandum no. 686[3] for the orientation and invigoration of the Austrian military leaders, are the standard which determines my *political* view. . . . As long as I am Minister, I shall not give my consent to a preventive war against Russia. . . . We shall not hesitate, as soon as a *casus foederis* exists, *i.e.*, a Russian attack upon Austria, to take up the war against Russia on our part, too, with all the forces which we can spare against France; but we shall neither take over an *attack* upon Russia ourselves, nor consider the *casus foederis* to exist if Austria undertakes it. In the expectation that the latter could appear to be necessitated by Austria's Balkan policy, we have successfully endeavored to bring Austria into closer relations with Italy and England. If these are so firm and reliable for Count Kálnoky[4] that Austria is certain to have both Powers, and then also the Porte, *actively* and not merely diplomatically on its side, then as an Austrian Minister I, too, would perhaps risk a clash of arms, but not *without* this. We cannot, in this case, *articulo foederis*, be counted upon. For us, a motive for war can never be found in the Balkan questions, but always only in the necessity to represent Austria's independence for our part, too, as soon as it is threatened by Russia. Austria has assumed

no obligation to intercede for us in French or Danish and other complications, and we not in the Oriental interests of Austria-Hungary which lie beyond its frontiers. This is to be firmly adhered to by both sides. Faced with the unpredictability of Russian policy, we must *both* be *heavily* armed against [a] Russian surprise attack, but we do not want to participate in an attack upon Russia, even if our military leaders are convinced that we could conduct the war under more advantageous conditions today than later.

.   .   .   .

In order not to blur the present clear delimitations of the *casus foederis*, we must not fortify the temptation, in which the Austrians already find themselves, of exploiting the situation in order to exhaust the strength of the German Army for Hungarian or Catholic ambitions in the Balkan area. We must not forget that there are aspirations in Austria to whom a decrease in Germany's present strength would not be unwelcome. We must try to bring it about that Austria becomes strong in order not to be overrun by a Russian attack, and in order to be a strong ally for us in such a case. In order to make Austria strong, we have endeavored to provide it with Italy's, and if possible also England's, support in case of war. But *under no circumstances* shall I have anything to do with a pledge of *our* support of Austria in case of an Austrian attack upon Russia. If I were to give His Majesty this advice, then we would place a premium upon Austrian policy to seek a quarrel.

If a Russian war occurs through an Austrian attack upon Russia, then the indicated action for us, in my opinion, is not participation in it, but rather an immediate attack upon *France,* and to make our position to the Russian war depend upon the success of our French war. *We must not encourage Austria at all to act aggressively towards Russia, only to be strong in a defensive posture.* Whether the Austrian army mistakenly believes that we have a defensive and offensive alliance for all eventualities is a matter of complete indifference to our policy; we can only regret that the Vienna Cabinet does not rectify this error at least in official civilian and military circles. . . .

We do not welcome a war under any circumstances. In addition to all the other reasons against it, there is the consideration of His Majesty the Emperor's age and of the health of His Imperial Majesty the Crown Prince.

Your Excellency will consider the preceeding statements as intended *for your personal orientation.*

No. 105   The Triple Alliance——20 May 1882[1]

Their Majesties the Emperor of Germany, King of Prussia, the Emperor of Austria, King of Bohemia, etc., and the King of Italy, animated by the desire to increase the guarantes of the general peace, to fortify the monarchical principle and to assure thereby the continued maintenance of the social and political order in their respective states, have come to an agreement to conclude a treaty which, by its essentially conservative and defensive nature, pursues only the objective of protecting them beforehand against the dangers which could menace the security of their states and the repose of Europe.

For this purpose, Their Majesties have appointed, to wit

His Majesty the Emperor of Germany, King of Prussia, Prince Henry VII von Reuss, Ambassador in Vienna,

His Majesty the Emperor of Austria, King of Bohemia, etc., Count Gustave Kálnoky, Minister for Foreign Affairs,

His Majesty the King of Italy, Count Charles de Robilant, Ambassador in Vienna,

who, provided with full powers which have been found to be in good and due form, have agreed upon the following articles:

ARTICLE I.

The High Contracting Parties mutually promise peace and friendship to each other, and will not enter into any alliance or engagement directed against one of their states.

They engage to proceed to an exchange of ideas concerning political and economic questions of a general nature which could arise, and further promise each other their mutual support within the limits of their own interests.

ARTICLE II.

In case Italy, without any direct provocation on its part, should be attacked by France for any reason whatsoever, the two other Contracting Parties shall be bound to lend to the attacked Party aid and assistance with their entire forces.

This same obligation shall be incumbent on Italy in case of an aggression not directly provoked by France against Germany.

ARTICLE III.

If one or two of the High Contracting Parties, without direct provocation on their part, should happen to be attacked and to find themselves engaged in a war with two or more Great Powers non-signatories of the present treaty, the *casus foederis* will exist simultaneously for all the High Contracting Parties.

ARTICLE IV.

In case a Great Power non-signatory of the present treaty should threaten the security of the states of one of the High Contracting Parties and the threatened Party should thereby see itself forced into going to war against it, the two others obligate themselves to observe a benevolent neutrality with regard to their Ally. Every one reserves to himself the right in this case to take part in the war, if he should judge it appropriate, in order to make common cause with his Ally.

ARTICLE V.

If the peace of one of the High Contracting Parties should happen to be threatened under the circumstances foreseen by the preceding Articles, the High Contracting Parties shall concert together in good time upon the military measures to be taken in view of an eventual coöperation.

They engage from this time on, in all cases of common participation in a war, to conclude neither armistice, nor peace, nor treaty except by common accord among themselves.

ARTICLE VI.

The High Contracting Parties mutually promise each other to keep both the content and the existence of the present treaty secret.

ARTICLE VII.

The present treaty shall remain in force during the space of five years from the day of the exchange of ratifications.

ARTICLE VIII.

The ratifications of the present treaty shall be exchanged in Vienna within a period of three weeks or earlier if that is possible.[2]

In witness whereof the respective Plenipotentiaries have signed the present treaty and have affixed thereto the seal of their arms.

Done at Vienna, the 20th day of May 1882.

(L.S.) H. VII P. REUSS.

(L.S.) C. ROBILANT.

(L.S.) KÁLNOKY.

Ministerial Declaration.

The Imperial and Royal Government declares that the stipulations of the secret treaty concluded on 20 May 1882 between Austria-Hungary, Germany, and Italy shall not—as has been previously agreed—in any case be regarded as being directed against England.

In witness whereof the present ministerial declaration, which shall equally remain secret, has been drawn up in order to be exchanged against identical declarations by the Imperial Government of Germany and by the Royal Government of Italy.

No. 106   The Reinsurance Treaty——18 June 1887[1]

The Imperial Courts of Germany and Russia, animated by an equal desire to consolidate the general peace by an understanding destined to assure the defensive position of their respective states, have resolved to perpetuate by a special arrangement the accord established between them, in view of the expiration, on the 15th/27th June 1885, of the validity of the secret treaty and protocol signed in 1881 and renewed in 1884 by the three Courts of Germany, Russia, and Austria-Hungary.[2]—

For this purpose, the two Courts have named as Plenipotentiaries:

His Majesty the Emperor of Germany, King of Prussia, Count Herbert von Bismarck, Secretary of State in the Foreign Ministry;

His Majesty the Emperor of All the Russias, Count Paul Schouvaloff, Ambassador in Berlin,

Who, furnished with full powers, which have been found to be in good and due form, have agreed upon the following Articles:

ARTICLE I.

In the event that one of the High Contracting Parties should find himself at war with a third Great Power, the other would maintain a benevolent neutrality with regard to him and would devote his efforts to a localization of the conflict. This disposition would not be applicable to a war against Austria or France in the event that this war would result from an attack directed against one of these two latter Powers by one of the High Contracting Parties.

ARTICLE II.

Germany recognizes the rights historically acquired by Russia in the Balkan Peninsula, and particularly the legitimacy of its preponderant and decisive influence in Bulgaria and in Eastern Roumelia. The two Courts engage not to accept any modification of the territorial *status quo* of the said Peninsula without a previous accord between them, and to oppose eventually any attempt to upset this *status quo* or to modify it without their consent.

ARTICLE III.

The two Courts recognize the European and mutually obligatory character of the principle of the closing of the Straits of the Bosporous and of the Dardanelles, founded on the rights of man,[3] confirmed by treaties, and recapitulated in the declaration made by the second Russian Plenipotentiary at the session of 12 July of the Congress of Berlin (Protocol 19).

They shall both be vigilant that Turkey should not make an exception to this rule in favor of the interests of any government whatsoever by lending that part of her Empire which forms the Straits to the warlike operations of a belligerent Power. In case of an infraction, or in order to prevent it if such an infraction were to be foreseen, the two Courts shall warn Turkey that, if such should be the case, they would consider her as having placed herself in a state of war towards the injured Party and as having deprived herself from that time on of the benefits of security to her territorial *status quo* assured by the Treaty of Berlin.

ARTICLE IV.

The present treaty shall remain in force during the space of three years, reckoning from the day of the exchange of ratifications.

ARTICLE V.

The High Contracting Parties mutually promise each other to keep both the content and the existence of the present treaty and of the Protocol annexed thereto secret.

ARTICLE VI.

The present treaty shall be ratified and its ratifications shall be exchanged in Berlin within a period of fifteen days or earlier if that is possible.

In witness whereof the respective Plenipotentiaries have signed the present treaty and have affixed thereto the seal of their arms.

Done at Berlin, on the 18th day of June 1887.

(L.S.) BISMARCK.   (L.S.) SCHOUVALOFF.

Additional and Very Secret Protocol.

In order to complete the stipulations of Articles II and III of the secret treaty concluded on this same date, the two Courts have come to an agreement on the following points:

1.

Germany shall lend, as in the past, its coöperation to Russia in order to re-establish a regular and legal government in Bulgaria.—It promises not to give its consent in any event to the restoration of the Prince of Battenberg.

2.

In the event that His Majesty the Emperor of Russia should find himself under the necessity of assuming the task of defending the entrance to the Black Sea himself in order to safeguard Russia's interests, Germany engages to accord its benevolent neutrality and its moral and diplomatic support to the measures which His Majesty should judge it necessary to take in order to guard the key of his Empire.

3.

The present Protocol forms an integral part of the secret treaty signed on this day in Berlin, and shall have the same force and validity.

In witness whereof the respective Plenipotentiaries have signed it and have affixed thereto the seal of their arms.

Done at Berlin, on the 18th day of June 1887.

(L.S.) BISMARCK.   (L.S.) SCHOUVALOFF.

No. 107   Germany Refuses to Renew the Reinsurance Treaty ——25 March to 29 May 1890[1]

Memorandum by Count von Berchem.[2]

Berlin, 25 March 1890.

The Treaty, whose renewal is involved, has the purpose of calling forth warlike events whose localisation is extremely improbable; we could, therefore, easily bring about a general war in this way, which we perhaps otherwise could avoid now and should avoid. . . . *One* Power would be deceived by us in any event by the Treaty which is to be renewed, but probably both of our eastern neighbors directly concerned would be mystified by it; . . . . The Treaty delivers us into the hands of the Russians even in times of peace; they receive a document with which they can disturb our relations with Austria, Italy, England, and Turkey at any moment.

The Treaty does not grant any reciprocity, Russia has the benefit of all of its advantages. France will not attack us without being sure of Russia's assistance. But if Russia starts an Oriental war, which is the purpose of the Treaty, and if France, as is probable, attacks us at the same time, then Russia's neutrality towards us can be assumed anyway under the circumstances, it is in Russia's interest in this case even without a Treaty. The Treaty, therefore, does not safeguard us against a French attack, but, on the other hand, grants Russia the right to take the offensive against Austria on the lower Danube and prevents us from taking the offensive against France, disregarding the fact that its tendency can hardly be reconciled with the Austro-German alliance. . . . The agreement is directly opposed, if not to the letter, then in all events to the spirit of the Triple Alliance, and will, if the Russians break loose in the south, probably bring us into opposition to friendly Powers. But the Treaty is also practically infeasible. . . .

. . . For it is a matter of urgent interest for our foreign policy not to discourage Russia's designs upon Bulgaria, since such discouragement would be turned against us, and at the same time to help maintain the resistance of other Powers against Russia in southeastern Europe. . . . The danger of a collaboration between France and Russia is smaller today than it still was several years ago, we have no interest in accelerating this collaboration by counselling a Bulgarian adventure at a time when we cannot desire a conflict with France. . . .

Memorandum by Caprivi.

Berlin, 28 March 1890.

Yesterday, the undersigned and Ambassador General von Schweinitz[3] had an audience with His Majesty concerning the eventual renewal of the Secret Treaty with Russia. They were both unanimously of the opinion that such a renewal would, it is true, have the effect of preventing Russia from entering into a coalition, but that it would hardly be possible to reconcile the stipulations of the Treaty, not so much with the letter as with the spirit of the Triple Alliance, with our present Treaty with Roumania, and with the influence which we are exerting upon England. . . .

His Majesty thereupon ordered that the Ambassador, upon his return to Russia, should explain to the appropriate authority that we, for our part, are determined to continue to maintain the best relations with Russia, but that the change of leadership, which has just occurred in Germany and which makes it desirable that we attempt to remain quiet and not enter into any kind of far-reaching negotiations for the time being, is the reason why we consider it advisable to refrain from renewing the Treaty.

Schweinitz to Caprivi.

SECRET.

St. Petersburg, 3 April 1890.

Soon after my return, on the evening of 31 March, I went to see Mr. von Giers,[4] who awaited me impatiently. I noticed immediately that Count Shuvalov[5] had only incompletely informed the Minister about the events of the past few days, ... I thus found Mr. von Giers still under the favorable impression caused by the Russian Ambassador's report on his audiences with our most gracious Emperor and Master;[6] . . . .

. . . I then gradually made it clear to Mr. von Giers that my Government did not intend at this time to renew the Treaty expiring on 18 June of this year. . . . Mr. von Giers was somewhat consternated. Without fully revealing his thoughts, the Russian Minister nevertheless indicated to me the kind of picture of the overall political situation this unrolled before his mind's eye: The three Central Powers of the Continent allied through loudly proclaimed treaties, England brought closer to Germany through repeated exchanges of courtesies and more recently through the visit of the Prince of Wales,[7] France somewhat moderated in her thirst for revenge by the population's unmistakable yearning for peace, Austria-Hungary set free from the wise and well-meaning, but strict control of Prince Bismarck, and in the face of all this, Russia alone, without any kind of agreement with us or with any other Power—this is about how his country's situation would appear to Mr. von Giers; . . . . . . , and no one should be surprised if he sought support elsewhere. . . .

Schweinitz to Caprivi.

SECRET.

St. Petersburg, 15 May 1890.

Mr. von Giers has not been feeling well for the past few days, . . . ; yesterday, however, he was able to receive the Diplomatic Corps. . . .

The Russian Minister then explained to me in a similar manner as in our conversation of 31 March, but with even greater earnestness, the reasons which made it seem regrettable to him that no more written agreement should exist between us from 18 June on; he attached no importance at all to the far-reaching stipulations of the Additional Protocol or to such adjectives as "preponderant and decisive," which had been brought in not by him but partly by Mr. Saburow, partly by Count Shuvalov; the one and only point that he was concerned about was that something written should exist which would make the essential foundation of the good relations now prevailing independent of a change in personnel. . . . "A Treaty is not really necessary," Mr. von Giers said, "an exchange of Notes would suffice—perhaps an exchange of letters between the monarchs."

Your Excellency may most graciously gather from these intimations by the Russian Minister that he must have weighty reasons to take up once more, in such an urgent manner, the request for a written agreement. . . . From the readiness of Mr. von Giers not only to drop the "Additional and Very Secret Protocol," which engages us to "coöperation in Bulgaria" and to "moral and diplomatic support" at the Straits, but to also renounce the recognition of "preponderant and decisive influence in Bulgaria and Roumelia," Your Excellency may further perceive that the Minister's motives are not to be found in the intention of taking aggressive action in the Balkan Peninsula. Therefore, while I dutifully bring the words of Mr. von Giers to Your Excellency's attention, I can only add that, in my respectful opinion, the moment is favorable to secure Russia's neutrality towards us in the event of a French attack without renewing engagements which are incompatible with our treaty obligations towards other Powers. I must not hereby fail to express my impartial personal view that, if we completely reject the Russian Minister's very conciliatory proposals, he or his successor would be forced to seek elsewhere the support which he cannot obtain from us. . . .

Memorandum by Holstein.

Berlin, 20 May 1890.

In the secret Russo-German Treaty with its Additional Protocol, we assume obligations for the support of Russia[a]

1. concerning Russian rights to Bulgaria;

2. concerning the closing of the Straits. Each of these obligations is mentioned once in the Treaty, once in the Additional Protocol.

General von Schweinitz now writes that the passage concerning Bulgaria shall be eliminated from the Treaty and the Additional Protocol, the passage concerning the closing of the Straits from the Additional Protocol. Therefore, the passage in the *Treaty* concerning the closing of the Straits would remain in force. Thus we are under the obligation of influencing Constantinople to a continued closing of the Straits. . . .

If we now renew the Straits clause, then we expect the Russians to keep secret a fact which, when communicated in confidence to the English, would sow the seeds of distrust between England and Germany, but on the other hand would bring Morier's[8] idea of an Anglo-Russian Entente closer to fruition. According to Morier's plan, England would give up its interests in the Balkan Peninsula if Russia promised no further approaches to India.

Apart from the Straits clause, the mere fact that a secret treaty existed between us and Russia would have a destructive effect on our treaty relations with Austria, Roumania, and Italy. . . . But anything which can arouse suspicion about Germany's foreign policy would be particularly effective at the *present* moment, since several recently revealed remarks by Prince Bismarck are in themselves capable of creating uncertainty among our allies. . . .

Marginal comment by Caprivi:
ªAlso neutrality in an Anglo-Russian war.

Memorandum by Caprivi.

Berlin, 23 May 1890.
At today's audience, His Majesty has been pleased to give his approval that the views contained in the enclosed sketch be made the basis of our diplomatic relations with Russia. Our gracious Sovereign also wishes that the Russian proposals not be treated dilatorily, but in such a manner that they are to be considered as definitively settled. . . .

ENCLOSURE.

Berlin, 22 May 1890.
Three times since Mr. von Schweinitz returned from here to St. Petersburg with a negative reply, he has reported on attempts by Mr. von Giers to bring about the renewal of a treaty with Russia: on 3 April, 1 May, and 15 May. The method changed, but the three attempts have in common: Italy is not taken into consideration. This, and Russia's attitude at the Brussels Conference,[9] justifies the conclusion: one wishes to destroy the Triple Alliance, and to alienate England as well as Italy from us. If this deduction were wrong, if Russia really only desired peace, then an alliance would not be necessary, for the world could expect a disturbance

of the peace only from Russia at this time; a "Bulgarian danger" does not exist if Russia does not want it to. . . .

If, therefore, we have no reason which would make us want to change the present situation in the East, it follows from Russia's repeated attempts that there the opposite interest has become urgent. Russia feels isolated, yet would like to—perhaps because the conditions in Bulgaria are consolidating to a greater degree than Russia finds desirable—take a further step towards Constantinople. Russia's dilemma develops from the fact that it can take this step only via the Black Sea. Nature has made the way through Armenia extremely difficult, the way through Roumania collides with the latter's ally. The way by sea, however, is endangered by the English. Therefore, above all close the Straits—this is the purpose of the latest proposal by Mr. von Giers.

Thus, a rapprochement between Germany and Russia would alienate our allies from us, damage England, and be incomprehensible and unsympathetic to our population which has increasingly come to accept the concept of the Triple Alliance. . . .

As for the possibility that Russia could seek elsewhere the support which it cannot obtain from us, only France and England come into question for such a purpose. For the step which Russia now seems to have in mind and which it obviously would like to take without causing a general war, the French alliance is worthless as long as the British fleet in the Mediterranean can intervene. Through an alliance with England, Russia would be able to gain what it wishes to receive at no cost from us only at some sacrifice in other places (Asia?), and probably weaken its relations with France. But an alliance which would include both England and France is, because of England's interests in the Mediterranean, altogether improbable. . . .[10]

No. 108 The Franco-Russian Entente——10 August 1892 to 8 January 1894[1]

Montebello[2] to Ribot.[3]

SECRET.

St. Petersburg, 10 August 1892.

General de Boisdeffre[4] today has seen General Obroutshev,[5] delegated by the Tsar to discuss the project of a convention. After a long discussion, the following text has been proposed:[6]

"France and Russia, being animated by an equal desire to preserve the peace and having no other aim than to guard against the demands of a defensive war provoked by an attack of the armed forces of the Triple Alliance against one of them or the other, have agreed upon the following stipulations:

1. If France is attacked by Germany, or by Italy supported by Germany, Russia shall employ all of her available armed forces to attack Germany.

If Russia is attacked by Germany, or by Austria supported by Germany, France shall employ all her available armed forces to combat Germany.

2. In the event that the armed forces of the Triple Alliance, or of one of the Powers which is a party to it, should come to be mobilized, France and Russia, at the first announcement of the event and without it being necessary that they concert beforehand, shall mobilize immediately and simultaneously all of their armed forces, and shall transport them as closely as possible to their frontiers.

3. The available armed forces which must be employed against Germany shall consist, on the part of France, of 1,300,000 men, on the part of Russia, of 7-to-800,000 men. These armed forces shall be engaged in depth and with all dispatch in such a manner that Germany shall have to fight in the East and in the West at the same time.

4. The General Staffs of the armies of the two countries shall consult together at all times in order to prepare and to facilitate the execution of the measures provided for above. They shall communicate to each other, even in peacetime, all the information concerning the armies of the Triple Alliance of which they have, or shall have, any knowledge. The ways and means of corresponding in times of war shall be studied and provided for in advance.

5. France and Russia shall not conclude peace separately.

6. The present convention shall have the same duration as the Triple Alliance.

7. All of the clauses enumerated above shall be kept strictly secret."

Boisdeffre to Freycinet.[7]

SECRET.

Camp of Krasnoeye-Selo, [18] *August 1892.*

To continue my report No. 4 of 10 August, I have the honor of giving you an account of what has happened since my arrival in camp. . . .

18 August.— . . . At 11 o'clock, I was received by the Tsar. . . . Finally, His Majesty repeated that the project was entirely satisfactory to him, and everything seemed to him to have been arranged in the best interests of the two countries. . . .

The Tsar then spoke to me about the mobilization which is the subject of Art. 2.

I remarked to him that mobilization was the same as a declaration of war:

that to mobilize was to oblige one's neighbor to do likewise;

that mobilization involved the movement of strategic transports and their concentration.

Without this, to let a million men be mobilized on one's frontier without simultaneously doing the same was to deprive oneself of any possibility of later action and to place oneself in the position of a man who, having a pistol in his pocket, would let his neighbor place a loaded one against his head without drawing his own.

"This is exactly how I understand it," replied the Tsar. . . .

Giers to Montebello.

VERY SECRET.

St. Petersburg, 15/27 December 1893.

After having examined, by my Sovereign's Order, the project of a military convention worked out by the Russian and French General Staffs in August, 1892, and having submitted my appraisal of it to the Tsar, it is my duty to inform Your Excellency that the text of this arrangement, as it was approved in principle by His Majesty and signed by Aide-de-Camp General Obroutshev and Major-General Boisdeffre, can henceforth be considered as having been definitively adopted in its present form. Thus, the two General Staffs shall be in a position to plan together at all times and to communicate to each other all the information which could be useful to them.

Montebello to Giers.

SECRET.

St. Petersburg, 24 December 1893.
4 January 1894.

I have received the letter which Your Excellency has done me the honor of addressing to me on 15/27 December 1893, by which you inform me that, after having, by your Sovereign's order, examined the project of a military convention worked out by the Russian and French General Staffs and submitted your appraisal to the Tsar, you find it your duty to advise me that this arrangement, as it was approved, in principle, by His Majesty and signed, in August, 1892, by Aide-de-Camp General Obroutshev and Major-General Boisdeffre, both appointed for this purpose by their respective governments, can henceforth be considered as definitively adopted.

I have hastened to inform my government of this decision, and I am authorized to declare to Your Excellency, while begging you to bring this resolution to the attention of His Majesty the Tsar, that the President of the Republic and the French Government likewise consider the said military convention, whose text is approved by both sides, as being now in force.

As a result of this accord, the two General Staffs shall be, from this time on, in a position to plan together at all times and to communicate to each other all the information which could be useful to them.

No. 109   Fashoda——25 September to 3 November 1898[1]

Rodd[2] to Salisbury.[3]

Cairo, 25 September 1898.

I have received the following telegram this morning from Sir Herbert Kitchener:—

"I have just returned from Fashoda where I found Captain Marchand, accompanied by eight officers and 120 men, located in the old government buildings, over which they had hoisted the French flag; I sent a letter announcing my approach the day before my arrival at Fashoda. . . .

"When we arrived at Fashoda, Captain Marchand and M. Germain came on board, and I at once stated that the presence of a French force at Fashoda and in the Valley of the Nile was regarded as a direct infringement of the rights of the Egyptian Government and of that of Great Britain, and I protested in the strongest terms against their occupation of Fashoda and their hoisting the French flag in the dominions of His Highness the Khedive. In reply, Captain Marchand stated that he had precise orders to occupy the country and to hoist the French flag over the government buildings at Fashoda, and that it was impossible for him to retire without receiving orders from his Government to that effect, but he did not expect that these orders would be delayed. On my pressing him to say whether, seeing that I had a preponderating force, he was prepared to resist the hoisting of the Egyptian flag at Fashoda, he hesitated and replied that resistance was impossible. I then caused the flag to be hoisted on a ruined bastion of the old Egyptian fortifications about 500 yards south of the French flag. . . . I appointed Major Jackson to be Commandant of the Fashoda district, where I left a garrison consisting of one Soudanese battalion, four guns, and a gun-boat, after which I proceeded to the Sobat. . . .

"The position in which Captain Marchand finds himself at Fashoda is as impossible as it is absurd. He is cut off from the interior, and his water transport is quite inadequate; he is, moreover, short of ammunition and supplies, which must take months to reach him; he has no following in the country, and nothing could have saved him and his expedition from being annihilated by the Dervishes had we been a fortnight later in crushing the Khalifa. The futility of all their efforts is fully realised by Captain Marchand himself, and he seems quite as anxious to return as we are to facilitate his departure. In his present position he is powerless, but I hope that Her Majesty's Government will take the necessary steps for his removal as soon as possible, as the presence of a French force and flag on the Nile is manifestly extremely undesirable. Captain Marchand only lost

four natives on the journey, and his expedition is all well. I am sending a complete despatch by Lord Edward Cecil,[4] who is leaving with it for Cairo at once."

Monson[5] to Salisbury.

SECRET.

Paris, 30 September 1898.

Minister for Foreign Affairs [Delcassé] says he wishes me to let you know unofficially that it is impossible for the French Government to give up Fashoda, their right to occupy which Her Majesty's Government do not even choose to discuss. Neither this nor any other Ministry could submit to what would be the humiliation of France. Any formal demand of this nature would be considered as an ultimatum and rejected.

Already by the occupation of Sobat, the Sirdar[6] has committed what is practically an act of war or at any rate a more than unfriendly act, of which, however, his Excellency does not yet wish to make official complaint. All his conversations of today he requested me to consider as unofficial, but as embodying a decision which would not be retracted. All France would resent such an insult to the national honour as is involved in the proposal to recall M. Marchand and to treat the French occupation of Fashoda as an unjustifiable act. He could not think that it is wished in England to go to war over such a question, but France would, however unwilling, accept war rather than submit.

I confined myself to saying that Her Majesty's Government had already through me signified their point of view, and that for my part I did not see how they could possibly retreat from it. All this was unofficial.

Monson to Salisbury.

Paris, 10 October 1898.

With reference to my telegram No. 165 of today's date, I have the honour to transmit to your Lordship herewith copy of a leading article published in the "Matin" on the subject of Fashoda, which, in view of the tone previously adopted by that organ with regard to the question, almost verges on the ludicrous, so sudden and complete is the change of front taken up.

"The abandonment of Fashoda is perfectly compatible with the preservation of the national honour"; such is the pith of the article. While doing full justice, says the writer, to the energy, perseverance, and indomitable tenacity of purpose which enabled Major Marchand to penetrate into the region of the Great Lakes before the arrival of the Sirdar's troops, and to hoist the French flag inside Fashoda whilst the English cocked snooks at him from without, yet we must realise that it is most imprudent to saddle ourselves with useless and extravagant territories, practically inaccessible from the French possessions on the Atlantic coast, annexations in the mountains of the moon, which might, for all the good they do us, as well be in the moon itself.

The article concludes by quoting extracts from the journal of a painter, M. Castellani, who accompanied the Marchand Mission, of a most gloomy and discouraging nature, which may, it is hoped, exercise a wholesome and blunting effect on the "hungry edge of appetite" lately exhibited by the Colonial party for the acquisition of fresh black territories, and for the responsibility of governing more cannibal tribes.

If a hint from the Government has inspired this article, the writer has carried out his instructions with a vengeance; and it will be interesting to observe whether this is but a solitary note, or whether the cry will be taken up by the whole pack.

Monson to Salisbury.

SECRET AND MOST CONFIDENTIAL.

Paris, 25 October 1898.

With reference to your Lordship's secret telegram of last night, I learn from a source which, in my opinion, is entirely trustworthy, that the advice which M. Delcassé received from Count Mouravieff[7] was almost textually as follows:—

"Do not give England any pretext for attacking you at present. At a later date an opportunity will be found by Russia for opening the whole question of Egypt."

This I believe to have been taken down in writing by M. Delcassé, to be submitted to M. Brisson[8] and the President.

My own opinion is that Count Mouravieff neither categorically refused, nor contingently promised, the support of Russia in the present emergency.

Monson to Salisbury.

Paris, 3 November 1898.

After the Cabinet Council this morning orders were telegraphed at once to French Ambassador to inform your Lordship that Fashoda would be evacuated with the least possible delay.

MM. Marchand and Baratier have been instructed to return to Fashoda to carry out this decision,[9] and Foreign Minister has expressed to me his hope that Her Majesty's Government will give them every facility to accomplish this. The mission has ceased to have any political character and must henceforth be considered a simple inoffensive troop armed only for its own defense against native attack. Foreign Minister said he would lose no time in settling the route to be taken by the mission, and is almost decided upon Eastern one *via* Tibouti or Obok.

No. 110.   Anglo-German Relations: William II and the Boers
———2 January 1896 to 2 March 1900

Letter, William II to Nicholas II.[1]

[*Berlin*] *New Palace, 1/2/1896.*

Dearest Nicky,

Radolin's[2] return to Petersburg gives me the opportunity of sending you a few lines. . . .

The political horizon is peculiar just now. Armenia and Venezuela are open questions England brought up,[3] and now suddenly the Transvaal Republic has been attacked in a most foul way as it seems not without England's knowledge.[4] I have used very severe language in London, and have opened communications with Paris for common defence of our endangered interests, as French and German colonists have immediately joined hands of their own accord to help the outraged boers. I hope you will also kindly consider the question, as it is one of principle of upholding treaties once concluded. I hope that all will come right, but come what may, I never shall allow the British to stamp out the Transvaal! I hope you have better news for your poor brother who has arrived as I see at the Riviera!

Please give my best love to dear Alix[5] and once more thanking you for all kindness to Stranz and his men, believe me, dear Nicky.

Ever,

Your most aff'ate cousin and friend,

⟨ Willy.

William II's Telegram to Kruger.[6, 7]

Berlin, 3 January 1896.

I convey to you my sincere congratulations that you, without appealing to friendly Powers for assistance, have succeeded with your people, by your own energetic action against the armed bands which invaded your country as disturbers of the peace, in again restoring the peace and in preserving the independence of the country against attacks from the outside.

Letter, Hatzfeldt[8] *to Holstein.*[9]

London, 21 January 1896.

There is nothing new to report, and, if no *new* incidents occur, it is perhaps to be hoped that the excitement will gradually die down on both sides.

In the meantime, we are dealing with a completely changed situation here, as you have undoubtedly long since become aware from the manifestations of the English press. What is involved here is not the displeasure of the English *Government,* but rather a profound bitterness among the *public* which has manifested itself in every way. I have been assured that, when the excitement was at its zenith, the Germans in the City could hardly do business any more with Englishmen. At well-known great Clubs, particularly at the Turf, an unbounded bitterness prevailed. I, myself, have received numerous anonymous abusive and threatening letters. The general mood was such—about this I have no doubt—that the Government, if it had also lost its head or had wanted war for any reason whatsoever, would then have had the full support of public opinion. . . .

Faced with this mood, Salisbury,[10] it must be admitted, did not lose his head, but instead maintained his conciliatory attitude towards me, probably in the expectation that calmness would return with time. But this is still no reason, in my opinion, why we should ever doubt for a moment that he has also thought about the opposite chances, and that he seeks to prepare himself for the eventuality that either a rupture occurs between us, or—what he is likely to consider as more probable, if not certain—that Germany now embarks upon a decidely Anglophobic foreign policy. . . . More serious is the obvious effort at a rapprochement with France. When I recently jokingly mentioned to Salisbury this new love for France, which must be rather strange for him, he went along with the joke but added that he did only what we were doing, too, and did not at all deny that better relations with France would not be unwelcome. . . .

Lascelles[11] to Salisbury.[12]

SECRET.

Berlin, 9 February 1900.

The Emperor sent me a message by telephone yesterday afternoon that he would call upon me at 7 o'clock. His Majesty arrived at the Embassy a few minutes after that time, and remained with me for upwards of an hour. His Majesty, after condoling with me on a personal loss which I have sustained in the war in South Africa in the person of a nephew, said that he wished to read to me some observations on the war which he had himself compiled and addressed to the Prince of Wales, to whom they had been delivered two days ago.[13] . . .

His Majesty then told me of the message which he had sent to the King of Italy, about three weeks ago, to the effect that he would raise no objection to Italian troops being sent to Egypt if Her Majesty's Government should consider it necessary to send the English garrison to South Africa. . . .

The Emperor replied that ' . . . we always seemed to forget that the German Empire was a young State which could not stand being kicked. What had been his own experience? He had constantly striven to promote the most cordial relations between our two countries, and just when his endeavours seemed to be crowned with success, he had received a kick on the shins which had upset all his endeavours. . . . His Majesty replied that he had seen Dr. Leyds[14] once in his life, shortly after the Jameson raid—about which His Majesty had expressed an opinion, for which he had been greatly blamed in England at the time, but which had since been endorsed by every English statesman, to whichever party he might belong, who had spoken on the subject. . . .

Lascelles to Salisbury.[15]

SECRET.

Berlin, 2 March 1900.

I had an opportunity yesterday of conversing with the German Emperor, ... His Majesty was most gracious to me, and expressed great satisfaction at hearing of the relief of Ladysmith, the news of which had just reached me before I left the Embassy. . . . He also most sincerely hoped that our recent successes might not blind us to the necessity of a complete reform of our military system. He understood the difficulty of introducing anything in the nature of universal service in England, and he was occupying himself with a scheme for the reorganisation of the British Army.

As regards himself, His Majesty had passed a hard winter in fighting against anti-English sentiments, and against the incitements, even in his immediate *entourage*, to intervene in the war. I had no doubt seen in the foreign press the arguments which had been put forward to induce him to take the initiative in intervening to put an end to the war.

I ventured to interrupt His Majesty by observing that I had gathered that the press of those countries which had demanded intervention had suggested that the initiative should be taken by some other country than their own.

His Majesty said that they all wanted him to take the task upon himself, which he had not the slightest intention of doing. He made politics with his head and not with his heart, and although he had had much to suffer from the attacks of the English press both on himself and on Germany in general, he would certainly take no action which would embarrass Her Majesty's Government, and he took great credit to himself for having prevented any hostile action on the part of France or Russia which any encouragement on his part would easily have produced. He thought it was only fair that it should be known and recognised in England that his action had influenced the conduct of France and Russia, or, as His Majesty expressed it, "that I have kept those two tigers quiet."

No. 111   Anglo-German Relations: Attempts at a Rapprochement——20 January to 19 December 1901[1]

William II to Bülow.[2]

London, 20 January 1901.

Crossing stormy, with violent movements, but sunny, you would not have liked it. Some gentlemen invisible. For six hours I faced the roaring ocean winds and have never felt better! It was wonderful! . . .

Prince of Wales very cordial and full of touching gratitude that I came.[3] . . . Baron von Eckardstein[4] tells me Chamberlain[5] had intimated confidentially that it was all over with "splendid isolation," England would have to choose between Triple Alliance and Russia-France. He wanted the former at all costs, part of the Cabinet the latter. Foreign Office the former; only if we did not go along, then a turn towards Dual Entente. Understanding over Morocco again desired by him, can occur as soon as Lord Salisbury has left for Cannes. Well, it looks like "they are coming to us," which is what we have been waiting for.

Bülow to William II.

Berlin, 21 January 1901.

. . . Your Majesty is completely right in the impression that the English must come to us. They have just taken quite a beating

in Africa, America proves to be uncertain, Japan unreliable, France filled with hatred, Russia perfidious, public opinion in all countries hostile. . . . now the realization is gradually dawning upon the English that they will be unable to defend their world empire against so many opponents with their own strength alone.

Now everything depends on neither discouraging the English nor letting ourselves be pinned down by them prematurely. The English difficulties will still increase during the next months, and that also increases the price which we can exact. . . . The understanding with the Dual Entente threatened by the English is a bugbear invented only for our intimidation, which they have been using for years. The sacrifices, which such an understanding would impose upon England, are so extravagant that the English Government decided against it even at the time when the tensions between us and England were at their height. . . .

Holstein to Metternich.[6]

PRIVATE.

Berlin, 21 January 1901.

The reason I am especially suspicious of the present vehement protestations of friendship by Chamberlain and his friends is because the threatened understanding with Russia and France is such a total fraud. An English retreat would postpone the battle for survival by a few years, but would then make it all the more certain because their opponents would be stronger, the English weaker in power and prestige. We can wait, time is on our side. A sensible agreement with England, *i.e.*, one in which the almost certain danger of war to which we thereby expose ourselves is properly taken into account, can only then be reached, in my opinion, when the feeling of being in a critical position has become more widespread in England than it is today.

Holstein to Eckardstein.

PRIVATE.

Berlin, 21 January 1901.

This whole threat of disarming the enmity of Russia and of France by a retreat out of China and the Persian Gulf is, of course, nonsense and a fraud. First of all, France does not get enough out of it. France could not be persuaded, either by this or by another concession, to hand over Tangier to England and with it the Straits of Gibraltar. If England were to make large concessions of territories and spheres of interest to Russia and France, it would thereby only whet the appetite of these two opponents and make the battle for survival, even if a few years later, more unavoidable than ever; a weakened England against strengthened enemies. . . .

Memorandum by Lansdowne.[7]

24 May 1901.

At the time when the Prime Minister was about to leave England, and during his absence, Baron Eckardstein several times recurred to the subject of an Anglo-German Alliance or understanding. . . . On the occasion of one of these interviews, Baron Eckardstein mentioned incidentally that Austria and Italy would have to be included in such an arrangement as he had proposed.

I said that this seemed to me a most important point. We had, I reminded him, until then, been discussing the possibility of a purely defensive alliance between England and Germany, against any other two Powers, and I had said to him that in my view the objection to such an arrangement was that this country might find itself dragged into a quarrel in which we had no concern, and which might have been in fact provoked by our ally, whose external policy might be quite beyond our control, although that ally was ostensibly defending itself from attack. These objections could, I thought, be urged with infinitely greater force if we were asked to enter into similar obligations to Austria and Italy as well as to Germany.

On the 23rd instant I had an interview with Count Hatzfeldt, . . . was I then, I said, to understand that the proposal was simply that we should join the Triple Alliance? Count Hatzfeldt answered in the affirmative. . . .

Lansdowne to Lascelles.

SECRET.

Foreign Office, 19 December 1901.

The German Ambassador called on me to-day on the eve of his departure for Germany. After a brief conversation on various matters which had already formed the subject of communications between us, I referred to the discussions which had taken place between his Excellency's predecessor, Count Hatzfeldt, and Baron Eckardstein, on the part of the German Embassy, and myself during the spring and summer of this year in regard to the possibility of establishing closer political relations between Great Britain and Germany. I reminded his Excellency briefly of the course of these discussions. . . . While, therefore, we certainly did not regard the German proposal with an unfriendly or indifferent eye, I did not think that for the moment we could afford to take it up.

Count Metternich replied that he was well aware of the history of the informal discussions which I had recapitulated; . . . . He had always thought that it was a magnificent opportunity for us, and he had wondered that we did not "jump at it." To his mind, our preference for isolation was unintelligible. . . . Count Metternich went on to say that he was glad I had given him these explanations, adding that he was bound to admit the justice of my observation to the effect that the present time was not a favourable one for further pursuing the question. He feared, however, that an opportunity so favourable as that which presented itself last summer might not again occur. In politics, his Excellency said, things never stood still, and his own opinion, which he expressed as one entirely personal, was that in the years which lay before us the tendency would be for Germany to move more and more towards Russia.

I replied that it would, to my mind, be most unfortunate if there should be any estrangement between our two countries, and I trusted that he would not consider that our inability to take so serious a step as that which had been proposed to us denoted any unfriendliness towards Germany. Speaking entirely for myself, I asked him whether, assuming that we could not accept the German proposal as it stood, it might not be possible for the two countries to arrive at an understanding with regard to the policy which they might pursue in reference to particular questions or in particular parts of the world in which they were alike interested?

His Excellency unhesitatingly replied that no such minor proposal was likely to find favour with the German Government. It was a case of "the whole or none."

At the close of the conversation, I expressed my hope that I had made it clear to his Excellency that if for the moment we regarded the object which the German Government had had in view as unattainable, we had come to this conclusion, not because we regarded the offer with indifference, but on account of practical difficulties the importance of which I had no doubt his Excellency would fully recognise.

No. 112   Statistics on the Naval Race——1898 to 1914[1]

Size of the Fleets

Great Britain:	1898	1902[2]	1906[3]	1910[4]	1914[4]
Battleships	52	52	55	56	58
Battle Cruisers	—	—	6	—	8
Cruisers	18	126	28	38	46
Light Cruisers	95	—	86	69	60
Coast Defence Vessels, Armoured	15	4	0	0	0
Torpedo Vessels	35	34	21	18	15
Torpedo Boat Destroyers	50	109	143	150	198
Torpedo Boats	98	92	87	116	106
Submarines	—	0	25	63	69

Size of the Fleets

France:	1898	1902[2]	1906[3]	1910[4]	1914[4]
Battleships	27	28	19	17	21
Battle Cruisers	—	—	10	—	0
Cruisers	9	46	19	19	24
Light Cruisers	30	—	37	16	8
Coast Defence Vessels, Armoured	14	15	9	5	0
Torpedo Vessels	13	15	14	5	3
Torpedo Boat Destroyers	0	10	31	60	80
Torpedo Boats	211	249	255	246	153
Submarines	—	12	39	56	50

Russia:					
Battleships	12	18	8	7	8
Battle Cruisers	—	—	4	—	0
Cruisers	10	21	3	4	12
Light Cruisers	3	—	9	11	2
Coast Defence Vessels, Armoured	15	14	6	2	0
Torpedo Vessels	17	17	7	6	0
Torpedo Boat Destroyers	1	27	68	99	95
Torpedo Boats	174	129	172	63	25
Submarines	—	0	13	30	25

Germany:					
Battle Ships	17	25	18	33	35
Battle Cruisers	—	—	13	—	4
Cruisers	3	38	6	9	9
Light Cruisers	7	—	26	35	43
Coast Defence Vessels, Armoured	11	11	11	7	0
Torpedo Vessels	2	2	1	1	0
Torpedo Boat Destroyers	0	21	43	84	131
Torpedo Boats	113	94	84	82	80
Submarines	—	0	1	8	24

United States:					
Battleships	5	10	14	30	30
Battle Cruisers	—	—	1	—	0
Cruisers	2	22	7	15	17
Light Cruisers	14	—	22	21	18
Coast Defence Vessels, Armoured	20	12	11	10	10
Torpedo Vessels	0	0	2	2	2
Torpedo Boat Destroyers	0	2	20	25	52
Torpedo Boats	8	24	32	30	21
Submarines	—	1	8	18	29

Naval Expenditures

	1898-1899	1902-1903	1906-1907	1910-1911	1914-1915
Great Britain	£23,880,876	£31,003,977	£31,472,087	£40,419,336	£51,550,000[6]
France	£12,144,020	£12,271,948	£12,245,740	£15,023,019	£25,387,306[6]
Russia	£6,728,926	£10,446,392	£12,490,444[6]	£9,723,574[6]	£26,149,294[6]
Germany	£6,083,874	£10,044,031	£12,005,000	£20,845,000	£23,284,531[6]
United States	£22,705,901[5]	£16,203,916	£21,358,199	£27,848,111	£30,331,364[6]

No. 113   The Anglo-Japanese Treaty——30 January 1902[1]

The Governments of Great Britain and Japan, actuated solely by a desire to maintain the *status quo* and general peace in the extreme East, being moreover specially interested in maintaining the independence and territorial integrity of the Empire of China and the Empire of Corea, and in securing equal opportunities in those countries for the commerce and industry of all nations, hereby agree as follows:—

ARTICLE I.

The High Contracting Parties, having mutually recognised the independence of China and Corea, declare themselves to be entirely uninfluenced by any aggressive tendencies in either country. Having in view, however, their special interests, of which those of Great Britain relate principally to China, while Japan, in addition to the interests which she possesses in China, is interested in a peculiar degree politically as well as commercially and industrially in Corea, the High Contracting Parties recognise that it will be admissible for either of them to safeguard those interests if threatened either by the aggressive action of any other Power, or by disturbance arising in China or Corea, and necessitating the intervention of either of the High Contracting Parties for the protection of the lives or property of its subjects.

ARTICLE II.

If either Great Britain or Japan, in the defence of their respective interests as above described, should become involved in war with another Power, the other High Contracting Party will maintain a strict neutrality, and use its efforts to prevent other Powers from joining in hostilities against its Ally.

ARTICLE III.

If in the above event any other Power or Powers should join in hostilities against the Ally, the other High Contracting Party will come to its assistance and will conduct the war in common, and make peace in mutual agreement with it.

ARTICLE IV.

The High Contracting Parties agree that neither of them will, without consulting the other, enter into separate arrangements with another Power to the prejudice of the interests above described.

ARTICLE V.

Whenever, in the opinion of either Great Britain or Japan, the above-mentioned interests are in jeopardy, the two Governments will communicate with one another fully and frankly.

ARTICLE VI.

The present Agreement shall come into effect immediately after the date of its signature, and remain in force for five years from that date. . . . But if, when the date fixed for its expiration arrives, either ally is actually engaged in war, the alliance shall, *ipso facto*, continue until peace is concluded.

In faith whereof the undersigned, duly authorized by their respective Governments, have signed this agreement and have affixed thereto their seals.

Done in duplicate at London, the 30th day of January, 1902.

(L.S.) LANSDOWNE.   (L.S.) HAYASHI.[2]

Diplomatic Note Accompanying the Agreement.

In reference to the Agreement concluded by us to-day on behalf of our respective Governments, I have the honour to inform you that the British/Japanese Government recognises that the naval forces of Great Britain/Japan should, so far as is possible, act in concert with those of Japan/Great Britain in time of peace, and agrees that mutual facilities shall be given for the docking and coaling of vessels of war of one country in the ports of the other, as well as other advantages conducing to the welfare and efficiency of the respective navies of the two Powers.

At the present moment Japan and Great Britain are each of them maintaining in the Extreme East a naval force superior in strength to that of any third Power. Great Britain/Japan has no intention of relaxing her efforts to maintain, so far as may be possible, available for concentration in the waters of the Extreme East a naval force superior to that of a third Power.[3]

No. 114   The Franco-Italian Agreement—— 30 June/10 July 1902[1]

Prinetti[2] to Barrère.[3]

SECRET.

Rome, 10 July[4] 1902.

As a result of the conversations which we have had concerning the reciprocal situation of Italy and of France in the Mediterranean basin, and concerning especially the respective interests of the two nations in Tripolitania-Cyrenaica and in Morocco, it has appeared to us opportune to clarify the engagements which result from the letters on this subject exchanged between Your Excellency and Marquis Visconti-Venosta,[5] on 14 and 16 December 1900, in the sense that each of the two Powers shall be able to develop freely its sphere of influence in the above-mentioned regions at the moment it shall judge opportune, and without the action of one of them being necessarily subordinated to that of the other. . . . We have ascertained that this interpretation leaves no divergence whatsoever remaining at present between our Governments concerning their respective interests in the Mediterranean.

On the occasion of these negotiations, and in order to eliminate in a definitive manner any possible misunderstanding between our two countries, I do not hesitate, in order to clarify their general relations, to spontaneously make the following declarations to Your Excellency in the name of the Government of His Majesty the King:

In the event that France were to be the object of a direct or indirect aggression on the part of one or of several Powers, Italy shall maintain a strict neutrality. The same shall apply in the event that France, as the result of a direct provocation,[6] should find herself compelled to take the initiative of a declaration of war for the defense of her honor or of her security. In this eventuality, the Government of the Republic should previously communicate its intention to the Royal Government, which would then be able to verify that it is indeed a question of a case of direct provocation.

In order to remain faithful to the spirit of friendship which has inspired the present declarations, I am furthermore authorized to assure you that there does not exist on Italy's part, and that there shall not be concluded by her, any protocol whatsoever, or military disposition of an international contractual kind, which would be in conflict with the present declarations.

I have to add that, except for the interpretation of the Mediterranean interests of the two Powers, which is of a definitive character in accordance with the spirit of the correspondence exchanged between Your Excellency and Marquis Visconti-Venosta on 14 and 16 December 1900, the preceding declarations being in harmony with the present international engagements of Italy, the Royal Government assumes that they shall remain in full force as long as it shall not notify the Government of the Republic that these engagements have been modified.

I would be grateful to Your Excellency if you would kindly acknowledge receipt of the present communication, which must remain secret, and if you would give me an official reply in the name of the Government of the Republic.[7]

No. 115   The Anglo-French Agreement——8 April 1904[1]

Convention between the United Kingdom and France respecting Newfoundland, and West and Central Africa.

.   .   .   .

ARTICLE I.

France renounces the privileges established to her advantage by Article XIII of the Treaty of Utrecht, and confirmed or modified by subsequent provisions.

ARTICLE II.

France retains for her citizens, on a footing of equality with British subjects, the right of fishing in the territorial waters on that portion of the coast of Newfoundland comprised between Cape St. John and Cape Ray, passing by the north; this right shall be exercised during the usual fishing season closing for all persons on the 20th October of each year.

The French may therefore fish there for every kind of fish. . . .

ARTICLE III.

A pecuniary indemnity shall be awarded by His Britannic Majesty's Government to the French citizens engaged in fishing or the preparation of fish on the "Treaty Shore," who are obliged, either to abandon the establishments they possess there, or to give up their occupation, in consequence of the modification introduced by the present convention into the existing state of affairs. . . .

ARTICLE IV.

His Britannic Majesty's Government, recognising that, in addition to the indemnity referred to in the preceding Article, some territorial compensation is due to France in return for the surrender of her privilege in that part of the Island of Newfoundland referred to in Article II, agree with the government of the French Republic to the provisions embodied in the following Articles:—

ARTICLE V.

The present frontier between Senegambia and the English Colony of the Gambia shall be modified so as to give to France Yarbutenda and the lands and landing-places belonging to that locality. . . .

The conditions which shall govern transit on the River Gambia. . . .

ARTICLE VI.

The group known as the Iles de Los, and situated opposite Konakry, is ceded by His Britannic Majesty to France.

ARTICLE VII.

Persons born in the territories ceded to France by Articles V and VI of the present convention may retain British nationality by means of an individual declaration to that effect, ...

ARTICLE VIII.

To the east of the Niger the following line shall be substituted for the [present] boundary . . . Starting from the point on the left bank of the Niger. . . .

ARTICLE IX.

The present Convention shall be ratified, and the ratifications shall be exchanged, at London, within eight months, or earlier if possible. . . .

Done at London, in duplicate, the 8th day of April, 1904.

(L.S.) LANSDOWNE. (L.S.) PAUL CAMBON.[2]

Declaration respecting Egypt and Morocco.

ARTICLE I.

His Britannic Majesty's Government declare that they have no intention of altering the political status of Egypt.

The Government of the French Republic, for their part, declare that they will not obstruct the action of Great Britain in that country by asking that a limit of time be fixed for the British occupation or in any other manner, and that they give their assent to the draft Khedivial Decree annexed to the present Arrangement, containing the guarantees considered necessary for the protection of the interests of the Egyptian bondholders, . . .

ARTICLE II.

The Government of the French Republic declare that they have no intention of altering the political status of Morocco.

His Britannic Majesty's Government, for their part, recognise that it appertains to France more particularly, as a Power whose dominions are conterminous for a great distance with those of Morocco, to preserve order in that country, and to provide assistance for the purpose of all administrative, economic, financial, and military reforms which it may require. They declare that they will not obstruct the action taken by France for this purpose, provided that such action shall leave intact the rights which Great Britain, in virtue of Treaties, Conventions, and usage, enjoys in Morocco, including the right of coasting trade between the ports of Morocco, enjoyed by British vessels since 1901.

ARTICLE III.

His Britannic Majesty's Government, for their part, will respect the rights which France, in virtue of Treaties, Conventions, and usage, enjoys in Egypt, including the right of coasting trade between Egyptian ports accorded to French vessels.

ARTICLE IV.

The two governments, being equally attached to the principle of commercial liberty both in Egypt and Morocco, declare that they will not, in those countries, countenance any inequality, either in the imposition of customs duties or other taxes. . . . .

ARTICLE VI.

In order to insure the free passage of the Suez Canal, His Britannic Majesty's Government declare that they adhere to the stipulations of the Treaty of the 29th October, 1888, . . .

ARTICLE VII.

In order to secure the free passage of the Straits of Gibraltar, the two Governments agree not to permit the erection of any fortifications or strategic works on that portion of the coast of Morocco comprised between, but not including, Melilla and the heights which command the right bank of the River Sebou. This condition does not, however, apply to the places at present in the occupation of Spain on the Moorish coast of the Mediterranean.

ARTICLE IX.

The two Governments agree to afford to one another their diplomatic support, in order to obtain the execution of the clauses of the present Declaration regarding Egypt and Morocco.

Done at London, in duplicate, the 8th day of April, 1904.

(L.S.) LANSDOWNE. (L.S.) PAUL CAMBON.[2]

SECRET ARTICLE I.

In the event of either Government finding themselves constrained, by the force of circumstances, to modify their policy in respect to Egypt and Morocco, the engagements which they have undertaken towards each other by Articles IV, VI, and VII of the Declaration of to-day's date would remain intact.

SECRET ARTICLE III.

The two Governments agree that a certain extent of Moorish territory adjacent to Melilla, Ceuta, and other *Présides* should, whenever the Sultan ceases to exercise authority over it, come within the sphere of influence of Spain, and that the administration of the coast from Melilla as far as, but not including, the heights on the right bank of the Sebou, shall be intrusted to Spain. . . .

SECRET ARTICLE IV.

If Spain, when invited to assent to the provisions of the preceding Article, should think proper to decline, the Arrangement between France and Great Britain, as embodied in the Declaration of to-day's date, would be none the less applicable.

SECRET ARTICLE V.

Should the consent of the other Powers to the draft Decree mentioned in Article I of the Declaration of today's date not be obtained, the Government of the French Republic will not oppose the repayment at par of the Guaranteed, Privileged, and Unified Debts after the 15th July, 1910.

Done at London, in duplicate, the 8th day of April, 1904.

(L.S.) LANSDOWNE. (L.S.) PAUL CAMBON.

Declaration concerning Siam, Madagascar, and the New Hebrides.

I.–SIAM.

The Government of His Britannic Majesty and the Government of the French Republic confirm Articles 1 and 2 of the Declaration signed in London on the 15th January, 1896, by the Marquess of Salisbury, then Her Britannic Majesty's Principal Secretary of State for Foreign Affairs, and Baron de Courcel, then Ambassador of the French Republic at the Court of Her Britannic Majesty.

In order, however, to complete these arrangements, they declare by mutual agreement that the influence of Great Britain shall be recognized by France in the territories situated to the west of the basin of the River Menam, and that the influence of France shall be recognized by Great Britain in the territories situated to the east of the same region, all the Siamese possessions on the east and south-east of the zone above described and the adjacent islands coming thus henceforth under French influence, and, on the other hand, all Siamese possessions on the west of this zone and of the Gulf of Siam, including the Malay Peninsula and the adjacent islands, coming under English influence.

The two Contracting Parties, disclaiming all idea of annexing any Siamese territory, and determined to abstain from any act which might contravene the provisions of existing Treaties, agree that, with this reservation, and so far as either of them is concerned, the two Governments shall each have respective liberty of action in their spheres of influence as above defined.

II.–MADAGASCAR.

In view of the agreement now in negotiation on the questions of Jurisdiction and the postal service in Zanzibar and on the adjacent coast, His Britannic Majesty's Government withdraw the protest which they had raised against the introduction of the customs tariff established at Madagascar after the annexation of that island to France. The Government of the French Republic take note of this Declaration.

III.–NEW HEBRIDES.

The two Governments agree to draw up in concert an Arrangement which, without involving any modification of the political *status quo,* shall put an end to the difficulties arising from the absence of jurisdiction over the natives of the New Hebrides.

They agree to appoint a Commission to settle the disputes of their respective nationals in the said islands with regard to landed property. The competency of this Commission and its rules of procedure shall form the subject of a preliminary Agreement between the two Governments.

Done at London, in duplicate, the 8th day of April, 1904.

(L.S.) LANSDOWNE. (L.S.) PAUL CAMBON.

No. 116   The First Moroccan Crisis——31 March 1905 to 20 February 1906

White[1] to Lansdowne.[2]

Tangier, 2 April 1905.

In continuation of my despatch No. 49 of yesterday's date, I have the honour to report that when the German Emperor landed on the pier[3] he was warmly greeted by Mulai Abdelmalek,[4] who saluted him in the Sultan's name and stated that His Shereefian Majesty's joy at receiving the visit was not only on His Majesty's own account but also on that of his subjects.

The Emperor replied that it gave him great pleasure and satisfaction to salute a near relative of the Sultan and he requested him to convey to the Sultan his thanks for having sent the special embassy to greet him, and also for the magnificent preparations made for his reception. His Imperial Majesty added that he was deeply interested in the welfare and prosperity of the Moorish Empire. It was to the Sultan as an independent sovereign that he was paying a visit, and he trusted that, under His Shereefian Majesty's sovereignty, Morocco would remain free, and open to the peaceful competition of all nations without monopolies or exclusion.

When later on at the German Legation Mulai Abdelmalek handed to the Emperor the Sultan's letter, his Highness said: "His Shereefian Majesty, recalling the friendship which has always existed between His Majesty's illustrious ancestors and the German Government, is animated by the desire to strengthen and extend that friendship by all means as far as possible. . . ."

The Emperor, in reply, thanked Mulai Abdelmalek, more especially for the expressions of sincere friendship contained in the message. He entirely concurred in the Sultan's sentiments. It proved emphatically the omnipotence of the divine wisdom, which, as the Ambassador knew, directed the fate of nations. He personally most sincerely wished the development and the prosperity of the Moorish Empire as much as for the good of His Shereefian Majesty's own subjects as for that of the nations of Europe trading in this country, as he hoped, on a footing of perfect equality.

His Imperial Majesty added that he had visited Tangier resolved to do all that lay in his power to efficiently safeguard German interests in Morocco. He considered the Sultan an absolutely independent Sovereign, and it was with His Majesty that he desired to come to an understanding as to a means of safeguarding those interests. . . .

Chérisey[5] to Delcassé.[6]

Tangier, 31 March 1905.

. . . I believe it my duty to report without any delay the words spoken to me by His Majesty, to whom I had been presented at the German Legation.

Emperor William . . . continued: "Yes, Morocco is a beautiful country, above all from a commercial point of view; I hope that the European nations shall do what is required to safeguard their commercial interests in this country. As far as I am concerned, I am indeed determined that the interests of German commerce here shall be respected.". . .

Barrère to Delcassé.[7]

Rome, 1 April 1905.

Mr. Luzatti[8] has reported to me a conversation which he has just had with the German Ambassador on the subject of Morocco. Mr. von Monts, after having sharply criticized the policy of the French Government, "which has treated Germany as a negligible quantity in this affair," attempted to cast upon it the whole responsibility for the difficulties which his Government could cause us. He did not try to dissemble that the latter would do its best to multiply them, that Germany would deal directly with the Sultan of Morocco, and that it would support him with its authority and its money in his resistance against us.

Memorandum by Grey[9] on Morocco.[10]

PRIVATE.

20 February 1906.

The German Ambassador asked to see me yesterday for the purpose of telling me that his Government had met the last proposal of the French about police in Morocco with a point blank refusal.

If the Conference[11] breaks up without result, the situation will be very dangerous. Germany will endeavour to establish her influence in Morocco at the expense of France. France, to counteract this, or even simply to protect herself and a neighbour from the state of disturbance which is now chronic in Morocco, will be driven to take action in Morocco, which Germany may make a *casus belli*.

If there is war between France and Germany, it will be very difficult for us to keep out of it. The *Entente*, and still more the constant and emphatic demonstrations of affection (official,[12] naval, political, commercial, Municipal, and in the Press), have created in France a belief that we should support her in war. The last report from our naval attaché at Toulon said that all the French officers took this for granted, if the war was between France and Germany about Morocco. If this expectation is disappointed, the French will never forgive us.

There would also, I think, be a general feeling in every country that we had behaved meanly and left France in the lurch. The United States would despise us, Russia would not think it worth while to make a friendly arrangement with us about Asia, Japan would prepare to re-insure herself elsewhere, we should be left without a friend and without the power of making a friend, and Germany would take some pleasure, after what has passed, in exploiting the whole situation to our disadvantage, very likely by stirring up trouble through the Sultan of Turkey in Egypt. As a minor matter, the position of any Foreign Secretary here, who had made it an object to maintain the Entente with France, would become intolerable.

On the other hand, the prospect of a European War, and of our being involved in it, is horrible.

I propose, therefore, if unpleasant symptoms develop after the Conference is over, to tell the French Ambassador that a great effort, and if need be some sacrifice, should, in our opinion, be made to avoid war. To do this, we should have to find out what compensation Germany would ask or accept as the price of her recognition of the French claims in Morocco. . . .

I have also a further point in view. The door is being kept open by us for a *rapprochement* with Russia; there is at least a prospect that when Russia is re-established[13] we shall find ourselves on good terms with her. An *Entente* between Russia, France and ourselves would be absolutely secure. If it is necessary to check Germany, it could then be done. The present is the most unfavourable moment for attempting to check her. Is it not a grave mistake, if there must be a quarrel with Germany, for France or ourselves to let Germany choose the moment which best suits her?

There is a possibility that war may come before these suggestions of mine can be developed in diplomacy. If so, it will only be because Germany has made up her mind that she wants war and intends to have it anyhow, which I do not believe is the case. But I think we ought, in our own minds, to face the question now, whether we can keep out of war, if war breaks out between France and Germany. The more I review the situation, the more it appears to me that we cannot, without losing our good name and our friends, and wrecking our policy and position in the world.

No. 117   The Anglo-Russian Agreement——31 August 1907[1]

Convention between the United Kingdom and Russia Relating to Persia, Afghanistan, and Thibet.

. . . .

Arrangement concerning Persia.

The Governments of Great Britain and Russia, having mutually engaged to respect the integrity and independence of Persia, and sincerely desiring the preservation of order throughout that country and its peaceful development, as well as the permanent establishment of equal advantages for the trade and industry of all other nations;

Considering that each of them has, for geographical and economic reasons, a special interest in the maintenance of peace and order in certain provinces of Persia adjoining, or in the neighbourhood of, the Russian frontier on the one hand, and the frontiers of Afghanistan and Baluchistan on the other hand; and being desirous of avoiding all cause of conflict between their respective interests in the above-mentioned provinces of Persia;

Have agreed on the following terms:—

ARTICLE I.

Great Britain engages not to seek for herself, and not to support in favour of British subjects, or in favour of the subjects of third Powers, any Concessions of a political or commercial nature—such as Concessions for railways, banks, telegraphs, roads, transports, insurance, etc.—beyond a line starting from Kasr-i-Shirin, passing through Isfahan, Yezd, Kakhk, and ending at a point on the Persian frontier at the intersection of the Russian and Afghan frontiers, and not to oppose, directly or indirectly, demands for similar Concessions in this region which are supported by the Russian Government. It is understood that the above-mentioned places are included in the region in which Great Britain engages not to seek the Concessions referred to.

ARTICLE II.

Russia, on her part, engages not to seek for herself and not to support, in favour of Russian subjects, or in favour of the subjects of third Powers, any Concessions of a political or commercial nature—such as Concessions for railways, banks, telegraphs, roads, transports, insurance, etc.—beyond a line going from the Afghan frontier by way of Gazik, Birjand, Kerman, and ending at Bunder Abbas, and not to oppose, directly or indirectly, demands for similar Concessions in this region which are supported by the British Government. It is understood that the above-mentioned places are included in the region in which Russia engages not to seek the Concessions referred to.

ARTICLE III.

Russia, on her part, engages not to oppose, without previous arrangement with Great Britain, the grant of any Concessions whatever to British subjects in the regions of Persia situated between the lines mentioned in Articles I and II.

Great Britain undertakes a similar engagement as regards the grant of Concessions to Russian subjects in the same regions of Persia.

All Concessions existing at present in the regions indicated in Articles I and II are maintained.

ARTICLE IV.[2]

. . . .

ARTICLE V.[2]

. . . .

Convention concerning Afghanistan.

The High Contracting Parties, in order to ensure perfect security on their respective frontiers in Central Asia and to maintain in these regions a solid and lasting peace, have concluded the following Convention:—

ARTICLE I.

His Britannic Majesty's Government declare that they have no intention of changing the political status of Afghanistan. His Britannic Majesty's Government further engage to exercise their influence in Afghanistan only in a pacific sense, and they will not themselves take, nor encourage Afghanistan to take, any measures threatening Russia.

The Russian Government, on their part, declare that they recognize Afghanistan as outside the sphere of Russian influence, and they engage that all their political relations with Afghanistan shall be conducted through the intermediary of His Britannic Majesty's Government; they further engage not to send any Agents into Afghanistan.

ARTICLE II.

The Government of His Britannic Majesty having declared, in the Treaty signed at Kabul on the 21st March, 1905, that they recognize the Agreement and the engagements concluded with the late Emir Abdur Rahman, and that they have no intention of interfering in the internal government of Afghan territory, Great Britain engages neither to annex nor to occupy, in contravention of that Treaty, any portion of Afghanistan or to interfere in the internal administration of the country, provided that the [present?] Emir fulfils the engagements already contracted by him towards His Britannic Majesty's Government under the above-mentioned Treaty.

ARTICLE III.

The Russian and Afghan authorities, specially designated for the purpose on the frontier or in the frontier provinces, may establish direct relations with each other for the settlement of local questions of a non-political character.

ARTICLE IV.

His Britannic Majesty's Government and the Russian Government affirm their adherence to the principle of equality of commercial opportunity in Afghanistan, and they agree that any facilities which may have been, or shall be hereafter, obtained for British and British-Indian trade and traders, shall be equally enjoyed by Russian trade and traders. Should the progress of trade establish the necessity for Commercial Agents, the two governments will agree as to what measures shall be taken, due regard, of course, being had to the Emir's sovereign rights.

ARTICLE V.

The present Arrangement will only come into force when His Britannic Majesty's Government shall have notified the Russian Government of the consent of the Emir to the terms stipulated above.

Arrangement concerning Thibet.

The Governments of Great Britain and Russia, recognizing the suzerain rights of China in Thibet, and considering the fact that Great Britain, by reason of her geographical position, has a special interest in the maintenance of the *status quo* in the external relations of Thibet, have made the following Arrangement:—

ARTICLE I.

The two High Contracting Parties engage to respect the territorial integrity of Thibet and to abstain from all interference in its internal administration.

ARTICLE II.

In conformity with the admitted principle of the suzerainty of China over Thibet, Great Britain and Russia engage not to enter into negotiations with Thibet except through the intermediary of the Chinese government. This engagement does not exclude the direct relations between British Commercial Agents and the Thibetan authorities provided for in Article V of the convention between Great Britain and Thibet of the 7th September, 1904, and confirmed by the Convention between Great Britain and China of the 27th April, 1906; . . .

It is clearly understood that Buddhists, subjects of Great Britain or of Russia, may enter into direct relations on strictly religious matters with the Dalai Lama and the other representatives of Buddhism in Thibet; the Governments of Great Britain and Russia engage, as far as they are concerned, not to allow those relations to infringe the stipulations of the present Arrangement.

ARTICLE III.

The British and Russian Governments respectively engage not to send Representatives to Lhassa.

ARTICLE IV.

The two High Contracting Parties engage neither to seek nor to obtain, whether for themselves or for their subjects, any concessions for railways, roads, telegraphs, and mines, or other rights in Thibet.

ARTICLE V.

The two governments agree that no part of the revenues of Thibet, whether in kind or in cash, shall be pledged or assigned to Great Britain or Russia, or to any of their subjects.

Annex concerning Thibet.[3]

.   .   .   .

The present Convention shall be ratified, and the ratifications exchanged at St. Petersburg, as soon as possible.[4]

In witness whereof the respective Plenipotentiaries have signed the present Convention and affixed thereto their seals.

Done, in duplicate, at St. Petersburg, the 18th/31st August, 1907.

(L.S.) A. NICOLSON.[5] (L.S.) IZVOLSKY.[6]

No. 118 Anglo-German Relations: Attempts at a Naval Agreement——16 July to 5 August 1908[1]

Metternich to Bülow.

SECRET.

London, 16 July 1908.

Sir Edward Grey invited me, together with Mr. Lloyd George,[2] to have breakfast in his home on the day before yesterday. The conversation soon turned to foreign policy. . . .

Both Ministers were of the opinion that the relations between England and Germany hinged on the question of their navies. The expenditures for the British Navy would, as a result of the German naval program[a]

Marginal comments by William II:

[a] wrong! as a result of the English lust for becoming a Super-Power and seeing ghosts everywhere.

and the accelerated[b] naval construction, increase to such an extent, and the feeling of a German danger would thereby reach such a degree of intensity, that the relations between the two countries could not be improved as long as they were trying to outdo each other in this naval competition.[c] Every Englishman would stake his last penny to retain naval superiority,[d] upon which depended not only England's position in the world, but also its existence as an independent state. The ruinous expenses, which were forced by the naval competition,[e] prevented the development of relations of trust and confidence between the two nations. Anyone who had even only a modicum of knowledge about England knew that the intention did not exist here to threaten[f] Germany with the British Navy or yet to attack Germany. An invasion was completely out of the question if only because of the condition of the British Army. As Mr. Lloyd George jokingly remarked, when, on some occasion or other, the conversation had turned to the subject of an English landing on the German coast, Prince Bismarck is supposed to have said that in such an event he would leave it up to the police to arrest the English landing force. The circumstances were still the same today, too, as far as a threat to Germany by England was concerned. For England, however, a powerful German fleet,[g] with a still more powerful army in the background, was a real danger.[h]

I replied that the notion of a "German invasion" was only a figment of the English imagination. No sensible person in Germany would think of it.[i] . . . Sir Edward Grey would first have to bring about a relaxation of political tension between the two countries, and, through his foreign policy, re-establish the belief in Central Europe that his Ententes could not one day be misused against us,[j] only then would the way be smoothed for an eventual discussion of the limitation of naval forces.[k] Not before. Mr. Lloyd George, who had taken an active part in the naval discussion, rejoined that a deceleration in the tempo of our naval construction[l] would contribute more of an immediate calming of tempers than any kind of political action could accomplish. We would find here the most sincere desire to meet us halfway in the creation of a common basis for the mutual limitation of naval construction.[m] The introduction of the Dreadnought class had

---

[b] is not accelerated!

[c] does not exist! ours is limited! by law!

[d] see *Nauticus*[3] they already have it threefold!!!

[e] England has never used such an arrogant tone, even in the days of greatest tension with Russia over Afghanistan! It has never dared to demand of Russia that she withdraw her troops from the frontier, or stop the troop transports for the reinforcement of the garrisons.

[f] ?! they have already done so permanently!

[g] will never be powerful against England! and even less of a danger than the already too powerful British Navy is for us.

[h] That, after my Guildhall speech, is really impudent!

[i] correct

[j] very good

[k] wrong! We will not discuss this subject at all! we shall never let anyone dictate the composition of our armaments to us.

[l] We have no accelerated tempo! And also do not have any *secret* "Dreadnoughts" under construction for other states—which are then purchased by England—or [which], made up to resemble battle cruisers, suddenly turn out to be battleships.

[m] The Engl.[ish] Minister should first try to present this completely unheard-of demand to Roosevelt, Clemenceau, Mirabello,[4] or Japan! The answers would give us a good laugh! Why *only* to *us*? Because they believe that my diplomacy is so scared it has made in its pants and lets itself be intimidated by clamors of war.

been a grave mistake on England's part. The Government here would give every possible guarantee[n] that no new class should be introduced[o] if we could reach an understanding. . . .[p]

Metternich to Bülow.

SECRET.

. . . . *London, 1 August 1908.*

On the same day [28 July], I had a long discussion with the Chancellor of the Exchequer, ... Mr. Lloyd George then again broached his favorite topic, a deceleration in the tempo of naval construction,[q] and tried to persuade me to make use of the time as long as the peaceful Liberal Government was in power. He estimated this time at three to four years. . . . It was perfectly clear to him that we must have a navy which inspired respect. He also understood perfectly that the present ratio between the German and British navies did not suit us, and that we wanted to come closer to the size of the British Navy.[r] There could be no objection to this because German interests overseas had increased to such an extent that we needed a strong navy to protect them. The present English Government interpreted the "Two-Power-Standard" to mean that the British Navy must be the equal of any two foreign navies,[s] but not that it must be twice as strong as the strongest foreign navy.[t] That is, as the German Navy plus another one, but not twice the Germany Navy. He would think that the ratio between the German and British navies should be fixed[u] at about 2:3. Because of the greater vital importance which the navy had for England than for Germany, the British Navy would always have to be quite a bit stronger than ours so that it would be capable of instilling the feeling of security which England demanded

---

[n] we do not need it!

[o] we couldn't care less.

[p] The Emperor's final comment:

Bravo! Metternich! He did an excellent job, except for one point, which is the most important one. The Ambassador completely overlooked the fact that he had no business, even if entirely informally and only as his private opinion,[5] the impudent request of the Engl.[ish] Ministers to make their peaceableness dependent upon the reduction of our naval armaments. He thereby ventured onto dangerous ground! I feel very sorry for him. He must be told that I do *not* desire a good relationship with England at the price of the expansion of Germany's navy. If England only intends to do us the favor of holding out its hand to us under the condition that we would have to limit the size of our Navy, then this is the height of impudence, which includes within it a shocking insult to the German people and their Emperor, which should have been rejected by the Ambassador at once! With the same right France and Russia can then demand a limitation of our ground forces. As soon as you permit a foreign state to interfere under any kind of pretense with your own armaments, you abdicate, like Portugal and Spain! The German Navy is not built *against* anybody, and also not *against* England! Rather for *our* needs! This is expressed very clearly in the Naval Law and has remained unchallenged for the past 11 years! Every single provision in this Law, down to the smallest one, will be carried out; whether the British like it or not makes no difference! If they want war, let them *start* one, we are not afraid of one!

[q] This is unheard-of! and results from the fact that Metternich recently agreed to discuss the idea at all.

[r] nonsense! has nothing at all to do with this!

[s] It has already reached a "3 Power-Standard"—without knowing it, of course!

[t] !! Jesuitical hair-splitting!

[u] well, well!? He has already reached that point!

of it [and] at the same time powerful enough to prevent the rise on our side of any reckless notions to attack.[v] . . . It was true that he could not speak in the name of the English Government in this matter, but could only express his personal opinion, yet he knew that we would find the most friendly reception by the Liberal Cabinet[w] if we were inclined to discuss a deceleration in the tempo of naval construction.[x] Even if we could only agree to construct *one* Dreadnought less each year on both sides, then that alone would bring about a complete change of mood towards us in England.[y] . . .

I replied that we first had to see some sign of good will in England's foreign policy before we could agree to consider the questions he had raised.[z] . . . It was to start at the wrong end, to place the cart before the horse, if we were to talk about naval programs before the atmosphere had been cleared of the present anxiety and mutual suspicion.

The Minister thought that precisely this would be most certainly achieved through a friendly agreement on the subject of naval construction.[aa] . . . [bb]

Bülow to Metternich.

SECRET.

Norderney, 5 August 1908.
His Majesty the Emperor and King has commented to your report of July 16th: "Bravo Metternich!"

Your Excellency was doubtlessly guided by the best of intentions in your discussions with the Ministers Sir Edward Grey and Mr. Lloyd George. . . . Nevertheless, we should be—and this was emphasized by His Majesty on the occasion of your report—under no illusion that the question which was discussed between you and the two Ministers is a very delicate one.

The German people are as sensitive as the English in questions of their security, independence, and dignity. . . . If a foreign country should demand of us unilateral limitations of our armaments at sea or on land, then no German Government would be able to render anything but an absolutely negative reply. The entire German nation would unanimously agree that it would be better to assume any burden, even a war fought on several fronts, than to suffer such an injury to its honor and its dignity. . . . What would the French say, and indeed the British as well, if we tried to force France to accept an agreement on the ratio between troop reserve strength and size of population, or a compromise concerning technical weapons or concerning the construction of frontier fortifications? What of the Russians if we demanded of them that they should follow our wishes in the disposition of their troops on their western frontier? What the whole world if we strove to achieve a Two- or yet a Three-Power-Standard for our army, upon which our fate depends no less than England's upon

---

[v] This is the kind of language that until now has been used only with China or Italy or such people! incredible!

[w] "bluff"!

[x] No! 3 times no! after the words above, *never!*

[y] hogwash!

[z] we won't do it!

[aa] No!

[bb] The Emperor's final comment:
This kind of conversation, as conducted here between L. George and Metternich, is really shameful and provocative for Germany! I must insist that in future he categorically reject such expectorations. . . . He just has to give these gentlemen, who want *to prevent the rise of "our reckless notions to attack,"* a rude answer, such as "You can lick my etc." So that these fellows first again become sensible! . . .

Metternich should be given a good strong kick in his —; he is too flabby!

its navy, [and] forbade other Powers from coming even close to this standard?

. . . I leave it to Your Excellency to decide whether it would be a tactically correct move if you should drop the hint in authoritative quarters at an opportune moment that we are constructing ships for purely defensive purposes, *i.e.*, particularly for the event that England should side with France in a war between Germany and France. Germany, unfortunately, would always have to be prepared for a French attack. If, however, England were to promise us neutrality in such an event, then it would be easier for us, of course, to decelerate even further the tempo of our naval construction.

. . . The question whether bilateral agreements between us and England over naval construction are possible at some future date can not be answered now with any certainty. In any case, the preliminary supposition for such an agreement would be a friendlier general policy, continued for some time, by England towards Germany. . . .

No. 119   The **Daily Telegraph** Interview——28 October 1908[1]

London, 28 October 1908.

We have received the following communication from a source of such unimpeachable authority that we can without hesitation commend the obvious message which it conveys to the attention of our readers.

Discretion is the first and last requisite in a diplomatist, and should still be observed by those who, like myself, have long passed from public into private life. Yet, moments sometimes occur in the history of nations when a calculated indiscretion proves of the highest possible service, and it is for this reason that I have decided to make known the substance of a lengthy conversation which it was my privilege during the present month to have had with His Majesty the German Emperor. I do so in the hope that it may help to remove that obstinate misconception of the character of the Kaiser's feelings towards England, which, I fear, is deeply rooted in the ordinary Englishman's breast. It is the Emperor's sincere wish that it should be eradicated. He has given repeated proofs of his desire by word and deed. But, to speak frankly, his large stock of patience is giving out, now that he finds himself so continually misrepresented, and has so often experienced the mortification of finding that any momentary improvement of relations is followed by renewed outbursts of prejudice, and a prompt return to the old attitude of suspicion.

As I have said, His Majesty honoured me with a long conversation, and spoke with impulsive and unusual frankness. "You English," he said, "are mad, mad as March hares. What has come over you that you are so completely given over to suspicions quite unworthy of a great nation? What more can I do than I have done? I declared with all the emphasis at my command, in my speech at the Guildhall, that my heart is set upon peace, and that it is one of my dearest wishes to live on the best of terms with England. Have I ever been false to my word? Falsehood and prevarication are alien to my nature. My actions ought to speak for themselves, but you listen not to them but to those who misinterpret and distort them. That is a personal insult which I feel and resent. To be forever misjudged, to have my repeated offers of friendship weighed and scrutinized with zealous, mistrustful eyes, taxes my patience severely. I have said time after time that I am a friend of England, and your press, or at least a considerable section of it, bids the people of England refuse my proffered hand and insinuates that the other holds a dagger. How can I convince a nation against its will?"

"I repeat," continued His Majesty, "that I am a friend of England, but you make it hard for me to remain so. My task is not of the easiest. The prevailing sentiment amongst large parts of the middle and lower classes of my own people is not friendly to England. So I am, so to speak, in a minority in my own land, but it is a minority of the best elements, just as it is in England with respect to Germany. That is another reason why I resent your refusal to accept my pledged word that I am the friend of England. I strive without ceasing to improve relations, and you retort that I am your arch-enemy. You make it very hard for me. Why is it?"

Thereupon I ventured to remind His Majesty that not England alone, but the whole of Europe had viewed with disapproval the recent action of Germany in allowing the German Consul to return from Tangier to Fez, and in anticipating the joint action of France and Spain by suggesting to the Powers that the time had come for Europe to recognize Mulay Hafid as the new Sultan of Morocco.

His Majesty made a gesture of impatience. "Yes," he said, "that is an excellent example of the way in which German action is misinterpreted. First, then, as regards the journey of Dr. Vassel. The German Government, in sending Vassel back to his post at Fez, was only guided by the wish that he should look after the private interests of German subjects in that city, who cried for help and protection after the long absence of a consular representative. And why not send him? Are those who charge Germany with having stolen a march on the other Powers aware that a French consular representative had already been in Fez for several months when Vassel set out? Then, as to the recognition of Mulay Hafid. The press of Europe has complained with much acerbity that Germany ought not to have suggested his recognition until he had notified Europe of his full acceptance of the Act of Algeciras[2] as being binding upon him as Sultan of Morocco and the successor of his brother. My answer is that Mulay Hafid notified the Powers to that effect weeks ago, before the decisive battle was fought. He sent, as far back as the middle of last July, an identical communication to the Governments of Germany, France, and Great Britain, containing an explicit acknowledgement that he was prepared to recognize all the obligations towards Europe incurred as Sultan by Abdul Aziz. The German Government interpreted that communication as a final and authoritative expression of Mulay Hafid's intentions, and therefore they considered that there was no reason to wait until he had sent a second communication before recognizing him as *de facto* Sultan of Morocco, who had succeeded to his brother's throne by right of victory in the field."

I suggested to His Majesty that an important and influential section of the German press had placed a very different interpretation upon the action of the German Government, and, in fact, had given it their effusive approbation precisely because they saw in it a strong act instead of mere words, and a decisive indication that Germany was once more about to intervene in the shaping of events in Morocco. "There are mischiefmakers," replied the Emperor, "in both countries. I will not attempt to weigh their relative capacity for misinterpretation. But the facts are as I have stated. There has been nothing in Germany's recent action with regard to Morocco which runs contrary to the explicit declaration of my love of peace, which I made both at the Guildhall and in my latest speech at Strasbourg."[3]

His Majesty then reverted to the subject uppermost in his mind—his proved friendship for England. "I have referred to my speeches," he said, "in which I have done all that a Sovereign can to proclaim my good will. But, as actions speak louder than words, let me also refer to my acts. It is commonly believed in England that throughout the South African War, Germany was hostile to her. German opinion undoubtedly was hostile, bitterly hostile. The press was hostile, the private opinion was hostile. But official Germany—what of that? Listen. What was it that brought to a sudden stop and absolute collapse the tour of the Boer delegates in Europe, who were striving to obtain European intervention? They were feted in Holland, France gave them a rapturous welcome. They wished to come to Berlin, where German people would have crowned them with flowers. They asked me to receive them. I refused. The agitation at once died away, and the delegation returned empty-handed. Was that, I ask the action of a secret enemy?

"Or again, when the struggle was at its height, the German Government was invited by the Governments of France and Russia to join with them in calling upon England to put an end to the war. The moment had come, they said, not only to save the Boer Republics, but also to humiliate England to the dust. What was my reply? I said that so far from Germany joining in any concerted European action to put pressure upon England and bring about her downfall, Germany would always keep aloof from politics that could bring her into complications with a Sea Power like England. Posterity will one day read the exact terms of the letter—now in the archives of Windsor Castle—in which I informed the Sovereign of England of the answer I had returned to the Powers which then sought to compass her fall. Englishmen, who now insult me by doubting my word, should know what were my actions in the hour of their adversity.

"Nor was that all. Just at the time of your Black Week, when disasters followed one another in rapid succession, I received a letter from Queen Victoria, my revered grandmother, written in sorrow and affliction, and bearing manifest traces of the anxieties which were preying upon her mind and health. I at once returned a sympathetic reply. But I did more than that. I bade one of my officers procure for me as exact an account as he could obtain of the number of combatants in South Africa on both sides, and of the actual position of the opposing forces. With the figures before me, I worked out what I considered to be the best plan of campaign under the circumstances, and submitted it to my General Staff for their criticism. Then I dispatched it to England, and that document,[4] likewise, is among the State papers at Windsor Castle, awaiting the severely impartial verdict of history. And, as a matter of curious coincidence, let me add that the plan which I formulated ran very much on the same lines as that which was actually adopted by Lord Roberts and carried by him into successful operation. Was that, I repeat, the act of one who wished England ill? Let Englishmen be just and say!

"But, you will say, what of the German Navy?[5] Is not that a menace to England? Against whom but England is it being steadily built up? If England is not in the minds of those Germans who are bent on creating a powerful fleet, why is Germany asked to consent to such new and heavy burdens of taxation? My answer is clear. Germany is a young and growing Empire. She has a world-wide commerce which is rapidly expanding, and to which the legitimate ambition of patriotic Germans refuses to assign any bounds. Germany must have a powerful fleet to protect that commerce and her manifold interests in even the most distant seas. She expects those interests to go on growing, and she must be able to champion them manfully in any quarter of the globe. Germany looks ahead. Her horizons stretch far away. She must be prepared for any eventualities in the Far East. Who can forsee what may take place in the Pacific in the days to come, days not so distant as some believe, but days, at any rate, for which all European Powers with Far Eastern interests ought steadily to prepare? Look at the accomplished rise of Japan, think of the possible national awakening of China, and then judge of the vast problems of the Pacific. Only those Powers which have great navies will be listened to with respect when the future of the Pacific comes to be solved, and, if for that reason only, Germany must have a powerful fleet. It may even be that England herself will be glad that Germany has a fleet when they speak together on the same side in the great debates of the future."

Such was the purport of the Emperor's conversation. He spoke with all that earnestness which marks his manner when speaking on deeply pondered subjects. I would ask my fellow countrymen who value the cause of peace to weigh what I have written, and to revise, if necessary, their estimate of the Kaiser and his friendship for England by His Majesty's own words. If they had enjoyed the privilege, which was mine, of hearing them spoken, they would doubt no longer either His Majesty's firm desire to live on the best of terms with England or his growing impatience at the persistent mistrust with which his offer of friendship is received.

No. 120   The Bosnian Crisis——25 June 1908 to 14 September 1909

No. 120-1.   Bülow to Schlözer.[1, 2]

VERY CONFIDENTIAL.

Berlin, 25 June 1908.

. . . .

For our attitude in the *Near East,* and especially in the Balkan peninsula, where we only pursue economic interests, the wishes, needs, and interests of Austria-Hungary, our close friend and ally, are, and shall remain, of decisive importance. . . . Germany and Austria-Hungary form a solid block which is capable of weathering any storm.[a] Their alliance, founded upon a solidarity of interests and the common championing of the monarchical concept of the state, is the best safeguard for the two monarchies against other Powers too often corrupted by revolutionary movements and ideas hostile to authority. Loyally standing together with Austria-Hungary shall and must remain also in future the highest principle of German foreign policy.[b]

. . . .

No. 120-2.   Bülow to Aehrenthal.[3, 4]

PRIVATE LETTER.

Norderney, 23 July 1908.

I avail myself of a quiet moment here on the seashore to thank you very much for your kind letter of June 12th, whose content I found most interesting, and which furnishes me with new and gratifying proof that agreement exists between us on all important questions. . . . The leading thought of our Near Eastern policy shall, as until now, so also in future, culminate in an effort to do justice to the wishes and interests of our Austro-Hungarian friend and ally. . . .

Marginal comments by William II on the copy:
[a] Yes

[b] correct

No. 120-3. Minutes of the Austrian Ministers' Conference held at Vienna on 19 August 1908.[5]

. . . .

SUBJECT: The question of the impact of the new era in Turkey[6] upon Bosnia and Herzegovina, and of the annexation of these provinces with the simultaneous withdrawal of the [Austro-Hungarian] garrisons from the Sandjak of Novi-Bazar, respectively.

Aehrenthal: . . . As far as the probable attitude of the Powers was concerned in the event of the transformation of the occupation into an annexation, the speaker commented first of all that one could indeed count absolutely upon Germany since this Power was now solely dependent upon Austria-Hungary, particularly after the rebuff which Emperor William had given to the King of England in Cronberg[7] on the latter's proposal to restrict the German naval construction plan already fixed by law. As for Russia, . . . it was the Minister's intention . . . to assure the St. Petersburg Cabinet that, if it would maintain a friendly attitude towards the Monarchy in the annexation question, he would be willing to maintain an equally friendly attitude in the event that Russia should bring up the question of the passage [of Russian warships] through the Dardanelles. Italy could not raise any demands for compensation on the basis of the Triple Alliance if the Monarchy should proceed with the annexation of Bosnia and of Herzegovina. Italy could only then demand compensation when Austria-Hungary went beyond the provinces now occupied on the basis of the Treaty of Berlin[8] and took possession of parts of Turkish areas. France was too much occupied in Morocco[9] at the moment for her to even think of taking an active role in the Balkan peninsula, and no opposition was to be feared from England either. . . .

Beck: The Minister-President posed the further question what the state of the Monarchy's military readiness was in the event of an armed conflict with a European Power.

Conrad: The Chief of the General Staff replied to this inquiry that, from his knowledge of the situation, Russia was not at this time in a position to conduct a war, and that the military situation in Turkey, too, was not presently such that an attack by it had to be feared. There was certainly no question at all about Germany, thus this left only Italy among the Great Powers, against whom the Monarchy was militarily ready. From a strictly military point of view of the relative strength on both sides, a war against Italy would even be almost desirable at the present moment since the Monarchy currently still possessed military superiority over Italy.

. . . .

No. 120-4. Schoen[10] *to Bülow.*[11]

CONFIDENTIAL.

Berchtesgaden, 5 September 1908.
. . . Finally, Baron Aehrenthal also spoke in some detail about his relations and negotiations with Mr. Izvolsky.[12] . . . Austria-Hungary, to be sure, could not avoid having to approach in time a definitive settlement of its relations with Bosnia and Herzegovina, and this solution could not, and would not, be any other than *annexation.* . . .

Finally, Baron Aehrenthal also indicated to me, with a certain trepidation and with a plea for the strictest secrecy, "the complete destruction of the Serbian revolutionary nest" as a further objective of his Balkan policy. He hoped to have our support for this. Serbia could be turned over to Bulgaria, which would also give Austria-Hungary the considerable advantage of having as neighbor a state with strong ethnographic boundaries.[13]

. . . .

No. 120-5.   Aehrenthal to Francis Joseph I.[14]

Vienna, 17 September 1908.
I report most obediently that yesterday's discussion in Buchlau[15] has furnished a satisfactory result. Mr. Izvolsky recognizes the forced situation in which the Monarchy finds itself, and has declared his agreement in principle to observe a friendly attitude in the event of annexation. As an equivalent, the Russian Minister suggested the same attitude by Austria-Hungary if Russia were to propose a change in the existing regulations for passage through the Straits. I held out this prospect to him, also only in principle. I hope to be able to submit to Your Majesty in the very near future a detailed draft concerning the regulations of the arrangement to be concluded.

No. 120-6.   Aehrenthal to Pallavicini.[16, 17]

SECRET.

Vienna, 18 September 1908.
. . . As I can inform you in strictest secrecy, diplomatic preparations for the action[18] have been completed insofar as this is possible, particularly through my interview with Izvolsky, and it is to take place in the first days of October. . . .

No. 120-7.   Stemrich[19] to Tschirschky.[20]

Berlin, 6 October 1908.
For Your Excellency's information and for any statements you may make.

The Imperial Chancellor [Bülow] thinks it particularly important that, in relation to the annexation question, there should not arise in Vienna any doubts whatsoever about our reliability, since it is for us an act of unquestioned loyalty that we firmly adhere to the alliance with Austria-Hungary, to which Europe owes, to a large extent, thirty years of peace. We make no secret of the fact that Austria-Hungary proceeded with the annexation on its own initiative,

as is only natural for a large and independent Monarchy.[21]

.   .   .   .

No. 120-8.   Bülow to Aehrenthal.[22]

PRIVATE LETTER.

Berlin, 30 October 1908.
Let me first repeat . . . that we firmly support Austria-Hungary in the Bosnian question. You may rest assured that we shall not let ourselves be influenced in our attitude as a friendly ally either by the apprehensions of Mr. Clemenceau or by possible Russian measures on our eastern frontier. Besides, I consider these two dark points as still a rather distant thunderstorm. . . . Mr. Izvolsky arrived here in an excited mood. I shall omit the personally prejudiced part of his remarks. More to the point, he expressed the opinion that Austria-Hungary's procedure in the Bosnian question constituted a treaty violation which would have to be submitted to the judgment of all the signatory Powers of the Treaty of Berlin. He could imagine a solution of the existing difficulties only in such a manner that Austria-Hungary should agree to have the question of the annexation of Bosnia and Herzegovina brought before an international conference, and that she grant territorial compensation to Serbia as well as to Montenegro. . . . In the event that these wishes should not be fulfilled, Mr. Izvolsky held out the prospect, not without considerable emphasis, of a breaking away by the Serbs and Montenegrians, of a general conflagration in the Balkan peninsula, and, finally, of a world war. While describing his own position as downright desperate, he demanded, finally, with an appeal to the century-old friendship between Russia and Prussia-Germany, that we should intercede with Austria-Hungary in favor of the acceptance of his wishes.

I replied to Mr. Izvolsky. . . . The firm and open support of our tried and trusted ally was for us not only an imperative of loyalty, but also justified by the facts of the situation. Given this premise, I could only state to him that we were not, to be sure, opposed to a conference in principle, but that we would have to decline to persuade Austria-Hungary into an acceptance of the role intended for it there. It did not seem to us compatible with the dignity of the Habsburg Monarchy that it should have to submit its decisions, imposed by the circumstances, to the criticism and arbitration of a conference, and that it should let such compensations to the small Balkan states be forced upon it by a conference. It went without saying that we would be unable to attend a conference if Austria-Hungary were to stay away from it. We considered a conference only then as possible when *complete* agreement among *all* the Powers on *all* the outstanding issues had actually previously been achieved.

. . . .

I know, through Mr. von Schoen, that you are coming to doubt more and more whether the present unappetizing conditions in Serbia can be tolerated much longer.[23] I have complete confidence in your judgment, [and] I furthermore say to myself in this special case that you can judge the Serbian circumstances and those connected with it more accurately than I can from afar. I shall, therefore, consider the decision which you shall eventually reach as the one necessitated by the circumstances.

No. 120-9.   Conrad to Moltke.[24,25]

By COURIER.

Vienna, 1 January 1909.
The present political situation makes it advisable that I confer with Your Excellency, and particularly in regard to the case, possible after all, that the Monarchy would have to reckon with a state of affairs leading to a war in the Balkans, then against Russia and Italy, and that it then would have Germany, according to the *casus foederis,* fighting on its side. The Minister for Foreign Affairs, after first consulting with His Serene Excellency Prince Bülow, has recommended to His Majesty that this step be taken. His Majesty was pleased to give his approval and to order that I am to initiate this consultation with Your Excellency, ...

This measure[26] by the Monarchy found a decidedly unfriendly reception, apart from England, especially in Italy and Russia, in the case of the latter above all as the leading Pan-Slavic Power. In Italy, calming assurances were issued on the part of the Government, so that the conviction prevails among the directors of our Foreign Ministry that this State will not assume a hostile attitude towards, or at least will not take the offensive against, the Monarchy, even in case the latter should become involved in difficulties in the Balkans; Russia's attitude shows itself to be less confidence-inspiring, so that it is reckoned as a possibility that Russia will, in case of an A.[ustro]-H.[ungarian] Balkan War, take hostile military measures in favor of the Monarchy's opponents, that is, mobilize against the Monarchy.

If, then, Germany ranges itself in this case on the side of the Monarchy in accordance with the Treaty of 1879,[27] then the question is raised first of all whether in this case France would also attack Germany, [or,] respectively, the opposite, if Germany should find it necessary to play the game of prevention against France. Thus, if war should break out, assuming Italy's neutrality, between France, Russia, Serbia, and Montenegro on the one hand, Germany and the Monarchy on the other, then it would be decisive above all for the attitude on our part whether Germany could become effective simultaneously on both sides with correspondingly strong forces, or whether it would launch the main blow with superior forces first against one, then against the other opponent, as well

which one of the two first, be-
____ would be co-determinant for the
Monarchy, too, whether it should first take
care of the Balkans quickly, energetically,
therefore with sufficient, consequently
strong, forces for this purpose, and only
then turn, together with the major German
forces, against Russia, or whether, with a
reduction to a minimum of the forces
destined against Serbia, it was, from the
very beginning, to launch the decisive blow
against Russia.

. . . .

No. 120-10.   Moltke to Conrad.[28]

SECRET.

Berlin, 21 January 1909.
I have received Your Excellency's valuable communication with the most vivid
interest. . . .

To begin with, permit me to give the
assurance—which is in accord with the
opinion expressed by His Majesty my Most
Gracious Master—that, if the *casus foederis*
occurs as the result of a Russian attack
upon the Monarchy, Germany shall, in
accordance with the Treaty of 1879, range
itself with all of its forces on Austria's
side. Complete agreement also prevails
on this point among the political leaders
on both sides. . . .

. . . It is to be expected that the moment
can arrive when the patience of the [Aus-
trian] Empire with regard to the Serbian
provocations will be exhausted. Then the
Monarchy will hardly have any other
choice than to invade Serbia. I believe that
only the invasion of Serbia by Austria
could trigger an eventual active intervention by Russia. With this, the *casus foederis*
would be established for Germany. . . .

At the same moment that Russia mobilizes, Germany shall also mobilize, and
all of its armed forces at that. Now the
time has come to consider also the attitude
of our other neighbors. For Austria this

means the conduct of Italy, for Germany
that of France. . . .

The condition of the Italian army, which
has not been improved by the activities
of the parliamentary investigating committee but has only been confused even more,
appears to me little suited to make a war
desirable for Italy, or, for that matter,
even possible. . . . If, however, Austria
were to be attacked by Italy, then I can
give the assurance that Germany shall consider the protection of its ally's rear as an
unquestioned duty.

More difficult, in my opinion, is the situation between Germany and France. It is
true that the prevailing impression amongst
us here is that France does not want war.
But it seems to me open to considerable
doubt whether this country, disposing of
an army almost as large as the German
armed forces, would be able to tolerate a
mobilized Germany at her border without
mobilizing in her turn. But two mobilized
armies, such as the German and the French,
will not be able to stand side by side without a clash of arms. . . .

I believe, then, that Germany, if it
mobilizes against Russia, must also reckon
with a war against France. Whether such a
war would not spread even farther and
extend overseas is a question I would not
want to discuss at this time.

. . . .

His Majesty the Emperor and His Gracious Excellency the Prince Imperial
Chancellor have been informed of the contents of the present letter.

No. 120-11.   Tschirschky to Bülow.[29]

Vienna, 24 February 1909.
. . . Baron von Aehrenthal remarked next
that, if the Powers could agree on a collective *démarche* in Belgrade, . . . then
Serbia would be called upon to make a
declaration that it intended to pursue a
peaceful and correct policy towards Aus-

tria-Hungary.ᵃ One would not have to demand more than this of Serbia, in his opinion.[30] . . .

Marginal comments by William II:
ᵃ Correct agreed.
Final comment by the Emperor:

It is necessary, considering the gravity of the situation, that we contact Paris *immediately* and demand of France that she join us in exerting pressure upon Russia, which forces this country to make its position towards Serbia clear (take part in the pressure upon Belgrade). It must be made clear to France that, in case of Russian intervention against Austria, the *casus foederis* is established without delay immediately[31] for us, *i.e.*, mobilization. France must be induced to a binding, clear declaration that in this case she will *not go to war* at all *against us*. A declaration of neutrality does not suffice. If France refuses this declaration, then that is to be interpreted by us as a *casus belli*, and the *Reichstag*, as well as the world, is to be told that France, in spite of our appeal to walk together with us along the only possible path leading to the preservation of Europ[ean] peace, has declined, therefore has *wanted* war.

This clarification, in this form, is necessary so that we fully utilize our mobilization against France first and finish her off. Under no circumstances can the Army permit itself to be placed in a situation where one half is fighting against Russia while the other half stands as protection against an uncertain France. We must commit all of it against the West or all of it against the East. . . .

Chief of the General Staff is in agreement with this.

No. 120-12.   *Bülow to Pourtalès.*[32, 33]

Berlin, 21 March 1909.
. . . Will you then inform Mr. Izvolsky that we would be willing to propose to the Austro-Hungarian Government to request the Powers, with reference to the Austro-Turkish Agreement[34] already communicated to them, to agree to the cancellation of Article 25 of the Treaty of Berlin. But before we make such a proposal to Austria-Hungary, we must definitely know that Russia will reply to the Austrian Note in the affirmative, and that it will declare its formal agreement, without any reservations, to the repeal of Article 25. Your Excellency will thereby tell Mr. Izvolsky in a firm manner that we expect a precise answer— yes or no—; we would have to regard any evasive or ambiguous answer, or one full of stipulations, as a rejection. We would then withdraw and let matters take their course; the responsibility for all subsequent events would then rest exclusively with Mr. Izvolsky, after we had made a last sincere effort to be of assistance to Mr. Izvolsky by clarifying the situation in a manner acceptable to him.

.   .   .   .

In any event, you are to say to Mr. Izvolsky that, in view of the increasingly provocative attitude of the Serbs, the matter is rapidly reaching a critical stage, and we therefore await an immediate *clear* reply to our question.

The question of an international conference has nothing to do with our *démarche*; the decision concerning its necessity and usefulness will have to continue to be reserved, now as before, for an exchange of views among the Powers. We would have to consider its intrusion into the present concrete question as an attempt at procrastination, and thereby as a rejection of our proposal.

No. 120-13.   *Nicolson*[35] *to Grey.*[36]

St. Petersburg, 23 March 1909.
M. Iswolsky asked me to call on him this afternoon. I found him agitated. He said that he had a great deal to communicate to me, but had I anything to tell him?

I replied in the negative. He said he would first begin with a peremptory "summons" which he had received yesterday afternoon from the German Ambassador. It was to the effect that the German Government found his reply to their last communication not sufficiently clear; and that they, therefore, requested to know precisely from the Russian Government whether, if Austria-Hungary sounded the Powers as to accepting the abrogation of Article 25 of the Treaty of Berlin, Russia would agree to the abrogation. The German Government wished to have a speedy reply in clear terms; and he had been told that if the reply was a refusal or evasion, Germany would "unleash Austria against Serbia." M. Iswolsky said that this summons, which had the character of a diplomatic ultimatum, was of so grave a nature that he had requested that a Cabinet Council should be summoned, and he had laid the question fully before his colleagues. . . . The Cabinet decided to authorize M. Iswolsky to accept the German proposal, and he would communicate their decision to the Emperor this evening and obtain His Majesty's sanction to it. He had made an appointment with Count Pourtalès tonight, and would give him the reply. He read it to me: it was a simple acceptance to consent to the abrogation of Article 25, should Austria-Hungary demand it; and he had added that he trusted that, in view of the ready acquiescence of the Russian Government, Germany would use her good offices at Vienna to induce the Austro-Hungarian Government to be conciliatory in the negotiations regarding Servia.[37]

I was, I confess, puzzled as to what to say. I should, I admit, have liked to have said a good deal on what seemed to me a surrender on the part of Russia, or, as he put it later to my French colleague, the "humiliation" of this country. M. Iswolsky was perfectly frank. He said the German summons was perhaps not an ultimatum

in the sense that it threatened war as an alternative, but it was a diplomatic ultimatum. He would like to have met it differently, but it was necessary to look the facts in the face. He thought that for some time past the two Central Powers had combined on their programme, and that they now considered that the moment had arrived for pushing Russia to the wall. The military preparations in Galicia were on a scale which was ominous, the immediate readiness of Germany for war was undoubted, and Russia was alone. France, even diplomatically, had supported Russia "very feebly," and she could not be depended upon; while, though England had been loyal throughout in her support, it was limited to diplomatic support. Russia was practically for active action isolated, and she was unable to face alone, in her present condition, the powerful combination of the Central Powers. Baron d'Aehrenthal was brow-beating Russia through Germany, and he had succeeded. It was useless to disguise the fact.

.   .   .   .

No. 120-14.   Nicolson to Grey.[38]

PRIVATE.

St. Petersburg, 24 March 1909.

I was surprised at the communication which Iswolsky made to me yesterday in regard to the German summons to "stand and deliver"; and I was astonished that the Russian Gov[ernmen]t capitulated with such promptitude and so completely. . . .

. . . My firm opinion is that both Germany and Austria are carrying out a line of policy and action carefully prepared and thought out. Algeciras had to be revenged, the "ring" broken through, and the Triple Entente dissipated. . . .

. . . The ultimate aims of Germany surely are, without doubt, to obtain the preponderance on the continent of Europe, and when she is strong enough—and apparently she is making very strenuous efforts to become so —that she will enter on a contest with us for maritime supremacy. In past times we have had to fight Holland, Spain and France for this supremacy, and personally I am convinced that, sooner or later, we shall have to repeat the same struggle with Germany.

If we could keep France and Russia on our side, it would be well; and if we could contract some kind of an alliance with Russia, we should probably also steady France and prevent her from deserting to the Central Powers.

You will, I daresay, consider that I am pursuing nightmares, but I will run this risk and lay my opinion before you.[39] . . .

No. 120-15.   Nicolson to Grey.[40]

St. Petersburg, 29 March 1909.

It was only on the morning of the 27th instant that the general public became aware that the Russian Government had consented, if asked by Austria-Hungary, to the unconditional abrogation of Article 25 of the Berlin Treaty, or, in other words, to recognize the annexation by Austria-Hungary of Bosnia and Herzegovina. . . . It was considered not only in the press but also, so far as I have been able to observe and ascertain, in all classes of society, that Russia had suffered a deep humiliation, and had renounced the traditional part which she had hitherto played in South East Europe and in the prosecution of which she had made so great sacrifices in the past. Even among those who take but little interest in foreign affairs, and who do not feel much sympathy for the smaller Balkan States, whom they regard as troublesome and ungrateful younger brethren, there was a feeling of bitter resentment that, at a most critical moment for two of the minor Slav States, their natural protector had abandoned them to the mercy of a German Power; and that Russia had consented,

without making any reservations in favour of those who had looked to her for assistance, if not material, in any case moral and diplomatic, to give her seal to an act which had been committed by Austria-Hungary to the detriment of Slav interests.

No. 120-16.   Pourtalès to Bülow.[41]

St. Petersburg, 1 April 1909.

An explanation for the mood prevailing in St. Petersburg at present can only be found in the peculiarities of the Slavic national character, in which feeling, passion, superficiality, and a lack of logic preclude any sober and impartial judgment. . . . The Slavophiles and their foreign patrons, whose political hopes and calculations have vanished into thin air, want to save at least one thing from the six months' long diplomatic and press campaign: The split between Russia and Germany must become ever deeper, Russia must draw ever nearer to the Western Powers, the great struggle between the Slavic and Germanic races,[a] for which Russia was not sufficiently armed at the moment, must be prepared with every means for a not too distant future. Hence the emphasis here that Germany had inflicted a wound upon Russia which she shall never forget, that Germany had incited Austria to her foreign policy of the past year in order to humiliate a Russia weakened by war and revolution.

These arguments do not fail to make an impression at the moment. The legend, spread by a familiar source,[b] that Germany had threatened here with the "mailed fist,"[42] finds credence in wide circles, and has had the result that there prevails here at this time a rather agitated feeling against us, which has also taken possession, to some extent, of circles ordinarily well-disposed towards us. . . .

Marginal comments by William II:
[a] how the yellow race will rejoice!
[b] England!

No. 120-17.　　　*Grey to Nicolson.*[43]

PRIVATE.

St. Petersburg,[44] *2 April 1909.*

I am not surprised at the reflections in your letter to me of the 24th.[45]

I do not think that it is practicable to change our agreements into alliances; the feeling here about definite commitment to a continental war on unforeseeable conditions would be too dubious to permit us to make an alliance. Russia, too, must make her internal government less reactionary—till she does, liberal sentiment here will remain very cool, and even those who are not sentimental will not believe that Russia can purge her administration sufficiently to become a strong and reliable Power. Meanwhile, let us keep an entente with Russia in the sense of keeping in touch so that our diplomatic action may be in accord and in mutual support.

It was unwise of Iswolsky to promise unconditional recognition of Austria's action without consulting us. I am glad you rubbed this point in yourself. Had he consulted us, he might have made the same stipulations as we have done, and Russia would have been saved the appearance of humiliation. There would have been no war—the result would have been just as it is now. . . .

Now, as to the result: Austria has scored by giving nothing to Servia; but Montenegro gets compensation by the removal of limitations on her sovereignty, and Austria has had to pay £2½ million to Turkey,[46] which she said originally she would never pay. The result would not be so bad, if only Iswolsky had withstood German hustling for 48 hours.

Russia has drawn closer to Bulgaria, who is worth many Servias—a result which twenty years ago would have been regarded unfavourably here, but which we now welcome as strengthening Russia's position. She has Bulgaria on her side, she has our goodwill, the Slav feeling is deeply apprehensive of Teuton advance and affronted by Teuton pressure, and it is at Russia's disposal; all these are improvements in her position if only she is cool enough to see them, wise enough to use them, and will reform her internal government. Germany will not make war upon her if not provoked, but Russia may have to withstand some provocation and bluff now and then; which, however, will cease if she makes her internal administration efficient and strong.

No. 120-18.　　　*Forgách*[47] *to Aehrenthal.*[48]

Belgrade, 3 April 1909.

It would still be premature at this time to want to pass definitive judgment on the consequences of our six months' long, so critical controversy with Serbia. . . . Only after much gnashing of teeth did the leading circles here decide upon submission, and upon the admission of their weakness and of their empty braggadocio. They do not deceive themselves at all that their retreat is as complete as it is shameful. Strange to say, our victory is also frankly admitted by the Serbian press. Whether the experience gained, and particularly Russia's conduct, will exert a lasting, salutary influence, seems doubtful to me. The Serbian Government will certainly act circumspectly for some time, and the movement for a Greater Serbia has received what is for us, especially in Bosnia, a very valuable blow. But the hatred against us, and the "Russian hypnosis," which Vladan Georgevitsh talks about with so much justification in his latest work, are too strong for me to be able to entertain any great hopes for a genuine turnabout and for a satisfactory formulation of our relations with Serbia. Today, everyone here still thinks about revenge, which can only be achieved in partnership with the Russian ally; the great Slavic Empire is not held to blame for its present conduct, which instead is ascribed to Mr. Izvolsky's incompetence. . . .

No. 120-19.   Nicolson to Grey.[49]

St. Petersburg, 8 April 1909.

ENCLOSURE—THE PRESS.

. . . The Near Eastern crisis has been followed by the entire Russian press with similar comments to those made throughout; European diplomacy is considered impotent to see that justice is done; M. Iswolsky's desertion of the Southern Slavs is criminal; the triumph of Germanism is complete and Russian influence in the Balkans is destroyed beyond all hope of remedy. The violence of these attacks has increased tenfold since it became known that M. Iswolsky had agreed to the abrogation of Article 25 of the Berlin Treaty; and the general tone of the press is best shown by the title of "diplomatic Tsushima"[50] by which the *Novoe Vremya* designated this step. . . .

No. 120-20.   Moltke to Conrad.[51]

PRIVATE.

Berlin, 14 September 1909.

I have the honor to acknowledge receipt of Your Excellency's communication of 10 April 1909. For the private letter[52] reaching me in the same envelope, I express my warmest thanks.

I do not need to assure Your Excellency that I reciprocate in full measure the feelings of confidence which were expressed therein to me in such a kind manner. Herein would have been found an immensely important guarantee for the successful execution of combined military operations if the kind of war had broken out on which we had reached agreement. I did not consider myself entitled to express an opinion to Your Excellency on the desirability or undesirability of such an event. In this private letter I may say that, together with Your Excellency, I most profoundly regret that an opportunity has passed by without being exploited, which is not likely to offer itself again soon under such favorable conditions. I am firmly convinced that it would have been possible to have localized the war between Austria-Hungary and Serbia, and, after its victorious conclusion, the Monarchy, fortified within, strengthened without, would have won a preponderance in the Balkans which could not have been shaken so easily any more. Even if Russia had become active and a European war had developed, the preconditions would have been better for Austria and Germany now than they presumably will be a few years hence. Be that as it may, Excellency, let us look with confidence to the future. As long as Austria and Germany stand shoulder to shoulder, ready to perceive in the welfare of the other the "need for your own action," we shall be strong enough to blast through any ring.[53] Many a person can break his teeth trying to crack this central European block.

May I also extend my congratulations to Your Excellency for the splendid execution of the preparatory measures in Bosnia and Herzegovina, as well as for the exemplary conduct of the troops. Both must give Your Excellency great satisfaction.

For the rest, our agreements remain in force. On our word of honor, and on our confidence in each other.

No. 121   The Final Crisis: Sarajevo——28 June to 4 August 1914

28 June 1914, Sarajevo, ca. 10:40 a.m. —Gavrilo Princip fires the shots that kill Archduke Francis Ferdinand and his wife.

2 July, Vienna—Francis Joseph I appeals to William II for support against Serbia.

No. 121-1.   Letter, Francis Joseph I to William II.[1]

. . . The murder of my poor nephew is the direct consequence of the agitation carried on by the Russian and Serbian Pan Slavists, whose sole aim is the weakening of the Triple Alliance and the destruction of my Empire.

According to all the information obtained until now, the bloody deed in Sarajevo was not the work of a single individual but the result of a well-organized plot whose strands reach to Belgrade, and even though it will probably be impossible to prove the complicity of the Serbian government, there can hardly be any doubt that its policy directed towards the unification of all South-Slavs under the Serbian flag encourages such crimes, and that the continuation of this situation represents a lasting danger for my House and my lands. . . .

Henceforth, the efforts of my government must be directed towards the isolation and diminution of Serbia. . . . . . . to form a new Balkan League, whose goal would consist in erecting a barrier against the advance of the Pan-Slavic flood-tide and in safeguarding the peace for our countries.

But this will only be possible if Serbia, which at the moment forms the fulcrum of Pan-Slavic policy, is eliminated as a political power factor in the Balkans.

After the recent terrible events in Bosnia, you, too, will carry the conviction that a reconciliation of the dichotomy which separates us from Serbia can no longer be considered possible, and that the stabilizing peace policy of all European monarchs will be in danger as long as this incubator of criminal agitation in Belgrade lives on unpunished.

5 July, Berlin, D 7:35 p.m.—William II assures Austria of Germany's complete support.

No. 121-2.   Szögyény[2] to Berchtold.[3, 4]

. . . After lunch, when I again emphasized seriousness of situation, His Majesty authorized me to report to our Most Gracious Sovereign that we could count with Germany's complete support in this case, too. As mentioned, he would first have to hear the Imperial Chancellor's opinion, but he had not the least doubt that Mr. von Bethmann Hollweg would completely agree with his view. This was particularly true regarding any action on our part against Serbia. But, according to his (Emperor William's) opinion, this action must not be delayed. Russia's attitude would be hostile in any case, but he had been prepared for this for years, and even if it should come to a war between Austria-Hungary and Russia, we could rest assured that Germany, with its customary loyalty of an ally, shall take its place at our side. However, as things were now constituted, Russia was not at all ready for war and would certainly think twice before resorting to arms. But it would incite the other Powers of the Triple Entente against us and fan the flames in the Balkans. He understood very well that it would be difficult for His Apostolic Majesty, with his well-known love of peace, to invade Serbia; but if we had really recognized the necessity of taking military action against Serbia, then he (Emperor William) would regret it if we did not take advantage of the present moment which was so favorable for us. . . .

6 July, Berlin, D 5:10 p.m.—Bethmann[5] joins William II in support of Austria.

No. 121-3.   *Szögyény to Berchtold.*[6]

. . . Accompanied by Count Hoyos,[7] have just had a long discussion with Imperial Chancellor and Under-Secretary of State. . . . As regards our relationship with Serbia, the German government takes the standpoint that we would have to judge what had to be done to clarify that relationship; in the process, we could count with certainty—whatever our decision might be—upon Germany, as the Monarchy's ally and friend, standing behind her. In the further course of the conversation, I noted that Imperial Chancellor, too, just as his Imperial Master, regards an immediate intervention on our part against Serbia as most radical and best solution of our difficulties in the Balkans. From an international standpoint, he considers the present moment as more favorable than a later one; he is in complete agreement that we do not notify either Italy or Roumania in advance of our eventual action against Serbia. . . .

7 July, Vienna—Austria's interpretation of the German statements.

No. 121-4.   *Conrad's Memoirs.*[8]

On the morning of 7 July, I received the news that Count Hoyos, who, on instructions from Count Berchtold, had to

ascertain Germany's attitude, had returned from Berlin with a favorable answer. I went to see Count Berchtold, in order to learn something definite about this, and was given the information that Germany would absolutely back us up, even if our action against Serbia should unleash the great war. Germany advised us to attack at once.

18 July, Belgrade—Serbia is confident of Russian support.

No. 121-5.   *Crackenthorpe[9] to Grey.*[10, 11]

In the course of a private conversation with the Secretary-General of the Servian Foreign Office this morning, . . .

The Secretary-General said he was aware that there was an influential party in Austria who wished to take advantage of the present conjuncture to press Servia to extremes. But the Servian Government had certain knowledge that restraint would be exercised on Austria from Berlin. Should, however, the worst come to the worst and Austria declare war, Servia would not stand alone. Russia would not remain quiet were Servia wantonly attacked, and Bulgaria would be immobilised by Roumania. Under present conditions a war between a Great Power and a Balkan State must inevitably, in the opinion of the Secretary-General, lead to a European conflagration.

21 July, Berlin—Bethmann insists on the localisation of the Austro-Serbian conflict.

No. 121-6.   *Bethmann to St. Petersburg, Paris, and London.*[12]

. . . no doubt can remain that the action center of the efforts to detach the South-Slav provinces from the Austro-Hungarian Monarchy and to join them to the Serbian Kingdom is to be sought in Belgrade, and that it develops its activities there with, at the least, the connivance of members of the government and of the army.

The Serbian intrigues have been going on for many years. Greater-Serbian chauvinism appeared in a particularly virulent form during the Bosnian crisis. . . . Under these circumstances, Austria-Hungary's action, as well as its demands, can only be considered moderate and just. Nevertheless, . . . the possibility cannot be excluded that the Serbian Government will refuse to comply with these demands, and that it will let itself be carried away into displaying a provocative attitude toward Austria-Hungary. The Austro-Hungarian Government, if it does not want to renounce forever its position as a Great Power, would then have no other choice but to obtain satisfaction of its demands from the Serbian Government by exerting strong pressure, and, if necessary, by resorting to military measures, in which case it must be left free to choose the means.

I have the honor to ask Your Excellency to speak to (name of the Foreign Minister) in the sense expressed above, and, while doing so, to especially place the greatest emphasis upon the view that the question here discussed involves a matter which is to be settled solely between Austria-Hungary and Serbia, and that to restrict it to these two direct participants must be the earnest endeavor of the Powers. We urgently desire the localisation of the conflict because any intervention by another Power would, as a result of the various alliance obligations, lead to incalculable consequences. . . .

21 July, St. Petersburg—Sazonov[13] warns Germany.

No. 121-7.   Pourtalès[14] to Bethmann.[15]

Mr. Sazonov, who spent several days last week on his country estate in the province of Grodno, is, since his return from there, very nervous because of the relations between Austria-Hungary and Serbia. . . . The Minister . . . insisted . . . that you cannot hold an entire country responsible for the deeds of some individuals.[a] . . . Mr. Sazonov thereupon commented that those persons in Austria who were advocating measures against Serbia apparently would not be satisfied with remonstrations in Belgrade, but that their objective was the annihilation of Serbia.[b] . . . The Minister continued excitedly that, in any case, if Austria-Hungary was thoroughly determined to upset the peace, in such an event it should not forget that it would have to reckon with Europe.[c] Russia would be unable to remain an indifferent spectator to any demand upon Belgrade which aimed at Serbia's humiliation. . . . Mr. Sazonov . . . commented further that Russia would not be able to tolerate it if Austria-Hungary used threatening language or took military measures against Serbia.[d] "Russia's policy," Mr. Sazonov said, "is pacific but not passive."

Marginal comments by William II:
[a] typically Russian
[b] would be the best thing, too!
[c] no! Russia yes! as the perpetrator and advocate of regicide!
[d] let's wait and see about that!

21 July, St. Petersburg—Poincaré[16] warns Austria.

No. 121-8.   Szápáry[17] to Berchtold.[18]

Mr. Poincaré received the diplomatic corps today, . . . he then inquired about the relations between Austria-Hungary and Serbia, . . . Mr. Poincaré then launched into a speech, made with great oratorical display and emphasis, in which he maintained that it was clearly only permissible to hold a government responsible for something if there existed concrete, accusatory evidence against it, unless this were to be nothing more than a pretext, which he would hardly expect of Austria-Hungary against such a small country. But in such a case one must not forget that Serbia has friends, and that hereby a situation would arise which would endanger the peace. . . . The President's conduct, . . . tactless, sounding like a threat, ...

23 July, Belgrade, 6:00 p.m.—Giesl[19] delivers Austria's ultimatum to Serbia.

No. 121-9.   Text of the Ultimatum— Berchtold to Giesl.[20]

. . . The history of recent years, and notably the painful events of 28 June, have proven the existence in Serbia of a subversive movement whose aim is to detach from the Austro-Hungarian Monarchy certain parts of its territories. . . . The Royal Serbian Government . . . has done nothing to suppress this movement: . . . The depositions and confessions by the criminal authors of the outrage of 28 June show that the Sarajevo murders were plotted in Belgrade, that the arms and explosives with which the murderers were found to be provided had been given to them by Serbian officers and officials belonging to the "Narodna Obrana,"[21] and, finally, that the passage into Bosnia of the criminals and their arms was organized and carried out by superiors of the Serbian border guard.
. . . The Imperial and Royal Government finds itself obliged to demand that . . . the Royal Government of Serbia shall have the following announcement published on the front page of the *Official Journal* on 26/13 July:
"The Royal Government of Serbia condemns the propaganda directed against Austria-Hungary, . . . The Royal Government regrets that Serbian officers and officials had participated in the above-mentioned propaganda, ..."
The Royal Serbian Government further undertakes
1. to suppress any publication which incites to hatred and contempt of the Monarchy, . . . ,

2. to dissolve immediately the society called "Narodna Obrana," . . . , and to proceed in the same manner against the other societies and their branches in Serbia which devote themselves to propaganda against the Austro-Hungarian Monarchy; . . . ,
3. to eliminate without delay from public instruction in Serbia, both as regards the teaching body and the means of instruction, all that serves or could serve to foment propaganda against Austria-Hungary,
4. to remove from the military service and the administration in general all the officers and officials guilty of propaganda against the Austro-Hungarian Monarchy, and whose names and deeds the I. and R. Government reserves the right to communicate to the Royal Government,
5. to accept the collaboration in Serbia of agencies of the I. and R. Government in the suppression of the subversive movement directed against the territorial integrity of the Monarchy,
6. to begin a judicial inquest against the participants in the plot of 28 June who are on Serbian soil,
7. to urgently proceed to the arrest of Commander Voija Tankosić and of a certain Milan Ciganović, employee of the Serbian State, implicated by the findings of the initial investigation at Sarajevo,
8. to prevent, by effective measures, the co-operation of Serbian authorities in the illicit traffic in arms and explosives across the border; to dismiss and severely punish the officials of the border guard at Schabatz and at Ložnica guilty of having aided the authors of the crime of Sarajevo by facilitating their passage across the border,
9. to give to the I. and R. Government explanations concerning the unjustifiable remarks by high Serbian officials, in Serbia as well as abroad, who, in spite of their official position, have not hesitated to express themselves in interviews after the outrage of 28 June in a manner hostile to the Austro-Hungarian Monarchy, finally
10. to notify the I. and R. Government

without delay of the execution of the measures included in the preceding points.

The I. and R. Government awaits the reply of the Royal Government not later than Saturday, the 25th of this month, at 6:00 p.m. . . .

24 July, St. Petersburg, 11 a.m.—Sazonov's reaction to Austria's ultimatum to Serbia.

No. 121-10.   Szápáry to Berchtold.[22]

. . . Mr. Sazonov commented, . . . "The fact is that you want war and have burned your bridges behind you." I replied, we were the most pacific Power in the world, what we wanted was only to safeguard our territory against revolution and our dynasty against bombs. "One sees how pacific you are since you are setting fire to Europe," Sazonov said. . . . In spite of the Minister's relative calm, his attitude was, as could hardly be expected otherwise, thoroughly negative and hostile. . . .

24 July, St. Petersburg, ca. 1:00 p.m. —Conference between Sazonov, Paléologue,[23] and Buchanan.[24]

No. 121-11.   Buchanan to Grey.[25]

. . . Minister for Foreign Affairs telephoned to me this morning saying that he had just received text of ultimatum presented by Austria at Belgrade yesterday that demands a reply in forty-eight hours. Step thus taken by Austria meant war, and he begged me to meet him at the French Embassy.

Minister for Foreign Affairs and French Ambassador told me confidentially that result of the visit of the President of the French Republic had been to establish the following points:—

1. Perfect community of views on the various problems with which the Powers are confronted as regards the maintenance of general peace and balance of power in Europe, more especially in the East.

2. Decision to take action at Vienna with a view to the prevention of a demand for explanations or any summons equivalent to an intervention in the internal affairs of Servia which the latter would be justified in regarding as an attack on her sovereignty and independence.

3. Solemn affirmation of obligations imposed by the alliance of the two countries.

Minister for Foreign Affairs expressed the hope that His Majesty's Government would proclaim their solidarity with France and Russia. He characterised Austria's conduct as immoral and provocative. Some of the demands which she had presented were absolutely inacceptable, and she would never have acted as she had done without having first consulted Germany. The French Ambassador gave me to understand that France would not only give Russia strong diplomatic support, but would, if necessary, fulfill all the obligations imposed on her by the alliance.

I said that I could not speak in the name of His Majesty's Government, but that I would telegraph all that they had said. I could personally hold out no hope that His Majesty's Government would make any declaration of solidarity that would entail engagement to support France and Russia by force of arms. We had no direct interests in Servia, and public opinion in England would never sanction a war on her behalf.[26] . . .

24 July, St. Petersburg, 3:00 p.m.— Russian Council of Ministers requests Nicholas II to approve partial mobilization.

24 July, St. Petersburg, 7:00 p.m.— Sazonov warns Germany.

No. 121-12.   Pourtalès to Bethmann.[27]

Just had long interview with Sazonov, . . . Minister, who was very excited,[a] and indulges in boundless accusations against Austria-Hungary, declared categorically that Russia could never permit the Austro-Serbian differences to be settled solely by the two participants.[28] . . . Austria could not be both prosecutor and judge in its own behalf.[b] . . . In the course of the conversation, Sazonov cried out: "If Austria-Hungary swallows Serbia, we shall go to war against it";[c] . . .

I expressed my conviction to the Minister that, in the most extreme case, only a punitive expedition by Austria against Serbia would be involved, and that Austria was far removed from thinking about territorial acquisitions.[29] Mr. Sazonov shook his head with incredulity at these explanations, and spoke of the far-reaching plans which Austria had. First, Serbia would be gobbled up, then it would be Bulgaria's turn, and then "we will have them at the Black Sea." . . .

Marginal comments by William II:
[a] good
[b] that's a matter of opinion!
[c] well, then, go to it!

25 July, St. Petersburg, a.m.—Nicholas II approves preparations for partial mobilization.

No. 121-13.   *Journal of the Russian General Staff Committee.*[30]

The Chief of the General Staff informed the members of the General Staff Committee that H. M. the Tsar has been pleased to declare that it was necessary to support Serbia, even if mobilization had to be proclaimed and military operations begun for this purpose, but not before Austrian troops had actually crossed the Serbian frontier.

According to the most recent information, some preparatory measures for mobilization were already being taken in Austria-Hungary and in Italy. Therefore, H. M. the Tsar has been pleased to approve the decree of the Council of Ministers that the

pre-mobilization period shall begin in the night from 25/12 to 26/13 July.

If it should prove to be necessary to proclaim mobilization, then, in view of the fact that operations would have to be confined solely against Austria alone, H. M. has ordered that the military districts of Kiev, Odessa, Kazan, and Moscow shall be mobilized. The other military districts shall only mobilize in the event that Germany joins Austria, not before, so that even greater diplomatic complications can be avoided. . . .

25 July, St. Petersburg, ca. 2:00 p.m.—Conference between Sazonov, Paléologue and Buchanan.

No. 121-14.   *Buchanan to Grey.*[31]

. . . Minister for Foreign Affairs then told us that at Council of Ministers held under his presidency this morning Emperor had sanctioned drafting of Imperial Ukase, which is only to be published when Minister for Foreign Affairs considers moment come for giving effect to it, ordering mobilisation of 1,100,000 men. Necessary preliminary preparations for mobilisation would, however, be begun at once. On my expressing earnest hope that Russia would not precipitate war by mobilising until you had had time to use your influence in favor of peace, his Excellency assured me that Russia had no aggressive intentions, and she would take no action until it was forced on her.

French Ambassador then said he had received a number of telegrams from Minister in charge of Ministry for Foreign Affairs, that no one of them displayed slightest sign of hesitation, and that he was in position to give his Excellency formal assurance that France placed herself unreservedly on Russia's side.[32]

. . . His Excellency said . . . They [the British public] did not understand that Austria's action was in reality directed against Russia. She aimed at overthrowing present *status quo* in Balkans and establishing her own hegemony there. . . .

I said all I could to impress prudence on Minister for Foreign Affairs, and warned him, if Russia mobilised, Germany would not be content with mere mobilisation, or give Russia time to carry out hers, but would probably declare war at once. His Excellency assured me once more that he did not wish to precipitate a conflict, but unless Germany can restrain Austria I can regard situation as desperate. Russia cannot allow Austria to crush Serbia and become predominant Power in Balkans, and, secure of support of France, she will face all the risks of war. . . .

25 July, Berlin, D 2:15 p.m.—Germany urges Austria to attack Serbia at once.

*No. 121-15.	Szögyény to Berchtold.*[33]

. . . It is generally considered certain here that an eventually negative Serbian reply will be followed immediately by our declaration of war, together with military operations. Every delay in beginning military operations is regarded here as a great danger concerning intervention by other Powers. We are most urgently advised to attack at once and to confront world with a *fait accompli.* I completely share this view by the Foreign Ministry.

25 July, Belgrade, 3:00 p.m.—Serbia orders general mobilization.

25 July, Belgrade, 5:58 p.m.—Pašić[34] hands Giesl Serbia's reply to Austria's ultimatum.

*No. 121-16.	Text of the Serbian Reply —Pašić to Giesl.*[35]

. . . Submitting, then, to the wish of the I. and R. Government, the Royal Government is willing to bring to trial any Serbian subject, regardless of his position or of his rank, for whose complicity in the crime of Sarajevo proof shall be furnished to it, and it undertakes especially to have the following announcement published on the front page of the *Official Journal* on 13/26 July:

"The Royal Government of Serbia condemns all propaganda which may be directed against Austria-Hungary, ... The Royal Government regrets that, according to the I. and R. Government's communication, certain Serbian officers and officials had participated in the above-mentioned propaganda, ..."

The Royal Government further undertakes

1. to introduce, (at the)[36] first regular convocation of the Skoupchtina, a provision in the press law through which the provocation of hatred and contempt of the Austro-Hungarian Monarchy shall be punished in the most severe manner, ...

2. The Government does not possess any proof—and the I. and R. Government's Note does not furnish it with any, either—that the "Narodna Obrana" society, and other similar societies, have committed, up to the present, any criminal act of this kind through the deed of one of their members. Nevertheless, the Royal Government shall accept the demand of the I. and R. Government, and shall dissolve the "Narodna Obrana" society and any other society which may agitate against Austria-Hungary.

3. The Royal Serbian Government undertakes to eliminate without delay from public instruction in Serbia (. . .)[37] all that serves or could serve to foment propaganda against Austria-Hungary whenever the I. and R. Government shall furnish it with facts and proofs of such propaganda.

4. The Royal Government also agrees to remove from the military service and from the administration the officers and officials who shall be proven guilty by a judicial inquest of acts directed against the integrity of the territory of the Austro-Hungarian

Monarchy, and it expects the I. and R. Government to communicate to it later on the names and the deeds of these officers and officials for the purpose of the proceedings which shall ensue.

5. The Royal Government must confess that it does not fully understand the meaning and the scope of the I. and R. Government's demand that Serbia undertake to accept within its borders the collaboration of agencies of the I. and R. Government, but it declares that it shall admit the collaboration which would agree with principles of international law and of criminal procedure, as well as with good neighborly relations.

6. The Royal Government—this goes without[38] saying—considers it to be its duty to open an inquest against all those who are, or who eventually may have been, implicated in the plot of 15 [28] June and who may still be within the territory of the Kingdom. As to the participation in this inquest by agencies of Austro-Hungarian authorities, who would be appointed for this purpose by the I. and R. Government, the Royal Government cannot accept it, for this would be a violation of the Constitution and of the law on criminal procedure. . . .

7. The Royal Government began to proceed, on the very evening of the delivery of the Note, with the arrest of Commander Voïslav Tankositch. As to Milan Ziganovitch, who is a subject of the Austro-Hungarian Monarchy . . . , he could not be found yet, and an order for his arrest has been issued. . . .

8. The Serbian Government shall reinforce and extend the measures taken to prevent the illicit traffic of arms and explosives across the border. It goes without saying that it shall immediately order an inquest, and shall severely punish the border officials in the Schabaz-Lozniza section who have failed in their duties and let pass the authors of the crime of Sarajevo.

9. The Royal Government shall willingly give explanations concerning the remarks made by its officials, in Serbia as well as abroad, in interviews after the outrage, and which, according to the I. and R. Government's assertion, have been hostile towards the Monarchy, as soon as the I. and R. Government shall have indicated to it the passages in question in these remarks, and as soon as it shall have demonstrated that the remarks used were, in effect, made by the said officials, on which subject the Royal Government shall itself take care to collect proof and evidence.

10. The Royal Government shall inform the I. and R. Government of the execution of the measures included in the preceding points, in so far as this has not already been done by the present Note,[39] as soon as each measure shall have been ordered and executed.

In the event that the I. and R. Government should not be satisfied with this reply, the Royal Serbian Government, considering that it is in the common interest not to precipitate the solution of this question, is ready, as always, to accept a pacific understanding, either by submitting this question to the decision of the International Tribunal at The Hague or to the Great Powers who had taken part in drafting the declaration which the Serbian Government made on 18/31 March 1909.

25 July, Belgrade, 6:10 p.m.—Giesl considers Serbia's reply unsatisfactory and breaks off diplomatic relations with Serbia.

25 July, Belgrade, 6:30 p.m.—Giesl and the staff of the Austrian Legation leave Belgrade by train.

25 July, Vienna, eve.—Reaction in the streets to the news from Belgrade.

No. 121-17. Bunsen[40] *to Grey.*[41]

. . . On the 24th July the note was published in the newspapers. By common consent it was at once styled an Ultimatum.

Its integral acceptance by Servia was neither expected nor desired, and when, on the following afternoon, it was at first rumoured in Vienna that it had been unconditionally accepted, there was a moment of keen disappointment. The mistake was quickly corrected, and as soon as it was known later in the evening that the Servian reply had been rejected and that Baron Giesl had broken off relations at Belgrade, Vienna burst into a frenzy of delight, vast crowds parading the streets and singing patriotic songs till the small hours of the morning. The demonstrations were perfectly orderly, consisting for the most part of organised processions through the principal streets ending up at the Ministry of War. One or two attempts to make hostile manifestations against the Russian Embassy were frustrated by the strong guard of police which held the approaches to the principal embassies during those days. The demeanour of the people at Vienna, and, as I was informed, in many other principal cities of the Monarchy, showed plainly the popularity of the idea of war with Servia, and there can be no doubt that the small body of Austrian and Hungarian statesmen, by whom this momentous step was adopted, gauged rightly the sense and, it may be said, the determination of the people, except presumably in portions of the provinces inhabited by the Slav races. There had been much disappointment in many quarters at the avoidance of war with Servia during the annexation crisis in 1908 and again in connection with the recent Balkan war. Count Berchtold's peace policy had met with little sympathy in the Delegations. Now the flood-gates were opened, and the entire people and press clamoured impatiently for immediate and condign punishment of the hated Servian race. . . .

25 July, Ischl, ca. 8:30 p.m.—Francis Joseph I orders partial mobilization against Serbia.

No. 121-18.   *Conrad's Memoirs.*[42]

. . . On 25 July, at 9:23 p.m., the Emperor's order for mobilization: "Plan B" —i.e., against Serbia and Montenegro—arrived. 27 July had been designated as the first alarm day, 28 July as the first mobilization day. By His Majesty's order, eight army corps, together with their first and second reserve units, were to be included in the mobilization, ...

26 July, Berlin, D 7:15 p.m.—Germany warns Russia.

No. 121-19.   *Bethmann to Pourtalès.*[43]

. . . preparatory military measures by Russia, which would be directed against us in any way, would force us to take counter-measures, which would have to consist in mobilizing our army. But mobilization would mean war, and would, moreover, have to be directed against Russia and France simultaneously since we are familiar, of course, with France's obligations towards Russia. . . .

26 July, St. Petersburg, eve.—Sazonov assures Germany that Russia urgently wishes peace with her.

No. 121-20.   *Pourtalès to Bethmann.*[44]

Military *attaché* reports on conversation with Minister of War: Sazonov had asked him to explain military situation to me. The Minister of War assured me, on his word of honor, that no mobilization order of any kind had been issued yet. Nothing but preparatory measures are being taken for the present, not a horse requisitioned, not a reservist called back. If Austria crosses Serbian frontier, military districts directed against Austria of Kiev, Odessa, Moscow, Kazan, will be mobilized. Under no circumstances on German front Warsaw, Vilna, Petersburg. We urgently wish for peace with Germany. . . . Had impression of great nervousness and anxiety. Consider wish for peace sincere, military information in so far accurate as that complete mobilization probably not ordered, but preparatory measures far advanced. They are obviously endeavoring to gain time for new negotiations and continuation of military preparations. . . .

27 July, Vienna, p.m.—Shebeko[45] delivers Sazonov's warning to Austria.

No. 121-21. Bunsen to Grey.[46]

The Russian Ambassador has had to-day a long and earnest conversation with Baron Macchio, Under-Secretary of State for Foreign Affairs. Having just returned to his post from St. Petersburg, he said that he was well acquainted with the state of Russian public opinion and with the views of the Russian Government. He could assure Under-Secretary of State that if actual war with Servia began it would be impossible to localise it, for Russia, which had yielded on previous occasions, and especially during annexation crisis in 1909, was not prepared to give way again. He earnestly hoped, therefore, that something might be done before an actual invasion of Servia took place. . . .

28 July, Berlin, 10:00 a.m.—William II's "Halt in Belgrade" proposal.

No. 121-22. William II to Jagow.[47, 48]

After having read the Serbian reply, which I received this morning,[49] I am convinced that the wishes of the Danubian Monarchy are, on the whole, fulfilled. The few reservations made by Serbia to individual points can well be clarified, in my opinion, through negotiations. But a capitulation of the most humiliating kind is thereby proclaimed to the whole world, and through it *all reason for war* falls to the ground.

Nevertheless, this piece of paper, together with its contents, has only limited value

as long as it is not translated into *action.* The Serbs are Orientals, hence untruthful, treacherous, and masters of procrastination. In order for these fine promises to become truth and fact, "gentle violence" must be applied. The way to do this would be for Austria to occupy a *security* (Belgrade) for the enforcement and performance of the promises, and to retain it until the demands are *actually* carried out. This is also necessary in order to give to the army, which has been mobilized for the 3rd time *to no purpose,* an outward "satisfaction of honor," the appearance of success in the eyes of foreign countries, and to enable it to have the realization of at least having stood on foreign soil. Without this, cancellation of the campaign might cause considerable ill will against the dynasty, which would be very serious. . . .

28 July, Vienna, 11:00 a.m.—Austria declares war against Serbia.

No. 121-23. Text—Berchtold to the Serbian Foreign Ministry.[50]

The Royal Government of Serbia not having replied in a satisfactory manner to the Note which had been handed to it by the Minister of Austria-Hungary in Belgrade on the 23rd of July 1914, the Imperial and Royal Government finds itself under the necessity of providing on its own for the safeguarding of its rights and interests, and for this purpose to have recourse to the force of arms. Therefore, Austria-Hungary considers herself from this moment on as in a state of war with Serbia.

28 July, St. Petersburg, p.m.—Paléologue assures Sazonov of France's full support.

No. 121-24. Daily Journal of the Russian Foreign Ministry.[51]

On instructions from his government, the French Ambassador declared to the Foreign Minister France's complete readiness to fulfill, if necessary, her obligations as an ally.

28 July, St. Petersburg, D eve.—Sazonov informs Germany and the other Powers of Russia's partial mobilization against Austria.

No. 121-25.   Sazonov to Bronewski.[52, 53]

Communicated to Vienna, Paris, London, and Rome.

As a result of Austria's declaration of war against Serbia, we shall announce the mobilization of the military districts of Odessa, Kiev, Moscow, and Kazan tomorrow. You are to inform the German Government of this, and you are to emphasize the absence of any aggressive intentions whatsoever by Russia against Germany. Our Ambassador in Vienna shall not be recalled from his post for the time being.

29 July, St. Petersburg, D 1:00 a.m. —Nicholas II appeals to William II.

No. 121-26.   Nicky[54] *to Willy.*[54, 55]

Am glad you are back. An *ignoble*[a] war has been declared to a *weak* country. The *indignation* in Russia *shared fully by me* is *enormous.*[b] I foresee that very soon I shall be *overwhelmed* by the *pressure* brought upon me and be *forced* to take extreme measures which will *lead to war.* To try and avoid such a calamity as a European War I beg you in the name of our old friendship to do what you can to *stop* your *allies*[c] from *going too far.*[d]

Marginal comments by William II:
[a] "ignoble" underlined twice, followed by "!"

[b] "enormous" underlined twice

[c] "allies" underlined three times, followed by "ally!"

[d] "what does that consist of? Confession of his own weakness, and attempt to push the responsibility onto me. The telegram contains a hidden threat! . . ."[56]

29 July, Nish, D a.m.—Strandtmann[57] reports Austria's bombardment of Belgrade.

No. 121-27.   Strandtmann to Sazonov.[58]

The last hopes have vanished. Belgrade has been bombarded and the bridge over the Save River blown up.

29 July, Berlin, D a.m.—Moltke's advice to the Chancellor.

No. 121-28.   Moltke to Bethmann.[59]

Memorandum for judging the political situation:

. . . Russia . . . declares its intention of mobilizing if Austria invades Serbia, ...

What will and must be the further consequence? Austria, if it invades Serbia, will face not only the Serbian army, but also a strong Russian superiority, it will not, then, be able to conduct a war against Serbia without protecting itself against Russian intervention. This means it will be forced to mobilize the other half of its army also, for it cannot possibly place itself at the mercy of a Russia ready for war. But the moment that Austria mobilizes its entire army, the clash between it and Russia will become inevitable. But that constitutes the *casus foederis* for Germany. If Germany does not want to be false to its word and let its ally succumb to annihilation through Russia's superior power, then it, too, must mobilize for its part. That will also bring about the mobilization of the remaining Russian military districts. But then Russia will be able to say, I am being attacked by Germany, and it can thereby be certain of the support of France, who is bound by treaty to take part in the war if her ally, Russia, is attacked. . . .

Germany does not want to bring about this terrible war. But the German Government knows that it would injure, to an ominous degree, the deeply rooted feelings of allied loyalty, one of the finest traits of German spiritual life, and would place itself at variance with all the sensibilities of its people, if it did not come to the aid of its ally at the moment which must decide over the latter's existence. . . .

Germany shall, therefore, if the clash between Austria and Russia is inevitable, mobilize and be ready to take up the struggle on two fronts. . . .

29 July, St. Petersburg, p.m.—Sazonov's reaction to Austria's bombardment of Belgrade.

No. 121-29.   *Szápáry to Berchtold.*[60]

. . . While we were thus engaged in a confidential exchange of views, the Minister received the news by telephone that we had bombarded Belgrade. His attitude changed completely, he tried to take up again all of his preceding arguments in a way which flew in the face of any logic, and remarked, he saw now how Tsar Nicholas had been right. "You only want to gain time with negotiations, but you go ahead and bombard an unprotected city!" "What else do you want to conquer anyway once you are in possession of the capital," and other similar childish declarations. . . . I left him in an extremely agitated mood, ...

29 July, St. Petersburg, p.m.—Nicholas II authorizes general mobilization.

No. 121-30.   *Daily Journal of the Russian Foreign Ministry.*[61]

. . . After examining the situation from every point of view, both Ministers[62] and the Chief of the General Staff reached the conclusion that, because of the small probability of avoiding war with Germany, it was necessary to prepare for it in every way in good time, and that, therefore, one could not run the risk of delaying general mobilization later by carrying out a partial mobilization now. The final decision of the conference was immediately communicated by telephone to His Majesty, who gave his approval for issuing the appropriate orders. This news was received with jubilation by the small circle of persons who had been initiated in the affair. Telegrams were immediately sent to Paris and London in order to inform these Governments of the decision taken. . . .

29 July, St. Petersburg, 6:30 p.m.—Pourtalès delivers Bethmann's warning to Sazonov.

No. 121-31.   *Text of the Warning—Bethmann to Pourtalès.*[63]

Please point out most earnestly to Mr. Sazonov that further progress of Russian mobilization measures would force us to mobilize, and that then European war could hardly still be avoided.

29 July, St. Petersburg, eve.—Sazonov considers war against Germany as "probably inevitable."

No. 121-32.   *Sazonov to Izvolsky.*[64, 65]

The German Ambassador informed me today that his government had decided to mobilize its armed forces if Russia did not cease her military preparations.[66] But we only made these preparations as a result of the already completed mobilization of eight army corps in Austria, and because the latter is obviously unwilling to agree to any kind of an arrangement for the peaceful settlement of its quarrel with Serbia.

Since we cannot grant Germany's wish, the only thing left for us to do is to speed up our armaments and to count with the probable inevitability of war. Will you please inform the French Government of this, and at the same time express our sincere gratitude for the declaration, which the French Ambassador made to me in its name, that we could count in full measure with the support of France as an ally.[67] This declaration is especially valuable to us under the present circumstances. . . .

29 July, St. Petersburg, 9:15 p.m.— Nicholas II revokes his order for general mobilization.

No. 121-33.   Daily Journal of the Russian Foreign Ministry.[68]

. . . At about 11 p.m., the Minister of War informed the Foreign Minister by telephone that he had received the Tsar's order to stop the general mobilization. . . .

*29 July, Berlin, ca. 10:00 p.m.—*Bethmann's bid for British neutrality.

No. 121-34.   Goschen[69] to Grey.[70]

(? Austria and) Servia. Chancellor having just returned from Potsdam sent for me again to-night and made the following strong bid for British neutrality in the event of war. He said he was continuing his efforts to maintain peace, but that (group omitted: ? in the event of) a Russian attack on Austria, Germany's obligation as Austria's ally might, to his great regret, render a European conflagration inevitable, and in that case he hoped Great Britain would remain neutral. As far as he was able to judge key-note of British policy, it was evident that Great Britain would never allow France to be crushed. Such a result was not contemplated by Germany. The Imperial Government was ready to give every assurance to the British Government provided that Great Britain remained neutral that, in the event of a victorious war, Germany aimed at no territorial acquisitions at the expense of France.

In answer to a question from me, his Excellency said that it would not be possible for him to give such an assurance as regards colonies.

Continuing, his Excellency said he was, further, ready to assure the British Government that Germany would respect neutrality and integrity of Holland as long as they were respected by Germany's adversaries.

As regards Belgium, his Excellency could not tell to what operations Germany might be forced by the action of France, but he could state that, provided that Belgium did not take sides against Germany, her integrity would be respected after the conclusion of the war. . . .[71]

*30 July, Vienna, p.m.—*Berchtold informs Russia of Austrian mobilization along Russian border.

No. 121-35.   Shebeko to Sazonov.[72]

Count Berchtold asked me to see him today, and declared, in the most amiable way, that, in view of our mobilization, Austria finds itself forced to likewise mobilize its troops along our border. He requested me to inform you that this measure did not contain any threat against Russia, since Austria had nothing against her and also wished to continue to maintain good relations with her. . . .

30 July, St. Petersburg, ca. 4:00 p.m.— Nicholas II reinstates his order for general mobilization.

No. 121-36.   Daily Journal of the Russian Foreign Ministry.[73]

. . . At about 11 a.m., the Foreign Minister met again with the Minister of War and the Chief of the General Staff. The information received during the night had strengthened even further the conviction they all held that it was urgently necessary to prepare without loss of time for a serious war. Accordingly, the Ministers and the Chief-of-Staff remained, as before, of the opinion which they had expressed on the preceding day that it was necessary to proceed to general mobilization. . . . General Janushkevitsh[74] asked the Minister

[Sazonov] that, if he should succeed in persuading the Tsar, he should immediately telephone the news to him from Peterhof so that he, Janushkevitsh, could take the necessary measures without delay, for it was necessary above all to change as quickly as possible partial mobilization, which had already begun, into general mobilization, and to replace the orders already sent out with new ones. "After that," Janushkevitsh said, "I will go away, will smash my telephone, and in general take all precautions to make certain that I cannot be found, just in case one wants to give me contrary orders in the sense of a renewed cancellation of general mobilization.". . .

At 2 o'clock, the Foreign Minister and Major-General Tatishtshev[75] drove to Peterhof, where both were received together by His Majesty in the Alexander Palace. For almost a whole hour, the Minister tried to show that war had become inevitable, for one could see from all indications that Germany was determined to let things develop into a conflict; otherwise, it would not have rejected all the peaceful proposals that had been made, and it could easily have brought its ally to reason. . . . The Tsar's fervent wish to avoid at any price a war whose horrors filled him with the utmost revulsion forced His Majesty, in the realization of the heavy responsibility resting upon him in this fateful hour, to explore every possible means in order to avert the approaching danger. . . . Finally, the Tsar admitted that under the prevailing circumstances it would be most dangerous not to prepare oneself in time for an apparently inevitable war, and he therefore gave his approval for general mobilization to begin at once.

S. D. Sazonov requested the Tsar's permission to immediately inform the Chief of the General Staff of this decision by telephone and after this was granted, he hurried to the telephone on the ground floor of the palace. He transmitted His Majesty's order to General Janushkevitsh, who was waiting impatiently for it, and, referring to their conversation of that morning, added: "Now you can smash your telephone." . . .

31 July, Vienna, R 7:45 a.m.—Moltke's telegram to Conrad.

No. 121-37.   Conrad's Memoirs.[76]

Stand firm against Russian mobilization;[77] Austria-Hungary must be preserved, mobilize against Russia immediately. Germany will mobilize. Force Italy to her treaty obligations through compensations.

31 July, Berlin, R 11:40 a.m.—Bethmann learns of Russian general mobilization.

No. 121-38.   Pourtalès to Bethmann.[78]

General mobilization Army and Navy ordered. First day of mobilization 31 July.

31 July, Vienna, D 1:00 p.m.—Francis Joseph I informs William II of Austrian general mobilization.

No. 121-39.   Francis Joseph I
to William II.[79]

. . . Conscious of my heavy responsibilities for the future of my Empire, I have ordered the mobilization of my entire armed forces. The action now in progress by my army against Serbia can suffer no interruption by Russia's threatening and provocative attitude. A renewed rescue of Serbia through Russia's intervention would have to entail the most serious consequences for my lands, and therefore I cannot possibly admit such an intervention. I am aware of the effect of my decisions and have taken them trusting in God's justice with the certainty that your armed forces shall, in immutable allied loyalty, stand by my Empire and the Triple Alliance.

31 July, Berlin, D 1:45 p.m.—Germany proclaims a "threatening danger of war."

No. 121-40. Bethmann to Tschirschky.[80, 81]

After Russian general mobilization we have proclaimed threatening danger of war, which presumably shall be followed by mobilization within 48 hours. This inevitably means war. We expect of Austria immediate *active* participation in the war against Russia.

31 July, Berlin, R 2:52 p.m.—Nicholas II appeals to William II.

No. 121-41. Nicky to Willy.[82]

. . . It is *technically* impossible to stop our military preparations which were obligatory owing to Austria's mobilisation. We are far from wishing war. As long as the negociations with Austria on Servia's account are taking place my troops shall not make [? take] any *provocative* action. I give you my solemn word for this. . . .

31 July, Berlin, D 3:30 p.m.—The German ultimatum to Russia.

No. 121-42. Text of the Ultimatum— Bethmann to Pourtalès.[83]

In spite of still pending mediation negotiations and even though we had not taken mobilization measures of any kind up to this moment, Russia had mobilized entire army and navy, therefore also against us. As a result of these Russian measures, we have been forced to proclaim, for the protection of the Empire, the threatening danger of war, which does not mean mobilization yet. But mobilization must follow if Russia does not stop all war measures against us and Austria-Hungary within twelve hours and does not give us definite assurance to this effect. Please notify Mr. Sazonov of this at once and wire time of

notification.[84] I know that Sverbejev[85] telegraphed yesterday to St. Petersburg that we had mobilized, which even up to this moment is not the case.[86]

31 July, Berlin, D 3:30 p.m.—The German ultimatum to France.

No. 121-43. Text of the Ultimatum— Bethmann to Schoen.[87, 88]

In spite of our still pending mediation action and even though we ourselves had not taken mobilization measures of any kind, Russia has ordered mobilization of her entire army and navy, therefore also against us. We have thereupon proclaimed threatening state of war, which must be followed by mobilization if Russia does not stop all war measures against us and Austria within twelve hours. Mobilization inevitably means war. Please ask French Government whether it intends to remain neutral in a Russo-German war. Answer must be given within eighteen (18) hours. Immediately wire time when question presented. Utmost speed required.[89]

Secret: If, as is not to be expected, French Government declares that it shall remain neutral, will Your Excellency declare to the French Government that we must demand, as security for neutrality, cession of the fortresses Toul and Verdun, which we would occupy and return after the war with Russia had ended. Answer to the latter question would have to be here by 4 o'clock tomorrow afternoon.[90]

31 July, London, p.m.—Grey refuses to assure France of British support.

No. 121-44. Grey to Bertie.[91, 92]

. . . M. Cambon[93] then asked me for my reply to what he had said yesterday. I said that we had come to the conclusion, in the Cabinet to-day, that we could not give any pledge at the present time. The commercial and financial situation was exceedingly serious; there was danger of a complete collapse that would involve us and everyone else in ruin; and it was possible that our standing aside might be the only means of preventing a complete collapse of European credit, in which we should be involved. This might be a paramount consideration in deciding our attitude. . . . Up to the present moment, we did not feel, and public opinion did not feel, that any treaties or obligations of this country were involved. Further developments might alter this situation and cause the Government and Parliament to take the view that intervention was justified. The preservation of the neutrality of Belgium might be, I would not say a decisive, but an important factor, in determining our attitude. . . .

M. Cambon expressed great disappointment at my reply. He repeated his question of whether we would help France if Germany made an attack on her.

I said that I could only adhere to the answer that, as far as things had gone at present, we could not take any engagement. . . .

31 July, Rome, D 11:45 p.m.—Italy announces its neutrality under certain conditions.

No. 121-45.   *Flotow*[94] *to Bethmann.*[95]

The Government here had already discussed Italy's position to the war in the meeting of the Council of Ministers which took place today. Marquis San Giuliano[96] told me that the Italian Government had examined the question thoroughly and had reached the conclusion once again that the Austrian action against Serbia must be considered as aggressive, and that therefore the *casus foederis* as defined in the Triple Alliance did not apply. Italy will therefore have to declare her neutrality.[97] Upon my vehement objections to this standpoint, the Minister further declared that Italy had not

been informed in advance of Austria's action against Serbia, it could therefore be all the less expected to take part in the war in that direct Italian interests were being damaged by Austria's action. The only thing he could tell me now was that the Government here reserved the right to examine whether it would be possible for it to intervene in the war on the side of the Central Powers at a later date if Italian interests were then adequately protected. . . . I have the impression that all hope for the future here does not have to be abandoned yet if an effort is made to meet the Italians halfway on their above-mentioned claim, that is to say, if they are offered compensations.[98]. . .

1 August, Berlin, D 12:52 p.m.—The German declaration of war against Russia.

No. 121-46.   *Text of the Declaration— Jagow to Pourtalès.*[99]

The Imperial Government has tried since the beginning of the crisis to bring it to a peaceful solution. Acceding to a wish expressed to it by H. M. the Tsar of Russia, H. M. the Emperor of Germany, together with England, had attempted to accomplish a mediating rôle between the Cabinets of Vienna and of St. Petersburg when Russia, without awaiting the result, proceeded to the mobilization of all of her land and sea forces.

As a result of this menacing measure, not justified by any military foreboding [? preparation] on Germany's part, the German Empire found itself faced with a grave and imminent danger. If the Imperial Government had failed to guard against this danger, it would have compromised the security and the very existence of Germany. Consequently, the German Government saw itself forced to address itself to the Government of H. M. the Tsar of all the Russias in order to insist upon the cessation of the said military acts. Russia (having refused to accede/not having thought it necessary to reply)[100] to this demand and having manifested by (this refusal/this attitude)[100] that her action was directed against Germany, I have the honor, on the order of my Government, to acquaint Your Excellency with the following:

H. M. the Emperor, my august Sovereign, in the name of the Empire, takes up the challenge and considers himself in a state of war with Russia.

1 August, Paris, D 1:05 p.m.—The French reply to Germany's ultimatum.

No. 121-47. Schoen to Bethmann.[101]

In reply to repeated firm question whether France would remain neutral in Russo-German war, Premier declared *hesitatingly*: France would do what her interests dictated. . . .

1 August, St. Petersburg, D 2:06 p.m. —Nicholas II's last appeal to William II.

No. 121-48. Nicky to Willy.[102]

. . . Understand you are obliged to mobilise but wish to have the same guarantee from you as I gave you, that these measures *do not* mean war and that we shall continue negociating for the benefit of our countries and universal peace dear to all our hearts.

1 August, Paris, 3:40 p.m.—France orders general mobilization.

1 August, Berlin, 5:00 p.m.—William II signs the order for general mobilization.

1 August, St. Petersburg, 7:00 p.m.— Pourtalès hands Sazonov Germany's declaration of war against Russia.

No. 121-49. Daily Journal of the Russian Foreign Ministry.[103]

. . . On entering the Minister's office, the German Ambassador asked whether the Imperial Government was willing to give a favorable reply to his Note of yesterday.[104] The Minister answered in the negative, but added that, even though the order for general mobilization could not be cancelled, Russia did not refuse to continue negotiations to find a peaceful solution to the present situation. Count Pourtalès, who was already very dejected when he arrived, began to show signs of increasing agitation. He took a folded sheet of paper from his pocket, and then once more addressed the same question to the Minister, emphasizing as he did so the grave consequences which must follow from Russia's refusal to accept Germany's demand for the cessation of mobilization. S. D. Sazonov firmly and calmly confirmed once more the answer he had just given. In ever growing agitation, the Ambassador asked the same question for the third time, and the Minister declared once again: "I have no other answer to give you." Deeply moved, breathing with difficulty, the Ambassador declared: "In that case, Your Excellency, I am instructed by my Government to hand you this Note," and with trembling hands he gave S. D. Sazonov the Note containing the declaration of war. . . .

The conversation between the Ambassador and the Minister took place while they were standing in the large conference room, and after the presentation of the Note, Count Pourtalès, who had lost all self-control, walked over to the window (the first from the corner), buried his head in his hands, broke into tears, and said: "I never would have believed that I would leave St. Petersburg under these conditions." . . .

1 August, London, p.m.—Grey repeats to Cambon that England is under no obligation to help France.

No. 121-50. Grey to Bertie.[105]

M. Cambon to-day . . . urged upon me very strongly our obligation to help France if she was attacked by Germany. . . .

As to the question of our obligation to help France, I pointed out that we had no obligation. France did not wish to join in the war that seemed about to break out, but she was obliged to join in it, because of her alliance. We had purposely kept clear of all alliances, in order that we might not be involved in difficulties in this way. I had assured Parliament again and again that our hands were free. . . .

2 August, Luxemburg, ca. 6 a.m.—German troops invade Luxemburg.

2 August, Berlin, R 11:47 a.m.—Lichnowsky[106] warns Bethmann.

No. 121-51.   Lichnowsky to Bethmann.[107]

The question whether we will violate Belgian territory in the war against France should be of decisive importance for England's neutrality. I am firmly supported in this impression by Sir E. Grey's remarks as well as by information from the Austrian Embassy and the local press. If we violate Belgium's neutrality and a war against the Belgians develops from this, then I do not believe that the Government shall be in a position to remain neutral very much longer in the face of the storm of public opinion which could be expected here. Were we to respect Belgian neutrality, however, then there is still a possibility of England's remaining neutral if, at our victory over France, we act with moderation. . . .

2 August, Berlin, D 2:05 p.m.—The German ultimatum to Belgium.

No. 121-52.   Text of the Ultimatum—Jagow to Below.[108, 109]

The Imperial Government is in possession of reliable information concerning the intended concentration of French armed forces along the Meuse River between Givet and Namur. There can be no doubt that it is France's intention to advance across Belgian territory against Germany.

The Imperial Government cannot help but fear that Belgium, in spite of the best intentions, shall be unable to repel, without assistance, a French invasion with such great expectations of success that therein can be found a sufficient safeguard against the threat to Germany. It is an imperative of survival for Germany to forestall the hostile attack. It would, therefore, fill the German Government with the deepest regret if Belgium were to consider it as an act of hostility against her that the measures taken by its opponents force Germany in self-defense to also enter Belgian territory in its turn.

In order to avoid any misunderstanding, the Imperial Government declares the following:

1. Germany intends no hostilities of any kind against Belgium. If Belgium is willing to adopt a benevolent neutrality towards Germany in the impending war, then the German Government undertakes to guarantee the possessions and independence of the Kingdom to their fullest extent at the conclusion of peace.

2. Germany undertakes, on the above condition, to evacuate the territory of the Kingdom again as soon as peace is concluded.

3. In case of a friendly attitude by Belgium, Germany is prepared, in coöperation with the Royal Belgian authorities, to purchase all the requirements of its troops by payment in cash and to make restitution for any damages which might be caused by German troops.

If Belgium were to confront the German troops with hostility, in particular cause difficulties for their advance by the resistance of the Meuse fortresses or by the destruction of railroads, streets, tunnels, or other public works, then Germany, to its regret, shall be forced to consider the Kingdom as an enemy. In that case, Germany could not assume any obligations towards the Kingdom, but would have to leave the later regulation of the relations between the two states to the decision of the battlefield.

The Imperial Government entertains the firm hope that this eventuality shall not occur, and that the Royal Belgian Government shall know how to take the appropriate steps in order to prevent incidents such as those mentioned above from taking place. In that case, the friendly ties which connect both neighboring states would experience a further and enduring strengthening.

Your Excellency shall communicate the above in strict confidence to the Royal Belgian Government this evening at 8 (eight) o'clock German time, and request it to give you an unequivocal reply within 12 (twelve) hours. Will Your Excellency report to me at once by telegram the reception given to your communication and the Royal Belgian Government's definitive reply.

2 August, Brussels, 7:00 p.m.—Below delivers the German ultimatum to Davignon.[110]

3 August, Brussels, 7:00 a.m.—Below receives the Belgian reply to Germany's ultimatum.

No. 121-53.   Text of the Belgian Reply—Below to Bethmann.[111]

. . . This Note has caused profound and painful astonishment to the Government of the King. The intentions which it attributes to France are in contradiction with the formal declarations made to us on 1 August in the name of the Government of the Republic. . . .

The treaties of 1839, confirmed by the treaties of 1870, perpetuate the independence and the neutrality of Belgium under the guarantee of the Powers, and notably of the Government of His Majesty the King of Prussia. . . . The blow to her independence, with which the German Government threatens [her],[112] would constitute a fixed

[? flagrant][112] violation of international law. No strategic interest justifies breaking the law. . . .

Conscious of the role which Belgium has been playing for more than 80 years in the civilization of the world, the Government refuses to believe that the independence of Belgium could only be preserved at the price [of the violation][113] of her neutrality. If this hope were to be deceived, the Belgian Government is firmly determined to repel any attack upon its rights with all the means in its power.

3 August, Berlin, D 1:05 p.m.—Germany declares war against France.

3 August, Paris, 6:45 p.m.—Schoen hands Viviani Germany's declaration of war against France.

No. 121-54.   Text of the Declaration— Schoen to Viviani.[114]

The German administrative and military authorities have verified that a certain number of flagrantly hostile acts have been committed on German territory by French military aviators. Several of the latter have clearly violated the neutrality of Belgium by flying over the territory of that country. One of them has attempted to destroy buildings near Wessel, others have been observed over the Eiffel region, another has dropped bombs on the railroad near Karlsruhe and Nuremberg.

I am instructed, and I have the honor, to inform Your Excellency that, in the presence of these aggressions, the German Empire considers itself in a state of war with France as a consequence of the acts of the latter Power.

I have, at the same time, the honor to bring to Your Excellency's attention that the German authorities shall detain the French merchant vessels in German ports, but that they shall release them if, within 48 (forty-eight) hours, complete reciprocity is assured.

My diplomatic mission having thus come to an end, it only remains for me to request Your Excellency to kindly furnish me with my passports and to take the measures which you consider useful to assure my return to Germany with the personnel of the Embassy, as well as with the personnel of the Bavarian Legation and of the German Consulate General in Paris.

4 August, Belgian frontier, ca. 8:00 a.m.—German troops invade Belgium.

4 August, St. Petersburg—Italy initiates discussions with Russia and France.

No. 121-55.   Sazonov to Izvolsky.[115]

The Italian Ambassador today resumed the discussion with me of the conditions under which Italy would decide to join us and France in the struggle against Austria.[116] He indicated that, in addition to the acquisition of the Trentino, Italy desired to secure the hegemony of the Adriatic, and for this purpose would like to receive Valona. It would also agree to a territorial increase on the part of Greece and Serbia on the Adriatic coast. Considering the fact that Franco-Italian relations are still not characterized by sufficient mutual trust, the Ambassador expressed the wish that the negotiations on this subject be conducted through our mediation. Expect your reply.

4 August, London, D 9:30 a.m.—The British ultimatum to Germany.

PART I.

No. 121-56.   Text of the Ultimatum— Grey to Goschen.[117]

The King of the Belgians has made an appeal to His Majesty the King for diplomatic intervention on behalf of Belgium. . . .

His Majesty's Government are bound to protest against this violation of a treaty to which Germany is a party in common with themselves, and must request an assurance

that the demand made upon Belgium will not be proceeded with, and that her neutrality will be respected by Germany. You should ask for an immediate reply.

4 August, London, D 2:00 p.m.—The British ultimatum to Germany.

PART II.

No. 121-57.   Text of the Ultimatum— Grey to Goschen.[118]

We hear that Germany has addressed note to Belgian Minister for Foreign Affairs stating that German Government will be compelled to carry out, if necessary by force of arms, the measures considered indispensable. We are also informed that Belgian territory has been violated at Gemmenich.

In these circumstances . . . we must . . . ask that a satisfactory reply to . . . my telegram No. 266 of this morning[119] be received here by 12 o'clock to-night. If not, you are instructed to ask for your passports and to say that His Majesty's Government feel bound to take all steps in their power to uphold the neutrality of Belgium and the observance of a Treaty to which Germany is as much a party as ourselves.

4 August, Berlin, 7:00 p.m.—Goschen hands Jagow the British ultimatum to Germany; subsequent events in Berlin.

No. 121-58.   Goschen to Grey.[120]

In accordance with the instructions contained in your telegram No. 266 of the 4th instant, I called upon the Under-Secretary of State[121] for Foreign Affairs that afternoon and enquired in the name of His Majesty's Government whether the Imperial Government would refrain from violating Belgian neutrality. Herr von Jagow at once replied that he was sorry to say that his answer must be "No" as, in consequence of the German troops having crossed the frontier that morning, Belgian neutrality had been already violated. Herr von Jagow again went into the reasons why the Imperial Government had been obliged to take this step—namely that they had to advance into France by the quickest and easiest way—so as to be able to get well ahead with their operations and endeavour to strike some decisive blow as early as as possible. . . .

During the afternoon, I received your telegram No. 270[122] and, in compliance with the instructions therein contained, I again proceeded to the Imperial Foreign Office. . . . Herr von Jagow replied that to his great regret he could give no other answer than that which he had given me earlier in the day, namely that the safety of the Empire rendered it absolutely necessary that the Imperial troops should advance through Belgium. I gave his Excellency a paraphrase of your telegram and, pointing out that you had mentioned 12 o'clock as the time when His Majesty's Government would expect an answer, asked him whether, in view of the terrible consequences which would necessarily ensue, it were not possible even at the last moment that their answer should be reconsidered. He replied that if the time given were even twenty-four hours or more his answer must be the same. I said that in that case I should have to demand my passports. . . .

I then said that I should like to go and see the Chancellor as it might be perhaps the last time I should have an opportunity of seeing him. He begged me to do so. I found the Chancellor very agitated. His Excellency at once began a harangue which lasted for about 20 minutes. He said that the step taken by His Majesty's Government was terrible to a degree, just for a word, "neutrality," a word which in war time had so often been disregarded—just for a scrap of paper, Great Britain was going to make war on a kindred nation who desired nothing better than to be friends with her. . . .

After this somewhat painful interview, I returned to the embassy. . . . At about 9:30 p.m., Herr von Zimmermann, the Under-Secretary of State for Foreign Affairs, came to see me. . . . In the meantime, after Herr Zimmermann left me, a flying sheet, issued by the "Berliner Tagesblatt," was circulated stating that Great Britain had declared war against Germany. The immediate result of this news was the assemblage of an exceedingly excited and unruly mob before His Majesty's Embassy. The small force of police which had been sent to guard the embassy was soon overpowered, and the attitude of the mob became more threatening. We took no notice of this demonstration as long as it was confined to noise, but when the crash of glass and the landing of cobble stones into the drawing-room where we were all sitting warned us that the situation was getting unpleasant, I telephoned to the Foreign Office an account of what was happening. Herr von Jagow at once informed the Chief of Police, and an adequate force of mounted police, sent with great promptness, very soon cleared the street. From that moment on, we were well guarded, and no more direct unpleasantness occurred. . . .

On the following morning, the 5th August, the Emperor sent one of His Majesty's Aide-de-Camps to me with the following message:—

"The Emperor has charged me to express to your Excellency his regret for the occurrences of last night, but to tell you at the same time that you will gather from those occurrences an idea of the feelings of his people respecting the action of Great Britain in joining with other nations against her old allies of Waterloo. His Majesty also begs that you will tell the King that he has been proud of the titles of British Field-Marshal and British Admiral, but that in consequence of what has occurred he must now, at once, divest himself of those titles."

I would add that the above message lost none of its petulant acerbity by the manner of its delivery. . . .

Before closing this long account of our last days in Berlin, I should like to place on record and bring to your notice the quite admirable behaviour of my staff under the most trying circumstances possible. One and all, they worked night and day with scarcely any rest: and I cannot praise too highly the cheerful zeal with which Counsellor, Naval and Military Attachés, Secretaries, and the two young Attachés, buckled to their work and kept their nerve, with often a yelling mob outside, and inside hundreds of British subjects clamoring for advice and assistance. . . .

4 August, London, 11:00 p.m.— Churchill[123] orders the British Navy to "Commence hostilities against Germany."

No. 121-59.   Churchill's Memoirs.[124]

. . . It was 11 o'clock at night—12 by German time—when the ultimatum expired. The windows of the Admiralty were thrown wide open in the warm night air. Under the roof from which Nelson had received his orders were gathered a small group of Admirals and Captains and a cluster of clerks, pencil in hand, waiting. Along the Mall from the direction of the Palace the sound of an immense concourse singing "God save the King" floated in. On this deep wave there broke the chimes of Big Ben; and, as the first stroke of the hour boomed out, a rustle of movement swept across the room. The war telegram, which meant "Commence hostilities against Germany," was flashed to the ships and establishments under the White Ensign all over the world.

I walked across the Horse Guards Parade to the Cabinet room and reported to the Prime Minister and the Ministers who were assembled there that the deed was done.

Notes

No. 100, pp. 229-231
[1] Hertslet (ed.). *Map of Europe*, IV, 2672-2693.
[2] See *No. 36*, above.—HNW.
[3] Ratifications exchanged at St. Petersburgh, 5/17 March, 1878.—Ed.

No. 101, pp. 231-233
[1] Hertslet (ed.), *Map of Europe*, IV, 2759-2799.
[2] In the following paragraphs, I have listed only the major title and office of each Plenipotentiary.—HNW.
[3] Ratifications were exchanged in Berlin by Great Britain, Germany, Austria-Hungary, France, Italy and Russia on 3 August 1878, and by Turkey on 28 August 1878.—HNW.

No. 102, pp. 234-235
[1] Germany. Auswärtiges Amt. *Die grosse Politik der europäischen Kabinette, 1871-1914:* *Sammlung der diplomatischen Akten des Auswärtigen Amtes*, eds. Johannes Lepsius, *et al.* (40 vols. in 54, Berlin, 1922-1927), III, 92-98. Hereafter cited as *Grosse Politik*. Translated by Herman N. Weill.
[2] Austrian Minister for Foreign Affairs.—HNW.
[3] Austrian Ambassador at Rome, who succeeded Andrássy as Minister for Foreign Affairs in 1879.—HNW.
[4] Russian Minister of War.—HNW.

No. 103, pp. 235-236
[1] *Grosse Politik*, III, 102-105. Translated by Herman N. Weill.
[2] Ratifications were exchanged at Vienna on 21 October 1879.—HNW.

No. 104, pp. 237-238
[1] *Grosse Politik*, VI, 24-28. Translated by Herman N. Weill.
[2] German Ambassador at Vienna.—HNW.

[3] In this memorandum, General Field Marshal Count Moltke summarized the development of Russia's armed forces since 1878, and reached the conclusion that Russia was preparing for an imminent war against Austria; see *Grosse Politik*, VI, 24-25, n.–HNW.

[4] Austrian Minister for Foreign Affairs.–HNW.

No. 105, pp. 238-239

[1] *Grosse Politik*, III, 244-247. Translated by Herman N. Weill.

[2] The exchange occurred on 30 May 1882.– HNW.

No. 106, pp. 239-241

[1] *Grosse Politik*, V, 253-255. Translated by Herman N. Weill.

[2] This refers to the Three Emperors' League, which Russia had refused to renew.–HNW.

[3] Probably meaning "international law."– HNW.

No. 107, pp. 241-244

[1] *Grosse Politik*, VII, 4-6, 9-13, 18-19, 22-23, 29-33. Translated by Herman N. Weill.

[2] Under-Secretary of State for Foreign Affairs. This memorandum is the result of a conference which had taken place at the Foreign Ministry on 23 March 1890, four days after Bismarck's dismissal, at which Berchem, Baron Friedrich von Holstein, First Counsellor in the Foreign Ministry, and L. von Raschdau, also First Counsellor in the Foreign Ministry, had urged the newly appointed Chancellor, General Leo von Caprivi, not to renew the Reinsurance Treaty. Holstein, the famous Gray Eminence of the German Foreign Ministry from 1890 until his dismissal in 1906, is usually considered to have been the driving force behind the non-renewal, a role for which he himself took credit; see *Grosse Politik*, VII, 10, n., and 47-49.–HNW.

[3] Schweinitz, German Ambassador at St. Petersburg, was in Berlin from 21-30 March 1890 for an initiation ceremony of the Order of the Black Eagle.–HNW.

[4] Russian Minister for Foreign Affairs.–HNW.

[5] Russian Ambassador at Berlin.–HNW.

[6] In the interview on 20 March 1890, William II had assured the Russian Ambassador that Bismarck's retirement had occurred solely for reasons of health, that this did not change Germany's policy towards Russia, and that he (William II) desired to renew the Reinsurance Treaty (see *Grosse Politik*, VII, 19-21). On the same day, Count Herbert von Bismarck, then Secretary of State in the Foreign Ministry, but who soon joined his father in retirement, sent William II a memorandum concerning the Reinsurance Treaty. On it, William II wrote: "Agree with renewal of the Treaty and authorize you to communicate this to Schuwaloff –20/III/90." (See *Grosse Politik*, VII, 3.) The Russian Foreign Minister's consternation was, therefore, caused as much by the undiplomatic abruptness with which William II had changed his mind, as it was by Germany's refusal to renew the Treaty.–HNW.

[7] Later King Edward VII; his son, Prince George, was one of those initiated into the Order of the Black Eagle at this time.–HNW.

[8] British Ambassador at St. Petersburg.–Ed.

[9] This refers to the Anti-Slavery Congress, which had been meeting in Brussels since the beginning of February and at which Russia had sought a rapprochement with England.– Ed.

[10] Caprivi sent a copy of this enclosure to Schweinitz, together with a cover letter dated 29 May 1890. In the latter, a curious additional argument against renewing the Treaty in any form was that Bismarck may have been capable of "selling" his complicated treaty system to the public, but now that he had left office, this was no longer possible (see *Grosse Politik*, VII, 34).–HNW.

No. 108, pp. 245-246

[1] France. Ministère des Affaires Étrangères. *Documents diplomatiques français relatifs aux origines de la guerre de 1914*, 42 vols. in 3 series (Paris, 1929-1940), 1e, IX, 643-644, 675, 679-681; X, 711-712; XI, 8-9. Hereafter cited as *Docs. diplom. français, 1871-1914*. Translated by Herman N. Weill.

[2] French Ambassador at St. Petersburg.–HNW.

[3] French Minister of Foreign Affairs.–HNW.

[4] French Army Vice-Chief of Staff.–HNW.

[5] Russian Army Chief of Staff.–HNW.

[6] The text which follows is the final version, including three minor corrections. It was signed by Generals Boisdeffre and Obroutshev on 17 August 1892.–HNW.

[7] French Minister of War.–HNW.

No. 109, pp. 246-248

1 Great Britain. Foreign Office. *British Documents on the Origins of the War, 1898-1914*, eds. G. P. Gooch and Harold Temperley, 11 vols., (London, 1927-1938), I, 167-168, 172, 178, 182, 188. Hereafter cited as *British Documents, 1898-1914*.

2 British Acting Agent at Cairo.—HNW.

3 British Secretary of State for Foreign Affairs. —HNW.

4 Kitchener's aide-de-camp.—HNW.

5 British Ambassador at Paris.—HNW.

6 Kitchener's title, equivalent to Commander-in-Chief.—HNW.

7 Russian Minister for Foreign Affairs, who was on a visit to Paris from 15 to 20 October 1898.—HNW.

8 French Premier.—HNW.

9 Marchand had left Fashoda, apparently on his own initiative, to make a personal report on the affair in Paris, and was then in Cairo; Captain Baratier had been sent to meet him by Delcassé with new instructions for Marchand (see *British Documents, 1898-1914*, I, 186).—HNW.

No. 110, pp. 249-251

1 Wilhelm II, German Emperor, *Briefe Wilhelms II. an den Zaren, 1894-1914*, ed. Walter Goetz, trans. Max Behrmann (Berlin, n.d.), pp. 300-301. The original text is in English.

2 German Ambassador at St. Petersburg.— HNW.

3 After the Armenian Massacres in the fall of 1895, England had taken the lead in putting pressure upon the Turks to introduce reforms. In the same year, England had become embroiled, first with Venezuela, and then with the United States, over the boundaries of British Guiana in South America.—HNW.

4 The attack referred to was the Jameson Raid, which had begun on 29 December 1895, and ended with the capture of Jameson and his men by the Boers on 2 January 1896.—HNW.

5 Empress Alexandra, Nicholas II's wife.— HNW.

6 *Grosse Politik*, XI, 31-32. Translated by Herman N. Weill.

7 President of the Transvaal Republic.—HNW.

8 German Ambassador at London.—HNW.

9 *Grosse Politik*, XI, 53-54. Translated by Herman N. Weill.

10 At this time Prime Minister as well as Secretary of State for Foreign Affairs.—HNW.

11 British Ambassador at Berlin.—HNW.

12 *British Documents, 1898-1914*, I, 249-252.

13 These observations, entitled "Aphorisms on the War in South Africa" and dated 4 February 1900, are printed in the German original in *Grosse Politik*, XV, 554-557, and in English translation in Sidney Lee, *King Edward VII: A Biography* (2 vols., London, 1925-1927), I, 807-810. Edward resented this rather amateurish attempt to second-guess the British military commanders in South Africa, but he was particularly incensed at the concluding paragraph: "Even the best football team, if it is beaten despite the most gallant defense, finally accepts its defeat with equanimity. Last year, in the great cricket match of England vs. Australia, the former took the victory of the latter quietly, with chivalrous acknowledgment of its opponent."—HNW.

14 Secretary of State of the Transvaal Republic, who had been sent to Berlin to enlist Germany's sympathy and support for the Boers.— HNW.

15 *British Documents, 1898-1914*, I, 253-254.

No. 111, pp. 251-253

1 The first four documents are from *Grosse Politik*, XVII, 19-23, translated by Herman N. Weill; the last two from *British Documents, 1898-1914*, II, 64-65 and 80-83, respectively.

2 German Imperial Chancellor.—HNW.

3 William II had hastened to London upon receiving the news that Queen Victoria, his grandmother, was gravely ill. She died on 21 January 1901.—HNW.

4 First Secretary at the German Embassy in London.—HNW.

5 Joseph Chamberlain, British Secretary of State for the Colonies. He had been involved in an attempt at an Anglo-German rapprochement once before when, in a speech delivered at Leicester in November 1899, he had publicly advocated closer ties between the two countries. Nothing had come of it, primarily because the Boer War had broken out in the preceding month and German public opinion was decidedly hostile to the British.—HNW.

6 German diplomat, who had accompanied William II to England. He was to succeed Count von Hatzfeldt as the German Ambas-

sador at London at the end of the year.—
HNW.

7 British Secretary of State for Foreign Affairs.
—HNW.

No. 112, pp. 253-255

1 "The Size of the Fleets of Great Britain,
France, Russia, Germany, and the United
States of America, and Their Naval Expendi-
tures," *British Parliamentary Papers* (1898),
Vol. 56; (1902), Vol. 60; (1906), Vol. 70;
(1910), Vol. 61; (1914), Vol. 54.

2 The tables for the year 1902 list only the
classification "Cruisers"; it may be assumed,
however, that the number of ships indicated—
e.g., 126 for Great Britain—includes "Light
Cruisers" as well as "Cruisers."—HNW.

3 The tables for the year 1906 distinguish between "Battleships, 1st, 2nd, and 3rd class,"
"Cruisers, Armoured," and "Cruisers, Protected,
1st, 2nd and 3rd class." These classifications are
not used in the other years. To keep the numbers comparable, I have combined "Battleships,
2nd and 3rd class" under "Battle Cruisers," and
"Cruisers, Protected, 1st, 2nd, and 3rd class"
under "Light Cruisers."—HNW.

4 The tables for the years 1910 and 1914 list
only "Battleships," "Battle Cruisers," and
"Cruisers" which are less than twenty years
old.—HNW.

5 Year of war with Spain.—Eds.

6 Estimated.—Eds.

No. 113, pp. 255-256

1 *British Documents, 1898-1914*, II, 115-120.

2 Japanese Ambassador at London.—HNW.

3 The British Ambasador at Berlin notified
William II of the Treaty on the evening of 5
February 1902, and the text was released to
the press on 11 February 1902; see *British
Documents, 1898-1914*, II, 122-125.—HNW.

No. 114, pp. 256-257

1 *Docs. diplom. francais, 1871-1914*, 2e, II,
391-392. Translated by Herman N. Weill.

2 Italian Minister for Foreign Affairs.—HNW.

3 French Ambassador at Rome.—HNW.

4 Most historians cite 1 November 1902 as the
date of this Agreement. In a cover letter, also
dated 10 July 1902 (see Barrère to Delcassé,
ibid., pp. 390-391), Barrère explained that
Prinetti felt a repugnance at signing the Agreement almost simultaneously with the renewal

of the Triple Alliance, which had occurred on
28 June 1902. It was, therefore, agreed to sign
two sets of documents, to date them 10 July
1902 and 1 November 1902, respectively, and
to destroy the set dated 10 July 1902 on 2
November 1902. This was done, according to
the editors (*ibid.*, p. 391, n.) and to Barrère
(*ibid.*, p. 696). Ten years later, in a lengthy
dispatch dated 10 March 1912 (*ibid.*, pp. 692-
699), Barrère explained to Poincaré, then
French Minister for Foreign Affairs, the circumstances leading to the Agreement, which,
he wrote, was signed on 30 June 1902. The
editors of the *Docs. diplom. francais* apparently prefer the date of 10 July 1902.—HNW.

5 Former Italian Minister for Foreign Affairs.
—HNW.

6 When Barrère pressed Prinetti to define
"direct provocation," the latter listed several
examples, including "The publication of spur-
ious dispatches by Prince von Bismarck in
1870; the refusal of King William to receive
Mr. Benedetti." As an example of an "indirect provocation," to which the Agreement
would not apply, he cited "the candidacy of
the Prince of Hohenzollern for the Spanish
throne." See Barrère to Delcassé, 20 July 1902,
ibid., p. 408.—HNW.

7 An identical Note, also dated 10 July 1902,
was delivered by Barrère to Prinetti; it is
printed *ibid.*, pp. 393-394.—HNW.

No. 115, pp. 257-260

1 *British Documents, 1898-1914*, II, 374-398.

2 French Ambassador at London.—HNW.

No. 116, pp. 260-262

1British Consul at Tangier.—HNW.

2 *British Documents, 1898-1914*, III, 63.

3 William II's visit to Tangier had taken place
on 31 March 1905.—HNW.

4 Great-uncle of the Sultan of Morocco.—
HNW.

5 French *chargé d'affaires* at Tangier.—HNW.

6 *Docs. diplom. francais, 1871-1914*, 2e, VI,
265-266. Translated by Herman N. Weill.

7 *Ibid.*, p. 273. Translated by Herman N. Weill.

8 Italian Minister of Finance.—HNW.

9 British Secretary of State for Foreign Affairs.
—HNW.

10 *British Documents, 1898-1914*, III, 266-267.

11 The Algeciras Conference, which had been
called to find a peaceful solution to the crisis.

For the results of its deliberations, see "General Act of the International Conference at Algeciras relating to the Affairs of Morocco, 7 April 1906. Ratifications deposited at Madrid, 31 December 1906," *British Parliamentary Papers* (1907), Vol. 99, "Treaty Series, No. 4-1907," pp. 1-36 (French text) and pp. 37-78 (English text).—HNW.

12 Beginning in May, 1903, with King Edward VII's famous visit to Paris, where he was given a tumultuous welcome by the French.—HNW.

13 Russia was still suffering from the after-effects of the Russo-Japanese War and the Revolution of 1905.—HNW.

No. 117, pp. 263-265

1 *British Parliamentary Papers* (1908), CXXV, 6-10. The original French text precedes the English translation, and is also printed in *British Documents, 1898-1914*, IV, 618-621.

2 Articles IV and V concern the repayment of Persian loans.—HNW.

3 The Annex primarily provides "that the occupation of the Chumbi Valley by British forces shall cease after the payment of three annual installments of the indemnity of 25,000,000 rupees."—HNW.

4 Ratifications were exchanged on 23 September 1907, the Great Powers were notified of the Agreement on 24 September 1907, and the public on the following day.—HNW.

5 British Ambassador at St. Petersburg.—HNW.

6 Russian Minister for Foreign Affairs.—HNW.

No. 118, pp. 265-269

1 *Grosse Politik*, XXIV, 99-104, 107-116, 117-119. Translated by Herman N. Weill.

2 At this time British Chancellor of the Exchequer.—HNW.

3 A widely read naval journal.—HNW.

4 Italian Minister of the Navy.—Eds.

5 One or more words are missing here to complete the sentence; perhaps "to seem to agree with."—Eds.

No. 119, pp. 269-272

1 *Grosse Politik*, XXIV, 170-174. For the origins, as well as some of the repercussions, of this famous interview between William II and a Colonel Stuart Wortley, an English admirer of the Emperor, see *ibid.*, pp. 165-210.—HNW.

2 See *No. 116*, above.—HNW.

3 On 30 August 1908.—Eds.

4 These are William II's "Aphorisms on the War in South Africa," mentioned in *No. 110*, above.—HNW.

5 See *No. 118*, above.—HNW.

No. 120, pp. 272-281

1 Prussian ambassador at Munich.—HNW.

2 *Grosse Politik*, Vol. 25-II, pp. 477, 478-479. Translated by Herman N. Weill.

The complete dispatch (*ibid.*, pp. 474-479) is a lengthy review of Germany's foreign policy.—HNW.

3 Austrian Minister for Foreign Affairs.—HNW.

4 Austria. Ministerium des Aeussern. *Oesterreich-Ungarns Ausenpolitik von der bosnischen Krise 1908 bis zum Kriegsausbruch 1914: Diplomatische Aktenstücke des österreich-ungarischen Ministerium des Aeussern*, eds. Ludwig Bittner, *et al.*, 9 vols. (Vienna, 1930), I, 14-15. Hereafter cited as *Oester.-Ungarns Aussenpolitik*. Translated by Herman N. Weill.

5 *Oester.-Ungarns Aussenpolitik*, I, 41-51. Translated by Herman N. Weill.

6 This refers to the Young Turk Revolution, which had broken out at the beginning of July, 1908, and which had largely determined the timing of the Austrian annexation.—HNW.

7 This personal meeting had occurred on 11 August 1908.—HNW.

8 See *No. 101*, above, particularly Article XXV.—HNW.

9 See *No. 119*, above.—HNW.

10 German Secretary of State for Foreign Affairs.—HNW.

11 *Grosse Politik*, Vol. 26-I, pp. 26-29. Translated by Herman N. Weill.

12 Russian Minister for Foreign Affairs.—HNW.

13 In a later conversation with Tschirschky, the German Ambassador at Vienna, Aehrenthal modified this plan so that Serbia would be divided between Austria and Bulgaria along ethnographic lines (see Tschirschky to Bülow, 20 October 1908, *Grosse Politik*, Vol. 26-I, p. 28, n.). Grey had a strong suspicion that this was Austria's ultimate aim, and strove hard to prevent the crisis from taking a turn which would serve as a convenient justification for an Austrian attack upon Serbia (see, e.g., Grey to Goschen, 25 March 1909, *British Documents, 1898-1914*, V, 740-741, and Grey

to Nicolson, 26 March 1909, *ibid.*, pp. 741-742). For this, as well as other, reasons, Aehrenthal changed his mind about invading Serbia at this time (see Tschirschky to Bülow, 28 March 1909, *Grosse Politik*, Vol. 26-II, pp. 723-725), a decision which was vehemently protested by Conrad, who was convinced that Austria was missing a golden opportunity to settle accounts with Serbia once and for all (see Conrad, *Dienstzeit*, I, 166-169).—HNW.

[14] *Oester.-Ungarns Aussenpolitik*, I, 92. Translated by Herman N. Weill.

[15] Since there were no witnesses present, we will never know exactly what transpired between the two Ministers at this famous meeting. Aehrenthal's memorandum of the meeting (printed *ibid.*, I, 86-92) is undated, and could have been written in the light of later events. Izvolsky, under the impression that the annexation would not take place until much later, continued his leisurely travels, and arrived in Paris on 4 October 1908, the very day that the news of the annexation was, through a misunderstanding, prematurely released in the French capital by the Austrian Ambassador. On the evening of that day, Izvolsky gave Sir Francis Bertie, the British Ambassador in Paris, his version of what had been said at Buchlau (see Bertie to Grey, *British Documents, 1898-1914*, Vol. 5, Nos. 292 and 293, both dated 4 October 1908, pp. 383-386). In the second dispatch, Bertie wrote: "From my interview with M. Izvolsky, I have the impression, I may say the conviction, that he did not quite tell the truth, the whole truth, and nothing but the truth." This conviction is still shared by many historians.—HNW.

[16] Austrian Ambassador at Constantinople.—HNW.

[17] *Oester.-Ungarns Aussenpolitik*, I, 93. Translated by Herman N. Weill.

[18] That is, the annexation of Bosnia and Herzegovina.—HNW.

[19] German Acting Secretary of State for Foreign Affairs.—HNW.

[20] *Grosse Politik*, Vol. 26-I, p. 106. Translated by Herman N. Weill.

[21] Rumors had been circulating that the annexation had occurred only after Austria had obtained Germany's approval. As a matter of fact, William II was quite upset that the Austrians had not taken him into their confidence beforehand, and that he was, as he put it, "the last person in all of Europe to have found out about it!" (see his final marginal comment, *ibid.*, p. 53)—HNW.

[22] *Grosse Politik*, Vol. 26-I, 224-227. Translated by Herman N. Weill.

[23] See *No. 120-4, above.*—HNW.

[24] Chief of the German General Staff. To distinguish him from his famous uncle of the same name, the Moltke of the Wars of German Unification, he is usually referred to as "Moltke the Younger."—HNW.

[25] Conrad [von Hötzendorf], *Aus meiner Dienstzeit, 1906-1918*, 5 vols. (Vienna, 1921-1925), I, 631-634. Hereafter cited as Conrad, *Dienstzeit.* Translated by Herman N. Weill.

[26] The annexation of Bosnia and Herzegovina. —HNW.

[27] The Dual Alliance—see *No. 103*, above.—HNW.

[28] Conrad, *Dienstzeit*, I, 379-384. Translated by Herman N. Weill.

[29] *Grosse Politik*, Vol. 26-II, pp. 623-624. Translated by Herman N. Weill.

[30] The most violent protests against the annexation had taken place in Serbia, which went so far as to mobilize its troops against Austria. The Serbs had at first been encouraged in this belligerent attitude by Russia, but when Russia yielded to German pressure (see *Nos. 120-12 and 120-13, below*), Serbia agreed to a Declaration drawn up by the Powers in which it recognized the annexation (for the text of the Declaration, see Ratibor to Bülow, 31 March 1909, *Grosse Politik*, Vol. 26-II, pp. 728-732). —HNW.

[31] The redundancy is in the original text.— HNW.

[32] German Ambassador at St. Petersburg.— HNW.

[33] *Grosse Politik*, Vol. 26-II, pp. 693-695. Translated by Herman N. Weill.

[34] The most important feature of this Agreement was that Austria agreed to pay Turkey compensation in return for Turkey's recognition of the annexation.—HNW.

[35] British Ambassador at St. Petersburg.— HNW.

[36] *British Documents, 1898-1914*, V, 727-729.

[37] The text of the Russian reply, forwarded by Pourtalès to Bülow on 24 March 1909, is printed in *Grosse Politik*, Vol. 26-II, pp. 702-

703.—HNW.

[38] *British Documents, 1898-1914,* V, 736-737.

[39] For Grey's reply, see *No. 120-17,* below.— HNW.

[40] *British Documents, 1898-1914,* V, 757-758.

[41] *Grosse Politik,* Vol. 26-II, pp. 735-737. Translated by Herman N. Weill.

[42] The Germans, then as later, vigorously denied that Bülow's demand of 21 March 1909 (see *No. 120-12,* above) was an "ultimatum," and they accused the British, especially Nicolson, of having originated what they considered to be a base canard (see the editor's discussion of the subject in a lengthy footnote in *Grosse Politik,* Vol. 26-II, pp. 693-695).—HNW.

[43] *British Documents, 1898-1914,* V, 771-772.

[44] An error; should be "London."—HNW.

[45] See *No. 120-14,* above.—HNW.

[46] The compensation provided by the Austro-Turkish Agreement, mentioned in *No. 120-12,* above.—HNW.

[47] Austrian Minister at Belgrade.—HNW.

[48] *Oester.-Ungarns Aussenpolitik,* II, 238-239. Translated by Herman N. Weill.

[49] *British Documents, 1898-1914,* V, 778.

[50] The naval battle in the Russo-Japanese War of 1904-1905, in which the Russian fleet was annihilated.—HNW.

[51] Conrad, *Dienstzeit,* I, 165. Translated by Herman N. Weill.

[52] In this letter to Moltke, as well as in memoranda to Francis Joseph I and to Aehrenthal, Conrad had insisted that Austria should have invaded Serbia (see *ibid.,* pp. 166-174).

[53] That is, the encirclement by the Entente Powers.—HNW.

No. 121, pp. 282-303

'Editor's note:

(1) The following abbreviations are used in the citations of this section:

BD   Great Britain. *British Documents on the Origins of the War, 1898-1914.*

DF   France. *Documents diplomatiques français relatifs aux origines de la guerre de 1914.*

IBR   Russia. *Die internationale Beziehungen im Zeitalter des Imperialismus.*

KD   Germany. *Die deutschen Dokumente zum Kriegsausbruch* (also known as the *Kautsky Documents*).

OUA   Austria. *Oesterreich-Ungarns Aussenpolitik, 1908-1914.*

(2) D - Dispatched, R - Received. The hour indicated is local time. In calculating the time at which a dispatch probably reached an addressee, allowance should be made for deciphering the dispatch and for time zones, e.g., one hour between London and Berlin, two hours between London and St. Petersburgh.

(3) To save space, several events are mentioned in brief entries, but the documentary evidence for them has been omitted.

(4) All translations are by Herman N. Weill unless otherwise noted.

[1] OUA, VIII, No. 9984.

[2] SZOGYENY, Count Marich von, Austrian Ambassador at Berlin.—HNW.

[3] BERCHTOLD, Count Leopold von, Austrian Minister for Foreign Affairs.—HNW.

[4] OUA, VIII, No. 10058.

[5] BETHMANN Hollweg, Theobald von, German Chancellor.—HNW.

[6] OUA, VIII, No. 10076.

[7] HOYOS, Count Alexander, Berchtold's *chef de cabinet,* who had personally brought Francis Joseph I's letter (No. 121-1) to Berlin.— HNW.

[8] Conrad, *Dienstzeit,* IV, 42. Conrad was, as previously mentioned (see *No. 120,* above), Chief of the Austrian General Staff.—HNW.

[9] CRACKANTHORPE, Dayrell, British *chargé d'affaires* at Belgrade.—HNW.

[10] GREY, Sir Edward, who, in the longest continuous tenure in that office in British history, was still Secretary of State for Foreign Affairs. —HNW.

[11] BD, XI, No. 80.

[12] KD, I, No. 100; the contents of this circular dispatch, its date, and the fact that it was not delivered in the capitals named until 24 July (see KD, I, Nos. 154, 157, 160, and BD, XI, No. 100), that is, on the day *after* Austria's ultimatum was presented in Belgrade *(No. 121-9),* has given rise to the accusation that Germany was not only fully informed of the contents of that ultimatum, but probably had a hand in drafting it.—HNW.

[13] SAZONOV, Serge, Russian Minister for Foreign Affairs.—HNW.

14 POURTALES, Count Friedrich von, German Ambassador at St. Petersburg.—HNW.

15 D 21 July, R 23 July, a.m.; KD, I, No. 120.

16 POINCARE, Raymond, President of the French Republic, who was in St. Petersburg on a state visit from 20 to 23 July.—HNW.

17 SZAPARY, Count Friedrich von, Austrian Ambassador at St. Petersburg.—HNW.

18 D 2:05 p.m. R 9:00 p.m.; OUA, VIII, No. 10461.

19 GIESL, Lt. General Baron von, Austrian Minister at Belgrade.—HNW.

20 D 20 July; OUA, VIII, No. 10395.

21 "National Defense," a secret organization devoted to a Greater Serbia; actually, it was the "Black Hand" organization which had plotted the assassination of the Archduke at Sarajevo.—HNW.

22 Szápáry reported his conversation with Sazonov in four telegrams, all dated 24 July and dispatched on the same day (OUA, VIII, Nos. 10616-10619); this is from No. 10619. —HNW.

23 PALEOLOGUE, Maurice, French Ambassador at St. Petersburg.—HNW.

24 BUCHANAN, Sir George, British Ambassador at St. Petersburg.—HNW.

25 D 5:40 p.m., R 8:00 p.m.; BD, XI, No. 101.

26 On 25 July, Grey informed Buchanan that he entirely approved of what Buchanan had said; see BD, XI, No. 112, p. 86.—HNW.

27 The report was sent in two telegrams, both dated 25 July: the first, D 1:08 a.m., R 3:45 a.m., KD, I, No. 160; the second, D 25 July, R 26 July, KD, I, No. 204.—HNW.

28 This refers to Bethmann's circular dispatch of 21 July (No. 121-6, above).—HNW.

29 This statement by Pourtalès is based upon an assurance Berchtold had given to Bethmann, but Sazonov's skepticism turned out to be justified for Berchtold later qualified it to such an extent that it became virtually meaningless; see, a.o., KD, II, No. 328, No. 380, No. 428. —HNW.

30 IBR, 1e, V, No. 79.

31 D 8:00 p.m., R 10:30 p.m.; BD, XI, No. 125.

32 It is interesting to note that Paléologue omitted this categorical assurance of French support from his own report of the conversation to Paris (DF, 3e, XI, No. 50). Considerable controversy still exists over the role he

played during these crucial days, especially over the apparent eagerness with which he supported Sazonov's increasingly belligerent attitude.—HNW.

33 R 8:00 p.m.; OUA, VIII, No. 10656.

34 PASIC, Nicholas, Serbian Prime Minister and Foreign Minister.—HNW.

35 OUA, VIII, Enclosure to No. 10648. When Berchtold later sent copies of the reply abroad, he added critical Austrian comments in parallel columns; for these, see ibid., Enclosure to No. 10860, and BD, XI, Appendix B.—HNW.

36 Both words left out in the original text.— Eds.

37 13 words crossed out (illegible).—Eds.

38 One word with about four letters crossed out (illegible.)—Eds.

39 One word with three letters crossed out (illegible).—Eds.

40 BUNSEN, Sir Maurice de, British Ambassador at Vienna.—HNW.

41 London, 1 September; BD, XI, No. 676, pp. 356-357.

42 Conrad, Dienstzeit, IV, 122.

43 KD, I, No. 219. Time of receipt of this telegram is not indicated, but on 27 July, Pourtalès reported to Bethmann that he had informed Sazonov of its contents; see KD, II, No. 282.—HNW.

44 D 1:00 a.m., 27 July, R 2:35 a.m., 27 July; KD, I, No. 242.

45 SHEBEKO, Nicholas, Russian Ambassador at Vienna.—HNW.

46 D 12:07 a.m., 27 [probable error, should be 28] July, R 10:30 a.m., 28 July, BD, XI, No. 199. See also Shebeko to Sazonov, dated 27/14 July, IBR, 1e, V, No. 139.

47 JAGOW, Gottlieb von, German Secretary of State for Foreign Affairs.—HNW.

48 R 29 July, p.m.; KD, II, No. 293.

49 It was on this occasion that William II made the marginal comment: "A brilliant achievement for a time-limit of only 48 hours! This is more than could be expected! A great moral success for Vienna; but with it, all reason for war disappears, and Giesl might as well have stayed in Belgrade! After that, I would never have ordered mobilization!" See KD, I, No. 271, p. 237.—HNW.

50 OUA, VIII, No. 10855, which, in the enclosure, contains the draft approved by Francis Joseph I, and ibid., No. 10862, which gives the

correction—part of one sentence was omitted—in the telegram actually sent.—HNW.

51 IBR, 1e, V, No. 172.

52 BRONEWSKI, Russian *chargé d'affaires* in Berlin.—HNW.

53 R not indicated, but the telegram's contents were delivered in the capitals named on 29 July; see, e.g., IBR, 1e, V, No. 241, for Berlin, and BD, XI, No. 258, for London.—HNW.

54 These nicknames were used by the monarchs themselves.—HNW.

55 R 1:10 a.m.; KD, II, No. 332. The original text is in English.

56 In his reply (dated 29 July, Berlin, D 6:30 p.m., R 9:40 p.m.; KD, II, No. 359) William II denied that this was an "ignoble war," and suggested "that it would be quite possible for Russia to remain a spectator of the Austro-Servian conflict without involving Europe in the most horrible war she ever witnessed."—HNW.

57 STRANDTMANN, Wassily, Russian *chargé d'affaires* at Belgrade.—HNW.

58 R 29 July (see *No. 121-29,* below); IBR, 1e, V, No. 257. The bombardment had begun in the early morning of 29 July.—HNW.

59 R 29 July; KD, II, No. 349.

60 D 11:00 p.m., R 11:00 a.m., 30 July; OUA, VIII, No. 11003.

61 IBR, 1e, V, No. 224.

62 Sazonov and General SUKHOMLINOV, Minister of War.—HNW.

63 D 12:50 p.m., R 4:35 p.m.; KD, II, No. 342.

64 Izvolsky, Alexander, Russian Ambassador at Paris (1910-1917), and formerly Russian Minister for Foreign Affairs (1906-1910).—HNW.

65 IBR, 1e, V, No. 221.

66 See *No. 121-31,* above.—HNW.

67 See *No. 121-24,* above.—HNW.

68 IBR, 1e, V, No. 224.

69 GOSCHEN, Sir William, British Ambassador at Berlin.—HNW.

70 D 1:20 a.m., 30 July, R 9:00 a.m., 30 July; BD, XI, No. 293.

71 The next day, Grey replied that Bethmann's proposal "cannot for a moment be entertained." See Grey to Goschen, 30 July, London, D 3:30 p.m.; BD, XI, No. 303.—HNW.

72 IBR, 1e, V, No. 307.

73 *Ibid.,* No. 284.

74 JANUSHKEVITSH, Nicholas, Chief of the Russian General Staff.—HNW.

75 TATISHTSHEV, Ilya, the Tsar's aide-de-camp, who had been his personal representative at the court of William II from 1905 to 1914.—HNW.

76 Conrad, *Dienstzeit,* IV, 152.

77 Moltke was referring to Russia's partial mobilization since he did not learn of Russia's general mobilization until 31 July.—HNW.

78 D 10:20 a.m.; KD, II, No. 473.

79 OUA, VIII, No. 11118.

80 TSCHIRSCHKY, Heinrich von, German Ambassador at Vienna.—HNW.

81 R 4:20 p.m.; KD, II, No. 479.

82 D 2:55 p.m.; KD, III, No. 487. The original text is in English.

83 R 11:10 p.m.; KD, III, No. 490.

84 Pourtalès delivered the ultimatum to Sazonov at midnight on 31 July (see Pourtalès to Bethmann, D 1:00 a.m., 1 August, R 1 August; KD, III, No. 536). Russia did not reply.—HNW.

85 SVERBEJEV, Sergei, Russian Ambassador at Berlin.—HNW.

86 Sverbejev's report apparently was based on rumors circulating in Berlin; see KD, III, No. 488.—HNW.

87 SCHOEN, Baron von, German Ambassador at Paris.—HNW.

88 R 31 July; KD, III, No. 491.

89 Schoen delivered the ultimatum to VIVIANI, the French Foreign Minister, at 7:00 p.m.—see Schoen to Bethmann, D 8:17 p.m., 31 July, R 12:30 a.m., I August; KD, III, No. 528.—HNW.

90 For the French reply, see *No. 121-47,* below.—HNW.

91 BERTIE, Sir Francis, British Ambassador at Paris.—HNW.

92 BD. XI, No. 367.

93 CAMBON, Paul, French Ambassador at London.—HNW.

94 FLOTOW, Hans von, German Ambassador at Rome.—HNW.

95 R 3:55 a.m., 1 August; KD, III, No. 534.

96 SAN GIULIANO, Antonio di, Italian Minister for Foreign Affairs.—HNW.

97 On the same day, Barrère—who was still the French Ambassador at Rome—drew San Guiliano's attention to the Franco-Italian Agreement of 1902 (see *No. 114,* above), but

his dispatch does not make clear to what extent the Agreement influenced Italy's decision to remain neutral; see Barrère to Viviani, dated 31 July, DF, 3e, XI, No. 411.–HNW.

[98] Apparently the compensation coveted by the Italian Government was the Trentino, but this was flatly rejected by Berchtold. The Italians then initiated discussions with the Entente Powers on 4 August—see No. 121-55, below.—HNW.

[99] R 5:45 p.m.; KD, III, No. 542. Pourtalès handed the declaration of war to Saznoov at 7:00 p.m.; see No. 121-49, below.–HNW.

[100] Pourtalès was expected to cross out one of these two versions— under the circumstances, the first one—but in his haste, or chagrin, he left both versions in the text he presented to Sazonov.–HNW.

[101] R 6:10 p.m.; KD, III, No. 571.

[102] R 2:05 p.m.; KD, III, No. 546. The original text is in English.

[103] IBR, 1e, V, No. 396.

[104] The German ultimatum; see No. 121-42, above.–HNW.

[105] BD, XI, No. 447.

[106] LICHNOWSKY, Prince Karl von, German Ambassador at London.–HNW.

[107] D 9:10 a.m.; KD, III, No. 641.

[108] BELOW Saleske, Baron von, German Minister at Brussels.–HNW.

[109] The text of the ultimatum, first drafted by Moltke on 26 July, had been sent to Below on 29 July in a sealed envelope, with orders not to open it until directed to do so (for the cover letter and the text, also dated 29 July, see KD, II, No. 375 and No. 376, respectively).

On 2 August, Jagow instructed Below to open the envelope and, after making several changes in the text, to present the ultimatum (D 2:05 p.m., R. ca. 4:00 p.m,; KD, III, No. 648). The changes have been incorporated in the text given here.–HNW.

[110] DAVIGNON, J., Belgian Minister for Foreign Affairs.–HNW.

[111] D 12:35 p.m., R 7:53 p.m.; KD, IV, No. 779.

[112] Added in the version given in the Belgian Gray Book.–Eds.

[113] Added in the version given in the Belgian Gray Book.–Eds.

[114] DF, 3e, XI, No. 678. The original text sent by Bethmann to Schoen (D 1:05 p.m., R 4:15 p.m.; KD, III, No. 734) arrived in Paris badly garbled, and Schoen had to recompose it as best he could. The text given here is, therefore, a copy—the original has disappeared from the French archives—of the text handed by Schoen to Viviani.–HNW.

[115] IBR, 1e, V, No. 529.

[116] See ibid., No. 521.

[117] BD, XI, No. 573.

[118] Ibid., No. 594.

[119] No. 121-56, above.–HNW.

[120] Dated Berlin, 6 August; R 19 August; BD, XI, No. 671.

[121] Should be Secretary of State.–Eds.

[122] No. 121-57, above.–HNW.

[123] CHURCHILL, Sir Winston, at this time First Lord of the Admiralty and Secretary of State for Home Affairs.–HNW.

[124] The World Crisis, 1911-1918 (London, 1932), p. 136.

INDEX

(Wherever possible, index entries carry parenthetical
annotations that explain the information in the book.)

313

322

Index

Fleury, Count (French general and diplomat), his interview with Bismarck (1863), 171, 215 (*No. 70*, n. 2)

Florence, 117, 118

Flotow, Hans von (German ambassador), and the outbreak of World War I (1914), 297

Forbes, Charles Stuart, Commander (British naval officer), his eyewitness account of Garibaldi's conquest of the Kingdom of the Two Sicilies (1860), 138-45

Forgách, Johann, Count von (Austrian Minister and Foreign Ministry official), and Serbian reactions to the Bosnian Crisis (1909), 280

Fould, Achille (French Minister of State), 83

Français, Le (French newspaper), and the Hohenzollern Candidacy (1870), 195

France, at the Congress of Vienna (1815), 4-5; and the Second Peace of Paris (1815), 14-16; agrees to the abolition of the Slave Trade (1815), 16; accedes to the Holy Alliance (1815), 18; and the Quadruple Alliance (1815), 18; and the Neapolitan Revolution (1820), 26; suppresses the Spanish Revolution (1823), 31; 32; and relations with Great Britain, 37; and the Crimean War (1853-1856), 45-50, 65, 66-67, 78, 83, 89-90, 91, 92, 93-94, 97 (*No. 35*, n. 19), 99; and the Unification of Italy (1858-1861), 99, 100, 101-6, 116-20, 121-22; concludes the Franco-Sardinian Alliance (1859), 123; and the War of 1859, 123-24, 125, 126, 127, 128, 129, 131; and her proclamation of War against Austria (1859), 132-33; 134, 135; concludes the preliminary Peace of Villafranca (1859), 135-36; and the cession by Sardinia of Savoy and Nice (1860), 137-38; and Garibaldi (1860), 140, 141, 142, 143; and the Unification of Germany (1863-1871), 149, 150, 151-55, 165, 166, 168-71; and Rhineland compensations (1863-1865), 171-77; 177-80; concludes the Austro-French Convention (1866), 181-82; assures Prussia of her neutrality in the coming Austro-Prussian War (1866), 182; 185; Venetia ceded by Austria and united with Italy (1866), 185, 189; 186, 187; and the proposed Franco-Prussian Treaty (1866), 191-192, 216 (*No. 84*, n. 1 and 3); and the Hohenzollern Candidacy for the Spanish Crown (1870), 192-98; makes her "à tout jamais" demand (1870), 154, 198-201;

France (*continued*)

and the Ems Dispatch (1870), 155, 202, 203; declares War against Prussia (1870), 203; and her conditions for peace in the Franco-Prussian War (1870), 213; and Napoleon III's surrender at Sedan (1870), 204-5; and the cession of Alsace-Lorraine to Germany (1870-1871), 208-10; concludes the preliminary Peace of Versailles (1871), 210-13; 220, 222; concludes the Treaty of Berlin (1878), 231-33; and the Dual Alliance (1879), 221, 234, 235, 236, 237, 238; and the Triple Alliance (1882), 238; 240, 241, 242, 243, 244; concludes the Franco-Russian Entente (1892-1894), 222, 245-46; 249, 250; and the Fashoda Crisis (1898), 222, 246-48; 251, 252; and the Naval Race (1898-1914), 253-55; concludes the Franco-Italian Agreement (1902), 256-57, 306 (*No. 114*, n. 4, 6 and 7); concludes the Anglo-French Agreement (1904), 223, 257-60; and the First Moroccan Crisis (1905-1906), 223, 260-62; 268, 269, 270, 271; and the Bosnian Crisis (1908-1909), 273, 275, 276, 277, 278, 279; and the outbreak of World War I (1914), 225, 226, 228; Germany insists on the localisation of the Austro-Serbian conflict (21 July), 283, 309 (*No. 121*, n. 12); warns Austria (21 July), 284; gives Russia assurances of her support (24 July), 286; is informed by Russia of Russian preparations for partial mobilization (25 July), 287; Paléologue assures Russia "that France placed herself unreservedly on Russia's side" (25 July), 287, 310 (*No. 121*, n. 32); 290; again assures Russia of her full support (28 July), 291; is informed by Russia of Russia's partial mobilization against Austria (29 July), 292; 293, 294; and the German ultimatum (31 July), 296, 311 (*No. 121*, n. 89); and Grey's refusal to assure her of British support (1 August), 296; and Italy's announcement of its neutrality under certain conditions (1 August), 297, 311 (*No. 121*, n. 97); and her reply to Germany's ultimatum (1 August), 298; orders general mobilization (1 August), 298; Grey repeats to Cambon that England is under no obligation to support France (1 August), 298; 299, 300; and Germany's declaration of war

DATE DUE